EXORBITANT ENLIGHTENMENT

Exorbitant Enlightenment

Blake, Hamann, and Anglo-German Constellations

ALEXANDER REGIER

OXFORD
UNIVERSITY PRESS

OXFORD
UNIVERSITY PRESS

Great Clarendon Street, Oxford, OX2 6DP,
United Kingdom

Oxford University Press is a department of the University of Oxford.
It furthers the University's objective of excellence in research, scholarship,
and education by publishing worldwide. Oxford is a registered trade mark of
Oxford University Press in the UK and in certain other countries

© Alexander Regier 2018

The moral rights of the author have been asserted

First Edition published in 2018
Impression: 3

Published in the United States of America by Oxford University Press
198 Madison Avenue, New York, NY 10016, United States of America

British Library Cataloguing in Publication Data
Data available

Library of Congress Control Number: 2018942144

ISBN 978-0-19-882712-2

Printed and bound by
CPI Group (UK) Ltd, Croydon, CR0 4YY

For Christian, Clara, and Thomas: Retter

Acknowledgements

It took many years to write this book. Throughout this process, I have benefitted from the support of many friends, colleagues, and institutions, some of whom I want to thank formally. During the research and writing of this project, I have enjoyed exemplary institutional backing from Rice University; I thank especially the Office of the Dean of the School of Humanities and the Department of English for their generosity and support. Several fellowships allowed me to research and complete parts of the book: thanks to the Alexander von Humboldt Foundation, CRASSH (Cambridge), Clare Hall (Cambridge), the Humanities Research Center (Rice), and the University of Exeter. I am grateful to the scholars and institutions that invited me to present parts of this project, including Arizona State University (Devoney Looser; Ron Broglio); Harvard University (Andrew Warren); Heythrop College, London (Francesca Knox); King's College, London (Rowan Boyson); University of California, Davis (Stefan H. Uhlig); the University of Cambridge (Simon Goldhill); the University of Oxford (Seamus Perry, Nick Halmi); and Queen Mary University of London (Angus Nicholls). Thanks also to the librarians who made this project possible; I thank Lorraine Parsons (Archives of the Moravian Church, British Province) as representative for them all. For help with preparing the manuscript, I am indebted to Mark Celeste and Theresa Grasso Munisteri. Jacqueline Norton at Oxford University Press is a tremendous editor, and I am deeply thankful to her for her wise counsel. The two anonymous reviewers for the press were very generous and constructive in their responses, and both deserve my thanks for spending the time and energy to read the manuscript so attentively. Portions of this book have appeared previously in my essay 'Anglo-German Connections in William Blake, Johann Georg Hamann, and the Moravians' published by *Studies in English Literature 1500–1900* 56.4 (2016).

There are many colleagues whose work, criticism, and advice have made this a much better book. Some of them read early drafts, chapters, and, in two cases, even versions of the whole manuscript. I want to mention a few of these people in particular for their generosity, intelligence, editorial help, and constructive criticism: Ian Balfour, who has more sense of Hamann than most; Ericka Beckman, a touchstone—textual, intellectual, and otherwise; Jim Chandler, who urged me to tell a positive story, not just a negative one; Peter de Bolla, mentor and friend, who gave the first and the last impulses for this book; James Faubion, a truly empathic thinker with a sense for the grotesque; Frances Ferguson, for pressing me on why this is a book about theory; Simon Goldhill, who asked a parsing question at a crucial stage; Paul Hamilton, *Freund und Kritiker*; Mary Jacobus, for her enthusiasm and for continuing to ask me encouraging questions; Betty Joseph, for pushing hard on everything, at HQ and elsewhere, and allowing me to see what I did *not* have to do; Jonathan Lamb, for convincing me that this was indeed a story; Marjorie Levinson, for her inimitable mixture of criticism and celebration;

Devoney Looser, without whose constant support and editorial advice this book would never have seen the light of day; Saree Makdisi, who reminded me not to write for Blakeans alone; Tim Morton for harping along; and Cary Wolfe, who helped at critical moments of gestation but also assured me that it was, indeed, time to stop. I admire all of these scholars greatly, and I am proud to call them my friends.

Finally, my most personal thanks go to my friends and family in Athens, Barcelona, Buenos Aires, Cambridge, Houston, London, Mendocino, Munich, New Delhi, New York City, Oxford, Philadelphia, Tempe, Ulm, Valencia, and Zurich. Love, trust, critical friendship, and their answers to Townes van Zandt's most demanding question make them central to all my endeavours.

Table of Contents

List of Illustrations

Introduction
Troubling Enlightenment

This book offers new ways to think about eighteenth- and early nineteenth-century literature and culture. It puts into view a constellation of Anglo-German relations in Britain, many of which are so radical—so exorbitant—that they ask us to rethink our own literary history of the Enlightenment and Romanticism. It is a polyglot study, and buoyantly so. The analysis of works across languages, as well as their respective literary or philosophical traditions, allows us to read authors in new, powerful ways. We uncover relations that we had not seen before. The set of Anglo-German relations that this book reveals does not fit into our standard understanding of the period, especially conventional accounts of the Enlightenment and its supposed opposition to Romanticism. Instead, these relations trouble conventional accounts in multiple ways, as the title of this Introduction declares. *Exorbitant Enlightenment* reveals a period in which significant figures are intellectual, artistic, and poetical radicals—exorbitants, as we will call them—many of whom continue to be neglected in scholarly accounts, even though they tell us important things about the period and our way of approaching it. Institutions such as the Moravian Church in London and individual figures such as William Blake and Johann Georg Hamann play important roles in this version of the Enlightenment that is rather different from the accounts we are used to. They are exorbitant not in the pecuniary sense of the term most common today, but rather in the first sense listed in the *OED*: that of '[l]eaving a specified track'.[1] This book gives an account of a set of thinkers and institutions that up-ends our view of literary history but does not try to create a systematic counter-narrative in its stead. We need to readjust the impulse of constructing grand narratives, however alternative or radical they are; if we do look for broader vantage points, a more productive focus will be to read across languages and literary traditions without trying to make them fit a particular historical or critical model. This Introduction will outline the work needed in such a project, offering two short examples of what this means in practice. The best way to understand the wider significance of the argument, both of the book and of the Introduction, is to get some factual misconceptions out of the way first, many of which have been occluding our critical view.

'It is a familiar fact that no Englishman read German literature in the eighteenth century', wrote Leslie Stephen.[2] His pithy 1898 assessment reflects a widely held

---

[1] *OED*, 2nd ed., s.v. 'exorbitant, *adj.* and *n*.', A1a.
[2] Leslie Stephen, 'The Importation of German', in *Studies of a Biographer*, 4 vols (London: Duckworth, 1898), 2: 39.

view that has been held in some circles up to the present day. It is an erroneous caricature that made it easy to treat these national literatures as completely distinct until the advent of Romanticism. By implication, it also allowed a neat and radical break between those two conceptual categories and periods when it came to Anglo-German relations. However, Anglo-German relations during the eighteenth century were, in fact, varied, rich, and complex. Their constancy and continuity suggest that to maintain a clear division between German and British canons—or Enlightenment and Romanticism, for that matter—is far too neat a way of arranging literary history and our understanding of these terms. The material and figures that come into view challenge the way we do both literary history and literary criticism, and they remind us of the need to work across languages if we want to get a sense of the complexity of certain historical realities at the time. The first few paragraphs of Daniel Defoe's *Robinson Crusoe* (1719) serve as an example here, since they frame that novel as a story about Anglo-German immigration, a novel whose main protagonist is meaningfully called Robinson Kreutznaer, a name pregnant with meaning in 1660—all of which are aspects that have been widely overlooked.

Defoe's *Robinson Crusoe* is one of the most commonly cited texts for marking the beginnings of the novel, a literary form said to signal the development of a new age. The genre of the novel went on to become the most influential form of modern realism. Defoe played a major part in shaping it as a form of social change and as a cultural turning point for the eighteenth century. Yet few have noticed how the very first paragraph of *Robinson Crusoe* presents readers with a significant Anglo-German connection. Defoe's narrator begins,

> I Was born in the Year 1632, in the City of *York*, of a good Family, tho' not of that Country, my Father being a Foreigner of *Bremen*, who settled first at *Hull*: He got a good Estate by Merchandise, and leaving off his Trade, lived afterward at *York*, from whence he had married my Mother, whose Relations were named *Robinson*, a very good Family in that Country, and from whom I was called *Robinson Kreutznaer*; but by the usual Corruption of Words in *England*, we are now called, nay we call ourselves, and write our Name *Crusoe*, and so my Companions always call'd me.[3]

Everyone familiar with *Robinson Crusoe* has his or her own interpretation of these significant opening lines. If we wanted to follow the question of the novel as form, then that interpretation might take us either to Ian Watt's *Rise of the Novel* or to Walter Benjamin's reflections on the genre. Some will think of *Robinson Crusoe* as a text about the formation of modern subjectivity. Others read those lines in terms of empire and postcolonialism, or as one of the most powerful articulations of the story of capital and the eighteenth-century beginnings of globalization. Still others think of this text as a prime example of how Protestantism becomes part and parcel of a new world order and how religious belief and the structure of society, including its work ethic and morals, intersect. It is, after all, also a story about loss and redemption. The novel, furthermore, remains the prime example for historians of the book illustrating a new level of literary dissemination.

---

[3] Daniel Defoe, *Robinson Crusoe*, ed. Thomas Keymer (Oxford: Oxford University Press, 2007), p. 5; italics in original.

Another approach, which none of the readings invoked above pay much attention to, is the opening lines' position on the cusp of different, specific geographies. Most of the readings that consider Crusoe's early life focus on the significance of his stubborn insistence on going to sea, despite the evidence (divine or otherwise) indicating that he should not. However, the first geographical crossing and sea voyage that is mentioned is, in fact, Crusoe's father's: he went from Bremen to Hull. The only way to do that is by ship, as Crusoe would have known all too well. What many critics discuss when it comes to Crusoe's paternal household is his father's suggestion to steer an even keel, but always on land, and never go to sea. Although the advice seems to be a well-meaning conservatism, it ought to prompt us to consider that Crusoe's father himself also took to the seas to find *his* island before his son did.

Crusoe's father is a German immigrant who has settled on an island; Crusoe himself is the son of a first-generation immigrant family. The opening of the novel insists on his Anglo-German background more than once: Crusoe's family is emphatically 'not of that Country' (England), 'my Father being a Foreigner of *Bremen*'. In fact, the Anglo-German status of his family is at the centre of the whole opening passage. Here is the first sentence again: 'I Was born in the Year 1632, in the City of *York*, of a good Family, tho' not of that Country, my Father being a Foreigner of Bremen'. Straightaway, Defoe sets the time and multiple places. As he does in other works such as the *Journal of the Plague Year* (1722), Defoe sets the action in the distant, yet not-too-distant, past of the text's publication. The other major piece of information we gain from the opening sentence of *Crusoe* is that the narrator's father is a northern German who settled in England and quickly assimilated. Defoe alludes to the cultural and religious dimensions of this process. He models the figure of the seventeenth-century Crusoe family on a type of assimilated Anglo-German household, often bilingual, that was increasingly common in eighteenth-century Britain. A telling detail is that Crusoe Sr marries a respectable Englishwoman (presumably an Anglican), thereby making assimilation in England easier. This union is a fictional instance of a development that the first part of my book will trace historically: there are several instances of German clergymen in eighteenth-century London who complained that English women drew men away from the German-Lutheran parishes into Anglicanism or, even worse, 'pulled' them into 'the English dissenting chapels'.[4] This marriage is only the first of many other historically real Anglo-German connections that Defoe invokes in these opening sentences.

As Crusoe's straightforwardly prepositional narration indicates, his immigrant background is noteworthy but not unusual. It is not presented in a dramatic or exculpatory way, giving us a sense of maybe how normal those relations were historically. Of course, this is a novel and not a field report. However, if we check our historical sources, then it transpires that such a transnational move was nothing

---

[4] '[S]o werden sie mit in die Englischen Dissenter-Kapellen gezogen' (Johann Gottlieb Burckhardt, *Kirchen-Geschichte der deutschen Gemeinde in London* [Tübingen: Fues, 1798], pp. 42–3). Also see Graham Jefcoate, *Deutsche Drucker und Buchhändler in London 1680–1811: Strukturen und Bedeutung des deutschen Anteils am englischen Buchhandel* (Berlin: De Gruyter, 2015), p. 32. Unless otherwise indicated, this and all translations from German throughout are mine.

unusual in Defoe's time and certainly within the realm of a realist novel. Nothing in the text leads us to imagine that Crusoe's father went directly from Bremen to Hull, though it is certainly likely we are supposed to do so. Defoe is drawing on the fact that in the 1620s (the supposed setting of the novel), as well as in the time of publication several decades later, it was already a busy route of exchange and commerce. In fact, it remained one of the most important routes from Germany to England and America, especially for immigrants, until the twentieth century. This allows us to see that this transnational connection might have had wider significance for some readers. For instance, how would German immigrants in 1720s London, around the publication date of the novel, read this text? They would certainly have picked up on the parallels with their own condition. Was this a novel about themselves, about their own experiences, or about those of their sons and daughters?

Robinson Crusoe, one of the first best-selling novels in British literary history, is about a family of immigrants and travellers. It must have given Defoe great pleasure to see that it was (and still is) widely understood to be a very English novel with a very English character, representing specifically Anglocentric values and ideas. It would have tickled him precisely because this is both mistaken and exactly right. It is blatantly a mistake if we are quick readers, believing Robinson to be a typically English figure à la John Bull, whose national identity is supposedly unproblematic. It is accurate if we read the novel in a spirit to which Defoe would have been more partial—namely, understanding the character of England to be the result of precisely the kind of immigration and cross-cultural exchange that the opening of the novel describes. In the preface to his popular poem *The True-Born Englishman* (1701), a work about the multicultural background of Britain, he eloquently explains that 'an Englishman, of all men, ought not to despise foreigners, as such; and I think the inference is just, since what they are to-day, we were yesterday, and to-morrow they will be like us'.[5] In this sense Crusoe *is* a typical Englishman because of, rather than despite of, his cross-national heritage and character. Such a reading of the novel makes us consider Crusoe as a British icon whose character and cultural background are the result of immigration, transnationalism, and a specifically Anglo-German context.

Economic migration sets the scene for Crusoe's upbringing, which is a story of cultural assimilation. And once more, Crusoe insists that this is directly tied to his Anglo-German identity. Here again is the second sentence of the novel, its focus still on the father: 'He got a good Estate by Merchandise, and leaving off his Trade, lived afterward at *York*, from whence he had married my Mother, whose Relations were named *Robinson*, a very good Family in that Country, and from whom I was called *Robinson Kreutznaer*; but by the usual Corruption of Words in *England*, we are now called, nay we call ourselves, and write our Name *Crusoe*, and so my Companions always call'd me'. Even Robinson Crusoe's name turns out to be an

    [5] Daniel Defoe, 'Explanatory Preface' to The True-Born Englishman, in *The Works of Daniel Defoe, Carefully Selected from the Most Authentic Sources, with Chalmer's Life of the Author, Annotated*, ed. John S. Keltie (Edinburgh: Nimmo, 1870), pp. 591–3, 592.

important site of his family's Anglo-German mixture. He presents his first, maternal name ('*Robinson*') as the traditional English part of the lineage.[6] '*Kreutznaer*' in contrast, is straightforwardly German. This goes beyond a narratorial nod towards the issue of immigration and assimilation that lies at the centre of the novel and also of Defoe's life. Paying attention to the exact nature of the Anglo-German connections helps us to see why this is a relevant and revealing example, not just for a fresh reading of the novel but also for the wider stakes, showing these national connections to be far more important than we have realized until now. The detail opens up *Crusoe* not just as a very British novel but also as a very Anglo-German novel. The text uses this Anglo-German dimension to set the scene for its exploration of the crossings and disruptions of both national languages and their literatures. It is revealing that Defoe wrote and published essays specifically about German immigrants to Britain, championing their presence in Britain. It gives the fact that Crusoe is one of these immigrants some extratextual poignancy too. (Chapter 1 will offer a detailed discussion of these essays.)

'*Kreutznaer*' is not a random name, and Defoe does not choose it by chance. The biblical 'Corruption of Words' that the narrator invokes only half-hides its deeper and important truth. '*Kreutznaer*' is itself a variant (actually a 'Corruption') of the name Kreutzer or Kreuzer, a word with much significance in the context of the novel.[7] *Kreuz* translates as 'cross' in all its many senses. A *Kreuzer* is a 'cruiser', a person or a ship that crosses the seas and oceans. Robinson's name is already a sign of his travels to come, of trying to create a grid of the oceans to explore. He can only do so by crossing his father, ignoring paternal advice. And 'Kreuzer' also refers to the Christian cross, so relevant for the Protestant undertone of the novel. Crusoe is a crusader, he brings modern Christianity with all its capitalist practices across to the island: he lives up to the potential (or is it a calling?) of his German name. As if by chance—though, of course, there is little chance here at all—his name also describes a literal intersection between these larger beliefs and the economic order that underlies them.

To make matters even richer and more complicated, a *Kreuzer* was a coin, the most common unit of exchange in German-speaking Europe between the sixteenth and nineteenth centuries. We still hear the echoes of this meaning today in the currency of the Brazilian *cruzeiro*, a currency unit that, at the end of the novel, Crusoe himself uses to estimate the value of his Brazilian plantation ('the Value of the Plantation encreasing, amounted to [38,892] Cruisadoes'), which will guarantee his wealth upon his return.[8] Like so many coins, the *Kreuzer* and *cruzeiro* bear the

---

[6] This is only somewhat straightforward, however, since 'Robinson', too, has a rather complicated and cross-national etymological history, including the migratory connotations of a robin—a topic that would take us too far afield here. For the history of 'Robinson' see Percy Reaney, ed., *A Dictionary of English Surnames*, 3rd. ed. (Oxford: Oxford University Press, 2005).

[7] To describe cultural assimilation in terms of how the 'Corruption of Words' has an impact on names and naming is an important detail here, especially when we consider Crusoe's naming of Friday and their biblical studies on the power of language. It is obviously also an invocation about the intrinsically tainted nature of language—i.e. that words are corrupt (they are fallen), and they do corrupt (people, ideas, and so forth).

[8] Defoe, *Crusoe*, p. 238.

visual representation of a cross, thereby marking the territory of its economic value as primarily Christian. One of the reasons we do not often think of *Robinson Crusoe* as an immigrant novel is because it is so powerful in sketching the protagonist's imperial ambitions—Crusoe's outward work, as it were. It is worth taking a moment to reflect on the intergenerational move across nations that facilitates this. The name Crusoe carries that move into the world and is, from the very beginning, marked as such. Robinson Kreutznaer is no incidental name. It contains within it many of the central aspects of Crusoe's life to come, which are only legible through their Anglo-German connection.[9]

What does this short reading suggest? One thing it directly puts to us is that there is a level of cross-cultural exchange—specifically between Britain and Germany—that is more complex than we might have realized. It behoves us to pay attention to it and study it carefully if we want to get a more precise picture of the historical, literary, and cultural trajectory of Europe in the eighteenth and nineteenth centuries. Of course, Defoe's novel presents only one instance, but there is plenty of further evidence, some of which is on display across the chapters of this book. There is a level of complexity here that is not reflected in scholarship to date, which we need to address. The ability to listen across languages is crucial to this endeavour. A monolingual construction of literary history does not get behind the story of Crusoe's name, which is representative here for a whole host of connections, genres, transmissions, and many other artistic forms that helped define the intellectual and cultural context of eighteenth-century Britain. Monolingual work has resulted in a restricted and simplified version of literary history. This is especially true if we understand some of these cultural products to be significant for our understanding of wider structures. If *Robinson Crusoe* is an iconic text that helps us comprehend the beginning of the Enlightenment, then we surely are in a better position to understand this larger category once we develop an appreciation for the novel as partly about polyglot transnationalism.

It is remarkable that so few scholars have paid attention to this pre-1790s Anglo-German context. The wealth of archival material is stunning: German churches, schools, and a German book industry in London, as well as an extensive web of intellectual currents, both public and private. All formed an important and serious network across the Channel. The British public consumed, much against later accounts, a considerable amount of German literature at the time. Seriously organized ecclesiastical and educational structures, such as the Moravians, overlapped with British nonconformist groups and the birth of Methodism. Plenty of reviews and translations by figures whom we thought we knew, such as the artist and writer Henry Fuseli, or the public intellectual Johann Caspar Lavater, reveal an active network of intellectuals, artists, writers, and scientists operating between the two countries. There were significant Anglo-German structures in commerce,

---

[9] Jacques Derrida uses this passage to explore a very different kind of Anglo-German connection, in this case between Defoe and Martin Heidegger, through a reading of Defoe's and, briefly, Crusoe's name in his second volume of *The Beast and the Sovereign*, trans. Geoffrey Bennington (Chicago, IL/London: University of Chicago Press, 2011), pp. 45–6.

ecclesiastical institutions, and educational establishments at the time. There was even a considerable institutionalization of multilingualism through publications, literary commerce, and translations. It emerges very clearly not only that there was Anglo-German life before 1790 but also that it had a remarkable penchant for producing unusual and philosophically significant figures.

BLAKE AND HAMANN: TWO EXORBITANTS

Once we have corrected our factual misapprehension about the level of complexity and nature of pre-1790s Anglo-German connections, including their relevance to our literary traditions, we have the chance to consider what theoretical consequences might follow from this insight. Some of these transnational connections are a sign for the stability, depth, and richness of London's multicultural and multilingual character at the time. As students of the period, we need to remind ourselves that the eighteenth century is far more polyglot than we usually appreciate. The Anglo-German relations are part of this, and we need to understand the level of their normality and comprehensiveness. From within that larger historical context, though, emerges an intriguing group of thinkers who catch our attention in a manner that changes our understanding of the period in a different, more substantial way.

Many of the Anglo-German connections and constellations that appear in this book understand history, language, and literature in forms that are radically different from those in standard accounts of the period. A substantial part of the Anglo-German Enlightenment that this book puts into view presents figures who are too excessive to be accommodated in the common narratives of Enlightenment and Romanticism. Within the larger Anglo-German culture of the period there is a substantial part, especially when it comes to the religious and philosophical spheres, that is heavily invested in developing a sensitivity for the unusual, a departure from the common canon. All the figures that are key to this book—the Moravians, Blake, Hamann, Fuseli, and Lavater—disturb the conventional historical account of Enlightenment and Romanticism, and their supposed opposition. They depart from the track that has provided our course and narrative of these periods and their conceptual imports. The astronomical and astrological terminology that this study employs throughout provides a powerful description of how the position of these thinkers and writers can be understood as a critical category: they are exorbitant because they are 'out of track', they are 'anomalous, not in accordance with the law'.[10]

The exorbitant is a figure who 'exceeds proper limits'.[11] Many of the figures that play a recurring and important role in this book are excessive in precisely this way. These authors and thinkers propel themselves outside of the normal forces of attraction and repulsion that govern the system of Enlightenment. We find a high number of these exorbitant thinkers in the Anglo-German context, authors whose

---

[10] OED, 2nd ed., s.v. 'exorbitant, *adj.* and *n.*', A1a and A2b.
[11] *OED*, 2nd ed., s.v. 'exorbitant, *adj.* and *n.*', B.

style of writing, arguing, and positioning themselves '[d]eviat[es] from the normal' and is '[e]ccentric, erratic, irregular'.[12] Thinkers such as the Moravians, Blake, Hamann, Fuseli, or Lavater break with the norms, and their practice departs from our model of how we account for the period. The exorbitant figures that emerge from the Anglo-German context in eighteenth-century London deeply challenge the way we produce literary and intellectual history.

Blake and Hamann emerge as the most exorbitant members produced in the Anglo-German context. That quality of irregularity, together with their remarkable affinity of interests in language, poetry, and thought, provides the rationale for making them my main pair in this book. Their arguments and writing are continuously exuberant and excessive. Their writing propels them outside the track, the orbit, of the Enlightenment and subsequent Romanticism, which is the model we usually use to understand the period. It is, thus, important to note that describing Blake and Hamann as exorbitant is not the same as marking them as outsiders. That difference is, as we shall see, behind one of the important methodological arguments of this book. In order to get a better sense of these larger questions, however, we will first turn to our second concrete example and consider a few of Blake's and Hamann's exorbitant positions.

Here is a scattershot of twelve statements, written between 1758 and 1821, that give us a sense of just how outside the common orbit and norms Blake's and Hamann's thinking is on language, thought, religion, and sexuality—the four aspects of their thought that this book mostly focuses on:

1. 'My coarse imagination is never able to imagine a creative Spirit without genitalia' (1786).[13]

2. 'God becomes as we are, / that we may be as he / is' (1788).[14]

3. [Immanuel] 'Kant makes God into an ideal without knowing that his pure reason is precisely the same' (1785).[15]

4. 'I am God O Sons of Men! I am your Rational Power! / Am I not Bacon & Newton & Locke who teach Humility to Man!' (1821).[16]

5. 'I am neither speaking about physics nor about theology—but language, the mother of reason and revelation, its A and Ω. It is the two-edged sword for all truths and lies' (1785).[17]

---

[12] *OED*, 2nd ed., s.v. 'exorbitant, *adj.* and *n.*', A2 and A2a.

[13] Gwen Griffith-Dickson, *Johann Georg Hamann's Relational Metacriticism* (Berlin: De Gruyter, 1995), p. 209. Griffith-Dickson translates the quotation from Johann Georg Hamann, *Briefwechsel*, ed. Walther Ziesemer and Arthur Henkel, 7 vols (Wiesbaden: Insel, 1955), 2: 415: 'Und meine grobe Einbildungskraft ist niemals im Stande gewesen, sich einen schöpferischen Geist ohne genitalia vorzustellen.' Subsequent references to Hamann's *Briefwechsel* are from this edition, edited by Ziesemer and Henkel, vols 4–7 edited by Henkel alone, hereafter cited as ZH, followed by volume and page number(s).

[14] William Blake, 'There Is No Natural Religion [b]', in *The Complete Poetry and Prose of William Blake*, ed. David V. Erdman, rev. ed. (New York: Anchor Books, 1988), pp. 2–3, 3.

[15] 'Kant macht Gott zum Ideal ohne zu wißen, daß seine reine Vernunft eben daßelbe ist' (ZH, 6: 163).

[16] Blake, *Jerusalem: The Emanation of the Giant Albion*, in *Complete Poetry and Prose*, pp. 144–258, 203, ch. 3, lines 16–17.

[17] 'Bey mir ist weder von Physik noch Theologie die Rede—sondern Sprache, die Mutter der Vernunft und Offenbarung, ihr A und Ω' (ZH, 6: 108).

6. 'He who sees the Infinite in all things sees God. He who sees the Ratio only sees himself only' (1788).[18]

7. 'Speaking is translation—from a tongue of angels into a human tongue, that is, thoughts in words—things in names—images in signs' (1762).[19]

8. 'Why is the Bible more Entertaining & Instructive than any other book[?] Is it not because [it is] addressed to the Imagination which is Spiritual Sensation & but mediately to the Understanding or Reason[?]' (1799).[20]

9. 'God reveals himself—the creator of the world: a writer' (1758).[21]

10. God '[t]o man the wondr'rous art of writing gave' (1808).[22]

11. '[T]he body or outward form of Man is derived from the Poetic Genius' (1795).[23]

12. '[T]he uterus of language, which is the *deipara* of our reason' (1780).[24]

Some of these statements were published, while others survived in unpublished drafts or letters. The authors are, in equal shares, Blake and Hamann.[25] We get an immediate sense for the deep affinity between them, partly because of their particular strangeness and idiosyncrasies. Their highly unusual ways of thinking about the status of poetry, thought, and the human body sidesteps the classical ways of empiricism, materialism, and idealism. The articulation of thinking is theoretically acute, sharp, intentionally shrill, and confrontational—plenty of readers, then and now, might be surprised or taken aback by them. These two thinkers, and their mode of expression, do not fit into our conventional picture of intellectual or cultural history of the Enlightenment and Romanticism; in fact, they fundamentally question this model of literary history. They remind us that there were certain forms of thinking available—about history and language in particular—that are strange to us now. These are forms of exorbitant thinking that not only are conceptually or stylistically unfamiliar but also disrupt our normal accounts of the history of ideas. What Blake and Hamann say does not fit into our normal account of the Enlightenment or British Romanticism, let

---

[18] Blake, 'There Is No Natural Religion [b]', p. 3.

[19] Griffith-Dickson, p. 413. Griffith-Dickson translates the quotation from Johann Georg Hamann, *Sämtliche Werke*, ed. Josef Nadler, 6 vols (Vienna: Herder, 1949–57), 2: 199: 'Reden ist übersetzen—aus einer Engelssprache in eine Menschensprache, das heist, Gedanken in Worte,—Sachen in Namen,—Bilder in Zeichen.' Subsequent references to Hamann's *Sämtliche Werke* are from this edition edited by Nadler, hereafter cited as N, followed by volume number and page number(s).

[20] William Blake to Dr Trusler, 23 August 1799, in *Complete Poetry and Prose*, pp. 702–3.

[21] 'Gott offenbart sich—Der Schöpfer der Welt ein Schriftsteller.' Johann Georg Hamann, *Londoner Schriften*, ed. Oswald Bayer and Bernd Weissenborn (Munich: Beck, 1993), p. 67.

[22] William Blake, 'To the Public', in *Jerusalem*, p. 145, line 4.

[23] William Blake, 'All Religions are One', in *Complete Poetry and Prose*, pp. 1–2.

[24] N, 3: 239: 'die Gebärmutter der Sprache, welche die DEIPARA unserer Vernunft ist'.

[25] Omitting the authorships of individual sentences will allow me to momentarily counteract the tendency we have to associate a particular way of thinking with a particular individual, a way of reading in which the concern for the coherence of a work, *oeuvre*, or subject, trumps most other criteria. As Simon Jarvis points out in a very different context, such ways of reading can inhibit our ability to read afresh because we feel an overriding impulse to already know how to read a particular idea, as, say, typically 'Blakean', including all the judgements that hang by it. See Jarvis, 'Introduction: Poetic Thinking', in *Wordsworth's Philosophic Song* (Cambridge: Cambridge University Press, 2007), pp. 1–32.

alone their supposed opposition. Neither do they fit neatly into the alternative binary of Enlightenment versus Counter-Enlightenment.

It is one thing to acknowledge the power of anthropomorphism—a discussion with a venerable tradition; it is another to state that one cannot 'imagine a creative Spirit without genitalia', implicitly challenging us to try this for ourselves. The coarseness of the formulation is not to be taken as an indictment: it is a slightly humorous way of indicating that genitalia are the best that are on offer, but that this might not be a terrible thing. Neither is mentioning the genitalia a pubescent joke about a God with a supposedly well-endowed sexual organ (although it is relevant that creative spirits tend to be male, at least in the imagination of philosophers and poets). Although the seeming rudeness of the formulation knowingly plays with the supposedly shocking conjunction of deity and genital, the statement is more about the deep anthropocentric quality of the imagination. For all its graphic quality, Hamann here makes a statement of fact regarding us as human animals. It is a statement that avoids both superiority and dejection. What is crucial and unusual is that the inability to imagine, to think, without genitalia (double meaning intended) is neither triumphant nor shameful. But the invocation of the sexual dimension is still key. Our nakedness is our compass precisely *because* it is the most human of things. It reminds us that we are human animals: beings that are, and always remain, physical in our experience and creative imagination. Nakedness is not a result of shame, as it is in much traditional Christian thought, but a proof for the positive and distinct quality of the human imagination.

The confessed lack of ability to imagine such a creative spirit is underwritten by a sense of humility, not arrogance, by reading value in the world, not projecting onto it. When we consider Blake's statement that 'God becomes as we are, / that we may be as he is', this also is a moment of thankfulness, not misplaced confidence. The reason that God transforms Himself into human terms is precisely so that we can understand and perceive Him as a creative spirit. Otherwise we would lack the ability to perceive anything at all. The phrase does indeed suggest that graceful condescension includes a potential for us to do the same as God—to become divine—not through self-apotheosis but rather through embracing His form of condescension, His creative spirit. This is how 'we may be as he is'. We are made in a divine image, but that of course means we have to humanize God, ontology, genitals, and all. By becoming 'as we are', which includes an embrace of our limitations, so that 'we may be as he is', we affirm our own state—not as something divine itself, but as something that can have a divine quality. In the end we can become 'as he is' by having our own creative spirit that will lead us to compose poems and produce other feats of the human imagination.

There is little room here for standard Enlightenment philosophy or conventional secularism. Neither classically idealist nor empiricist thinkers would invoke a creative spirit with genitalia. Most thinkers in the period attempt to locate creativity and thought in the mind alone. Rather than admitting our anthropomorphic limits of thoughts, such idealism produces an apotheosis by deifying reason: 'I am God O Sons of Men! I am your Rational Power! / Am I not Bacon & Newton & Locke who teach Humility to Man!' This is human rational power *as*

God, whose humility will mean something very different than the humility implied in the first thesis. Capitalized 'Humility' is more akin to humiliation, a perverse and forced version of acknowledging human limits. True humility is the last thing a reigning 'Rational Power' will produce. To admit we can only imagine a creative spirit without genitalia—*that* is humble. To exclaim in sentences that attempt to be Godlike in their pseudo-prophetic force and authoritative, declamatory style that one is himself God is human vanity parading as humility. Blake and Hamann will fight tooth and claw against such a Newtonian, supposedly enlightened, vision of the world. According to them, leaving the orbit of such thought is the only way to avoid a banalization of the world.

Deifying reason will either turn into atheism, self-deception, or both. The unholy trinity Blake had already accused of deifying 'Rational Power' illustrates this well: 'Bacon Locke & Newton are the three great teachers of Atheism or Satan's Doctrine'.[26] Importantly, the claim here is not only that Locke is 'an Atheist' but also that he is guilty of 'wilful [*sic*] deception'.[27] Importantly, this is not only the intentional deception of others, but also unintentional *self*-deception. Locke and others cannot resist the lure they have themselves constructed; the 'Rational Power' has truly turned into a deity that they in turn worship. This type of apotheosis is deeply related to atheism (and hence makes Bacon, Locke, and Newton its teachers) since they are both the result of zealous overconfidence in one's own rational power, a narcissism that suggests an anxiety to make everything intelligible. It is this narcissism that lies at the heart of wanting to absorb everything into intelligibility. One problem with this form of thinking is that it substitutes divine ability with a version of human ability. Similar to crude fantasies of usurpation, it retains the structures of explanation, yet it simplifies them according to its own agenda. Hamann describes this as a philosophy that 'turns God into the ideal without knowing that . . . pure reason is precisely the same'. The 'pure reason' here is a direct reference to Kant, of course, who joins 'Bacon & Newton & Locke' as a representative target of those attacks. According to Hamann, Kant's *Critique of Pure Reason* (1781) has done two things. First, it turned God into an ideal, something that exists in the realm of the mental alone and relates to human experience in only a mediated way. The Kantian God is certainly not a creative spirit with genitalia. Second, it has made 'pure reason' not just into an ideal but also into God itself. This describes the apotheosis of reason, which masquerades as something neutral and ideal. For Hamann, this is even worse than proclaiming, 'I am God'.

Blake and Hamann emerge as sharp critics of an ideology of reason and over-confident forms of thinking, including unintentional ones. Kant, for instance, did not know that he turned pure reason into his God. But if we want to avoid a similar mistake, we need to understand the reasons why Kant did not notice this slippage.

---

[26] William Blake, qtd. in Henry Crabb Robinson, 'Reminiscences' (1852), appendix 1, part F, of G. E. Bentley, *Blake Records: Documents (1714–1841) concerning the Life of William Blake (1757–1827) and His Family, Incorporating Blake Records (1969), Blake Records Supplement (1988), and Extensive Discoveries since 1988*, 2nd ed. (New Haven, CT: Published for the Paul Mellon Centre for Studies in British Art by Yale University Press, 2004), pp. 692–706, 697.

[27] Crabb Robinson, 'Reminiscences', p. 699.

According to Hamann, it is because he did not pay attention to language that is both 'the mother of reason and revelation' and 'the centre point of the misunderstanding of reason with itself'.[28] We need to turn to the relation between language and thought in order to step outside a system that deifies ourselves or reason. In their alternate ways, both Hamann and Blake maintain that thought always involves language and that we need to reconsider poetry, philosophy, reading, and their own writing in this light.

For many of the exorbitant thinkers presented in this book—and especially for Blake and Hamann—language is a privileged model for understanding our relation to the world. It is not privileged because it is an effective, transparent tool; it is privileged neither for its supposedly neutral powers of abstraction nor because we can control its semantic instability. It is precisely the opposite of all of these: it is privileged because language itself is part of the production of language and thought. Language has ontological power that goes beyond science, human control, or what we might call religion. As Hamann states, he is 'neither speaking about physics nor about theology—but language, the *mother* of reason and revelation, its A and Ω. It is the two-edged sword for all truths and lies' (my emphasis). Language produces all of revelation: it encompasses the beginning and end as well as the process in the middle, which includes the reading of the text of the world. Since reason and language belong to one another, the production of thought is always linguistic. Whatever world we find and construct, it involves language as a medium without which we will not be able to comprehend physical or mental reality. Crucially, there is no suggestion or pretence that this 'mother' is neutral.

What Hamann gets to when he speaks of language and thought is not simply the description of a mental faculty but a description of a much more complicated and enmeshed relation between a whole array of mental faculties and our construction of the world. According to him—and Blake would assent here—if our idea of language is reduced to a simple way of assisting reason to define and express its epistemological insights as clearly as possible, it will inevitably lead to a form of self-deception. As Blake puts it, 'He who sees the Ratio only sees himself only'. A banal theory of language will lead to a simple, limited perception. Only 'He who sees the Infinite in all things sees God'. We will turn in due course to the issue of how to understand such statements in the context of a world that considers itself to have completed a linguistic turn. The idea that language and thought are inextricably connected strikes many of us as powerfully convincing. The question here, however, is what Blake and Hamann understand by 'language' and 'thought'. The fact that language is, for both Blake and Hamann, a medium with visionary, even divine qualities, whose prime function is definitely *not* to assist the continuing enlightenment, clarification, and secularization of the world, suggests that this is not a straightforward issue.

The elliptical suggestion that 'God reveals himself—the creator of the world: a writer!' combines the visionary and readerly qualities of Blake and Hamann. For

---

[28] '[D]ie Mutter der Vernunft und Offenbarung' (ZH, 6: 108); 'Sprache ist auch der Mittelpunct des Missverstandes der Vernunft mit ihr selbst' (N, 3: 286).

both of them revelation is real, and it comes through the medium of language, through the text of the world. God speaks to us through his writing, which constitutes external and internal existence. This is not a tempered Enlightenment God of secular eighteenth-century humanism. Biblical interpretation might be contingent, but for Hamann or Blake that tells us more about our limited abilities of understanding the divine word than about the text. Thus, when Blake claims that 'I know that This World Is a World of Imagination & Vision I see Every thing I paint In This World', this 'see[ing]' includes visions, representations that do not accord with the normal way we explain physical and mental reality.[29] They are part of God's writing that we read as the language of the world. In turn, we transform our reading of God's word into art and poetry. What we see in this world we can paint, and our 'see[ing]' here goes beyond passive reception.

The way Blake speaks about seeing and painting the world makes it clear that we all, according to him, actively participate in shaping it. Ultimately, God is the author, but in reading what he has written, we also take part in the work's linguistic construction. Making sense of the world and articulating this process are akin to translation: 'Speaking is translation—from a tongue of angels into a human tongue, that is, thoughts in words—things in names—images in signs'. When we see and read the world, we interpret it, and that means we translate it. For the excessive thinkers this book is primarily concerned with, such translation is not a functionalist decoding activity or a fact-finding mission for the scientific or real structure of the universe whose puzzles we need to solve. Rather, it is a creative act that is sensitive to the fact that we as humans both need to and can transpose from one language into another. Once more language retains its privileged status: when we translate 'thoughts in words' or 'things in names' or 'images in signs', this is a linguistic activity: it is trans-lation, a carrying over, not a straight substitution or a mathematical equation. The point here is that linguistic translation is, to a degree, always opaque. It is part of an account of language that retains a trace of opacity at its centre. Translation does both: it reveals by transposing from one language to another, but it also conceals, since that transport is never completely transparent or successful. We have by now understood that 'languages' and 'translation' here do not just mean translating from one natural language to the next (say, from English to German). Translation concerns all systems of signification, even ones we only grasp marginally, such as the tongue of angels. For the people who want to read Blake's and Hamann's privileging of language as in tune with our contemporary proclivities, it becomes increasingly difficult to see how all this talk of angels, images, and signs will translate into standard twenty-first-century norms and tracks.

Let us consider some translations, forms of transposition, that have proven to be especially powerful or lasting for Blake and Hamann, especially in the sphere of literature and culture. They coincide in their prime and most important example: the Bible. As Blake tells us, the biblical text still remains 'more Entertaining & Instructive than any other book'. The main reason for such historical staying power is not ideological or philosophical but rather poetical. The Bible is so powerful

---

[29] Blake to Dr Trusler, p. 702.

because it is 'addressed to the Imagination which is Spiritual Sensation & but mediately to the Understanding or Reason'. Revelation is addressed to imagination. It is not addressed to 'Understanding or Reason'—that is, it is not philosophy's version of epistemology but rather a translation into a language that can keep the deeper qualities of its form. The power of the story of Genesis, the naming of the animals, the Tower of Babel, the narrative of Isaac and Abraham, or the Sermon on the Mount, does not lie in their appeal to the understanding, in a development of reason either to do with history (how old is the earth really?), translation (the exact location of the Tower of Babel?), ethics (what role does faith play in our moral decisions?), or politics (what are our codes and structures of representation?). The power of these stories, and many others besides, lies in how they speak to the imagination—how they translate outside of our normal understanding—and what, in that sphere, is revealed. When Ezekiel speaks of the wheels within wheels, that is not about comprehending the history of myth; it is about how God as a writer reveals Himself in the Bible and the poetical text of the world, and about how we can understand such writing in our own way and we represent it in turn.

It is evident by now that Blake and Hamann privilege not just language but poetic and expressive language in particular. Poetry defines our account of language from the beginning, and it is that poetic quality that the Bible has retained, much unlike other texts of supposed instruction that aim for unambiguous clarity. For Blake and Hamann, this is not just about the chronological primacy of poetry, like so many other eighteenth-century theories of language. For both of them, poetry continues to be the defining characteristic of all language until today, which, remember, is at the heart of all translation. Language's tropological nature adds to meaning rather than subtracts from it. Once more, this sounds similar to a particular version of poststructuralist thought, yet there is a deep assumption about the religious dimension to the tropological significance. As we will see, the claims by Hamann are qualitatively different from, say, Paul de Man's insistence on the inescapably figural structure of language, but no less radical.

Through the privileging of language, and tropological language in particular, the status of poetic expression becomes important and far more encompassing than we normally assume. In the extreme case of Blake's and Hamanns's thought, it goes beyond the imaginative or spiritual self-definition of the human and comprehends the sphere of the physical body. When they contend that we are defined through tropes and poetry, this includes the body itself: '[T]he body or outward form of man is derived from the Poetic Genius'. The poetic genius makes our body tangible and real. Blake's point suggests that there is a special place for the intersection between the material and the immaterial, and that this intersection directly relates to the overlap between the bodily and the poetical. If our outward form is 'derived from the Poetic Genius', then the relation between these two spheres is crucial, including how the 'translation' works from one sphere into another and what powers the 'deriv[ation]' from poetic genius into outward form. We should take seriously the insistence on the physical dimension of language, an aspect that, of course, is of considerable interest to contemporary criticism, especially when it comes to the sexual and gendered dimensions of the body and how they are figured in language.

Against most thought from both Enlightenment and Christian quarters, Blake and Hamann deeply believe not only that the body is a constitutive element of the word but also that this material connection should be celebrated. Remember that the invocation of genitalia in relation to imagining God was positive, not shameful. Similarly, in one of the most memorable phrasings of eighteenth-century language theory, Hamann speaks about 'the uterus of language, which is the *deipara* of our reason'. The image is as intriguing as it is drastic: language is the uterus that produces thought, the way that we construct the world. *Deipara* is the mother of God, and thus language becomes, in a variation of the sexual image, the holy mother of our reason. By referring to the 'uterus of language' (the uterus that *is* language), we are invited to think of it not as a mental, abstract, or neutral process but one that is gendered, physical, and literally sexual. There is no doubt the formulation is explicit, and, just like the first thesis ('My coarse imagination is never able to imagine a creative Spirit without genitalia'), playfully so. But, crucially, for all its playfulness, the formulation 'language is the uterus of thought' is neither a simile nor an analogy. The physicality of the phrasing is well considered: it is not that language is *like* a uterus, but rather that we are pushed to think about what that real equivalency might mean. In another context we read of language as the '*organon*' of reason: it connects, shapes, and forms, the mind and body.[30] It is a structural and structuring entity: giving birth to ideas, novels, or axioms does actually involve a body. Physical form is tied to their actual production as well as giving an account of them. This, of course, brings us back to the anthropological dimensions and limitations of our way of thinking with which we started—the creative spirits with genitalia. There is nothing to be embarrassed about when it comes to our uterus of thought and our inability to imagine a creative genius without genitalia. It is vital for Blake and Hamann that the link between sexual body, language, and creativity is celebrated, and celebrated loudly.

Once we are confronted with this strange pair of authors and their unusual statements, our first question as literary critics and intellectual historians is: How does such odd thinking fit into the model of literary history, into the divisions of Enlightenment and Romanticism? And what might this explanation tell us about the period's contemporary relevance? The reception of Blake and Hamann is telling on both accounts, since it attempts to tame their deeply unorthodox qualities in order to fit them into a familiar narrative that will make sense to us. This is the narrative of Enlightenment and Romanticism but also, much more fundamentally, the narrative that thinks of literary history in terms of the central and the marginal, the inside and the outside. Blake and Hamann are integrated into their respective national traditions in remarkably similar ways. They are what is best termed canonical outsiders. Blake and Hamann are classified and domesticated as exceptional artists or thinkers whose work is intriguing but historically too atypical to be truly critically relevant on its own terms. As we will see in due course (Chapter 3), even some of the early instances of comparative work follow this critical model.

---

[30] Griffith-Dickson, p. 520; emphasis in original. 'Organon' (N, 3: 284).

This book suggests that such a domestication is a mistake. Rather than domesticate them as outsiders, we need to unlock the theoretical-critical potential of these thinkers in a different way. Reading across languages helps us in this endeavour, but what is even more important is that we take these thinkers seriously, try and understand them on their own exorbitant terms, and attempt to read the period from a position that is not so much at the margins but rather outside of the track. This approach is different from the historical reception that Hamann and Blake have experienced in their respective literary and philosophical traditions. One of the most common reactions to their writings, both in their time and now, is that while they are undoubtedly interesting thinkers, they are also too hermetic, wilfully obscure, or simply too difficult to understand. This reception reveals a curious mixture of, on the one hand, admiration for their extraordinary creativity with, and on the other hand, an uneasiness about the excessiveness of their arguments and style. Although there is a certain intrigue about both Blake and Hamann, for many readers what ultimately prevails is the sense that their writings fundamentally cannot be placed in the context of known discourses. Their exaggerated tone and rhetorical flourishes mark them as extreme writers whose contributions are 'deep' but 'incomprehensible', 'creative' but 'mad'.

Two representative examples of how this critical reception tries to make sense of them in traditional ways are William Wordsworth commenting on Blake and Johann Wolfgang von Goethe writing on Hamann. Wordsworth's verdict openly reflects on his ambiguity: 'There is no doubt this poor man was mad'.[31] It is not a question of whether or not Blake is mad; there is 'no doubt' about it, even if that is precisely what makes him intriguing as an unusual figure. (Wordsworth goes on to say that it is Blake's 'madness' that makes him interesting.) We find variations of Wordsworth's patronizing assessment throughout British literary history: Blake is introduced as the quirky artist, the loveable but eccentric poet. Robert Southey speaks about Blake as a 'decided madman'; Robert Hunt talks about him as 'an unfortunate lunatic, whose personal inoffensiveness secures him from confinement'.[32] Later on in the nineteenth century, John Ruskin talks about Blake as 'diseased and wild' yet 'wise'.[33] Contemporary scholarship, as well as counterculture that celebrates Blake, often repeats this initial narrative of the wild yet canonical genius.[34] In all of these accounts,

---

[31] Qtd in Crabb Robinson, 'Reminiscences', p. 693. While the singularity of Blake and Hamann is important, it is a myth that they are completely unknown or obscure. Consider the level of their contemporary readers (William Wordsworth, Johann Wolfgang von Goethe). For a good contextualizing discussion, see Wayne C. Ripley, 'William Blake and the Hunt Circle', *Studies in Romanticism* 50, 1 (Spring 2011): 173–93.

[32] Bentley, *Blake Records*, pp. 310 and 283.

[33] John Ruskin, 'Expenditure', in *The Works of John Ruskin: Time and Tide, by Weare and Tyne. Twenty-Five Letters to a Working Man of Sunderland on the Laws of Work* (New York: John Wiley and Sons, 1889), pp. 18–21, 21.

[34] There is plenty of excellent secondary literature to make these points in much more detail, so I will leave it there for the moment. The best introductions to Hamann's thought available in English currently are Oswald Bayer, *A Contemporary in Dissent: Johann Georg Hamann as a Radical Enlightener* (Grand Rapids, MI: Eerdmans, 2012); John R. Betz, *After Enlightenment: The Post-Secular Vision of J. G. Hamann* (Malden, MA: Wiley-Blackwell, 2012); and Griffith-Dickson, *Hamann's Relational Metacriticism*. I mention more specialized studies later.

Blake is the addle-brained figure whose work is intriguing but, in the end, one who is too radical to be truly comprehensible as a thinker, and he is absorbed as such. We include him in a historical survey, and we even advertise that his work maintains a certain sense of impenetrability that, once identified as such, does not need to be engaged with at face value. For all his historically important presence, he is framed as a difficult figure who is part of the picture but who is coherently framed at the margins.

In Germany, there is a strand of Hamann reception that follows pretty much the same pattern. He was and still is widely regarded as an important yet ultimately mysterious figure of the period. As Goethe puts it, 'Here one sensed a profoundly thinking, well-grounded man who, although thoroughly familiar with the visible world and literature, still accepted the existence of something secret and inscrutable, and spoke about it in a highly individual manner. Of course, the literary arbiters of the day considered him an abstruse dreamer'.[35] This reaction is very common in the intellectual circles at the time and becomes somewhat of a historical norm. A generation after Hamann's death, G. W. F. Hegel describes Hamann's writing as a 'tiresome riddle'.[36] From early on, Hamann's nickname was the 'Magus of the North', a description that emphasizes the mysterious, even mystical aspect of his work that ultimately absorbed him into a traditional understanding of literary or philosophical discourse, an outsider.[37] Thus, both Blake and Hamann become figures who are deep, inscrutable thinkers who end up at the margins. They are seen as highly talented, yet literary history has reacted to their incapacity or unwillingness to insert themselves into traditional stylistic and historical trajectories of poetry and of philosophy by making them representatives of peripheral thinking. The only way in which they are legible is as mad creative geniuses who remain at the edge of the period.

---

[35] Johann Wolfgang von Goethe, *From My Life: Poetry and Truth; Parts One to Three*, trans. Robert Heitner vol. 4 of *Goethe's Collected Works* ed. Victor Lange; Eric Blackall; Cyrus Hamlin 12 vols (Princeton NJ: Princeton University Press, 1994–5), p. 379. 'Man ahndete hier einen tiefdenkenden gründlichen Mann, der, mit der offenbaren Welt und Literatur genau bekannt, doch auch noch etwas Geheimes, Unerforschliches gelten ließ und sich darüber auf eine ganz eigne Weise aussprach. Von denen, die damals die Literatur des Tags beherrschten, ward er freilich für einen abstrusen Schwärmer gehalten' (Johann Wolfgang von Goethe, *Goethes Werke*, 6 vols [Frankfurt am Main: Insel, 1965] 5: 463). Goethe wanted to edit Hamann's works, a task he never completed (see Goethe, 5: 464). On the complex relation between Goethe and Hamann, see the excellent article by Arthur Henkel, 'Goethe und Hamann. Ergänzende Bemerkungen zu einem Geistergespräch', *Euphorion* 77 (1983): 453–69.

[36] Lisa Marie Anderson, *Hegel on Hamann*, trans. Anderson (Evanston, IL: Northwestern University Press, 2008), p. 7.

[37] Often it is assumed that Hamann gave himself this name to underline his link to Christian thought and mediation. In fact, the name was coined by one of his supporters, President Moder of Darmstadt. See Karl C. Carvacchi, *Biographische Erinnerungen an Johann Georg Hamann, den Magus in Norden* (Münster: Friedrich Regensberg, 1855), p. 20. Hamann used the name with a certain irony and bemusement, though he was surely flattered by it and adopted it in his intricate play with identity. At one point he suggests that 'my Chinese name is Mien-Man-Hoam', but that answers to his writings should be directed to the 'Magus of the North, resident at 758 Alter Graben at Königsberg in Prussia' (Mein chinesischer Name ist Mien-Man-Hoam. Richten Sie aber... Ihre Antwort an den Magum in Norden, haussässig am alten Graben No. 758. zu Königsberg in Preußen) (N, 3: 77).

The problem with this model of reception and criticism is that it basically domesticates them *as* canonical outsiders, *as* marginal figures. It blunts their critical edge since it is a model that presses them into a version of history, theory, and language that they completely and forcefully reject. My suggestion is that we need to read figures such as Blake and Hamann in a way that takes seriously their status as exorbitants, not peripherals, as having left the common tracks of our historical and literary understanding. What that also means is that we resist the urge to claim for these figures a central—instead of a marginal—position. My argument is not that we need to put Blake, Hamann, the Moravians, or Fuseli at the centre of the period. That is what happens in familiar literary criticism, especially in projects that recover marginal or forgotten thinkers. In contrast, this book argues for something that is theoretically more experimental: How might we figure out what it means to read from a vantage point that is *outside* the tracks (*ex-orbita*) of literary history altogether, an exorbitant position?

The claim of this book is that its most prominent figures, especially Blake and Hamann, offer a way of approaching the period that reveals a historical and philosophical complexity and depth that we have not appreciated. Their views on language, for instance, are extremely difficult to reconcile with some of our basic assumptions formed in the *longue durée* about epistemology and ontology. Their strangeness of thought taken seriously yet retained *as* strange alerts us to the orthodoxies of these assumptions that have come to us to feel natural. We have to resist our impulse to normalize these figures, to pretend that we can recover them by putting them at the centre. Such a move, just as their domestication as canonical outsiders, does not engage with their full critical power. This book will continuously try and resist the strong temptation of the critical move of putting exorbitants at the centre because, I believe, there is something to be gained when we engage with these excessive ways of thinking as being out of orbit.

Ultimately, the engagement with the exorbitant thinkers of the Anglo-German Enlightenment suggests that we should explode the difference between Enlightenment and Romanticism. This argument obviously implies a radically different literary history that sidesteps conventional chronology. It also works with a model that does not arrange authors in terms of contrast between these two categories. Of course, both of these traditional ways of doing literary history are very powerful, which is why it is difficult to think our way out of their dominance. Most conventional histories work well when they are told monolingually. They are often either presented as neat consecutive developments, like beads on a rosary, or in a Bloomian scheme of influence that has a telos or point of reference. In literary criticism of the eighteenth and nineteenth centuries, such a model helps us to connect history and literary history. It allows us to read literature in what sometimes might be called a 'historical way' because it maps the way that Enlightenment and Romanticism function as terms across disciplines and allows us to talk about their different local valences in an intelligible manner that we understand throughout history. However, for all the uses of these models, the underlying assumptions are deeply problematic. It will be useful to consider them in turns.

WHY TAKE THE TROUBLE?

The most basic example for the type of literary history that *Exorbitant Enlightenment* seeks to dispel is scholarship that relies on a sharp contrast between Enlightenment and Romanticism. Despite all the evidence that alerts us to the complexity of the period, once it comes to explaining how the Enlightenment relates to Romanticism, much scholarship goes for a model of clear contrast and juxtaposition. The old story that the rationalist Enlightenment violently clashed with an emotional Romanticism is alive and well. Even an immensely experienced contributor on the eighteenth century such as T. J. Reed makes the claim in his *Light in Germany* (2015) that 'the Romantic movement...and more crudely and brutally the later stages of German history' were responsible for 'rejecting the Enlightenment and all of its values in favour of a more "profound", uniquely German, intellectual (or more precisely anti-intellectual) tradition. It was difficult for defenders of reason to confront declared irrationalism'.[38] Similarly to Isaiah Berlin, Reed intimates a line from German Romanticism to the Third Reich, seeing each as an irrational reaction against an Enlightenment that was solely interested in reason, rationality, and clarity. It is a version of history that crassly simplifies the role of reason ('no high-falutin affair', apparently) and also historical events themselves.[39]

The proclamation of the exceptional status of the French Revolution in many narratives that pitch Enlightenment against Romanticism is a good example for a vision of history that is overinvested in a model of dialectical progress through a sequence of ruptures. The event is the classic locus used to posit a beginning to Romanticism, a new epoch that radically changed everything and everybody, thereby marking the end of Enlightenment. Supposedly, this is immediately clear to late eighteenth-century authors in Britain, such as Wordsworth or Samuel Taylor Coleridge. One of the many problems with this story is that, as Michael Sonenscher and Nicholas Halmi have pointed out in powerful ways, there have to be in place certain ideas to make the Revolution legible as the type of event that begins a new epoch.[40] Although 1789 was important, it did not mark a complete Foucauldian epistemic shift; and even though discourse changed as a result of the historical realities that Romanticism created, there was a continuity of ideas between these two periods, much of which was acknowledged at the time. We need to deconstruct our notions of the Enlightenment and Romanticism as juxtaposed and temper the myth of rupture that has become an unconscious motor of many accounts that pitch these two complex concepts and historical periods against one another. It pays off, in other words, to be less enraptured with rupture, especially if this rupture ultimately ends up creating a rather smooth, conventional narrative.

---

[38] T. J. Reed, *Light in Germany: Scenes from an Unknown Enlightenment* (Chicago, IL: University of Chicago Press, 2015), p. 2.

[39] Reed, *Light in Germany*, p. 13. It is not entirely clear whether this is Reed's view or his ventriloquism of Kant. Either way, it seems egregiously wrong. I will discuss Berlin's role shortly.

[40] See Michael Sonenscher, *Before the Deluge: Public Debt, Inequality, and the Intellectual Origins of the French Revolution* (Princeton, NJ: Princeton University Press, 2007); and Nicholas Halmi, *The Genealogy of the Romantic Symbol* (Oxford: Oxford University Press, 2008).

One attempt at such more granular scholarship has been to develop what Vivasvan Soni describes as 'A New Passion for Enlightenment', which includes an excitement about its diversity.[41] This passion opens a space that has been cleared by historical works—including J. G. A. Pocock's arguments about the multiplicity of Enlightenments and Jonathan I. Israel's *Radical Enlightenment*—to give two prominent examples.[42] Scholars as different as Srinivas Aravamudan, John Bender, Peter Mortensen, or Pascale Casanova have brought many of these general historical insights to the table when it comes to specific issues of the variety of Enlightenment history and culture in literary studies.[43] There is also work that pays particular relation to polyglot philology and the Anglo-German context, though, again, much of this focuses on the nineteenth century.[44] What holds all of these accounts together is an investment in telling a story about the Enlightenment that is different from an account that was, and in certain places remains, standard: the story that defines the Enlightenment mostly as a philosophically homogenous movement whose advance took place hand in hand with secularism throughout Europe. Charles Taylor's monumental *A Secular Age* (2007) articulates a similarly diverse vision, which inspired many others in its wake.[45] All of this scholarship has shown that there was much more contact between Berlin, Paris, Edinburgh, and what we used to call 'the East' than we might have assumed. As has become clear through the discovery of an Anglo-German network, it also pays off to foreground the relation between Königsberg (Kant's and Hamann's home) and Blake's London in this map. Some scholars will be tempted to understand these different interacting sources across nations and languages in terms of network theory, whether it be in

[41] Vivasvan Soni, 'A New Passion for Enlightenment', review of John Bender, *Ends of Enlightenment*; Hina Nazar, *Enlightened Sentiments: Judgment and Autonomy in the Age of Sensibility*; John C. O'Neal, *The Progressive Poetics of Confusion in the French Enlightenment*; and Wolfram Schmidgen, *Exquisite Mixture: The Virtues of Impurity in Early Modern England*, *Eighteenth-Century Studies* 48, 2 (Winter 2015): 239–45.

[42] See J. G. A. Pocock, *Barbarism and Religion*, 6 vols (Cambridge: Cambridge University Press, 2000–15), esp. vol. 1, *The Enlightenments of Edward Gibbon, 1737–1764*; Pocock, 'Enlightenment and Counter-Enlightenment, Revolution and Counter-Revolution; A Eurosceptical Enquiry', *History of Political Thought* 20, 1 (January 1999): 125–39; and Jonathan I. Israel, *Radical Enlightenment: Philosophy and the Making of Modernity 1650–1750* (Oxford: Oxford University Press, 2001).

[43] See Srinivas Aravamudan, *Enlightenment Orientalism: Resisting the Rise of the Novel* (Chicago, IL: University of Chicago Press, 2011); John Bender, *Ends of Enlightenment* (Stanford, CA: Stanford University Press, 2012); Peter Mortensen, *British Romanticism and Continental Influences: Writing in an Age of Europhobia* (Houndmills, Basingstoke: Palgrave, 2007); and Pascale Casanova, *The World Republic of Letters* (Cambridge, MA: Harvard University Press, 2004). Also see Ian Hunter, *Rival Enlightenments: Civil and Metaphysical Philosophy in Early Modern Germany* (Cambridge: Cambridge University Press, 2001).

[44] See Kristina Mendicino, *Prophecies of Language: The Confusion of Tongues in German Romanticism* (New York: Fordham University Press, 2017); and Gregory Maertz, *Literature and the Cult of Personality: Essays on Goethe and His Influence* (Stuttgart: Ibidem, 2017).

[45] See Charles Taylor, *A Secular Age* (Cambridge, MA: Harvard University Press, 2007). Also see Colin Jager, *The Book of God: Secularization and Design in the Romantic Era* (Philadelphia, PA: University of Pennsylvania Press, 2007); Jon Mee, *Dangerous Enthusiasm: William Blake and the Culture of Radicalism in the 1790s* (Oxford: Clarendon, 1992); Betz, *After Enlightenment*; Paul Hamilton, *Metaromanticism: Aesthetics, Literature, Theory* (Chicago, IL: University of Chicago Press, 2003); and Thomas Pfau, *Minding the Modern: Human Agency, Intellectual Traditions, and Responsible Knowledge* (Notre Dame, IN: University of Notre Dame Press, 2015).

Caroline Levine's recent sense or a more theoretical one such as Franco Moretti's.[46] The growing body of work arguing for different, parallel versions of the Enlightenment also has prompted descriptions of whole counter-movements. Already E. P. Thompson, for instance, locates a '*counter*-enlightenment... in London in the 1780s' and links it to 'an explosion of anti-rationalism', a formulation that was echoed by Berlin in his own account of a counter-Enlightenment that focuses on Hamann, Johann Gottfried Herder, and Giambattista Vico.[47] More recently, scholars such as Christian Thorne have produced a so-called dialectic of counter-Enlightenment, charting a genealogy of scepticism through eighteenth-century thought.[48]

All of this work explains much more satisfactorily the late eighteenth century than the story of a standoff between Enlightenment and Romanticism, especially when it comes to accounting for the importance of transnational and translinguistic influences. That said, all these accounts still function by creating a narrative of duality (Enlightenment versus Counter-Enlightenment) or dialectics (centre versus margin). Like most recuperations, they either argue that we have missed the central, historical importance of a figure (or a movement) or, alternatively, they suggest that we need to focus on the importance of a figure that was historically marginalized but turns out to be central for modernity. If we have missed it historically, then we should address this by putting this outsider at the centre (such as how Israel locates Baruch Spinoza at the centre of *Radical Enlightenment*). In the second case, we tell the story of how a formally marginalized figure came to stand at the centre of contemporary thought (e.g. framing Friedrich Nietzsche as a figure who was once marginal and now is central).

The literary history told in *Exorbitant Enlightenment* challenges these common dialectical models. It suggests that certain literary cultures and histories organized themselves in multidimensional and multilingual spaces that do not follow such a margin/centre principle. One of these spaces can be found in the Anglo-German context in eighteenth-century Britain. This includes singular figures such as Blake, Hamann, Fuseli, Lavater, or James Hervey, some of whom are so radically different that their thought sidesteps the tracks that we use to explain the period to ourselves in terms of inside and outside. It also covers institutions, such as the Moravians, who are a group that, although a strong part of the London cultural scene (i.e. we would normally move them more towards the centre), actively maintain their integrity as outsiders through their multilingual practices, as shown in Chapters 3 and 5.

[46] See Caroline Levine, *Forms: Whole, Rhythm, Hierarchy, Network* (Princeton, NJ: Princeton University Press, 2015); and Franco Moretti, *Graphs, Maps, Trees: Abstract Models for Literary History* (New York: Verso, 2005).
[47] E. P. Thompson, *Witness against the Beast: William Blake and the Moral Law* (New York: New Press, 1993), p. xiv. Also see Isaiah Berlin, *Three Critics of Enlightenment: Vico, Hamann, Herder* (New York: Random House, 2000). For a thorough exposition of Berlin's influence, see Timo Günther, 'Mythos und Irrationalismus: Isiah Berlins Blick auf Hamann', in *In the Embrace of the Swan: Anglo-German Mythologies in Literature, the Visual Arts and Cultural Theory*, ed. Rüdiger Görner and Angus James Nicholls (Berlin: De Gruyter, 2010), pp. 353–68.
[48] Christian Thorne, *Dialectic of Counter-Enlightenment* (Cambridge, MA: Harvard University Press, 2009).

All of these figures place a high importance on keeping the integrity of their non-belonging. It becomes a central part of the cultural and literary practice. In this sense, they show how this radical, exorbitant quality not only is a critical term but also describes a method, a positioning, that moves them away from the normal way of doing literary history or analysis.

Blake and Hamann are the two most powerful examples of authors in the period to use this method: they are prime examples to show us what it means to think exorbitantly, which is why I pay special attention to them. Both of them carve open a space in which thinking outside of the normal lanes of criticism and theory is possible. It is a space that follows a different logic, that can be excessive, overboard, sometimes even incomprehensible, but never with the desire to be reconciled or be at the centre. It is no surprise that both Blake and Hamann saw themselves as authors who were not really writing for anybody but themselves and for whom normal models of history did not really apply. They open up a space to think about language, epistemology, sexuality, and history in ways that are exorbitantly different. The most powerful approach to deal with this way of thinking is not to recover it historically in order to slot it into a history but, rather, to explore the avenues it opens.

In order to explore the space that figures such as Blake and Hamann carve open we need to attempt to think about the Enlightenment and Romanticism in a way that avoids the continuous switch to the model of inside/outside or the axis of centre/periphery. The heuristic that this book suggests has a theoretical purpose to it that goes beyond historical recovery. The theoretical purpose is to outline the nature of these exorbitant thinkers, which means to avoid falling back into the model of substituting centre with periphery. Such an approach disturbs our normal account of the *longue durée* significantly. And it allows us to understand how thinking of a very different kind is enabled and expressed, without shutting down a central part of it. Many of the critical strategies that we have inherited via the nineteenth century—the classic ways of doing historicism or literary criticism up to poststructuralism and after—have been distracting. That includes the many ways in which poststructural criticism has treated marginal figures, not just in its more philosophical forms (e.g. the work of Jacques Derrida), but also in feminist or postcolonial work. Although these approaches have been tremendously important in many ways, they have also shut down our capacity to recognize what it is to escape that model, to move to a space that is beyond the margins or the track, and to be curious about the possibilities that are provided of viewing the world from such a place. These approaches are so concerned with the status of the centre that they do not allow excessive or unusual thinking to continue *as* unusual thinking that is not defined in relation to a centre.

'Romanticism' and 'Enlightenment' are constricting and unhelpful categories if we want to understand exorbitant thinkers and institutions, several of which deeply add to our understanding of the eighteenth century. That does not mean, of course, we should give up completely on these words or categories. The distinctions continue to be powerful when it comes to making particular, important arguments that help us understand the period in certain ways, and there is no doubt that they are here to stay. However, we also must understand that these same distinctions are less than helpful when we want to understand certain other complex cultural relations and positions and their theoretical import. Not all authors, institutions, or ideas can be moved like pieces on a board, from the periphery to the centre: that suggests a different version of literary history, not all of which can be subsumed under the same model. The exorbitant Enlightenment is one we have been missing so far, and one that demands our attention if we want to understand the suppleness of the eighteenth century better.

READING ANGLO-GERMAN CONSTELLATIONS

One obvious yet important question remains: *How* does one tell an exorbitant literary history? This methodological issue brings the subtitle of this book—Anglo-German Constellations—into view. The image of a constellation serves my task well here because it sidesteps, just like my main objects of study, a model of historical analysis that is primarily monolingual, causal, dialectical, and sequential. In contrast, a constellation breaks with the linear and monolingual construction of literary history that has led to the silos of narrow national literature or periodization. What emerges across the book are connections that a more conventional way of ordering the material may not suggest as readily. The book's chapters are best understood as stars in a constellation, relating to each other in various ways but not in a uniform, regular, or consecutive pattern. The chapters span a multitude of topics, areas, and authors. They cover modes of cultural production, religious institutions, and literary genres, and they analyse in detail how some authors discuss particular topics such as the origin of language; the connection between philosophy, politics, and religion; the importance of aesthetics for religious experience; or the irreducibly physical character of the linguistic sign. A key suggestion of this book is that these elements all belong *together*—but that the relations between these chapters and figures are not simple. And the most illuminating ones are often not sequential. Thus, the chapters in the book resemble not so much beads on a string as an irregular pattern of interrelated case studies.

Constellations also have a spatial, geographical dimension that adds to their diachronically disruptive form. What we see here are a set of relations that cross borders and languages across time and space. They unveil a set of linguistic connections between figures and institutions that remain hidden if we approach these sources in a traditional, monolingual way. And their irregular but meaningful arrangement is a much more accurate reflection of the complexity of the materials at hand than what a linear story would be able to capture. In practice, this covers direct historical influence, such as, say, Fuseli's translations (discussed in Chapter 3), but also broader concerns, such as an understanding of how much a polyglot culture was, in fact, part of British society at the time (described in Chapter 1). The London Moravians and their Anglo-German hymns (discussed in Chapters 5 and 7), which became a model for Methodism, are a perfect example that this account follows an inadequate model which we need to redress. The geographical dimension and its multilingual quality include Blake and Hamann, and putting their work in a polyglot relation to one another means that their writings on language (discussed in Chapter 4), religion (Chapter 6), or sexuality (Chapter 8) can unfold their full radicality. Instead of being marginal figures of their respective national literary histories, Blake and Hamann become two important exorbitant stars that illuminate Anglo-German constellations across the eighteenth century and beyond.

One of the most fertile thinkers in relation to the operative terms and methods in this book—exorbitance, Enlightenment, Romanticism, constellations—is Walter Benjamin. Although his name does not appear much in the main body of the text, his ideas helped to shape the material substantially, including the rationale for its arrangement. Benjamin is a crucial figure not only for the theoretical underpinnings of the idea of constellation but also, of course, for the understanding of how these claims relate to a deeper theoretical dimension for our contemporary moment.[49] Two of Benjamin's main critical targets are a dialectical version of history and an impoverished account of language, both of which are topics that are pivotal to my readings throughout. Similarly to his sustained interest in the relation between theological language and history, Benjamin wrote about constellations throughout his life and works. We find considerations about them in his early essays on language and the mimetic faculty in his later *Origin of German Tragic Drama*, as well as in his last work, the *Arcades Project*. It is a topic that for him connects issues of history, the relation between Ideas and concepts, as well as his ideas on language and hermeneutics.

For this book, the most important aspect of Benjamin's scattered writings on constellations is the early argument about a link between language and reading through mimesis. For Benjamin, an expert on Hamann and Romanticism himself, in modernity our ability to perceive certain relations, and thus to actively produce similarities through our mimetic faculty, has changed. A transformation has taken place, which we, as historians and philosophers, must take into consideration.

> [T]his is the question: is it the case that the mimetic faculty is dying out, or has perhaps a transformation taken place? Some aspects of astrology may indicate, even if indirectly, the direction in which such a transformation might lie. For as inquirers into the

---

[49] The idea and the term of the constellation has been taken up by a variety of scholars over the years, especially in relation to Walter Benjamin, as well as to Theodor Adorno, Friedrich Nietzsche, and other figures of philosophy, theology, or politics. In Anglophone literary studies of Romanticism, the idea of a constellation as a critical principle is mentioned with relative frequency, especially in relation to Benjamin, yet, with the exception of Colin Jager's, these studies generally invoke the term rather than discuss it in any detail. In contrast, in German studies of the nineteenth century there is a whole technical field of *Konstellationsforschung*, developed by Dieter Henrich in his study of German idealism. See Jacques Khalip and Forest Pyle, ed., *Constellations of a Contemporary Romanticism* (Oxford: Oxford University Press, 2016); Colin Jager, *Unquiet Things: Secularism in the Romantic Age* (Philadelphia: University of Pennsylvania Press, 2015), pp. 205–23; Andreas Lehr, 'Kleine Formen: Adornos Kombinationen: Konstellation/Konfiguration, Montage, und Essay' (PhD dissertation, University of Freiburg, 2000); Dieter Henrich, *Konstellationen: Probleme und Debatten am Ursprung der idealistischen Philosophie (1789–1795)* (Stuttgart: Klett-Cotta, 1991; Martin Mulsow and Marcelo Stamm, ed., *Konstellationsforschung* (Frankfurt: Suhrkamp, 2005); and Helmut Lethen, Annegret Pelz, and Michael Rohrwasser, ed., *Konstellationen: Versuchsanordnungen eines Schreibens* (Vienna: Vienna University Press, 2013).

old traditions we must take into account the possibility that human beings might have perceived manifest formations, that is, that objects had a mimetic character, where nowadays we would not even be capable of suspecting it. For example, in the constellation of the stars.[50]

At this point we have lost the possibility of meaningfully describing the relation between the constellation and the individual, just as we find it almost impossible to understand the exorbitant. Although this book is not an exercise in astrology, I do want to insist that Benjamin's argument needs to be taken seriously, especially as he develops it when it comes to language. Even though we may 'no longer possess what once made it possible to speak of a similarity which might exist between a constellation of stars and a human being', we 'nonetheless... possess a canon on the basis of which we can bring towards clarification the obscurity attached to the concept of the non-sensuous similarity. And that canon is language'.[51] Language, not only for the early Benjamin, is a way to access relations that are not easily perceptible. Its powers are ontological and magical, a quality that we need to remember if we want to understand this language well. Of course, this is a deeply Hamannian point and a view that has significant ties to a Blakean understanding of the power of the word. For Benjamin, the ability to read this language is what becomes central to historiography and heuristics alike.

The idea of reading, especially with such a metaphysically charged account of language, is not unambiguous.[52] Benjamin himself points out that 'reading' has 'profane and magical senses', a set of connotations that is intensified in German, since 'lesen' means not just 'to read' in all its different ways but also 'to collect' or 'to gather'. It is worth providing the full context of Benjamin's argument:

The pupil reads his ABC book, and the astrologer reads the future in the stars. In the first clause, reading is not separated into its two components. But the second clarifies both levels of the process: the astrologer reads off the position of the stars in the heavens; simultaneously he reads the future and fate from it.

If, in the dawn of humanity, this reading from stars, entrails, and coincidences represented reading *per se*, and further, if there were mediating links to a newer kind of

---

[50] Walter Benjamin, 'Doctrine of the Similar (1933)', trans. Knut Tarnowski, in special Walter Benjamin issue of *New German Critique* 17 (Spring 1979): 65–9, 66. 'Die Frage ist nur die: ob es sich um ein Absterben des mimetischen Vermögens oder aber vielleicht um eine mit ihm stattgehabte Verwandlung handelt. In welcher Richtung eine solche jedoch liegen könnte, darüber läßt sich, wenn auch indirekt, einiges der Astrologie entnehmen. Wir müssen nämlich als Erforscher der alten Überlieferungen damit rechnen, daß sinnfällige Gestaltung, mimetischer Objektcharakter bestanden habe, wo wir ihn heute nicht einmal zu ahnen fähig sind. Zum Beispiel in den Konstellationen der Sterne' (Walter Benjamin, *Aufsätze, Essays, Vorträge*, vol. 2, part 1, of *Gesammelte Schriften*, 7 vols, ed. Rolf Tiedemann and Hermann Schweppenhäuser (Frankfurt: Suhrkamp, 1991), p. 206.
[51] Benjamin, 'Doctrine of the Similar', p. 66–7. '[I]n unserer Wahrnehmung dasjenige nicht mehr besitzen, was es einmal möglich machte, von einer Ähnlichkeit zu sprechen, die bestehe zwischen einer Sternenkonstellation und einem Menschen. Jedoch besitzen wir einen Kanon, nach dem die Unklarheit, die dem Begriff von unsinnlicher Ähnlichkeit anhaftet, sich einer Klärung näher bringen läßt. Und dieser Kanon ist die Sprache' (Benjamin, *Gesammelte Schriften*, 2.1, p. 207).
[52] See Bettine Menke, 'Magie des Lesens', in *Namen, Texte, Stimmen: Walter Benjamins Sprachphilosophie*, ed. Thomas Regehly and Iris Gniosdorsch (Stuttgart: Akademie der Diözese Rotenberg, 1993), pp. 109–37.

reading, as represented by the runes, then one might well assume tht [*sic*] the mimetic faculty, which was earlier the basis for clairvoyance, quite gradually found its way into language and writing in the course of a development over thousands of years, thus creating for itself in language and writing the most perfect archive of non-sensuous similarity. Language is the highest application of the mimetic faculty: a medium into which the earlier perceptive capabilities for recognizing the similar had entered without residue, so that it is now language which represents the medium in which objects meet and enter into relationship with each other, no longer directly, as once in the mind of the augur or priest, but in their essences, in their most volatile and delicate substances, even in their aromata. In other words: it is to writing and language that clairvoyance has, over the course of history, yielded its old powers.[53]

Benjamin insists that language has a particular and privileged access to certain forms of knowledge. It is more than coincidence that this book pushes multilingualism as a particularly powerful form of analysis, especially in order to see relations that we have not seen before. The focus on authors whose strongest works are on language— Blake, Hamann, the Moravians, Lavater, Fuseli—and literary genres (rather than, say, visual culture) is also not coincidental. All of this is not to say that the constellations I propose here are somehow readings on the magnitude Benjamin refers to. Nevertheless, they come from a methodological place that believes it is worth entertaining some of the ways that Benjamin, Hamann, or Blake articulate these issues. Admittedly, such a turn leads this book into highly difficult and choppy waters when it comes to issues of history, theory, theology, or metaphysics. But just because these case studies and their arrangement complicate these larger categories and do not solve them does not mean we should ignore them.

If we truly want to understand our literary history and theoretical position within it better, then we need to risk engaging with material that will trouble both us and the objects of our study. Thus, this constellation of chapters asks fundamental questions of our critical practice. The case studies ask us to query our accounts of sequential historicity and often draw upon a theory of language that is utterly different from the way we generally think about this topic. Not in that they are applications of a Benjaminian theory; any such crass mechanical model would be directly contravening what is at stake here methodologically. It is more that in both

---

[53] Benjamin, 'Doctrine of the Similar', 68. 'Der Schüler liest das Abcbuch und der Astrolog die Zukunft in den Sternen. Im ersten Satze tritt das Lesen nicht in seine beiden Komponenten auseinander. Dagegen wohl im zweiten, der den Vorgang nach seinen beiden Schichten deutlich macht: der Astrolog liest den Gestirnstand von den Sternen am Himmel ab; er liest zugleich aus ihm die Zukunft oder das Geschick heraus.

Wenn nun dieses Herauslesen aus Sternen, Eingeweiden, Zufällen in der Urzeit der Menschheit das Lesen schlechthin war, wenn es weiterhin Vermittlungsglieder zu einem neuen Lesen, wie die Runen es gewesen sind, gegeben hat, so liegt die Annahme sehr nahe, jene mimetische Begabung, welche früher das Fundament der Hellsicht gewesen ist, sei in jahrtausendlangem Gange der Entwicklung ganz allmählich in Sprache und Schrift hineingewandert und habe sich in ihnen das vollkommenste Archiv unsinnlicher Ähnlichkeit geschaffen. Dergestalt wäre die Sprache die höchste Verwendung des mimetischen Vermögens: ein Medium, in das ohne Rest die frühern Merkfähigkeiten für das Ähnliche so eingegangen seien, daß nun sie das Medium darstellt, in dem sich die Dinge nicht mehr direkt wie früher in dem Geist des Sehers oder Priesters sondern in ihren Essenzen, flüchtigsten und feinsten Substanzen, ja Aromen begegnen und zu einander in Beziehung treten. Mit andern Worten: Schrift und Sprache sind es, an die die Hellsicht ihre alten Kräfte im Laufe der Geschichte abgetreten hat' (Benjamin, *Gesammelte Schriften*, 2.1, p. 209).

cases the full critical potential only unfolds if we do not try and domesticate it into our own more orthodox narratives and critical assumptions. We need to let the invocation of a Benjaminian constellation, or a Hamannian metacritique, or a Blakean prophecy unfold their full critical power. Much criticism does not let this happen simply because it ignores the more unusual parts of their thinking, treating these aspects as archival oddities, an approach that actually denies them their ability to unsettle our own critical assumptions.

The constellations that this book presents are examples of how polyglossia can help us see relations across language and history that are otherwise uncovered. Blake, Hamann, the Moravians, and Fuseli are all unlocked through multilingualism. There is a wider dimension to this, of course. Hamann speaks of the multilingual, Babelian condition of the world in the following terms: 'The confusion of language is a history, a phaenomeon, a continuing miracle, and a parable, through which God still continues to speak to us'.[54] In a similar vein, Benjamin states that '[t]he multiplicity of histories resembles the multiplicity of languages'.[55] Although each language is distinct, we need to compare and contrast that multiplicity of languages if we want to understand our critical understanding, its history, and their articulation better. Such an attention to the method of multilingualism compels us to revisit the growing body of literature in Enlightenment studies with new questions and an alternate focus. Polyglot criticism not only is additive, but it also allows us to see different relations. It must also be open to a way of putting things in unusual ways, reading them in terms that we do not immediately recognize. The point here is that in some cases it might help us to switch out of our critical predilections and orthodoxies. In our case here this means that reading across languages can help us perceive certain connections that were not visible before.

Language is however, *pace* Hamann, not everything. The comparativism that allows the serious questioning of the literary-historical categories of Enlightenment and Romanticism are multiple. As we know, comparative work is by definition at once totalizing and yet desperately incomplete. Benjamin's qualification about the multiplicity of languages in comparative work makes this point in a suggestive way: 'Universal history in the present-day sense, can never be more than a kind of Esperanto. The idea of a universal history is a messianic idea'.[56] Even comparative work needs to understand that it is patchwork, a made-up Esperanto that deals with fragmented histories, which constitute the reality of the world. The impulse to compare does not mean we fall foul of assuming that we will see or resolve everything through this comparison. Just as there is no one machine that will make everything run, the comparativisms in this book are multiple.

---

[54] 'Die Verwirrung der Sprache ist eine Geschichte, ein *Phaenomeon*, ein fortdauerndes Wunder, und ein Geichnis, wodurch Gott noch immer fortfährt mit uns zu reden' (Hamann, *Londoner Schriften*, p. 282).
[55] Walter Benjamin, 'Paralipomena to "On the Concept of History"', in *1938–1940, vol. 4 of Walter Benjamin: Selected Writings*, trans. Edmund Jephcott and others, ed. Howard Eiland and Michael W. Jennings, 4 vols (Cambridge, MA: Belknap Press of Harvard University Press, 1996–2003), pp. 401–11, 405. 'Die Vielheit der "Historien" ist eng verwandt wenn nicht identisch mit der Vielheit der Sprachen' (Benjamin, *Gesammelte Schriften* 1.3, p. 1235).
[56] Ibid. 'Universalgeschichte im heutigen Sinn ist immer nur eine Sorte von Esperanto'.

Most comparative scholarly approaches focus on one of the aspects or relations that their material presents. Many of them look comparatively at the historical aspects, or they turn towards the institutional; some other works focus on issues of transmission; and another set, especially in literary studies, are attentive to comparisons between literary forms or genres. The ambition of this book is to run many of these comparative methods simultaneously, side by side. Together, they form the Anglo-German constellations that reveal more than either their sequential arrangement would, or than would a focus on only one aspect of the material. *Exorbitant Enlightenment* is thus a book about the power of multiple comparativisms. It argues that such a method, in its many different forms, is a necessary heuristic for a serious assessment of the period by presenting an irregular arrangement of problems and suggests how we might work them with precision and theoretical acuity. The book does not pretend to have solved them. My hope and aim is that other scholars can think about and work with these constellations and the problems they present, approach them in multiple ways, or illuminate new ones through their own work.

It remains, as is customary, to briefly explain a few technical issues, including what this study is not, even though most of the book's antagonistic relation to linear history, ideas of progress, or presentism, will be obvious by now. Overall, the study has a commitment to the deep study of primary texts, their historical contexts, and their conceptual import. As a result, much of the main body of this book is on primary sources and the close analysis of that material. A lot of the discussions of scholarly conversations are relegated to the book's footnotes, which therefore are extensive. The notes offer readers who are interested in the metadimension the chance to pursue important sources and discussions further, but they also allow readers whose investment lies in the insights that emerge directly from the historical material to follow the main argument of the book more easily.

Of course, the constellations presented in this book cannot, by definition, make claims for being comprehensive. There are topics that directly relate to the issues raised in this book, but which are so far beyond my expertise I simply cannot cover them. One such topic is a deeper study of music, especially understood as a language. The Moravians, Blake, Hamann, and the many Protestant connections in the Anglo-German context in London—all are deeply shaped by musical practice, theory, and transmission. For the most part, even in the chapter on the hymn, I had to leave out the technical discussion of the performance and possible sound of the performance. I hope a later study will address these matters. Similarly, many of the transatlantic connections, especially when it comes to the export of nonconformist Protestantism in the eighteenth century (for instance, the Moravians in Pennsylvania), have been left aside so I could keep the focus on Europe. I am aware of the irony that, in a study that argues for the importance of transnationalism and polyglot scholarship, I am still on only one continent and covering only two languages. However, I think of these limitations as invitations for further study and hope that the insights and methodologies presented here will open up territory for further polyglot literary studies and cultural histories.

Much of the analysis in this book is on language, and it is central to the examples and figures that I discuss in detail. Other scholars might have chosen a different approach, instead focusing more on science, technology, questions of material culture, or visual art. At no point was the aim to build an all-encompassing alternative account of the period as a whole or to claim that it is only through language that we can understand any version of the Enlightenment.

Let me close with a small but important issue of nomenclature. In this book, sometimes the reader will come across terms and categories that were not historically available at the time in the same way that they are now. The formulation of 'Anglo-*German* Constellations' is the most obvious example. German, in this operative way, refers specifically to a language and far less specifically to a geographical or political entity. In a way this is obvious since Germany as a nation state, of course, came into existence only in 1871 and thus did not exist in the eighteenth century. However, despite this lack of political unity, which in itself remains much more unstable than many other national identities, it does make sense, I want to suggest, to speak of German literature or culture. It is a field that is mostly identified through language, then and now. This is not an easy topic, especially since it is linked up with a whole discussion of nationalism from Herder (and before) onward. The way I use 'German' is very capacious: it includes Swiss nationals, such as Fuseli and Lavater, and authors whose origins are as different as Prussia, Saxony, or Bavaria. All of these sources were treated as 'German' by the British public at the time; it is a category that, at least in printed translations and cultural identification, was readily used and understood in eighteenth-century Britain. The Hanoverians were German, John Wesley referred to the Moravians as 'the Germans', and the Savoy Chapel in London was the German church. Byron, Percy Shelley, and Thomas De Quincey learned the language by looking at German literature written by authors as different as Salomon Gessner or Hamann, all of whom were identified as German. Crabb Robinson imagined Blake's ideal readership to be 'German'. All of these designations were and are intelligible then and now, and I do think it is both reasonable and productive to accept such cultural designations as meaningful, even though we know that they cover a rather large and heterogeneous field. The only argument about the explicitly *national* literature of Germany in this book is about how its definition and reception in effect unduly restricts our understanding of authors such as Hamann. Thus, while we, of course, need to be aware of the rise of the political nation state, and its links to languages, we should not prevent ourselves access to the capacious understanding that the eighteenth century had of language as one among many important ways of understanding the exchange between cultural spheres and national communities, both real and imagined.

The two critical touchstones of this book are that, first, polyglot approaches to literary and cultural history allow us to discover important new critical patterns, including highly unfamiliar ones, and that, second, it is important that we take these unusual, excessive, and sometimes even exorbitant figures seriously, precisely because they cannot be successfully absorbed into our conventional literary history. We need to understand the power of exorbitant thinkers such as Blake or Hamann and how their scepticism tells us something about the orthodoxies we have inherited. It is only if we resist the temptation to absorb and to domesticate exorbitant thinking that we can get a sense of how the critical power of their alternative accounts of a language, full of ontological power and creativity, might be relevant for our own thinking about linguistics, history, or even the world. To do that takes trouble, just as it takes trouble to work comparatively or to rethink the relation between Enlightenment and Romanticism. The suggestion of this book is that all of those are worth it, and that we should take on these troubles without immediately opposing them or straightaway wanting to end them.

1

Unexpected Connections
Anglo-German Contexts in Pre-1790s Britain

THE 'FAMILIAR FACT THAT NO ENGLISHMAN READ GERMAN LITERATURE'

In 1898, Leslie Stephen stated that '[i]t is a familiar fact that no Englishman read German literature in the eighteenth century. One sufficient reason was that there was no German literature to read.... It would, I imagine, be difficult to find a single direct reference to a German book in the whole English literature of the eighteenth century'.[1] This is probably the most condensed and certainly the most memorable expression of what we might call the 'official line' on German literature of the eighteenth century in Britain.[2] Although the context of Stephen's claim is by no means as anti-German as his phrasing here might suggest, he is more than clear on his view of the role of Anglo-German relations prior to Romanticism. There are various reasons for this, many to do with nineteenth-century politics, but what is most important here is that it is a view he inherits historically and, in turn, passes on with great success. The origin of Stephen's account lies in the Romantic period itself, was solidified in Victorian scholarship, and is still the basis of standard accounts of literary Anglo-German history. However, it does not match the historical facts and severely limits our understanding of the period. This chapter will explain why that is the case and how we might come up with a more accurate and sophisticated narrative.

Most good stories provide a powerful account of their own origin. Stephen's is no exception. The single most commonly cited event in the development of Anglo-German relations in the eighteenth and nineteenth centuries is Henry Mackenzie's 1788 lecture on Friedrich Schiller's *The Robbers*. While Mackenzie's own influence remains relatively minor, his lecture has become the supposed Ur-moment not only of Romantic Anglo-German relations but also of Anglo-German relations *tout court*. Samuel Taylor Coleridge's nightly reading of Schiller's play in 1794 epitomizes the self-dramatization of the lecture for literary history. He had picked up the drama only to find himself utterly involved in it: 'I had read, chill and trembling.... I could

---

[1] Leslie Stephen, 'The Importation of German', in *Studies of a Biographer*, 4 vols (London: Duckworth, 1898), 2: 39 and 42.

[2] Henry Bett, similarly, claims that '[i]t would be possible to count on the fingers of one hand the distinguished Englishmen who knew German in 1740' (*Hymns of Methodism in Their Literary Relations* [London: Charles H. Kelly, 1913], p. 12).

read no more. My God, Southey, who is this Schiller, this convulser of the heart?...I tremble like an aspen leaf. Upon my soul, I write to you because I am frightened....Why have we ever called Milton sublime?'[3] Coleridge, here of course, acts as a cipher for English literary culture as a whole. His captivation is metonymic for a larger trend. After 1790, so the story goes, there is an explosion of interest in Germanic writing, especially drama, which is so rapid and successful that ten years later William Wordsworth already complains about the ubiquitous 'sickly and stupid German tragedies'.[4] The mania for August von Kotzebue's works was in full swing and Gottfried August Bürger's *Leonore* becomes a point of reference for poets such as Coleridge and, indeed, Wordsworth himself.[5] Wordsworth's complaint in the preface to *Lyrical Ballads* signals a cooling of this engagement, yet it is also a testament that German intellectual culture had quickly been established from absolute dearth to a serious presence by the first decade of the 1800s, a development that will continue and proliferate via the writings of Thomas De Quincey, Henry Crabb Robinson, and Thomas Carlyle—all the way to George Eliot.

Crucially, this story of Romanticism is based on a two-pronged contrast with the preceding age. According to this contrast, there was (a) no interest in German language and culture before 1790, and (b) nothing of interest in German language and culture before 1790. (The reader will notice the irony: these claims are pretty much exactly parallel to Stephen's pronouncement a generation later.) Many of the publications imply that it was only after 1790 that the British were getting acquainted with German sources. Most contemporary accounts start telling the history of Anglo-German relations after 1790, classifying them as having their origins in the 'Romantic'.[6] The implication is that there was no interest in such matters before, and it was a way for the first decade of the nineteenth century to contrast itself with the period directly preceding it. In 1813 the *Edinburgh Review* writes about the 1780s: 'Thirty years ago, there were probably in London as many Persian as German scholars.'[7] The context makes it plain that the article neither contrasts London with another town that would have *more* Persian scholars (I take that to mean scholars *of* Persian), nor does it claim that there was an abundance of Persian (or German) scholars around. The primary point is to draw a sharp contrast with what supposedly went on '[t]hirty years ago', between British life in the 1780s and that in the early nineteenth century. The supposed lack of interest in German directly links to the second prong—namely, that there was little of cultural interest prior to Schiller and what would become German Romanticism. At different

[3] Samuel Taylor Coleridge to Robert Southey, November 1794, in *Letters of Samuel Taylor Coleridge*, 2 vols (London: William Heinemann, 1895), 1: 95–101, 96–7.
[4] William Wordsworth, preface to *Lyrical Ballads, with Other Poems*, 2 vols, 2nd ed. (London: printed for T. N. Longman and O. Rees by Biggs, 1800), pp. v–xlvi, xix.
[5] See Mary Jacobus *Tradition and Experiment in Wordsworth's 'Lyrical Ballads' (1798)* (Oxford: Clarendon, 1976).
[6] Such an assumption underlies even such powerful contributions as James Pipkin's classic collection of essays *English and German Romanticism: Cross-Currents and Controversies* (Heidelberg: Carl Winter, 1985). Also see Görner and Nicholls, *In the Embrace of the Swan*.
[7] [Review of Madame de Stael's] 'De l'Allemagne', *Edinburgh Review* 22, 43 (October 1813): 198–238, 201.

points Coleridge, Wordsworth, and Lord Byron all ridicule pre-Schillerian German literature as facile, boring, or aesthetically inferior. As I will reveal, their relation is, in fact, rather more ambivalent, but their main tenor is clear: there was little of interest for the British reader in German eighteenth-century literature, already forming the basis for Stephen's later statement.

The question posing itself is simple: how does the insistence of the negative judgement square with the claim that nobody was familiar with the material? It seems that plenty of people, including many Romantic poets, *were* familiar with German literature, albeit not with the kind that they were to champion in their own prime. The epistemic break of Mackenzie's lecture seems both too neat and too agenda-driven: Germany becomes interesting at the precise point that it becomes sufficiently like us. So much like us, in fact, that we can then start imitating it. What came before is rejected, forgotten, or, in embarrassed fashion, simply ignored. For instance, Byron, Percy Bysshe Shelley, and others hold up Salomon Gessner, an eighteenth-century German author, for derision. However, once we dig a little deeper, we find out that Byron and Shelley actually used Gessner to learn German as children. Such instruction not only suggests the German language and its literature were, in fact, considered far more useful as cultural commodities than later statements make us want to believe but also will help us to reveal, in due course, that there is a much larger, active, and important Anglo-German historical and literary context in pre-1790s Britain than is commonly assumed. It seems, then, that the initial story about the absence of German literature is more than a little muddled, which leads to an equally muddled history of reception. Let me illustrate how this narrative is constructed and then continued in scholarship by returning to Stephen's claim and comparing it with the archival evidence of the period.

Stephen claims that 'there was no German literature to read' in the period. As he puts it, '[I]t would, I imagine, be difficult to find a single direct reference to a German book in the whole English literature of the eighteenth century'. Again, I am not so interested in following up on the obvious nationalism on display here (though it does bear repeating that Stephen is not a Germanophobe). What is interesting to me is Stephen's implicit claim not only that there would have been no literature around that was worthwhile to read but also that the eighteenth-century British public indeed shared that view.[8] For Stephen, and for much scholarship after him, there is an immediate translation from the perceived inferiority of eighteenth-century German literature to the assumption that there was no historical interest in these texts. This is oddly naive and, as it turns out, historically completely inaccurate. The Englishmen in whose taste Stephen had so much confidence in fact embraced their German contemporaries. Contrary to his assertion, the British, across the board, displayed an intense interest in German literature in translation, and German texts in translation made up a good share of the book market. No doubt

---

[8] Eric A. Blackall provides a comprehensive account that, contrary to Stephen's, charts eighteenth-century literary language and claims that 'it was between 1700 and 1775 that the German language developed into a literary language of infinite richness and subtlety' (Eric A. Blackall, *The Emergence of German as a Literary Language 1700–1775*, 2nd ed. [Ithaca, NY: Cornell University Press, 1978], p. 2).

this also normalized the presence of the Anglo-German community in their midst. The point here concerns a wider point that I am making throughout this book: the eighteenth-century cultural sphere in Britain was a much more complex and multilingual sphere than we commonly assume, a quality that became part of the conditions of possibility for the context against which we need to read both larger historical changes (the Enlightenment) and radical individual authorships (William Blake and Johann Georg Hamann).

Take London, for instance, or even Soho alone, the part of London in which both Hamann and Blake lived. In the period that Hamann visits, and throughout Blake's life, these places provided a cosmopolitan and multidisciplinary world. Alexander Gilchrist describes it with Blake in mind, though we can imagine also Hamann soaking up this atmosphere some twenty years before:

> In 1780, Fuseli, then thirty-nine, just returned from eight years' sojourn in Italy, became a neighbour, lodging in Broad Street, where he remained until 1782.... Artists' homes as well as studios abounded then in Broad Street and its neighbourhood. Bacon the sculptor lived in Wardour Street, Paul Sandby in Poland Street, the fair *R.A.*, Angelica Kauffman, in Golden Square, Bartolozzi, with his apprentice Sherwin, in Broad Street itself, and at a later date John Varley, 'father of modern Water Colours', in the same street (No. 15). Literary celebrities were not wanting: in Wardour Street, Mrs. Chapone; in Poland Street, pushing, pompous Dr. Burney, of Musical *History* notoriety.[9]

This is not only a bunch of names. The reason for including this dense description here is that I want to draw attention to the sheer variety and difference within the group that is described by Gilchrist. These are people from a variety of backgrounds, languages, and geographical regions—all living in a very condensed space. This is a picture of a London that was connected to the world and connected the world in turn. We will see a lot of these types of connections in this book, so I wanted to give the reader a concentrated impression of the types of connections that we ought to keep in mind. Evidently, in this case it shows us a London whose landscape was far more heterogeneous and multilingual than we often assume.

Importantly, this heterogeneity and multilingualism was not just a reality for a small, educated upper crust but rather part of the daily life that many Londoners or visitors led, including figures such as Blake and Hamann. Take David Wilkie's account that gives us a similarly colourful picture of this part of London, stressing its cosmopolitan character in the local taverns where artists from all over Europe would spend time, including the King's Arms, a pub a few doors down from where Blake lived and where he had 'the advantage of hearing all the languages of Europe talked with the greatest fluency, the place being mostly frequented by foreigners.... [T]here are Corsicans, Italians, French, Germans, Welsh and Scotch'.[10] Among the voices in this Babelian tavern might very well have been Hamann's at the time of Blake's birth; a few years later Blake himself probably 'ate there on

---

    [9] Alexander Gilchrist, *The Life of William Blake* (Mineola, NY: Dover, 1998), p. 35.
    [10] David Wilkie to James Wilkie, [1805], in Allan Cunningham, *The Life of Sir David Wilkie; with His Journals, Tours, and Critical Remarks on Works of Art; and a Selection from His Correspondence*, 3 vols (London: John Murray, 1843), 1: 80; qtd in Bentley, *Blake Records*, p. 743.

occasion, or at least bought his porter' there.[11] My point in speculatively invoking how Hamann's and Blake's paths crossed in London over time is to suggest we consider the complexity and richness of the wider structures that would have made multilingual encounters (albeit not between the two of them, since they are two decades apart in age) not just likely but certain; even more importantly, it would have been normal, a fact we need to account for if we want to understand the period.

It is somewhat odd that as Western, twenty-first-century scholars who are supposedly so globally connected we not only have lost some of the knowledge about how cultural connections worked in the past but also immediately assume that somehow these eighteenth-century figures were less connected than we are now. My sense is that this comes of thinking about connectivity in a very narrow way. (For instance, multilingualism was probably more common then than it is now; other forms of spatial or virtual connections are evidently much easier today.) In any case, we do well to remind ourselves that there was a highly functioning network that worked with increasing rapidity. Johann Wolfgang von Goethe's *Sorrows of Young Werther* was first available in English a mere five years after its original publication in 1774. Johann Caspar Lavater's popular *Physiognomy* was translated and published in English a year after *Werther* appeared. These are two prominent examples from a much larger set. Among the writers and works familiar to the English public we find Friedrich Gottlieb Klopstock's *Messiah* and *Death of Adam*, Christoph Martin Wieland's *Trial of Abraham*, Johann Jakob Bodmer's *Noah*, Johann Jacob Rambach's *Pious Aspirations and Meditations*, Carl Heinrich von Bogatzky's *A Golden Treasury*, and Gottlieb Wilhelm Rabener's satirical letters.[12] Many of these authors were regularly discussed in periodicals, and the writings became known as the 'German stories'. Plenty of them were translated and published in London by the booksellers we will turn to shortly.[13] The numbers and details of their distribution clearly suggest that there was a variety of German authors who were widely read and whose works formed part of the common literary fabric in Britain. As Garold N. Davis puts it, '[T]hese translations blended immediately into the cultural pattern'.[14] By my count, in the years 1680–1790 there were at least 135 volumes published in London alone that were translations from the German to English.[15] The significant numbers show

---

[11] Bentley, *Blake Records*, p. 743.

[12] See Garold N. Davis, *German Thought and Culture in England 1700–1770: A Preliminary Survey*, Studies in Comparative Literature 47 (Chapel Hill, NC: University of North Carolina Press, 1969).

[13] Johann Christoph Haberkorn's successor Carl Heydinger illustrates best how the Anglo-German book market was very much part of the wider exchanges throughout Europe. He started to import texts via the book fair in Leipzig and to facilitate translations of authors such as Albrecht von Haller and Christoph Martin Wieland. See Jefcoate, pp. 278–312.

[14] Davis, p. 96. It is worth mentioning here that these authors were very popular in their native context, too. Johann Georg Hamann's library shows copies of works of all the authors just mentioned, except Wieland (an author Hamann was likely familiar with despite not owning his books). For the full record, we should mention that between 1778 and 1788 there was no German bookstore in London. During this time readers got their German books by ordering them at English bookstores that specialized in foreign imports. After the turn of the decade, that movement reversed itself again.

[15] I have combined the information available in Garold N. Davis and Graham Jefcoate and added to it further items I found independently.

that there was a steady market for a variety of these books. All the authors I just mentioned see their works not just imported but also published in London, alongside other Germans such as Christian Fürchtegott Gellert, Christoph Otto von Schönaich, Justus Möser, Haller, Gotthold Ephraim Lessing, Christian Wolff, and Sophie von La Roche. These were not specialized publications for a few dedicated Germanophiles; they encompassed literature, travelogues, philosophy, aesthetics, art history, politics, history, and theology. Rather than demonstrating an aversion to German sources, what this information shows is a plethora of genres and a continuous demand for them, which was matched by a strong structure of translation and wide distribution—especially since all of the sources I have listed here were monographs. Many further, shorter pieces by German authors were published in periodicals and other formats.[16] Taken together, this large set of publications adds a distinctly German flavour to the wider literary, religious, and political context of the period. It also reminds us that there is a larger European context in which Britain actively participated and which was present in London.[17]

All of this information prompts us to return to the study of the historical sources and gain a more accurate picture of what was, in fact, happening on the ground. What was the historical relation the British had to the German literary scene, both through immediate presence and through translation? Byron, Coleridge, and Shelley give us a good entry point into answering this question, as all of them mention the German author Salomon Gessner as a representative author. Gessner in fact was the most popular of all German writers in eighteenth-century Britain. He was famous mainly as the author of *Tod Abels (Death of Abel)* (1758) and *Idyllen (Idylls)* (1756), works of religious and pastoral poetry. Already popular in his native Germany, he enjoyed even more success in England, despite a relatively poor translation by Mary Collyer, which was immediately superseded by another (though, as happens often, the original translation remained the more widely circulated).

Once we dig into the historical record we see just how popular a writer he was. Within a year, a second edition of *Death of Abel* was printed in England. Four years later the work was in its seventh edition, and by 1766 in its eleventh, a rise that would continue long into the nineteenth century. Similarly, the *Idylls* went through several translations and editions.[18] The British engaged with these German works throughout the eighteenth century and well into Romanticism. Over 120 reviews of Gessner's work appeared in British periodicals between 1760 and 1810, attesting to his wide appeal and suggesting much more continuity of interest and style than a supposed rupture around 1790 would explain. The popularity of these 'German

---

[16] See Bayard Quincy Morgan, A. R. Hohlfeld, and Walter E. Roloff, *German Literature in British Magazines, 1750–1860* (Madison, WI: University of Wisconsin Press, 1959).

[17] All the books I mentioned here were familiar to Hamann, too, and most of them even appear in his library.

[18] We all know through William St Clair's work that the number of editions of a work does not necessarily equate with its popularity. In Salomon Gessner's case, however, the numbers stack up: his work enjoyed high circulation and prominence across intellectual circles and beyond. See William St Clair, *The Reading Nation in the Romantic Period* (Cambridge: Cambridge University Press, 2004), pp. 131, 539, and 751.

stories' during that whole time show that such texts played a major part in shaping the transition between what we now call the Enlightenment and Romanticism.

This shift in understanding the transition and our growing sense of the inter-connectedness of literary culture across nations and languages fits in with Gessner's own background of being highly polyglot. He was part of a set of Anglophile, Swiss-German academics and writers whose role in the history of Anglo-European relations has been woefully neglected. The main figures of this Zurich intelligentsia were academics, such as Johann Jakob Bodmer (first translator of Milton into German); Johann Jakob Breitinger (Fuseli's and Lavater's teacher); theologians, such as Lavater; and public scholars or intellectuals, such as Henry Fuseli Sr, a respected art historian.[19] These men fostered intellectual, scholarly, and artistic connections throughout Europe, and it is in this context that Gessner composes the verses that end up being so popular in Britain. The members of this circle maintained their connections across borders and languages for several generations. Gessner himself was godfather to Fuseli, which is one of the reasons why they remained important to each other after Fuseli's travels to London.

All of Gessner's writings, not just his more famous poetry, were expressly conducted on a European scale. Take, for instance, his book *Briefe über die Landschaftsmahlerey* (1772), a treatise that he wrote expressly for Henry Fuseli Sr. Four years after its initial publication it was translated as *Letter on Landscape Painting* (1776) and published in London. Together with works by Johann Joachim Winckelmann, William Hogarth, Lessing, and others, Gessner's *Letter* formed part of the active exchanges of aesthetic discourse between England and Germany. They point towards a neglected genealogy of Anglo-German aesthetic writing that Leonard Trawick calls Blake's 'German connection'.[20] Gessner's contribution not only prefigures expressive theories of art, as Trawick explores, but also strongly suggests potential influences that deserve fuller exploration.

Gessner's most famous work, *Death of Abel*, is an epic poem that mixes canonical genres of the eighteenth century; it has been accurately described by Gabrielle Bersier as 'a sentimental narration of Cain's destruction of the primeval idyll'.[21] In the opening book of the poem the speaker exclaims: 'Stehe du mir bey, Muse, oder edle Begeisterung, die du des Dichters Seel erfüllest, wenn er in stiller Einsamkeit staunt, bey nächtlichen Stunden, wenn der Mond über ihm leuchtet, oder im Dunkel des Hayns, oder bey der einsam beschatteten Quelle.'[22] Collyer's translation reads:

---

[19] It is no surprise that Hamann, always at the centre of intellectual and literary exchange, is familiar with all these members of Zurich circles and corresponds with many of them.

[20] Leonard Trawick presents a suggestive reading of William Blake's knowledge of German aesthetics, the *Laocoön* in particular, and his relation to Johann Caspar Lavater and Henry Fuseli ('William Blake's German Connection', *Colby Library Quarterly* 13 [1979]: 229–45). On Blake and Lessing, see also Frederick Burwick, 'Blake's Laocoon and Job: Or, on the Boundaries of Painting and Poetry', in *The Romantic Imagination: Literature and Art in England and Germany*, ed. Burwick and Jürgen Klein (Amsterdam: Rodopi, 1996), pp. 125–55.

[21] Gabrielle Bersier, 'Arcadia Revitalized: The International Appeal of Gessner's Idylls in the 18th Century', in *From the Greeks to the Greens: Images of Simple Life*, ed. Reinhold Grimm and Jost Hermand (Madison, WI: University of Wisconsin Press, 1989), pp. 34–47, 35.

[22] Salomon Gessner, 'Der Tod Abels', in *Salomon Geßners Schriften*, 3 vols (Zurich: Orell, Geßner, Füeßlin, 1774), vol. 1. pp. 5–157, 5.

'Come, thou noble Enthusiasm! that warmest and fillest the mind of the rapt poet, who, during the silent hours of night contemplates in the thick grove, or at the side of a clear stream glimmering with the moon's pale lamp'.[23] Much of this sounds more than a little tired to our ears. The translation shows us the proclivities of the age, leaving 'Muse' untranslated and rendering 'Begeisterung' as 'Enthusiasm'. As we know, this type of graveyard poetry was typical and highly topical on both sides of the Channel. Edward Young's *Night Thoughts* was a continuous reference point across the European eighteenth and early nineteenth centuries. Blake admired and illustrated Young's work, and Hamann translated it. Authors such as Young, Thomas Gray, William Cowper, or Robert Blair belong centrally in our account of the period, especially Romanticism, as Marilyn Butler and James Chandler have so persuasively shown in different ways.[24] So does, I want to argue, Gessner.

Consider that for a while Gessner was, in fact, more popular than Young, even in Britain, and that his writings were consumed by the reading public as well as by all major British authors of the period. Many of the reviews well into the nineteenth century actually thematize the popularity of Gessner's work by highlighting both its ubiquity and its status in an increasingly international marketplace of novels. *The Eclectic Review* writes, 'The Death of Abel, during the last half-century, has rivalled the Pilgrim's Progress and Robinson Crusoe in popularity'.[25] Echoing this very same formulation, *The Quarterly Review* states that '[n]o book of foreign growth has ever become so popular in England as the Death of Abel.... [I]t has been repeatedly printed at country presses, with worn types and on coarse paper; and it is found at country fairs, and in the little shops of remote towns almost as certainly as the Pilgrim's Progress and Robinson Crusoe'.[26] The German poem takes its place next to the works of British prose that shape the modern form of the novel. Its proselytizing power covers the whole of Britain: it reaches the cities as well as the country and becomes universally available even for readers who can only afford 'coarse paper'. The article in *The Quarterly Review* openly acknowledges that there are many cultural products of 'foreign growth' that have both intellectual and economic impact in Britain. The fact that we are dealing with an increasingly complex and international context is reflected in the weekly publications at the time, making this topic part of public discussion and awareness.

Gessner and the German stories were a mainstay in Britain while the first-generation Romantics grew into the poets we know today. Similar to Gray or Young, Gessner was eventually rejected as outdated, despite, or maybe because of, his influence. What makes the rejection of his work so interesting for me is not only that Gessner was formative for many central figures of Romanticism but also that

---

[23] Salomon Gessner, *The Death of Abel: In Five Books; Translated from the German of Mr. Gessner*, trans. Mary Collyer (London: printed for C. Cooke [1796]), p. 7.

[24] See Marilyn Butler, *Romantics, Rebels, and Reactionaries: English Literature and Its Background, 1760–1830* (Oxford: Oxford University Press, 1981); and James Chandler, *England in 1819: The Politics of Literary Culture and the Case of Romantic Historicism* (Chicago, IL: University of Chicago Press, 1999).

[25] 'The Death of Abel, by Solomon [sic] Gessner', *Eclectic Review* 6, 2 (October 1810): 946–7, 947.

[26] Review of '*The World before the Flood, a Poem, in Ten Cantos; with Other Occasional Pieces*, by James Montgomery', *Quarterly Review* 11, 21 (April 1814): 78–87, 78. See also Davis, p. 100.

he was so explicitly as a German source. Eight-year-old Byron learned German with Gessner's book in hand: 'Abel was one of the first books my German master read to me.'[27] The poem stuck with Byron. His celebrated *Cain* (1821) was a direct response to the German author. Blake, in turn, of course refers to Byron's poem in his own *The Ghost of Abel*.[28] Some of Coleridge's earliest exposure to German literature came through Gessner. As Davis points out, 'Gessner was constantly used as a source of ideas by Coleridge'.[29] The German appears in Wordsworth's *Prelude* alongside Shakespeare as 'he who penn'd the other day / The Death of Abel'.[30] In the only study of Gessner and English literature, Bertha Reed points out various other examples of his influence upon writers of the age, including Walter Scott and Felicia Hemans, who translated his work.[31]

Why is it, then, that we know relatively little about these writings? There are several reasons. I will quickly sketch four of them here. The first is scholarship's myopic obsession with the French Revolution for the definition of the transition between Enlightenment and Romanticism, mentioned in the introduction. Second, traditional scholarship of High Romanticism reads the German idealist influence on British Romanticism as crucial, thus turning our attention (and the period's construction) away from the historically strong presence of eighteenth-century German literature in Britain, such as that of Gessner or Klopstock. Third is the politically charged situation after the First World War, the widespread anti-German sentiment in Anglophone universities that led to a suppression of German studies in Britain in the aftermath of 1914.[32] Of course, the Second World War did not exactly improve matters on this front. The fourth and main reason lies in the period itself—namely, in the actual disavowal of these eighteenth-century sources by the major Romantic poets and how they shaped and dominated subsequent reception.

The genesis of Coleridge's *The Wanderings of Cain* is a good example. In 1798 Coleridge and Wordsworth engaged in a writing competition of sorts, imitating Gessner's poem. The venture was a failure, since, according to Coleridge, Wordsworth did not find the task either possible or truly enjoyable. The whole scheme 'broke up in a laugh: and the Ancient Mariner was written instead'.[33] The spin of the story is clear: instead of imitating eighteenth-century poetry, German or English, a new experimental venture beckoned to these poets. The relationship of these Romantics to their eighteenth-century German sources and language textbooks

---

[27] Qtd in Davis, p. 105.

[28] For a discussion of Lord Byron (George Gordon), and Blake that also makes reference to Hamann, see Ágnes Péter, 'A Second Essay in Romantic Typology: Lord Byron in the Wilderness', *Neohelicon* 26, 1 (January 1999): 39–54.

[29] Davis, p. 105.

[30] William Wordsworth, The Prelude ['AB-Stage Reading Text'], in *The Thirteen-Book Prelude*, ed. Mark L. Reed, 2 vols (Ithaca, NY: Cornell University Press, 1991), pp. 95–324, 207, lines 559–60.

[31] Bertha Reed, *The Influence of Solomon [sic] Gessner upon English Literature*, Americana Germanica, n.s., 4 (Philadelphia, PA: Americana Germanica, 1905), pp. 5 and 52.

[32] In the nineteenth century this was different: Americans went to the Germans for the model of the modern research university, for instance, while Britain was less touched by these developments. The fandom for Germany in both countries ended in the early twentieth century.

[33] Samuel Taylor Coleridge, *The Wanderings of Cain* [reading text], ed. Nikki Santilli, *Romantic Circles*, 2003, https://www.rc.umd.edu/editions/cain/readingtext.html.

became increasingly uneasy; Byron, Coleridge, and Wordsworth all exhibit an anxious reluctance to admit just how formative Gessner might have been on their writings.

Although by the late 1780s Gessner was still an important poetic referent, a cultural touchstone whose familiarity was taken for granted, he was also beginning to be turned, like so many other pre-1790s poets, into a representative of an aesthetic that Romanticism overcame. The narrative was set. Here is Byron continuing the description of his German language lesson: 'Whilst he [his teacher] was crying his eyes out over its [*The Death of Abel*'s] pages, I thought that any other than Cain had hardly committed a crime in ridding the world of so dull a fellow as Gessner made brother Abel. I always thought Cain a fine subject, and when I took it up, I determined to treat it strictly after the Mosaic account'.[34] It is not simply that Gessner himself is dull, though the fact that he made Abel a dull fellow does not inspire confidence. Byron here is a fairly typical instance of Romantic authors whose relation to Gessner is torn between understanding him as an important figure of European literature and sensing that he will be superseded by their own writing. Once he grows into a full-blown Romantic, Byron supposedly goes back to the 'Mosaic' account, rather than to Gessner's derivative, to write his own poem.

The way that Byron and Coleridge diminished Gessner's authorship was crucial for putting in place the myth that before the 1790s there was no real interest in German writing, and thus no real Anglo-German culture in Britain. In this erroneous story, Romanticism discovers its own contemporaries in Germany: British authors become fascinated with German literature as what they perceive as fellow 'Romantic' literature. We might think of Coleridge's infatuation with Schiller, for example. Obscuring the earlier Anglo-German connections makes it look as if the interest in Continental materials is something new, in step with the changing aesthetics in Britain. Yet whatever enthusiasm Byron or Coleridge have for Goethe, Schiller, and others post-1790, the first time they were excited by German literature would have been, despite any later embarrassment, through Gessner or one of his eighteenth-century contemporaries.

Coleridge's and Byron's moves exemplify the crossing point of two problematic issues that have haunted literary history ever since. First is the degree to which the narrative by many Romantics of a supposed independence from eighteenth-century poetical influences became a canonical story. It has become increasingly

---

[34] Qtd in Davis, p. 105. René Wellek mentions a variation of this story in Walter Scott's work in connection with the early reception of Immanuel Kant in England, specifically the German speakers who came to England during the 1790s, including a certain Anthony Willich who had studied with Kant and came to Edinburgh: 'In 1792 he [Willich] taught German there to a class of young men which had the distinction of including Walter Scott. Scott gives an amusing account of these hilarious study-periods in his "Essay on the Imitation of the Ancient Ballad". Six or seven friends formed a group and "Dr. Willich (a medical gentleman)" read with them Gessner's sentimental "Death of Abel". "At length, amidst much laughing and little study, most of us acquired some knowledge, more or less extensive, of the German language, and selected for ourselves, some in the philosophy of Kant, some in the more animated works of the German dramatists, specimens more to our taste than the 'Death of Abel'" (Scott, *Poetical Works IV* (1830), p. 36; qtd in Wellek, *Immanuel Kant in England 1793–1838* (Princeton, NJ: Princeton University Press, 1931) (p. 11). For a more recent study of the dissemination of Kantian ideas in England, see Monika Class, *Coleridge and Kantian Ideas in England, 1769–1817* (New York: Bloomsbury, 2012).

clear that their departure from existing poetics was more akin to a transition than a radical break. Second, literary history has lost a sense of the international nature of many Romantics' eighteenth-century background that they came to reject but that was still important to them. Byron's and Coleridge's eventual disavowal of Gessner, and the Victorians' willingness to adopt the Romantics' self-stylization of their rejection of the German source, paved the way for a retrospectively mono-lingual literary history. It obfuscates the influence of German literature at the time and diminishes the relevance of the Anglo-German context in London before 1790. We must change this narrative fundamentally if we want to get a better sense of the intellectual and cultural parameters that are in place while this shift to Romanticism occurs.

Once the discussion of Anglo-German connections is focused on the period after 1790, the supposed previous disregard for German language becomes part of the narrative of English literary history. If the Romantics fashioned themselves as the group that discovered German literature and culture, then many of the Victorians repeated this flawed account. Of course, the Victorians had plenty of interest in German sources post-1790. For instance, Leslie Stephen himself was deeply invested in German culture and literature, and Alexander von Humboldt's prom-inence among Victorians is a good indicator that he was not alone. Yet this interest was centred on the nineteenth century, still stylizing the preceding period as a cul-tural wasteland. In an odd echo of the comparisons of Persian and German scholars cited earlier, when J. E. Austen-Leigh in 1870 described his aunt Jane Austens's childhood and education, he ruled out that Austen learned German, since '[i]n those days German was no more thought of than Hindostanee, as part of a lady's education'.[35] In the eighteenth century, anything that lay beyond the North Sea was deeply foreign, be it Germany or India. According to this view there was no need (or even maybe no way) to learn these languages before the turn of the century.

This version of events has been historically very robust, well into the twentieth century. Yet hardly any scholarly accounts of Anglo-German relations pay attention to possible German influences before the 1790s. Many ignore them altogether. Most gloss over them quickly, dismissing them as irrelevant, sometimes even in the face of their own amassed evidence. Stephen *'imagines'* it would 'be difficult to find a single direct reference to a German book in the whole English literature of the eighteenth century' (my emphasis). Literary histories survey the literature and find German materials but, nevertheless, conclude that Stephen imagines correctly. V. Stockley's 1929 book, *German Literature as Known in England 1750–1830*, is typical. Despite its generous titular chronological range, and in odd contrast with many of the sources it amasses, Stockley's book not only repeats but also reinforces the myth of the 1790 turning point when she sets out assuming that 'not until after

---

[35] J. E. Austen-Leigh, *A Memoir of Jane Austen and Other Family Recollections*, ed. Kathryn Sutherland (Oxford: Oxford University Press, 2002), p. 71. As Devoney Looser points out, '[T]his book was published in December 1869 but had an imprint of 1870. Most sources will list it as 1870. Interestingly, Austen has her fictional character Lady Susan mention what a waste of time it is for a young woman to study "French, Italian, and German"—a line we are clearly supposed to think is wrong' (private correspondence with Looser, 8 August 2016).

that date [1790] was there in England anything like a real appreciation of the general development of German literature'.[36] The vast majority of the book is dedicated to post-1790 output, and the discussion of the earlier eighteenth-century connections is further minimized by its focus on literature proper. It is a critical move that we will encounter more than once: Stockley notes political and economic ties, and even German language learning, 'but for purposes purely utilitarian and commercial', thus almost contrasting any interest in German with interest in anything cultural or literary.[37] The structure that F. W. Stokoe produces in *German Influence in the English Romantic Period 1788–1818* (1926) is very similar. It offers what became a standard list of the main reasons for the disregard of German sources in Britain during that time—namely, the Thirty Years' War (resulting in subpar German cultural output), the dominance of French taste across Europe, the low number of German speakers in Britain, and the scarcity of German literary materials on the island.[38]

Later twentieth-century literary theory adopts a similar model. John Mander's book *Our German Cousins: Anglo-German Relations in the 19th and 20th Centuries* (1974) sets out to make postwar Britons see how close they are historically to their German 'cousins'. Once more, though, this is a story that begins only in the nineteenth century. And once again the blame for this development lies mostly with the supposedly inferior German cultural situation before: 'Until about 1800, then, the English were largely unaware that the Germans had a *Kultur* at all: indeed the Germans were mostly unaware of it themselves.... It was only with Coleridge and his followers, and somewhat later with the great figures of Carlyle, of Thomas and Matthew Arnold, of G. H. Lewes and George Eliot, that *Deutsche Kultur* can be said to have come into its own'.[39] The obvious question—What counts as *Kultur*?— illustrates that, like all these literary histories, Mander's story also contains a theoretical claim. In his project, *Kultur* is precisely the kind of construct that reinforces a story in which German Romantic thought starts *ex nihilo* and provides the theoretical backbone for European Romanticism.

Because they are theoretically so invested in a particular form of literary history, these accounts ignore the avenues I suggested for myself in the introduction—for instance, multilingual archival work. What is particularly telling is that accounts such as Stokoe's or Mander's even mention this type of material, yet dismiss it without further thought. That is, some of Anglo-German literary history is so solidified and theoretically entrenched in its views that in critical moments it simply glosses over the kind of empirical evidence that, in other moments, it considers to be crucial. Take Mander's brief qualification that '[i]t is not quite true that the Germans and their *Kultur* were unknown to the English before that date [1750],

---

[36] V. Stockley, *German Literature as Known in England 1750–1830* (London: G. Routledge and Sons, 1929), p. 2.

[37] Stockley, pp. 2–3.

[38] See F. W. Stokoe, *German Influence in the English Romantic Period 1788–1818, with Special Reference to Scott, Coleridge, Shelley, and Byron* (1929; Cambridge: Cambridge University Press, 2013).

[39] John Mander, *Our German Cousins: Anglo-German Relations in the 19th and 20th Centuries* (London: John Murray, 1974), pp. 8–9.

but it is as true as to make no difference'.[40] The way that this literary history ends up claiming something that is, by its own admission, 'not quite true' is by dismissing some of the materials it has amassed as irrelevant. In this case, Mander does so because they do not adhere to a later aesthetic standard: 'It was not, then, that the books were wholly unavailable; but rather that the selection was unfortunate'.[41] Again, much of this problem lies with how one wants to define *Kultur* or what would have been 'fortunate'. Simply put, if what you are looking for is by definition post-Romantic, it's no surprise that it cannot be found in a pre-Romantic period. For Stokoe, it is not so much a question of aesthetics (though that does also play a role) than one of disciplines. In that way, her mention of pre-1790s Anglo-German material is even more revealing than Mander's: quite against her general account, she mentions that '[t]he magazines of the time' were 'replete with notices of German philosophical, theological, legal and scientific works'.[42] She does not follow or discuss these texts further, though, paying them no heed. Yet somebody in the eighteenth century would have written and read those notices in German; and they must have been about something that actually happened in Britain at the time. One way to understand what is going on here is to look at Stokoe's parallel claim that these magazines 'contain but one review of a work purely literary in character'.[43] In her study, it is only literature that counts, and it is a pretty narrow definition of literature at that. It is not just that today much more extensive research methods can show that there was a more intense engagement with literary works than we thought. More importantly, we realize that many of the historical claims about the dearth of interest only cover a very limited number of genres and disciplines. Since we now think that much of the philosophical and theological writing that circulates in the British context is of direct relevance to the imaginative output, we need to revisit those publications, starting with Daniel Defoe's historical and economic essay on the German refugees in 1607, to which I will turn in a few moments.

Before I do so, I would like to mention an exception to the scholarly rule I have been presenting here. It remains the great distinction of Davis's *German Thought and Culture in England 1700–1770* that it recognized the sheer variety and complexity of Anglo-German literary relations during the eighteenth century and their relevance today. One reason that Davis developed a sense for this complexity is that he did not follow the traditional disciplinary model used by Stokoe and others. Against 'champions of literary isolation', his work developed a sharp eye for the overlap between theology, music, and literary work, realizing that Anglo-German life extended across all of these spheres.[44] Now, of course, cross-disciplinary work in such a vein is encouraged. And yet there are very few examples of it, which is one of the reasons why Davis's work never made the impact it ought to have made.[45]

---

[40] Mander, p. 19.

[41] Mander, p. 20. Mander continues: 'At the risk of boring the reader, here is a list of what was actually translated in the thirty years after 1750' (ibid.). The apologetic tone shows just how little he is actually interested in the literary history of the eighteenth century.

[42] Stokoe, p. 15.   [43] Ibid.   [44] Davis, p. 108.

[45] It did not help, of course, that the bookend of his inquiry (1770) made it easy for scholars invested in a 1790s break simply to pass it by.

The larger point that transpires is that even scholarship that is interested in Anglo-German relations has tended to perpetuate the myth there is a clear break with the French Revolution, which supposedly coincides with the rise of Romanticism. Yet there are clear signs that Anglo-German exchanges and life before 1790 are much more complex and that the break between these two periods is not as neat or radical as it may look initially. Thus, we can draw much larger conclusions about the cultural and literary impact such multilingual, transnational networks have in the period. Defoe's writings on German refugees in London, to which I now turn, provide a timely and powerful illustration.

TWO WAVES OF GERMAN ARRIVALS IN LONDON: 1708 AND 1764

One simple reason for the rise of the Anglo-German community in eighteenth-century London was simply that comparatively many German immigrants came to Britain. While we do not have exact numbers for the whole nation, it is certain that the German community numbered 8,000 in London alone by 1785, a number that fifteen years later had risen to 30,000, or around 3 per cent of the total population.[46] German immigrants, their culture, and the Anglo-German contexts they created become an important part of the story about the increasingly heterogeneous Britain. It is no coincidence that Defoe developed an interest in this steadily more influential group that was mixing with the British. He believed England to be a mongrel nation ('Thus, from a mixture of all kinds, began, / That het'rogeneous thing, an Englishman'), a diverse people whose amazing quality was to assimilate foreign influence.[47] Earlier I offered an illustration of how this translates into Defoe's fiction via *Robinson Crusoe*, aka Robinson Kreutzner, himself the mongrel son of a German immigrant. Next, I will focus on historical data and how Defoe and some of his contemporaries reacted to the actual German migration to Britain. The 1708 and 1764 arrival of two large groups of Palatines in London serves as a useful barometer for the increasing size and importance of the Anglo-German context in Britain, as well as the British reaction. We can see how quickly German integration proceeded, and how much Anglo-German culture became a part of everyday life in London.

In 1709, Defoe published an essay entitled *A Brief History of the Poor Palatine Refugees, Lately Arriv'd in England*. The piece, which is more than a 'brief history', helps us appreciate how the influx of Germans, many of them economic refugees, prepared the ground for a complex Anglo-German cultural context. The direct material cause for Defoe's essay is the arrival of between 13,000 and 15,000 Germans in London in a matter of weeks. Most of these were agricultural labourers looking for work. Many were migrants whose eventual goal was to reach the Americas.

---

[46] See Jefcoate, p. 22. Also see Stefan Manz, Margrit Schulte Beerbühl, and John R. Davis, eds, *Migration and Transfer from Germany to Britain 1660–1914* (Munich: K. G. Saur, 2007).

[47] Defoe, *The True-Born Englishman: A Satire* (Leeds: Alice Mann, 1836), p. 17.

In the meantime, they were housed (or, rather, they housed themselves) in what we would now consider a refugee camp east of the City. London and its inhabitants debated what to do about them, and Defoe's essay joined other publications discussing the Anglo-German influx.

Much as in his other essayistic work during this period, Defoe's *Brief History* champions social and economic liberalism with a view that England is a multilingual and international space. The *History* is a passionate defence for the free labour movement and the trust in economic prosperity that it will produce. In the most general terms, Defoe's *History* makes an argument about the economic, ethical, and cultural advantages of migration; in this specific case, Defoe argues that the character of these German arrivals in particular will not only help them assimilate but also, in fact, will have a positive effect on the British workforce.

Defoe is not just international in his argument. He also brings a comparative practice to his reading and writing. At a crucial moment in the *History*, he refers to scholarship in German ('a printed Relation in the German Tongue') or to related legislation ('late Act of *Naturalization of foreign Protestants*') to bolster his argument.[48] Defoe's reading of foreign sources on economic migration was by no means something special or far-fetched for his time. Just as his prose style and his political argument suggest, the crossing of linguistic barriers through print, travel, and other forms of exchange was just part of a new reality for an increasing number of people, certainly in Europe. In this sense, Defoe's essay is a testament to the internationalization of the argument of economic liberalism and the immediate impact such views have for the reality on the ground that these German migrants will experience in London. Defoe mentions a moral imperative to provide shelter for refugees from religious persecution, but in the end, what is most important are the practical reasons to welcome these migrants as potentially beneficial and productive members of society.

It is a familiar argument: poor migrant, and eventually immigrant, labourers, as long as they are well behaved, are likely to work harder than the native population and, thus, will serve as an encouraging example to the English poor. Once resettled, the integrated arrivals will generate work and business in the rural and unproductive parts of the country. Finally, after their naturalization, maybe over a generation or two, the children and grandchildren of these immigrants will be an integral part of the country and, for Britain, a crucial help towards its expansive colonial projects. Defoe intimates that it would be best to preserve the efficient and productive German character of the migrants and, at the same time, make them part of English imperial ambitions. They are members of the kind of international commonwealth that Defoe imagines England to be.

Obviously, the political implications of Defoe's views regarding migration are not uncontroversial. Plenty of scholars today would be sceptical about the faux simplicity of his economic liberalism or the celebration of 'free' movement of labour. Historically, however, such criticism was formulated in terms of national self-interest.

---

[48] Defoe, *A Brief History of the Poor Palatine Refugees, Lately Arriv'd in England* (London: J. Baker, 1709), pp. 5–6; ECCO ESTC T094068.

For instance, the political pamphlet *The Palatines' Catechism, or, a True Description of Their Camps at Black-Heath and Camberwell: In a Pleasant Dialogue between an English Tradesman and a High-Dutchman* (1709) dramatizes the events around the refugees in a fictionalized conversation. While the dialogue is 'pleasant', the piece ultimately takes a dim yet familiar view of the new arrivals: 'I think our Charity ought to begin at Home.... The *Palatines* may be Poor enough, but their coming hither can never make us Rich (as has too often been learnedly worded).'[49] This attitude attempts to keep the foreign influence at bay, avoiding the vision that Defoe has developed in the *History* (precisely the kind of source that here is termed 'learnedly worded') and the reality that in effect will prevail. Either way, there is a clear awareness that this is a discussion about the internationalization of Britain and thus the nation's place in a wider European and global context.

Neither the arrival of these economic migrants nor Defoe's *Brief History* are isolated events.[50] The arrival of the Palatinates in 1708 was a sign of what was to come. Throughout the first half of the eighteenth century, German immigration to London continued to grow, and with it the Anglo-German community. Over time, it helped to create facts on the ground. That is, it translated into the development of a complex, visible, and important community, which began to be an integral part of London life. The reaction to another large wave of German migrants in 1764 illustrates that by that time the Anglo-German community was well established, and that we need to integrate their presence into a larger account of eighteenth-century Britain.

The Germans who arrived en masse in 1764 were economic migrants, the victims of human traffickers. An officer (or a man posing as such) had brought several hundred Germans to London with the promise of passage to America, only to abandon them upon arrival. Similar to the incident in 1709, the group of migrants suddenly depended on the charity of Londoners. The city's reaction, a generation after Defoe's essay, is instructive, since it shows us how much had changed. While there were still concerned voices, these were much more easily appeased, mostly because the German community in London was well established enough to offer financial help. In turn, that meant that they could coordinate their activities with the city officials, suggesting an implicit level of official recognition of the Anglo-German community and its importance. The mixture between public and semi-official status is well reflected in how these events were recorded by the protagonists themselves. It was not just the British who wrote on the subject, as Defoe had written on the migrants and immigrants, but both British and Anglo-Germans alike.

---

[49] *The Palatines' Catechism, or, a True Description of Their Camps at Black-Heath and Camberwell: In a Pleasant Dialogue between an English Tradesman and a High-Dutchman* (London: printed for T. Hare, 1709), p. 4; ECCO ESTC T043561.

[50] As Susan Reed points out, many of these discussions ignored the fact that the migrants' preferred destination was America, not Britain. While eventually many of the refugees settled in London, some of them made it to their original destination. Similarly to Defoe's suggestions, the British made them resettle not just in the British Isles but also in New York and Pennsylvania, where their German influence is still felt. See Reed, 'The Poor Palatines: An 18th-Century Refugee Crisis', *British Library* (4 September 2015), http://blogs.bl.uk/european/2015/09/the-poor-palatines.html#.

As late as 1787, the Anglophile Johann Wilhelm von Archenholtz in his two-volume travelogue *England und Italien* (*England and Italy*) relates what had become the standard account of events surrounding the arrival of the migrants. Gustav Anton Wachsel, a pastor of one of the German-Lutheran parishes formalized in the 1760s as part of the Anglo-German context, published in the *Daily Advertiser* an account of the Palatinates' desperate situation on the outskirts of London. Once the news of their plight travelled across London, the Germans received ample gifts and charity. Archenholtz describes the actions of the English in heroic terms: 'The effect of this letter was incredible and exceeded all expectation.... Guineas and banknotes rained down upon the worthy Wachsel; everyone rushed to Goodman's Field; coffee houses were set up to receive distant contributions and subscriptions; men were appointed guardians for the unfortunate people.... [P]hysicians, apothecaries, male nurses, and interpreters were designated; in short, by midday the entire troop of abandoned people had been housed, fed, their sorrows eased, and a fortunate future secured for them'.[51] Although this is evidently an idealized account, it gives us an idea how unproblematic the presence of Germans had become, including Germans who had already settled and were, of course, some of the Londoners who helped. Crucially, this latter group is best characterized as Anglo-German since at no point is this a story of a ghettoized or marginalized community, which also explains why the story about the help the newcomers received was repeated in various forms across the Anglophone press. This narrative highlights how the German arrivals were absorbed without much complication, partly because the English and Anglo-German Londoners were so incredibly generous, partly because their arrival actually created more economic activity.

These accounts were not all hyperbole. As part of the overall charitable effort, a committee was in fact appointed to coordinate help efforts and logistics. They were official and organized enough to produce a publication, the *Proceedings of the Committee Appointed for Relieving the Poor Germans, Who Were Brought to London and There Left Destitute in the Month of August 1764*. These *Proceedings* assemble and distribute all the relevant press coverage regarding the arrival and subsequent treatment of the Palatines. The idea was to raise funds for the migrants through subscription to the *Proceedings*, a plan that seems to have been moderately successful. The committee consisted of '21 Gentlemen', many of whom were established figures in the Anglo-German community.[52] They included Wachsel and Johann Christoph Haberkorn, the latter of whom was responsible for publishing the *Proceedings* and

[51] Johann Wilhelm von Archenholtz, *England: From the 1787 Expanded Edition of 'England und Italien'*, ed. and trans. Lois E. Bueler (Lanham, MD: University Press of America, 2014), pp. 42–3. For the original German text, see Archenholtz, *England und Italien*, 2 vols (C. G. Schmieder, 1787), 1: 80–1: 'Die Wirkung dieses Briefes war unglaublich, und übertrifft alle Vorstellung. Guineen und Banknoten regneten so zu sagen auf den würdigen Wachsel; alles stürzte nach Goodmansfield; man bestimmte Kaffeehäuser zu fernern Wohlthaten und Subscriptionen;...man nahm Aerzte, Apotheker, Krankenpfleger und Dolmetscher an; kurz, ehe der Mittag herankam, war die ganze Schaar der Verlassenen untergebracht...und konnte auf eine glückliche Zukunft rechnen.'
[52] *Proceedings of the Committee Appointed for Relieving the Poor Germans, Who Were Brought to London and There Left Destitute in the Month of August 1764* (London: J. Haberkorn, 1765), p. iv; ECCO ESTC T058314.

whose influence I will discuss later on in the chapter.[53] I highlight these two examples because both of them have strong institutional affiliations and professional contexts, and thereby hint at the settled and developed nature of the Anglo-German cultural context.

As Defoe predicted in 1709, over the course of the eighteenth century many of the new German arrivals brought skills that made them thrive in Britain and thus helped to establish them as full members of society. We find them taking up businesses as book binders, sugar bakers, traders, musicians, and a variety of other professions that made them part of the growing commercial and cultural complexity of London that formed the cultural background to the writings of Defoe, Blake, or Hemans. When Wordsworth reflected on the city with its 'domes, theatres, and temples', or when De Quincey had to decide between wandering the streets looking for Ann and pondering Kantian metaphysics, the Anglo-German community was already a constitutive part of this wider historical fabric.[54] We often forget not only that by the turn of the century there were plenty of Germans in Britain but also that they had settled in ways that made them an active part in shaping daily life in London and beyond.

The increasing presence of the Anglo-German community even encompasses institutional structures we often think of as highly monolithic, such as the judicial system. In actuality, these institutions often deal with a much more fluid and multilingual concrete situation, a complexity that they themselves archive in their records. For instance, by the end of the eighteenth century the Old Bailey had a whole system of translators and multilingual jurors in place. We read in a set of 1783 court proceedings that '(*The prisoner being a German, was asked by the Court, whether he chose to have one half of the Jury composed of his own countrymen, to which he replied in the affirmative, and the following Jury were sworn)*'.[55] Like so many parenthetical statements, this little aside contains a whole set of assumptions, ideas, and suppositions about what is normal, some of which are useful to unpack here. The parenthesis suggests, almost casually, that it was relatively common to compose half a jury by assembling '*his own countrymen*' and that it would be no problem to find them. It is likely that they were members of an established Anglo-German community, some of them multilingual, who had the education, time, and interest to serve as part of what had become an increasingly international and multilingual court that was trying to regulate an increasingly complex and polyglot city. We should note that it is the court itself that suggests the possibility of an Anglo-German jury; it is not an unusual plea by the accused but a standard option given to him as a matter of course, a pattern we find in many other Old Bailey proceedings

---

[53] There is an interesting subplot to the story of the 1764 arrival: it illustrates the power of print and the importance of the developing press, real or imagined. It is through periodicals that the news of their arrival travelled and that the Germans could be saved. Considering this aspect, it is relevant that the Anglo-German community made sure it had its own printing presses.

[54] William Wordsworth, 'Composed upon Westminster Bridge, Sept. 3, 1803 [*sic*]', in *Poems, in Two Volumes* (London: printed for Longman, Hurst, Rees, and Orms, 1807), 1: 118.

[55] [Trial of Charles Bairnes], 26 February 1783, in *Proceedings of the Old Bailey*, pp. 292–6; rprt in *The Old Bailey Proceedings* (Harvester Microform, 1983), pp. 64–8; *Old Bailey Proceedings Online*, t17830226–38.

throughout the eighteenth century.[56] While bilingual courts are always a sign for a barrier, they are also a marker for the societal acceptance and common presence of different languages. '[B]eing a German' in this context primarily suggests not continued distance but, rather, a familiarity that has been structurally accommodated. There is a certain effortlessness here that suggests that the presence of German culture and language was significant and extensive.

Thus, the Anglo-German community had its own structures, including trade, ecclesiastical and literary life, German churches, and the German book trade, among many others. For instance, there was George Frederic Handel's influence in music alongside other Germans, which ended up as the Royal Society of Musicians. Artists were well represented and it is certainly 'significant that one of the "founders" of the Royal Society was German'.[57] There are others that I will only touch upon briefly, such as the Hanoverian Court, with the understanding that these are partial snapshots. As I mentioned before, it is my ambition here not to give the fullest possible description of this culture but, rather, to provide enough evidence for us to see that there is a level of social and cultural complexity that deserves attention. These connections and contexts create the conditions of possibility for the emergence of particular forms of thought, including exorbitant versions of it, that are relevant beyond their historical specificity. In other words, Anglo-German structures were an integral part of London during the period. We need to incorporate their multifaceted presence into our account of British cultural life if we want to claim a real understanding of how that culture has shaped the present.

ANGLO-GERMAN INSTITUTIONALIZATION: CHURCHES, BOOK INDUSTRY, AND BILINGUAL PUBLICATIONS

Some of the most important and visible signs of Anglo-German life in London were the multiple religious congregations and churches throughout the city. People like Wachsel, the pastor of the Georgenkirche who wrote the initial account of the German refugees in 1764, were deeply important for newly arrived migrants, thus shaping the community they were becoming a part of. Highly self-aware of their institutional function, they actively chronicled their own development and documented how the growing Anglo-German community was connected to an increasing number of Anglo-German congregations throughout London. As a result,

---

[56] It is interesting to see that there seemed to have been little fear that one's '*own countrymen*' would be biased, predisposed to decide in favour of one of their own. Many of these cases record the presence of interpreters and juries that were, at least partly, composed of foreigners. There were even cases wherein the prosecution, rather than the defence, used a German interpreter since the initial accusation came from a visiting German who did not speak any English. Far be it from me to suggest that the Old Bailey was a place without its nationalist prejudices, but it is worth noting that by 1780 this English institution had evolved to the degree that it provided the resources even for foreign visitors to prosecute British citizens successfully.

[57] That is, Theodor Haak (Davis, p. 76).

the most comprehensive account of German-speaking churchgoers was written almost simultaneously with their initial development: in 1798 Johann Gottlieb Burckhardt published a church history of the German congregations in London, the *Kirchengeschichte der deutschen Gemeinden in London* (*Church History of the German Congregations in London*). This extensive work gives an overview of the number, state, activities, and personal involvements of the German-speaking clergy, leaving no doubt that they formed part of the wider intellectual and cultural fabric of the city.[58] The publication of the book suggests that to Burckhardt and others the relevance of Anglo-German church life is so obvious to anybody living in eighteenth-century London that it would seem odd not to record it. Although there is clearly a difference between standard English Anglican churches and German congregations, it is also evident that the latter played an active enough part in London life that they touched almost every Londoner (churchgoer or not) during the period.

The first openly self-identifying German church in London was the Lutheran Hamburg Church, founded in 1669 in Trinity Lane. It received its Royal Charter in 1763. As the name suggests, the northern German and Protestant character of much of the early Anglo-German community was decisive. In the eighteenth century, the most important congregation for Anglo-German relations were the Moravians and the congregation of St Mary. The latter group became better known as the Savoy Church, named after the chapel building that housed them once they had split from the Hamburg congregation in 1694. The Savoy Chapel was active for many years and became almost synonymous with the German congregation. Its location was, as the name suggests, at the Strand, close to Fetter Lane, where the Moravians worshipped. The Savoy congregation was dominated by Pietists, a group with growing influence and whose importance for Protestant thinking and culture in London could be keenly felt. Scholarship in recent years has rectified the view of Pietism as a purely German phenomenon. While its most important roots were certainly in Halle, its intellectual power was present across northern Europe, often through travelling missionaries, theologians, and merchants. As Graham Jefcoate points out, 'The influence of Halle Pietism on the protestant-Lutheran congregations in London cannot be overestimated. . . . The court pastor [Friedrich Michael] Ziegenhagen is to be regarded as one of the most influential Germans in eighteenth century London'.[59] Although the exact impact of the particular

---

[58] See Burckhardt, *Kirchengeschichte*.

[59] 'Der Einfluss des Hallischen Pietismus auf die evangelisch-lutherischen Gemeinden in London kann kaum überschätzt werden. ... Der Hofprediger Ziegenhagen, seinerzeit bedeutendster Vertreter des Hallischen Pietismus in England, ist als einer der einflussreichsten Deutschen in London im 18. Jahrhundert zu betrachten' (Jefcoate, pp. 43–4). Hamann was, of course, in London at the same time as Ziegenhagen was exerting this influence, both intellectually and administratively. There is a certain anti-institutional, Pietist dimension to Hamann's thinking—John Milbank, Catherine Pickstock, and Graham Ward go so far as to describe him as a 'radical pietist'—and the group's anti-institutional character was certainly an aspect that would have impressed both Hamann and Blake (introduction to *Radical Orthodoxy: A New Theology*, ed. Milbank, Pickstock, and Ward [New York: Routledge, 2002], pp. 1–20, 6). See also Christopher B. Barnett, 'Socrates the Pietist? Tracing the Socratic in Zinzendorf,

brand of Halle Pietism for English Protestantism remains to be understood, it is clear that its Anglo-German outpost in London was nothing if not active and well. Its presence contributes to the general importance of a certain Anglo-German intellectual milieu.[60]

There are plenty of examples of how widespread the Anglo-German institutions were and how much they began to interact with the British intelligentsia, especially through distinguished German clerics across the reformed congregations in London. Take, for instance, Carl Gottfried Woide (or Charles Godfrey Woide) (1725–90), an immensely learned Orientalist scholar who resided in London from 1770 onward. One of the foremost experts on Egyptian languages, he ended up working at the British Museum. He was a central figure in Orientalist scholarship until his death, which occurred after a fit he suffered at Sir Joseph Banks's house. During his time as reader and chaplain at the Savoy Chapel, Woide was in touch with European intellectuals such as Johann David Michaelis, also a major interlocutor for Hamann later on in that century. The memorial sermon for Woide was given by another German cleric in London and published by J. Young after his death in 1790.[61] Woide was succeeded at the Savoy Chapel by Peter Will, who became one of the most important translators of German authors such as Kotzebue or Lavater into English.[62] We will turn to some of the more prominent individual members of the Anglo-German intellectual context (Lavater, Gessner, Fuseli) shortly, but what is already clear is that in the eighteenth century there was an institutional framework for these thinkers that not only overlapped with the British literary and artistic circles, but also was part of the wider complex of cultural life in London. Anglo-German culture in London was not a sum of refugees or anonymous travelling merchants but, rather, an established public that was institutionally and intellectually represented through ecclesiastical and economic structures. It is important to understand that this culture was an active part of the historical shift that we now call the Enlightenment.

There was an Anglo-German network of intellectuals, clergymen, and academics who knew each other, corresponded with one another, publicly commented on each other's work, and formed connections that established solid structures of exchange. One of the most fascinating areas of these networks is the German book trade in eighteenth-century London and its captivating products such as dual-language books, printed both in English and German. It might come as a surprise to many scholars that there even was a culture of German booksellers in eighteenth-century

---

Hamann, and Kierkegaard', in *Kierkegaard's Late Writings*, ed. Niels Jørgen Cappelørn, Hermann Deuser, and K. Brian Söderquist, special issue, *Kierkegaard Studies Yearbook* [15] (2010): 307–23, 311.

[60] Some argue that it is this active Anglo-German congregation that allowed the survival of a version of Halle Pietism that had disappeared on the Continent. According to Garold N. Davis, it was the 'sweet singing of the Moravians' that saved Halle Pietism (p. 94).

[61] G. J. H. Röhrs, *Predigt bei der Beerdigung des am 9ten May 1790. ganz unerwartet verstorbenen Herrn Dr. C. G. Woide* (London: Young, 1790). Also see Jefcoate, p. 537.

[62] See Jefcoate, pp. 43 and 360–1. Also see Peter Will's translation of *Horrid Mysteries* (1797) in *Gothic Readings: The First Wave 1764–1840*, ed. Rictor Norton (London: Leicester University Press, 2000), pp. 122–8.

London. Much of the work on transnationalism in the period has neglected non-Anglophone research on the history of the book. Other accounts of the period have not been looking out for bilingual publications or publications in foreign languages. As James Raven points out, 'Many accounts of the early modern trade in Britain are remorselessly anglocentric, isolating the English—and British—trade in books from that of Europe, and severely underestimating the market for imported books'.[63] It is not only that the markets were underestimated, but also that scholarship has avoided examining the multilingual communities and practices that these markets served. Neither is it a matter of understanding the importance of *imported* non-English books only, since there were plenty of German and Anglo-German books that were composed, edited, published, and distributed in the British capital.

The fact that almost nobody has paid attention to this wider development demonstrates the widespread problems that result from a monolingual focus on English primary and secondary material only. It shows how certain linguistic–nationalistic proclivities, no matter how multidisciplinary, still prevent us from developing an adequately complex understanding of the networks that created the intellectual culture from which figures such as Blake and Hamann emerged. There is a transnational, polyglot element to book history that has often been overlooked by Anglophone literary criticism on the eighteenth and nineteenth centuries. This includes book history done today in Germany, which has had relatively little impact on Anglophone scholarship, although it reveals crucial aspects of the period in Britain.

Graham Jefcoate's groundbreaking work is a case in point. His *Deutsche Drucker und Buchhändler in London 1680–1811* (2015) reveals with great power and detail that there was a serious and thriving German book industry in eighteenth-century England. Jefcoate's meticulous work on the history of German books, publications, and printing houses in Britain provides us with a complex and fascinating overview of the Anglo-German literary culture of the times. It also allows us to see that this culture intersected directly with the broader literary life in Britain: just as the German churches were an integral part of the wider ecclesiastical life in London, Anglo-German print houses formed a visible part of the wider landscape of cultural production in eighteenth-century London.

The German books published in London cover all areas of public intellectual interest, especially religion, language, and literature. Many of them are Bibles and grammars, of course, but there are publications in plenty of other fields. The *Lutherbibel* was widely printed in German, sometimes in Fraktur, or what is commonly known as 'German print'.[64] The numbers, consistency, and distribution of Anglo-German, bilingual editions, and German printings all suggest that these are not incidental but rather the output of an established structure. This structure is

[63] James Raven, *The Business of Books: Booksellers and the English Book Trade 1450–1850* (New Haven, CT: Yale University Press, 2007), p. 143. See also Jefcoate, p. 107.
[64] As Jefcoate points out, the matter of Fraktur is helpful in identifying the possible printers at the time. Some printers were clearly committed enough, culturally and financially, to buy the additional materials (letters and so on) to print these materials, a fact that shows this was not just an ancillary activity. See Jefcoate, pp. 401–6.

not a historical blip: it exists solidly throughout the eighteenth century. To illustrate its constancy and variety, and also to give a sense of the players that are involved in it, I turn to three German publishers—Johann Christian Jacobi, Haberkorn, and Johann Andreas Linde—whose works made an impact and whose lives span the century. It gives a sense of the larger structure and the cultural and linguistic capital at stake. I next turn my attention to the most fascinating examples of this book industry: bilingual texts and dual-language productions. On each of their bilingual pages, these books illustrate how English and German overlapped productively and consistently in London.

It is now well known that the world of publishers and booksellers in eighteenth-century London was intensely interesting and constantly shifting. Many of the booksellers were located around St Paul's Cathedral, Soho, or the Strand. The German booksellers are no exception, as you can see in these two maps, showing the locations of German book stores and printers in London. The first shows German book shops and institutions around the Strand (see Figure 1.1).

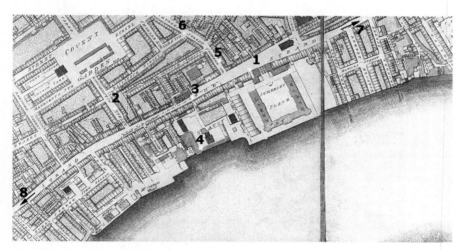

Figure 1.1 Map 1, German book shops and institutions around the Strand, from Graham Jefcoate, *Deutsche Drucker und Buchhändler in London 1680–1811* (De Gruyter, 2015, pp. 19–20).

1. J. C. Jacobi, 'next door but one to Sommerset-House in the Strand', ca. 1709–11
2. J. C. Jacobi, 'Southampton Court, Southampton Street', ca. 1712–17
3. J. C. Jacobi, 'Exeter Exchange, the Strand', ca. 1717
4. Marienkirche [Church of St. Mary] (from 1694) and Deutsche Reformierte Kirche [German Reformed Church] (from 1697), in the Freedom Savoy Palace
5. A. Linde, Catherine Street, Strand, ca. 1749–59; U. Linde, ca. 1759–67
6. U. Linde, Bridges Street, ca. 1767–74; C. Heydinger, 'No. 6, Bridges Street', ca. 1776–81
7. C. Heydinger, 'No. 274, The Strand, opposite Essex Street', ca. 1771–75
8. Deutsche Lese-Bibliothek, 'No. 65 Charing Cross', ca. 1794–96 '444 The Strand', ca. 1797–99[65]

[65] Reproduced with permission from Jefcoate, p. 19.

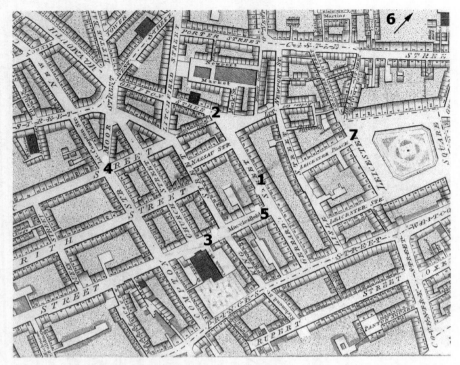

Figure 1.2 Map 2, German presses, book shops, and some other German institutions in Soho and Leicester Fields, from Graham Jefcoate, *Deutsche Drucker und Buchhändler in London 1680–1811* (De Gruyter, 2015, pp. 19–20).

1. J. C. Haberkorn, 'next door to Mill's Coffee-House', Gerrard Street, ca. 1749–59
2. J. C. Haberkorn, Grafton Street, ca. 1759–67; C. Heydinger, ca. 1768–70
3. C. G. Seyffert, 'at the corner of Kings Street in Dean Street opposite St Anns', ca. 1755–60
4. C. Heydinger, 'at the Black Moore's Head, in Moor-Street, the end of Compton Street', ca. 1766–67
5. H. Escher, 'No. 14 Gerrard Street', ca. 1798–1807
6. J. H. Müller, 'Fountain Court, opposite the Bell Bagnio, St. Martin's Lane', 1758–60
7. Sans Souci Theatre: F. Schirmers 'Deutsches Theater' [German theatre], ca. 1805–06[66]

The second map (Figure 1.2) indicates German presses, book shops, and some other German institutions in Soho and Leicester Fields.

Jacobi, who located his offices next to the Savoy, was known to his contemporaries as '[t]he German bookseller in the Strand', a description that was included in his prints.[67] He opened his shop in 1709, the same year that Defoe published his *History* welcoming the Palatines. When Defoe mentioned that he had consulted foreign sources, he might very well have been referring to works purchased at Jacobi's shop. Principally, however, Jacobi dealt with books on German Pietism, becoming a key player in the way that theological discussion was shaped. His close connections to the Society for Promoting Christian Knowledge and, especially, to

---

[66] Reproduced with permission from Jefcoate, p. 20.   [67] Jefcoate, p. 128.

the Society's influential Joseph Downing made Jacobi an important figure in the disseminating of what was considered edifying literature. Like his colleagues, Jacobi published books in German and English, as well as bilingual editions. Another major source of his income was his import and distribution of books from Germany, especially Bibles. As Jefcoate mentions, 'In the time around 1710 Jacobi's business consisted in importing German books while also selling writings, edited in London, near the Strand in collaboration with Joseph Downing'.[68] The fact that one of the first German booksellers in London worked in collaboration with a Brit is a further example of how their worlds intersected. This activity was not just a lonely endeavour of a single German but, rather, a collaboration that was based on a common understanding that there was a wider intellectual and financial market to enter.

Around the middle of the century, the German editorial work and printing presses in London experienced somewhat of a boom. The most important business to emerge was the Teutsche Druckerey (German Printing House) in Soho, founded by Haberkorn and Johann Nicodemus Gussen in 1749.[69] Haberkorn was a major player among the Anglo-German community in mid-eighteenth-century London. His store connected people: he advertised it as a place to meet those interested in German language lessons and who wanted to acquire grammars, literature, or other materials. An experienced *émigré* and businessman, it was he who published the *Proceedings* composed by the committee overseeing the second wave of Palatine refugees that I have already discussed. It was no coincidence that he was involved in this venture. Although almost entirely unknown—apart from Jefcoate, there is almost no work on him, even in German—Haberkorn's case illustrates well why the book trade is an excellent barometer for the diverse presence of the Germans then in London at the time. Many of the texts he published were, like the imports, religious in nature. A milestone was his 1750 printing of a *Neues Testament*, basically a *Lutherbibel* that was being sold in German. This is the type of Bible that was useful for Germans travelling through England or for people who wanted to read German at school and at home. It reminds us that there was an active set who formed part of a cultural context that we all-too-easily think of in static or monolingual terms.

Haberkorn was a busy man. His catalogue gives us an idea of the size and multidisciplinary scope of German books at the time (always, of course, assuming that there was a meaningful relation between production and demand). As Jefcoate describes, more than a hundred prints from Haberkorn's press in Soho are known from the period between 1749 and 1767, and they 'represent only a part of his overall production'.[70] Considering that they are only a small, interdisciplinary but

[68] 'In der Zeit um 1710 bestand Jacobis Geschäft also darin, deutsche Bücher zu importieren und gleichzeitig, meist in Zusammenarbeit mit Joseph Downing, in London verlegte Schriften in der Nähe des Strand zu verkaufen' (Jefcoate, p. 139).

[69] In addition, during the following decade, two Moravian presses were established. See Ch. 4 for a detailed discussion.

[70] 'Inzwischen sind über hundert Drucke aus der Zeit von 1749 bis 1767 bekannt, die aus Haberkorns Presse in Londons Soho stammen. Diese entsprechen aber nur zu einem Teil seiner Gesamtproduktion' (Jefcoate, p. 145).

representative sample, it suddenly becomes apparent that there was a considerable, influential German publication scene in London. Unfortunately, what may be Haberkorn's most interesting publication has been lost. It is a fortnightly newspaper, *Das Deutsche Magazin; oder Schatzkammer Miscellanischer Schriften* (*The German Magazine, or, the Treasure Room of Miscellaneous Writings*). It was announced in November 1750 in the *Daily Advertiser*, and the announcement was repeated after the magazine had already been published. The fact Haberkorn advertises his German publication in English periodicals indicates that there was a sizeable number of people who were capable not just of reading both in German and in English but also doing it as a regular part of consuming information. Reading during the eighteenth century was a much more eclectic, multilingual activity than we have realized. Haberkorn, for instance, not only published translations of German material into English but also vice versa, including a 1751 version of John Bunyan's *Pilgrim's Progress* (*Eines Christen Reise nach der seligen Ewigkeit*). The press produced newspapers in French and English and extensive publications in Italian and Latin. Between 1749 and 1768, Haberkorn alone published forty-one titles in English, forty-four in German, twenty-three in French, four in Italian, and four in Latin—all printed and sold in London.

Moving between different languages was a common and a normal activity for all of these printers and editors, who presented their work in multilingual forms. This suggests that they expected a similar linguistic capacity and flexibility from their potential reader-clients. As with the proceedings from the Old Bailey, a bilingual advertisement suggests a need for translation but also a certain level of interest and proficiency. This is how best to make sense of a bilingual advertisement such as the following, published in 1754: 'Denen respectiven Bücher-Liebhabern füge hiermit zu wissen, dass wann sich einige Liebhaber sowohl von Englisch, Französisch [*sic*], Latein- und Teutsche Büchern finden sollten, selbige in Menge sowohl sauber gebunden, als auch roh bey mir um civilen Preis zu haben sind; ... A N D R. L I N D E, Buchhaendler in Catherine-Street, L O N D O N. G E N T L E M E N may be furnished at very reasonable prizes [*sic*], with all sorts of English, French, Latin and German books, neatly bound or in quires.... their humble servant A. L I N D E'.[71] The nonchalance and familiarity with the multilingual environment, which includes multiple languages on the page of the advertisement, suggests that there is a certain normality to this multilingual practice that has been historically forgotten. We would do well to remind ourselves that these multilingual and varied publications are part of the intellectual and cultural context into which a figure such as Blake is born. These polyglot booksellers in Soho are part of the cultural complexity that forms his intellectual and material background into what we call the Enlightenment.

Who were all these publications for? The answer is probably just as varied and eclectic as the publications. Immigrants must have had to replace their own German Bibles at some point, and the *Lutherbibel* was used as the standard work

---

[71] Advertisement for *An English and Danish Dictionary: Containing the Genuine Words of Both Languages with Their Proper and Figurative Meanings*, ed. Andreas Berthelson (London: printed by John Haberkorn and A. Linde, 1754), sig. Kkkk3v.

at German schools and for language classes. Other purchaser-readers presumably included travellers coming through London, such as the missionaries on their way to the Americas, Australia, or the two Indies who wanted to spread the Christian word, often in German. But Haberkorn's titles also serviced a great variety of English people at home, such as *The Theory and Practice of Brewing* (1762), which became a surprisingly popular work, much used throughout the century. In the same year, Haberkorn also published *The Antiquities of Athens* (1762), one of the most sumptuously produced books of the decade in any language. The volume, put together by James Stuart and Nicholas Revett, had luxurious illustrations, and it became central to the creation of what was termed 'the Greek style' in nineteenth-century Britain. Thus, Haberkorn was not just an important German publisher but also a figure whose business illustrates the international character of the London publishing scene during the mid-eighteenth century.[72]

Once we have a sense of the target audience of these books in German, we can ask ourselves about how Haberkorn and others would have reached these readers, an insight that would tell us about the social fabric of this eighteenth-century marketplace of ideas. Although Haberkorn acted sometimes as a printer and as a distributor, other printers still relied on specialized booksellers, such as Linde, another key figure in the dissemination of Anglo-German material. As Jefcoate notes, Linde started out as a book binder, also dealing in paper, but quickly added the selling of books to his business, which was located, like so many other German bookshops, near the Strand. After 1752, Linde was mainly active as a bookseller and editor, though he also worked as a translator—a side activity many of these figures had in common. For roughly ten years (1749–59), he was one of the most important figures when it came to the dissemination of the kind of material Haberkorn was editing and printing. We can find around 170 advertisements regarding his publications in London newspapers after 1749.[73] He complemented the material by Haberkorn with translations of German scientific publications and English titles against the Moravians—a remarkable thing, given their prominence in Anglo-German affairs.

A few details from Linde's publications are indicative of the vibrant Anglo-German culture in England at the time. The best examples are Linde's advertisements and catalogues of 1753–54, which appeared separately and additionally to the advertisements I mentioned. Putting together such catalogues was standard for booksellers at the time, and these documents are some of the most valuable sources in figuring out what was sold and in circulation and how these titles were mar-keted. Each catalogue ran between 2,200 and 2,500 titles, many of which were German originals, translations from the German, and translations into German. Take the first page of the 1753 catalogue, which lists three books: *A Compleat German Grammar*; *Neue Englische Grammatik*; and *A Candid Narrative of the Rise*

---

[72] Haberkorn's life is an intriguing example of the increasing mobility and globalization of the period. After leaving London in 1770, he worked for the East India Company and then returned to Germany, which he subsequently left to settle in Copenhagen.

[73] See Jefcoate, p. 199.

and Progress of the Herrnhuters, Commonly Called the Moravians. Linde was very active in distributing titles such as these and managed to create one of the larger bookselling ventures in London at the time. Just like Haberkorn, he would eventually run into financial troubles—all of which was relayed to debtors and observers back in Germany—and retire, but his titles remain as good examples of the kind of Anglo-German culture that was developing and taking root in London.

To learn more about the kinds of books that Jacobi, Haberkorn, Linde, or others would have sold, I have selected a set of dual-language books, texts that were published in both English and German, either on the same or on alternating pages. They vividly exemplify the status of multilingual relations. These are not bizarre texts, but rather remarkable for their normalcy in subject matter and self-representation. None of them is advertised as an unusual book, even when they are produced in two different fonts (which required considerable effort from the printers). They are remarkably practical: grammars, handbooks for religious instruction, and cultural guides for life in England. If they look unusual to us now, then it is because we underestimate how normal, and normalizing, such publications were.

Over the course of my archival research, I have identified at least eighteen dual-language books published in Britain between 1706 and 1790, materials that add to Jefcoate's account. Of course, some of them are a continuation of a practice that was common use for grammars.[74] Yet they also include bilingual titles on topics such as cultural assimilation or daily religious instruction, both of which illustrate the increasing expansion and normalization of the Anglo-German context. Take, for instance, John King's/Johann König's *A Compleat English Guide for High-Germans / Ein vollkommener englischer Wegweiser fur Hoch-Teutsche* (1706), a 250-page manual that, besides its grammar, provides extensive instruction for behaviour in the London Anglo-German world, as well as a contextualization of its cultural sphere (it was republished in extended form in 1758). The preface gives us the reason for the existence of this *Guide*: 'Among the vast Concourse of Foreigners that resort to this Flourishing Kingdom, the *Germans*, since their happy Alliance with the *English*, are not the least considerable'.[75] In the early eighteenth century, the considerable influx of Germans still required a guide, but it was a guide to something that was establishing itself as a stable institution. The reader and user of the guide would help establish its cultural as well as its linguistic structures. Figure 1.3 shows a concrete example.

There are several hundred pages such as these, covering phrases, expressions, and even fictional dialogues, very much along the lines of what we still use in second-language instruction. The selection and character of these passages is a self-conscious choice, 'that nothing might be wanting that wou'd render this Tract compleatly Useful, and really Instructive, I have added such Dialogues as were thought most Convenient, and to the Purpose'.[76] What is indeed instructive is what King thinks

---

[74] The famous grammar *The Dutch Minerva* (1680), by Daniel Higgs, is the most obvious example.
[75] John King/Johann Konig, *A Compleat English Guide for High-Germans / Ein vollkommener englischer Wegweiser fur Hoch-Teutsche* (London: printed for W. Freeman / Wilhelm Frieman and B. Barker, 1706), p. [i]; ECCO ESTC T101126.
[76] King/Konig, p. [v].

Englifcher Wegweifer. 161

What is to pay?	*Was bin ich fchuldig?*
	Was ift die Rechnung?
Two Shillings and fix Pence.	*Eine halbe Krone.*
How can that be?	*Wie kan das feyn?*
Yes, Sir, there is fo much indeed; a Shilling Meat, a Penny Bread, Two Pence Cheefe Three-pence Sallad, and Twelve Pence Wine.	*Ja mein Herr, es ift gewifs foviel; für einen Schilling Fleifch, für einen Stüber Brod, zwey Stüber Kefe, drey Stüber Salat und zwölf Stüber wein.*
It is very right, there's your Mony.	*Es ift gar recht; da habt ihr euer Geld.*
Welcome, Sir.	*Der Herr ift willkommen.*

The VIII. Dialogue. Das VIII. Gefpræch.

Of Buying and Selling. Von kauffen und verkauffen.

WHat will you buy, Sir? Have you got any good Cloth, Ribbands, good Hats, good Gloves or Stockings?	*WAs will der Herr kauffen? Habt ihr gut Tuch oder Lacken, Bänder, gute Hüte, gute Handfchuh oder Strümpffe?*
Yes, Sir, the beft in Town.	*Ja mein Herr die beften in der Stadt.*
Shew me a piece of good Cloth.	*Zeiget mir ein Stuck gutes Lacken.*
Black or coloured?	*Schwartz oder gefærbt?*
There's Cloth for you, Sir, if you like the Colour.	*Hier ift gutes Tuch woferne dem Herrn die Farbe gefält.*
What's this a Yard?	*Wie theuer die Elle?*
Twenty Shillings.	*Zwanzig Schillinge.*
How? Twenty Shillings? you take me for a Stranger, I fee.	*Wie? zwanzig Schillinge? ihr fehet mich fur einen fremden an, wie ich mercke.*
No, Sir, we are not in *France*. We fell no dearer to a Stranger in this Country than to an *Englifh-Man*.	*Nein mein Herr, wir find allhier nicht in Franckreich. Man verkaufft hier den Fremden nicht theurer alfs den Engelandern.*
Well, I'll give you fixteen Shillings.	*Wohl, ich will euch fechzehen Schilling geben.*
M	Upon

Figure 1.3 John King/Johann Konig, *A Compleat English Guide for High-Germans / Ein vollkommener englischer Wegweiser fur Hoch-Teutsche* (London: printed for W. Freeman / Wilhelm Frieman and B. Barker, 1706), p. 161. © The British Library Board. General Reference Collection DRT Digital Store 1490.l.11.

'Useful' for a German coming to London in 1706: most of the examples and materials are for a quotidian life that is shaped by conversations about daily socializing, food, drink, housing, transportation, commerce, and faith. The examples ('*Dialog. Between an* English *and a* German Gentleman') throughout the book follow this pattern.[77] The fictional situations from which they take their examples

---

[77] King/Konig, p. 187.

invoke themes from social life ('Of Eating and Drinking in a Cook's-Shop') to traffic and postal service between England, Holland, and Germany ('when do you Sail for *England?*'; 'How have you done, since I saw you at *Amsterdam?*').[78] They are about the details of moving belongings from one country to the next, sending money, but also having arrived and settling ('Have you no Acquaintance at Court? / No Sir, none at all. / I will bring you acquainted').[79] The mock dialogues and descriptions are set in restaurants and inns, and cover everything from cock fights and the royal palaces to a description of Bedlam. The many and varied examples cover conversations with and among many social classes and professions who range from servants, laundresses, and tailors to doctors, postmasters, and members of the nobility. The phrases that King/Konig provides as likely to be of use ('Virtue cannot agree with Vice / *Die Tugend und das Laster koennen sich nicht vereinigen*') follow this pattern of diversity and suggest shared experiences.[80] The *Guide* is not a specialized publication in business or ecclesiastical English for travelling merchants or priests but, rather, a guide that is aimed at facilitating the creation of a full, rounded life in a new environment. As an overall guide to London, King's/Konig's indirect description would already be a remarkable publication. What makes it even more important is that it is presented in a continuous form of polyglot pages. It serves to shape the reality it describes, which turns out to be a multilingual, rapidly developing context. The fact that King's *Guide* was followed by very similar publications and, in one form or another, that such bilingual extensive guides were published at least throughout the first six decades of the eighteenth century shows us that they were continuously helping to form the diverse Anglo-German community on the ground.

Bilingual publications were not only for new arrivals; they included books for people who had already settled. Since the churches and ecclesiastical structures were crucial in this regard, it is not surprising many of these publications came out of this arena, such as several bilingual catechisms for adults and children that were published throughout the eighteenth century. In 1709 we see the London publication of *Der kirchen-Catechismus* [*sic*] / *The Church Catechism* for the use of the Palatine Refugees (Figure 1.4).[81] Later in the century (1770) we encounter a further Lutheran catechism, '*published together with the German*'.[82] Just as the common phrases in the *Guide*, the English and German texts here are also printed on facing sides, enumerating phrases of everyday religious life. There is a 'Daily Manual' that provides English and German versions of daily morning and evening prayers, graces before and after meals, and similar situations.[83] Providing these kinds of prayers in two languages suggests that the book seeks to bridge the linguistic gap

---

[78] King/Konig, pp. 160, 153, and 182.   [79] King/Konig, p. 182.

[80] King/Konig, p. 24.

[81] *Der kirchen-Catechismus: Welchem einige der auserlesensten Sprüche der Heiligen Schrifft hinzugesetzet worden* (London: Downing, 1709).

[82] The full title of the work gives us a flavour of the wider context: *The Shorter Catechism of Martin Luther, translated from the Latin into English by a Clergyman of the Church of England; and now published together with the German, for the use of the school belonging to St. George's Lutheran Chapel, in Little Ayliffe-Street, Goodman's Fields, London. By Gustavus Anthony Wachsel, D. D. Pastor of the said Church* (London, 1770).

[83] *The Shorter Catechism*, p. 49.

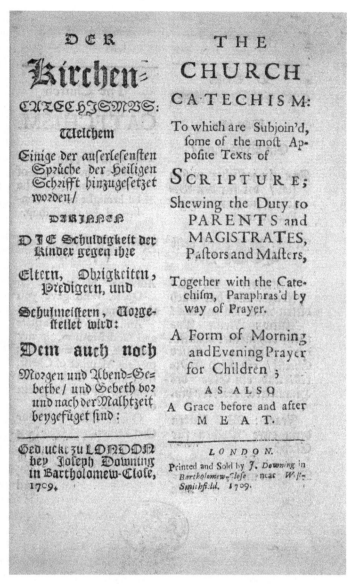

Figure 1.4 *Der kirchen-Catechismus: Welchem einige der auserlesensten Sprüche der Heiligen Schrifft hinzugesetzet worden* (London: Downing, 1709), p 1.© The British Library Board. General Reference Collection DRT Digital Store 3504.e.28.

between them every day. Conversely, the book promotes the idea that it is in the everyday that the most relevant religious habits and linguistic practices are located. There is an investment here that comes from understanding how important daily life was and, thus, that the church needed to help shape this experience that then was multilingual. These bilingual publications are, therefore, a perfect example that the Anglo-German community avoids ghettoization or segregation along linguistic lines.

These multilingual publications are not for the debates between highly educated theologians but, rather, a way of forming the daily intellectual context of religious life and practice in London. The catechisms give the regulation of daily life in a bilingual list of 'Duties' (*Haustafel*), which covers the expected behaviour of the clergy and political subjects, along with details on how husbands, wives, parents, and children ought to behave. The advice is a mixture of biblical passages on the abstract and the specific ('Let him, that is taught in the word, communicate unto him that teacheth, in all good things'; 'A bishop must be blameless, the husband of a wife vigilant, sober, of good behaviour, given to hospitality, apt to teach, not given to wine'), which is not unusual and would have been rather helpful for language instruction.[84] As can be expected, the advice is rather conservative (wives submit to husbands, children to parents, slaves to masters) and invested in the status quo. Contra figures such as Blake and Hamann, the catechism shows a deep commitment to religious institutionalism, traditional positions on gender roles, and parental or institutional authority. These bilingual catechisms are very much about keeping the status quo, albeit in a newly forming linguistic environment. Parallel to this occasional conservatism, however, the Anglo-German ecclesiastical context is a world wherein multilingualism is an accepted, promoted, and encouraged part of cultural life.

It is worth reminding ourselves that the German churches and their publications were spaces where immigrants could formulate much of their Anglo-German life for themselves and their children. These texts play an important part in the shaping of that context. Many of the bilingual schools were attached to churches, and most of them used publications such as a catechism. The quotidian aspect of these books thus remains important beyond their perpetuation of particular cultural norms (such as are formulated in the list of 'Duties'). They also made a difference in the way that people began to think about the multilingual arena in which they were moving. The readers of the bilingual catechism—children during language instruction, adults who were learning to fit into their new world—came not only to learn and memorize the word of God but also to learn how to live by His word in more than one language. The wider significance of the *Catechism* in this context is that it is akin to a hermeneutic manual. The most common phrase in the *Catechism* is 'What do these words mean?' to which the student needs to learn the answer: 'Geheiligt werde dein Nahme. *Was ist daß?* Gottes Nahme ist zwar an ihm selbst heilig; aber wir bitten in diesem Gebet, dass er auch bey uns heilig werde.... Hallowed be thy name. *What meaneth this Petition?* The name of God truly is of itself holy, but we ask in this petition, that it may be hallowed by us.'[85] Learning that answer in more than one language is bound up in learning the word of God in multiple ways.

The most explicit example for this metadynamic is when the *Catechism* self-consciously turns to the wider signification of language instruction. It states that the manual is all about the way that 'the Word of God is taught with purity and sincerity, and we as becometh children of God live godly according thereto'.[86] We learn that the word of God connects the two natural languages, and we learn how to express our daily thanks in both of them. Through this process we begin to understand that these natural languages point towards a higher level of hermeneutic—namely, a language of God that encompasses the world and transcends the limits of natural languages. The *Catechism* is a reminder that we can celebrate God in multiple languages, and that continuing to do this is part of how the Anglo-German community can and ought to distinguish itself.

In many of these publications there is a self-reflexivity about their contributions to emerging Anglo-German culture and how it shapes daily lives in Britain. There is even an archivization of the way in which this knowledge is constructed, especially via guides that describe Britain either to reflect back onto the Anglo-German community itself or to help the German reader outside of Britain understand it better. Take, for instance, Gebhard Friedrich Wendeborn's addition to the field of Anglo-German discourse, his German *Contributions to the Knowledge of Great Britain in the Year 1779* (*Beyträge zur Kentniss Grosbritanniens vom Jahr 1779*).[87] Wendeborn had lived in London for over twenty-five years, and worked as a pastor at one of the German churches mentioned before. He had travelled widely and had already published a travelogue about western and southern England.[88] As the book's title suggests, the *Contributions* are an expansive and thorough study of the country that was Wendeborn's home for many years. It became the 'most thorough and reliable study of England' and 'the recognized guide-book on this country'.[89] This distinctly Anglo-German contribution to the description of Britain's complex social structure becomes one of the most accurate guides of the larger historical context. The book itself grew to four volumes, and an abridged version was published in London. It remains one of the most intriguing portrayals of late eighteenth-century England, often more investigative than similar books by native authors. It includes chapters, among others, on the king and taxes, the character of the English, the provisions for the poor, and curiosities in and around London. It suggests that the Anglo-German experience is comprehensive, varied, and self-aware rather than a specialized or insubstantial phenomenon that can be easily neglected.

Wendeborn's was by no means the only self-aware study of the Anglo-German community at the time. Archenholtz's multivolume *England und Italien* recounts the history of the Palatinate refugees living in England for quite some time (1769–79). Archenholtz published some essays about his visits in the early 1780s and his more substantial travelogue in 1785, which was translated throughout Europe, including into English. Later on, Archenholtz embarked on a fascinating project that gives us an immediate idea of the degree to which the Anglo-German community continued to exist and represent itself to itself even beyond the borders of Britain.

---

[86] *The Shorter Catechism*, p. 21.
[87] See Gebhard Friedrich Wendeborn, *Beyträge zur Kentniss Grosbritanniens vom Jahr 1779. Aus der Handschrift eines Ungenannten* (Lemgo: Meyer, 1780).
[88] See Percy Ewing Matheson, *German Visitors to England 1770–1795 and Their Impressions* (Oxford: Clarendon, 1930).
[89] W. D. Robson-Scott, *German Travellers in England 1400–1800* (Oxford: Basil Blackwell, 1953), p. 163.

For over a decade, Archenholtz published a yearly report on the most important events in England (*Annalen der Britischen Geschichte*) which, just like Wendeborn's work, included all parts of society, from courthouses to prostitutes. By chronicling Anglo-German context and the degree to which it touched British life in the eighteenth century, works such as Wendeborn's and Archenholtz's are a central part of English *and* German literary and cultural histories. They add to the picture provided throughout this chapter, enriching our sense, not only that this Anglo-German context existed, but also that it was a vital part of a larger intellectual matrix that allowed people like Hamann or Blake to thrive. The work of Wendeborn, Archenholtz, and many others illustrates why it is blinkered and insufficient to look at these texts within the context of a national literature alone, especially if we want to get a sense of the depth of the context in which subsequent generations produce Romantic literature, be it in English or German.

GERMAN VISITORS TO LONDON
AS CHRONICLERS OF BRITAIN

Mobility obviously played a major role in the creation of the eighteenth-century transnational context in London and beyond. With the exception of Blake, most of the important and influential authors that I cover in this book travelled extensively. Many of them, like Archenholtz, Fuseli, or Robinson Crusoe's fictional father, stayed for decades or even resettled in their newly adopted country. Some shuttled in-between. Most of the authors I focus on were based in the capital or continuously connected to it in some way—a group of travellers whose presence in Britain was more fleeting, yet who added something more to our overall understanding of the period.

Occasional travel between Germany and Britain was not only a major part of the cultural and financial exchange between the two countries but also the source of considerable writing and publishing, most of which remains untranslated and therefore largely unexamined. While we have excellent scholarship on more canonical travel routes, such as the Grand Tour, there has been a relative lack of interest in the depth of travel writing between those two countries. The existing research in this area typically focuses on the period post-1790, in keeping with much other Anglo-German work.[90] We are yet to understand what these writings can tell us about the specifically Anglo-German culture in eighteenth-century Britain. Yet German travellers' reports about their time in Britain delivers insights not only on general life in the country but also, more specifically, commentary on the Anglo-German communities there, especially in London. This is true for the long-term visitors, such as Wendeborn and Archenholtz, whose works I've discussed earlier. But even short-term travellers, the conversations they create, and the records of

---

[90] One exception is Alessa Johns, though even she does not consider much before 1780. See Johns, *Bluestocking Feminism and British–German Cultural Transfer, 1750–1837* (Ann Arbor, MI: University of Michigan Press, 2014).

those conversations they produce—each of them shows us a small Anglo-German contact zone, an addition to the larger Anglo-German context. It is a mistake to assume that these travellers simply came and went; they brought things with them and took others away, transforming the context which they temporarily inhabited. Thus, we should think of German visitors to Britain, even if they only stayed for a short time, as an active part of the Anglo-German sphere that was helping to shape the nation's multilingual and cross-national intellectual landscape.

Many of the German visitors to Britain were Anglophiles and came with a deep cultural and political interest in recording the cultural structures of their host country. They were attracted by the growing importance of Britain as the home of John Locke, Adam Smith, and David Hume, a society defined by an emerging empiricism that would eventually end up as the British Enlightenment. English literary luminaries such as Henry Fielding, Samuel Richardson, or Laurence Sterne were widely read on the Continent, and the German craze for Shakespeare fell into the same period. (It was instrumental in shifting Germany's taste from neoclassical theatre to the kind modern drama that Wordsworth would later describe as 'sickly and stupid German tragedies'.) Yet these were not just literary, economic, or political travellers. They were also invested in seeing what such a country looked like on the ground, how the literature and philosophy they had read and discussed in Germany compared to the quotidian life in the English Parliament, in the London theatre, and in its streets. They really did participate in, and formed part of, the Anglo-German life at the time.

It would be a mistake, however, to think of these visitors as having a particular goal in mind or even following a regularized travel programme. The sheer number of German travellers to England, their heterogeneous interests and circumstances, make it difficult to discuss them as one coherent group. According to W. D. Robson-Scott, the 'critical admiration of the travellers of the Aufklärung gives way to an uncritical enthusiasm for everything English, an enthusiasm so unbalanced in its more extreme forms that it justly deserves the name of anglomania'.[91] This assessment seems a little extreme and certainly too invested in a break between such *Aufklärung* and an uncritical Romanticism. While there is certainly a rise in German Anglomania, there are plenty of studied and critical approaches well into the 1780s. I will discuss two of the most important ones here—namely, Georg Christoph Lichtenberg and Sophie von La Roche, both of whom connect their abstract interests in England with a concrete, self-aware study of quotidian life in ways that are telling for us today.[92] They were both learned, observant travellers

---

[91] Robson-Scott, p. 161.

[92] So that the reader can get a sense of the sheer number and complexity of these visitors, all of whom provide us with accounts of the intellectual atmosphere in Britain, it will be useful to mention a few of them. There were visitors whose expertise and interest in British literature is paramount, such as Johann Christian Fabricius, Franz de Paula Anton von Hartig, Friedrich von Günderode, Carl Friedrich Bardt, and Johann Wilhelm von Archenholtz, who all write on British contemporary literature. Travellers such as Baron Karl Ludwig von Pöllnitz, Béat Ludwig von Muralt, Baron Jakob Friedrich von Bielfeld, or Peter Sturz were more interested in Britain's political culture. Bielfeld visited the House of Commons and, like Muralt, he saluted 'England as the home of common sense' (qtd. in Robson-Scott, p. 139). Sturz, a great admirer of William Pitt the Elder, combined political and literary

with a particular eye for the social and cultural complexities, including the relations to their own home nation.

The German Anglophile Lichtenberg (1742–99) was a fascinating figure by any standard. Known today primarily as a satirist and inventor of the German aphoristic tradition, and as the author of his *Sudelbücher* (Scrap Books) and his pointed attacks on Lavater's *Physiognomy*, Lichtenberg held the first German chair for experimental physics at the University of Göttingen. One of the most fiercely intelligent minds of his age, he was deeply aware of the growing intellectual interconnectedness across Europe, conducting his conversations across all important nations and languages. Before taking up his chair in Göttingen, Lichtenberg undertook two journeys to England, in 1770 and 1774–75. Like many other travellers, he was well prepared and connected. Most importantly, his English, at least according to David Garrick, was so good that he 'might have almost passed for an Englishman'.[93] Such proficiency would certainly have allowed him to interact with ease across social classes and registers. During his visits he met King George III, Joseph Priestley (and thus, one would imagine, Joseph Johnson), James Watt, and many other leading figures of the London scientific and artistic circles. He was a tutor and friend to the aristocrat William Henry Irby (they visited Sterne's grave together, venerating the great British author who had become a European sensation) and Daniel Solander, the librarian of the British Museum. When their conversations were not about art, most of these men talked politics, especially about the developments in the American colonies (in the years of his second visit, from 1774–75, there was no hotter political topic), including the writings of Richard Price.[94]

But Lichtenberg as a traveller did not restrict his interactions to intellectuals or distinguished members of society. His interests also included the daily life of London's social institutions, which led him to visit the theatre frequently as well as the Old Bailey and explore some of the seedier parts of London. Lichtenberg's connections and wide interests give us a good idea of the kind of conversations that were going on during that time between German visitors and British subjects, whether they were intellectuals or common people on the streets. Lichtenberg's diaries and essays record all of these voices. Despite his many publications on England and the fact that in 1793 the Royal Society appointed Lichtenberg a member, he barely registers now in our accounts of the period. Recovering his work as a recognized member of the Anglo-German intellectual exchange allows us to gain a sense of the complexity of the period and develop an understanding for the importance of transnational perspectives within it.

---

interest, meeting James MacPherson, David Garrick, and Samuel Johnson, with whom he ended up having a conversation about (presumably German) loan-words in English. His letters and essays also show familiarity with British art, especially that of Hogarth and Angelica Kaufman (see Robson-Scott, pp. 140–4).

[93] Qtd in Robson-Scott, p. 137. For further material on Georg Christoph Lichtenberg's travels, see Otto Deneke, *Lichtenbergs Leben* (Munich: Ernst Heimeran, 1944), pp. 100–6 and 222–61.

[94] In his writings, Lichtenberg often imagines being a British subject, either within the colonies or at home, and reflects on how he would feel as such, compared to how he feels as the German subject that he is; the result of this thought experiment is that he would sympathize with the claims for more independence.

Lichtenberg's *Letters from England* (*Briefe aus England*) (1774–75) and his diary give us an extraordinary picture of the arts scene in London, especially theatre and opera. He was obsessed with the stage and its budding celebrity culture, so he quickly gained access to the most important actors of the age, such as Garrick and the main female actors who played alongside him (Ann Street Barry and Frances 'Fanny' Abington). Lichtenberg was especially taken by the actor's ability to remain, an 'acutely perceptive man, who keeps the most exact register on his nation's taste'.[95] He translates this interest in aesthetics and contemporary life to his essays on Joshua Reynolds and William Hogarth.[96] In his discussions and writings, Lichtenberg was interested in the contemporaneous moment in Britain, including its increasing exposure to the outside world that allowed people like him to be part of the Anglo-German context within it. He was only too aware that the 'nation's taste', which included science and politics, was also influenced and shaped by visitors like himself.

Known primarily as a novelist today, von La Roche is one of the relatively few public female examples of Anglo-German travel writing during the eighteenth century.[97] Von La Roche had toured England in 1786, having prepared by studying all the relevant secondary and primary literature. Her diary is one of the most meticulous and attentive records we have of English life during this era, despite one critic who declares it 'entertaining gossip of a blue-stocking and society lady, equipped with a warm heart and the somewhat tearful sensibility of the age'.[98] Her detailed recordings of high and low life in London are as revealing as are her discussions with some of her British hosts. Von La Roche met various members of the Windsor Court, visited with Frances Burney and with Warren Hastings. Yet she also witnessed daily London life with its poor and its prostitute 'light girls' in the theatre.[99] For all their idealization, her writings nevertheless discuss her visit to Bedlam and her view of the East India Company, showing that von La Roche's diaries and essays are far more than mere gossip and, as Alison Martin suggests, 'self-conscious to a degree rarely found in accounts by her male counterparts'.[100] They present a treasure trove of analysis and observations across English classes, often with a sharp eye towards gender and politics.[101]

---

[95] Georg Christoph Lichtenberg, *Schriften und Briefe*, 5 vols (Munich: Hanser, 1967–74), 3: 347. On Garrick and Lavater, see vol. 4, pp. 252–3.

[96] The essay 'Extensive Explanation of Hogarth's Copper Etchings' (*Ausführliche Erklärung der Hogarthischen Kupferstiche*), still ranks among the standard commentaries on the artist, at least in German scholarship. It provides discussions of all the major works, including *The Harlot's Progress, The Rake's Progress, Marriage à la Mode*, and *Industry and Idleness* as well as contemporary Hogarth scholarship. See Lichtenberg, 3: 660–1060.

[97] On von La Roche and also nineteenth-century examples of German travelogues, male and female, see Alison Martin, *Moving Scenes: The Aesthetics of German Travel Writing on England 1783–1830* (London: MHRA, 2008).

[98] Robson-Scott, p. 181.

[99] 'Freudenmädchen'. Sophie von La Roche, *Sophie in London, 1786: Being the Diary of Sophie v. la Roche*, trans. Clare Williams (London: Jonathan Cape, 1933), p. 133. See also, Sophie von La Roche, *Tagebuch einer Reise durch Holland und England* (Offenbach, Ger.: Brede, 1788), p. 288.

[100] Martin, p. 46.

[101] Helen Lowry, '"Reisen, sollte ich reisen! England sehen!" A Study in Eighteenth-Century Travel Accounts: Sophie von La Roche, Johanna Schopenhauer and Others' (PhD dissertation, Queen's University, Kingston, Ontario, 1998), p. 63.

Take, for instance, her confrontation with the politician Lord George Gordon, name-giver of the Gordon Riots: 'I am amazed that you, with your gentle mien, could be responsible for the death of so many hundreds of London's inhabitants, and for bringing misfortune to hundreds of others.'[102] It puts the Anglophile German in a position of an astute critic whose sympathies lie beyond the boundaries of nations. In another instance, von La Roche provoked Burney to explain why she thought the German's visit to Bedlam highly inappropriate. Here we not only learn something about the German's interest in British institutional life and the daily circumstances and treatment of its sick, but also see how von La Roche uses her diary to record a cultural clash on decorum.[103] Von La Roche presents an Anglo-German example that turns the visitor's gaze onto the British themselves and, thereby, becomes part of their history.[104] What is true for von La Roche is also the case for the huge number of other travelogues composed by German visitors. They deserve to be classified and contextualized in greater detail. But even the cursory view that I have provided of these short-term visitors provides a good sense of how these figures contributed actively to Anglo-German relations.

Once we appreciate the level and the persistence of interaction between Britain and Germany, we need to alter the way that we see the supposedly sudden turn from a British Enlightenment devoid of German influence to a Romanticism whose members engage with German sources that have been active in Britain consistently and for quite some time. We have to cut through the nationalistic assumptions and linguistic proclivities that prevent us from having an adequately complex understanding of the conditions of possibility for the emergence of relations between figures such as Blake, Hamann, Fuseli, or Lavater. The work of this chapter has been to offer a sense of the complexity of the social and cultural production, through at least three main case studies. The first was establishing a considerable German presence in eighteenth-century London that included a keen British interest in German cultural productions. The second concerned the structural traces of the German presence in London—ecclesiastical and economic—and how their inter-action with the English formed an Anglo-German context showcased in bilingual publications. The last was on the international nature of linguistic and cultural exchange through travel writings, especially through actual German visitors to London during that period. Taken together, these case studies reveal an Anglo-German context that demands to be accounted for in our historical understanding of this period. We need to know who was travelling where during this period and what they read, wrote, sold, and produced in order to understand fully the

---

[102] 'Ich wundere mich, daß Sie, mit dem Ansehen von Sanftmut, den Anlaß geben konnten, daß so viele hundert Einwohner von London ihr leben verloren, und so viele hundert andere unglücklich wurden!' (von La Roche, *Sophie in London*, p. 150; von La Roche, *Tagebuch*, 316).

[103] See Lowry, p. 50; and Bernd Heidenreich, *Sophie von La Roche: Eine Werkbiographie* (Frankfurt am Main: Peter Lang, 1986).

[104] Incidentally, von La Roche also wrote similarly insightful letters about her visits to Zurich and the lively intellectual circles that included Lavater, Johann Jakob Bodmer, the Fuselis, and others who played an important part in Swiss Anglophile circles. See von La Roche, *Begegnungen mit Zürich im Ausgehenden 18. Jahrhundert* (Zurich: Berichthaus, 1962), pp. 1–44.

interlinguistic and cultural conditions that shaped this period and thereby also its influence upon us.

The exchange between Germany and England of literature, arts, print, institutions, and philosophical and religious thought is vigorous and serious. Such exchange between Britain and France has received significant scholarly attention and has become almost a canonical part of understanding the period. It is high time that we show that there was a serious Anglo-German network from even before the Hanoverian period, extending well into the 1780s. The 'familiar fact that no Englishman read German literature' must be laid to rest. Instead of isolationism, there were active and sustained connections between the two countries throughout the eighteenth and early nineteenth centuries. We need to change our understanding of the period accordingly and flesh out our understanding of these connections.

What emerges is a historical background that shows that some of these Anglo-German connections are not peripheral but, rather, that they are a central part of British identity. Yet they also contain a high proportion of strange and unusual figures. Between the historical context and the off-track figures, it helps us understand a new aspect of the eighteenth century from within and from without. Recovering this network shows that it is through concrete evidence and close readings that we put ourselves into a position to be able to productively challenge the monolingual accounts that have dominated much of our scholarship. Far more material exists to do so, beyond the brief overview of this chapter. Once we start looking in a comparative and detailed way, there are Anglo-German sources and connections that cover all manner of aspects of social, cultural, and intellectual life in the eighteenth and nineteenth centuries.

What is remarkable is the high proportion of unusual, strange, and exorbitant figures that emerge out of the Anglo-German context. That includes Blake and Hamann, the focus of Chapter 2, but also other figures that have left the track of the standard Enlightenment. The chapters that follow show how these figures form a constellation that presses us to think differently about this period. Each chapter illuminates the next, revealing hitherto disregarded historical connections among important individuals (Blake, Hamann, Lavater, Fuseli) and unearthing archival materials on relevant institutions (the Moravians), as well as remapping both literary and intellectual history. The case gets cumulatively stronger, as the constellations become clearer and more detailed. Thus, once we have absorbed that Anglo-German relations had created a level of normality in Britain, we can focus our attention on the outliers and exorbitants in these contexts. They radically challenge our notions of what is central, marginal, and excessive in this period.

2

Blake and Hamann
Exorbitants

INTRODUCTION

William Blake and Johann Georg Hamann are two exorbitant thinkers whose works explode the neat division between Enlightenment and Romanticism. The two men are the two most radical and idiosyncratic thinkers to emerge out of the eighteenth-century Anglo-German context that this book charts across geographical and temporal boundaries. They have connections to plenty of the other strange and unusual figures of this context, yet their positions turn out to be particularly powerful, especially since they emerge as a dazzling and instructive pair. Their remarkable conceptual affinities are, in fact, deeply revealing about the period as a whole and help to show how our common differentiation between Enlightenment and Romanticism is only of limited use. Their positions are contrarian and at odds with their respective environments, and their connection allows us to see how the way we perceive these environments traditionally—through conventional literary periods and national literatures—needs to be challenged via a form of literary history and criticism that engages with their deeply unsettling and exorbitant power.

Blake and Hamann believe in the inextricability of language and thought, that thinking is always linguistic, and that language itself has ontological power. They also agree on the irreducibly poetical quality of language, thereby suggesting the category of poetical thought. Both thinkers are radically anti-systematic, though neither of them is a straightforward nominalist. With their anti-systematicity comes a deeply held conviction in the power and philosophical relevance of the particular over the abstract. As we will see, this pair belongs to the most radical critics of an epistemology and history that places the ratio at the centre of explaining the world or our place in it.[1] While not irrationalists, they completely reject instrumental reason as an inadequate way of engaging with the world. Both of them agree that it is precisely this model of reasoning that is the most destructive motor behind ideological formations, such as institutional religion, or our self-understanding.

---

[1] A longer genealogy of such views would reach back to the polylingual work of Giambattista Vico, especially his suggestion of a poetic logic, and the work of Jacob Boehme whose work was well known to Hamann and Blake. Boehme's exorbitant theory of language, in particular, represents a common historical connection between them. In connection to Boehme's eighteenth-century reception in England, see B. J. Gibbons, *Gender in Mystical and Occult Thought: Behmenism and Its Development in England* (Cambridge: Cambridge University Press, 1996), pp. 180–208.

With their scepticism of instrumental reason (discussed in detail in Chapter 4) comes a celebration of the bodily dimension of human existence, including sexuality (discussed in detail in Chapter 8). Very different from traditional forms of Christianity, they rejoice in the erotic dimension of the human body and its creations. Although, of course, all of these similarities are expressed in rather different forms—Blake is a poet and Hamann a philosopher—the tone and tenor of the expression is remarkably similar: they are the loudest, shrillest, and most unusual voices of the period, and this tone is part of their argument. In their views and their expressions, both of these remarkable figures simultaneously look backward and forward: motivated by deep religiosity and a fascination for origins, they hold positions that *seem* extremely (post)modern but turn out to be even more radical.

Normally, these two authors are not imagined as a pair. There are many reasons for this, most of them connected to their canonization within their respective national traditions, which I already briefly alluded to in the introduction. Their status as canonized outsiders has mistakenly domesticated their views, bringing them safely back into the orbit of traditional literary history. The motivation behind this trend was partly an unwillingness to deal with their challenge to the most fundamental tenets of epistemology and ontology, but it also had political and pragmatic reasons. Their role as the mad but talented outsiders of a national literature reinforced the linguistic and geographical boundary of that construction in ways that they would have found deeply puzzling and offensive.

Blake, for instance, in some versions has become a very *English* oddball, an idiosyncratic author who writes about Albion and whose connections to the outside, if any, are to his immediate surroundings rather than to a wider European context. The fact that people think of 'And did those feet in ancient time', played at the royal wedding of Prince William and Catherine Middleton, as a form of English national anthem is a grotesque example of such a reception.[2] Such a restricted understanding of Blake and Hamann also reinforces their position as particular period examples for English Romanticism or German counter-Enlightenment. That they are at the fringes does not mean that their own status or what they at the margins *of* will be questioned. Again, such a model is tied to national literary history and period divisions. For instance, even though Anglo-German Romanticism is an area with a long and solid tradition of scholarship, there is a curious lack of interest for the period immediately before, which has allowed this ossification between periods to feel natural.[3] As a result, the few transnational readings that do exist of

---

[2] William Blake, 'Milton a Poem in 2 Books', in *Complete Poetry and Prose*, pp. 95–144, 95, line 1.

[3] This is true for accounts whose primary interest is theoretical (Philippe Lacoue-Labarthe and Jean-Luc Nancy, Andrew Bowie, Kathleen M. Wheeler, and Paul Hamilton) or historical (Eugene Stelzig). It also covers accomplished studies that are tied to particular authors, traditionally Coleridge (Paul Hamilton) and more recently also Wordsworth (John Williams). See Lacoue-Labarthe and Nancy, *The Literary Absolute: The Theory of Literature in German Romanticism* (Albany: State University of New York Press, 1978); Bowie, *From Romanticism to Critical Theory: The Philosophy of German Literary Theory* (London: Routledge, 2012); Wheeler, *Romanticism, Pragmatism, and Deconstruction* (Oxford: Blackwell, 1993); and Paul Hamilton, *Metaromanticism*. See also Stelzig, *Henry Crabb Robinson in Germany: A Study in Nineteenth-Century Life Writing* (Lewisburg, PA: Bucknell University Press, 2010); Paul Hamilton, *Coleridge and German Philosophy: The Poet in the Land of Logic* (London:

their work are misunderstood or unknown today. These studies, which I discuss in some detail, paint a different picture, presenting Blake and Hamann as related, breaking up the sharp difference between periods in engaging ways. However, even these studies domesticate the violence of Blake's and Hamann's thought. What we need to do is to go beyond the comparative, transnational approach that some of these forgotten studies suggest. We need to engage with these authors as offering us a vision that is outside of the normal orbit of thinkers at the time and that allows us to understand the limitations of our own thinking about history and criticism.

EARLY COMPARATIVISM

The unspoken assumption about Hamann's work is that it was not really known in Anglophone circles until the twentieth century. However, just as with the myth that Britons are not interested in German material before 1790, this idea of the completely unknown Hamann turns out to be incorrect. Hamann's work was, in fact, disseminated by Germans who visited Britain, and there is evidence that his writings did make an impression. For instance, when Thomas De Quincey in his *Confessions of an English Opium-Eater* speaks about his 'first lessons in German' and his 'first acquaintance with German literature', he describes it as an encounter with the works of Johann Paul Friedrich Richter, Theodor Gottlieb von Hippel, 'and Hamann'.[4] Thus, De Quincey, one of the main authors to introduce Immanuel Kant and German literature more widely to Britain, starts with Hamann. Not surprisingly, the special status of this influence is immediately policed. In the *Confessions*, De Quincey suggests that Hamann was a writer 'singularly obscure, whom I have never seen in the hands of any Englishman except once of Sir William Hamilton'.[5] De Quincey picks up the narrative of Hamann's obscurity and makes it part of his reception. And yet he must have learned about Hamann throughout his reading in German sources, especially in connection with his study of Johann Gottfried Herder.[6] Similarly, the figure that De Quincey mentions initially, Hamilton, a professor of logic and metaphysics, not only had a copy of Hamann's work, as De Quincey suggests, but also actively mentions, quotes, and misquotes

---

Bloomsbury, 2007); and Williams, *Wordsworth Translated: A Case Study in the Reception of British Romantic Poetry in Germany, 1804–1914* (London: Continuum, 2009).

[4] Thomas De Quincey, *Confessions of an English Opium-Eater, 1821–1856*, ed. Grevel Lindop, vol. 2 of *The Works of Thomas De Quincey*, 21 vols (London: Pickering and Chatto, 2000), p. 183. The instructor of German is a 'Mr De Haren', a figure about whom—according to Lindop—'nothing more is known' (De Quincey, Works, 2: 355n321). Patrick Bridgewater suggests that it was Pieter Willem van Haren, a Dutchman (Patrick Bridgewater, *De Quincey's Gothic Masquerade* [Amsterdam: Rodopi, 2002], p. 33).

[5] De Quincey, *Confessions*, p. 355. William Hamilton was 'Professor of Logic and Metaphysics at Edinburgh University, an authority on Kant and Aristotle, and a lifelong friend of De Quincey, who was introduced to him in 1814 by John Wilson' (De Quincey, *Works*, p. 355n322).

[6] See De Quincey's essay 'Death of a German Great Man', in which he discusses studying Johann Gottfried Herder's biographies that amply mention Johann Georg Hamann's importance (De Quincey, 'Death of a German Great Man', in *Articles and Translations from the 'London Magazine', 'Blackwood's Magazine', and Others, 1821–1824*, vol. 3 of *Works*, pp. 114–24).

Hamann's essays and letters in his published writings, in which he describes Hamann as 'one of the shrewdest thinkers'.[7]

De Quincey's and Hamilton's references are not the only sign of Hamann's presence in early nineteenth-century Britain. His name appears regularly in periodical literature, which was deeply interested in foreign texts and authors. There was a lively culture of discussion and reviews across national borders, languages, and disciplines. Future scholarship needs to look at concrete examples of the dynamic that Karen Junod describes when she states that 'in Britain, periodicals like the *European Magazine*, the *Monthly Magazine*, the *Monthly Review*, and the *Monthly Repository* contributed effectively to the dissemination of German literature and culture in England'.[8] This dissemination included discussions of Hamann in reviews such as Thomas Carlyle's seminal essay 'State of German Literature' (1827) and others. Carlyle picks up the rhetoric about Hamann as a genius outsider, already a standard move in the German press at the time. He describes Hamann as able to 'meditate deep thoughts' but 'defective in the power of uttering them with propriety'.[9]

What emerges from the British periodical press in the first decades of the nineteenth century is that Hamann was an integral part of Anglo-German discussions going on across the Channel. In 1830 *Fraser's Magazine* published a translation of Jean Paul Friedrich Richter's review of Germaine de Staël's *De l'Allemagne*, in which Hamann is mentioned, again as an unusual writer.[10] In the same year, a review of Herder's works in the *Monthly Repository* highlights Hamann as a 'principal friend' and as 'one who perhaps exercised the most powerful influence on the future bent of his [Herder's] taste and genius'. In this review, Hamann's residence in London and his knowledge of English combine with his 'moral and religious principle', thereby also introducing his biographical Anglo-German ties.[11] Throughout the 1830s Hamann appears in various reviews, none of which, as far as I know, have been previously discussed. He is mentioned casually in them, assuming knowledge of or about his work. That includes pairing him in 1837 with his German contemporaries who all 'formed a powerful opposition against the efforts of scepticism and sensualism'.[12] Several different British journals note him as a scholar, a key reader of biblical hermeneutics, a public intellectual, a moral thinker, and a mystical

---

[7] Sir William Hamilton, *Discussions on Philosophy and Literature, Education, and University Reform* (London: Longman, 1853), p. 300.

[8] Karen Junod, 'Crabb Robinson, Blake, and Perthes's *Vaterländisches Museum* (1810–1811)', *European Romantic Review* 23, 4 (August 2012): 435–51, 437. In support of this claim Junod cites John Boening, 'Pioneers and Precedents: The "Importation of German" and the Emergence of Periodical Criticism in England', Internationales Archiv für Sozialgeschichte der deutschen Literatur 7 (1982): 65–87.

[9] Thomas Carlyle, 'State of German Literature', *Edinburgh Review* 46, 92 (October 1827): 304–51, 322.

[10] Jean Paul Friedrich Richter, 'Jean Paul Friedrich Richter's Review of Madame de Stael's "Allemagne"', *Fraser's Magazine for Town and Country* 1, 4 (May 1830): 407–13, 408.

[11] [Rev. John James Taylor, 'Some Account of the Life and Writings of Herder', *Monthly Repository and Review*, n.s., 4, 47 (November 1830): 729–38, 734..

[12] The review describes this as a group including 'Klopstock, Hamann, Claudius, Jacobi, Lavater, Herder, and Göthe' ([Edmund S. Williams], 'German Literature', *Foreign Quarterly Review* 20, 39 (October 1837): 121–36, 134.

writer.[13] Many reviews of Herder's works include Hamann in their summaries or discussions, suggesting that Hamann's name was probably familiar to Anglophone students of German sources and, certainly, to readers of Herder.

One such reader would have been Samuel Taylor Coleridge, who might very well have been aware of Hamann. In his marginalia to Richard Hooker's works, Coleridge uses the phrase 'Schools of psilology (the love of empty noise)' to distinguish 'psilology' from real philosophy.[14] Hamann had already used the same word in a similar, ironic way in his writings and given it much importance. He spoke to Johann Caspar Lavater about 'Psilosophy or psilology, a word that I have invented for *pure reason*'.[15] As far as the *OED* is concerned, both 'psilology' and 'psilosophy' are of Coleridge's doing. He himself does not mention a source and presents them as his own neologisms. However, it seems highly likely that Coleridge directly or indirectly profited from Hamann's thinking on this matter. The point here is not

[13] See [Francis Watts], 'Life and Writings of John Albert Bengel', *Eclectic Review* 3 (January 1838): 21–37, 31; and [J. S. Blackie], 'Jung Stilling: Religious Literature of Germany', *Foreign Quarterly Review* 21, 42 (July 1838): 247–83. Also see 'Schlegel's *Lectures on Ancient and Modern Literature*', *Monthly Review, or, Literary Journal* 81 (December 1816): 506–16; 'Reminiscences of the Latter Days of Kant', *Athenaeum* 129 (17 April 1830): 232–3; 'Prussian Schools', *British Critic, and Quarterly Theological Review* 25, 49 (January 1839): 76–95; [George Irvine], 'Recollections of the Life of Johann Gottfried von Herder', *Dublin Review* 14, 28 (May 1843): 505–34; 'Works Recently Published on the Continent', *Foreign and Colonial Quarterly Review* 1, 2 (April 1843): 660–7; [Jane Sinnett], 'Johann Gottlieb v. Herder', *Foreign Quarterly Review* 37, 74 (July 1846): 281–304; 'Jean Paul Richter', *British Quarterly Review* 12 (November 1847): 375–407, 396; and 'German Pantheism and Its Influence on Criticism', *Christian Remembrancer* 15, 60 (April 1848): 353–95. Furthermore, I found announcements of the publication of Hamann's works in the *Foreign and Colonial Quarterly Review*.
[14] Samuel Taylor Coleridge, *Marginalia 2*, ed. George Whalley, in *The Collected Works of Samuel Taylor Coleridge*, 23 vols (Princeton, NJ: Princeton University Press, 1969), 12.2: 1147.
[15] 'Psilosophie oder Psilologie, ein von mir selbst erdachtes Wort für reine Vernunft' (ZH, 5: 294). Hamann's neologism characterizes the supposed purity of thought as emptiness, a charge he levelled not only against Kant but also against Spinoza: 'In my eyes, Spinoza's superstitious belief in mathematical form is already a deception, and a very unphilosophical jugglery. With the examination of the 15 definitions and axioms, the whole first book of the *Ethics* is knocked on its head. This type of grit does not hold a building, hardly one made out of paper. Therefore, the *tabula votiua* remains: Metacritique on the Purism of Language and Reason in psilological and psilosophical (billets-doux or) little love letters. You notice probably that I have it in for two of the most meritorious men, and that I do not want to insult either of them; I would rather touch with light hand and gentle wand the prejudices that are detrimental to their good cause, touch them in play or, as the prophet says, with the tool of a simple shepherd just for the benefit of bright and dignified readers who would have had been served with a *Sapienti sat!* and who can be helped on better ways' (In meinen Augen ist schon Spinozas Aberglaube an die mathematische Form <schon> ein Blendwerk, und eine sehr unphilosophische Gaukeley. Mit der Untersuchung der 15 Erklärungen u Grundsätze fällt das ganze erste Buch der Ethik über den Haufen. Ein solcher Streusand trägt kein Gebäude, kaum ein papiernes. Die *tabula votiua* bleibt also: Metakritik über den Purismum der Sprache und Vernunft in psilologischen und psilosophischen [Billets-doux oder] Liebesbrief<ch>en. Sie merken wohl, daß ich zwey der verdientesten Männer aufs Korn habe, und daß ich keinen von beyden <nicht zu> beleidigen, sondern ihre der guten Sache nachtheilige Vorurteile gern mit leichter Hand und dem Stabe Sanft, im Spielen oder wie der Prophet sagt, mit dem Geräthe eines thörichten Hirten berühren möchte, zum bloßen besten kluger und würdiger Leser, denen mit einem *Sapienti sat!* gedient wäre, und die auf beßere Spuren geholfen werden könnten' [ZH, 6: 107–8]). Hamann's objective here is not only to insult but also to suggest humorously that systematicity—mathematics (or geometry) for Spinoza and pure reason for Kant—more often than not turns out to rely on articles of faith rather than on a supposedly neutral ground or coherent thought. Hamann's neologism of 'psilology' and 'psilosophy' enacts his argument through his style. 'Psilo' suggests a 'bare' or 'empty' dimension to this 'vacuous chatter', thus leading to 'shallow philosophy'.

to litigate Coleridge's plagiarism but, rather, to illustrate just how entangled Hamann's British presence might have been at the turn of the century. He gets mentioned and leaves his mark both in superficial and in conceptually substantive ways as part of the Anglo-German context in eighteenth-century Britain.

The reception of Blake in Germany is a little easier to follow than Hamann's in Britain. Through G. E. Bentley we know that by 1789 Blake was known well enough 'to be listed in a German dictionary of engravers' and that his engravings for Edward Young's *Night Thoughts* were circulating among German literati, including Jean Paul Richter.[16] This interest reached a new level of intensity, though, when in 1811 Henry Crabb Robinson's introduction to Blake titled *Artist, Poet, and Religious Mystic* was published in a German translation in the periodical *Vaterländisches Museum*.[17] As a scholar interested in Anglo-German relations, Robinson thinks of Blake in comparative terms; describing Blake's work, Robinson notes how 'a host of expressions occur among them which one would have expected from a German rather than an Englishman'.[18] Robinson's description comes from an informed place: he had met Herder several times and his knowledge of German thinkers included Lavater, Kant, von La Roche, and Johann Wolfgang von Goethe. Like Lavater, Crabb Robinson wrote on physiognomy; he was, like Blake, a dissenter, and also was deeply familiar with German thought. It is highly likely that he would also have known about Hamann's work and very possible that he later shared some of that information with Blake in conversation. Crabb Robinson 'became a leading figure in the transmission to Britain of German idealist philosophy, and of German literature and criticism in Britain', as Karen Junod points out, complementing Eugene Stelzig's important work. Specifically, she argues that 'within the wider context of transnational and intercultural relations... Crabb Robinson's article on Blake breaks new ground and asserts integral, yet complex, connections between Anglo-German interaction, periodical culture, and literary and artistic networks'.[19] These rich Anglo-German networks were well established by the time Blake started to write and publish.

Crabb Robinson was not alone in exploring the idea of Blake's comparative 'Germanness'. In the *London University Magazine* we read that 'if Blake had lived in Germany, by this time he would have had commentators of the highest order'. The review considers Blake together with Novalis (Georg Philipp Friedrich Freiherr von Hardenberg [incidentally, a great admirer of Hamann]) and how they both

[16] Bentley, *Blake Records*, p. 54. Also see Bentley, Blake Records, pp. 113–14; and Jean Paul Richter, *Vorschule der Aesthetik*, 3 vols (Stuttgart: Cotta, 1813), 3: 844–8.

[17] On this publication, see Junod. Friedrich Christoph Perthes, the editor of the journal, played an important role in the Anglo-German traffic of information and publications. Intriguingly, he defended Hamann against Karl Wilhelm Friedrich Schlegel, making it perfectly possible that he discussed this matter with Crabb Robinson. For Crabb Robinson's Anglo-German mediation of German thought, see Henry Crabb Robinson, *Essays on Kant, Schelling, and German Aesthetics*, ed. James Vigus (London: MHRA, 2010).

[18] Henry Crabb Robinson, 'William Blake, Künstler, Dichter, und religiöser Schwärmer', *Vaterländisches Museum*, vol. 1 (January 1811), appendix 1B to Bentley, *Blake Records*, pp. 594–603, 599.

[19] Junod, pp. 435–6. One of these connections was Blake's link to Henry Fuseli, a figure whose key function as part of these wider Anglo-German constellations will be discussed in Chapter 3.

'contemplated the natural world as the mere outbirth of thought'.[20] As a result, there is the hope, which never came to pass, that 'the German nation certainly in a still higher degree even than the English, must take in the contemplation of such a character'.[21] The implication here is that we should read Blake across national registers and landscapes. It also plays on the ideas of national stereotypes—namely, that Blake would have a better home in the supposedly philosophically more inclined German landscape than in England. What emerges is that there was, from the beginning, a small number of critics whose reception of these writers through an Anglo-German lens resisted the more common national and monolingual narratives. In relation to Blake and German thought, Eudo Mason and Leonard M. Trawick are more contemporary examples of such work, arguing that part of 'Blake's similarity to his German contemporaries . . . may be attributed to temperamental affinity'.[22] All of these efforts show that there is a small but constant critical tradition that has been interested in keeping the Anglo-German dimensions of Blake's work alive.

What comes into focus is that there is a neglected but powerful set of publications in the reception of Blake and Hamann that illustrates how they are part of the wider context that was much keener on comparative discussions than we often assume. The handful of contemporary books that do mention both Blake and Hamann do not investigate their possible connection or into earlier literature that explores it. There are two exceptions to this, both fascinating historical examples that directly connect Blake and Hamann and both written by women whose work has been neglected. The first example is an 1872 review of Hamann's works by the feminist critic Edith Simcox in a journal entitled *The Academy*.[23] The second is a 1930s essay on Blake and Hamann by Helene Richter, a remarkable Austrian literary and cultural critic.[24] Both of them belong to a set of early comparative scholarly efforts that deserve to be reintroduced into criticism and whose history we need to make part of our own efforts to understand Blake and Hamann. Writing under her pseudonym H. Lawrenny, Simcox's review is the most extensive publication on Hamann in English before the twentieth century. Extraordinarily, no previous

---

[20] 'The Inventions of William Blake, Painter and Poet', *London University Magazine* 2 (March 1830): 318–23; qtd in Bentley, *Blake Records*, pp. 510–17, 512 and 514.

[21] Robinson, 'Künstler, Dichter', p. 603.

[22] Leonard M. Trawick, 'William Blake's German Connection', p. 245.

[23] H. Lawrenny [Edith Simcox], 'Hamann's Life and Works', *Academy* 3, 62 (15 December 1872): 463–6. In relation to Simcox, see Rosemarie Bodenheimer, 'Autobiography in Fragments: The Elusive Life of Edith Simcox', *Victorian Studies* 44, 3 (Spring 2002): 399–422; Bodenheimer, *The Real Life of Mary Ann Evans: George Eliot, Her Letters, and Fiction* (Ithaca, NY: Cornell University Press, 1994), pp. 252–6; and Brenda Ayres, 'Edith Simcox's Diptych: Sexuality and Textuality', in *Women in Journalism at the Fin de Siècle: 'Making a Name for Herself'*, ed. F. Elizabeth Gray, Palgrave Studies in Nineteenth-Century Writing and Culture (New York: Palgrave Macmillan, 2012).

[24] See Helene Richter, 'Blake und Hamann: Zu Hamanns 200. Geburtstag', 3 parts, *Archiv für das Studium der Neueren Sprachen und Literaturen* 158 (1930): [part 1] 213–21; vol. 159 (1931): [part 2] 36–45; vol. 159 (1931): and [part 3] 195–210. Helene Richter was an autodidact who published books on Mary Wollstonecraft, a massive Percy Bysshe Shelley biography, and a history of English Romanticism, as well as works on Shakespeare and contemporary drama. In 1931 she received honorary doctorates from the University of Heidelberg and the University of Erlangen. In 1942 she was deported to Theresienstadt, where she died the same year.

scholar has discussed this essay. Her review of Hamann, his life, work, and editorial history shows that he was better known in Britain than is generally assumed.[25]

Simcox's text itself plays with the supposed unfamiliarity of Hamann to English readers, which she claims is already wrong and old hat: 'The complaint that Hamann's life and writings are not so well known or so highly valued as they ought to be has been repeated so often as almost to answer itself'.[26] Throughout the article we encounter Simcox's barely tempered impatience both with Hamann's work and with his reception. Rather than recover Hamann from obscurity, as post-1950s scholarship felt it had to, for Simcox the matter is one of entrenched ideology already: 'The fact is that nothing will ever make Hamann popular, while his eminence is already conceded on all hands.'[27] The difference between importance and popularity is not just one of a genius and an unreflecting public, however. It is based on Hamann's form of writing and thinking, which has both his detractors and his defendants equally confused. As Simcox wittily puts it,

> Even his self-selected champions do little to increase his fame, because the difficulty of his writings, both in style and substance, is not to be explained away by pious admiration: it is easy to agree with him without understanding him, very difficult to understand him, as Goethe did, without agreeing with him, and yet hardly worth while to agree with him merely for the sake of fathoming his oracles, or of being persuaded that they were worth fathoming.[28]

While she does not deny that there is a depth to Hamann, 'pious admiration' will not do since such intuitive agreements seldom fully understand the object of their enthusiasm.[29] It is no wonder that Hamann will end up an outsider, and, in Simcox's view, there is nothing wrong with that. Her healthy scepticism is intriguing, especially as it comes out of an evident interest in the topic. What connects it with earlier reviews is that there is an odd mixture of, on the one hand, an assumption of familiarity and, on the other hand, a conviction that Hamann is and will remain an ultimately obscure figure.

Simcox's review covers Hamann's biography, what he called his 'marriage of conscience' to his lifelong partner as well as other aspects of his character, and is particularly remarkable because it links Blake and Hamann, the first such instance to my knowledge.[30] She articulates the familiar criticism of Hamann's style as obscure, but she does so through a comparative move when she writes of Hamann that '[i]f his contemporaries had been candid, they might have described Hamann's attraction, that like Blake, he was "uncommonly good to steal from"'.[31] Simcox

---

[25] Simcox probably introduced Hamann's work to George Eliot: Simcox paid her first visit to the priory in the same month that the review was published.
[26] Simcox, 'Hamann's Life and Works', p. 463.
[27] Ibid. It is a complaint that is echoed in contemporary work, too. Take the opening sentence of Robert Alan Sparling's book: 'The work of Johann Georg Hamann has been at once the steady object of admiration and neglect' (*Johann Hamann and the Enlightenment Project* [Toronto: University of Toronto Press, 2011], p. vii).
[28] Simcox, 'Hamann's Life and Works', p. 463. [29] Ibid.
[30] 'GewissensEhe' (ZH, 3: 263). [31] Simcox, 'Hamann's Life and Works', p. 466.

connects Hamann and Blake through the context of their style and thought. On the one hand, they are inaccessible, their ways of writing are hermetic and impenetrable; on the other, they are inspiring, more than commonly good to steal from. Simcox's reference makes the Anglo-German connection between Blake and Hamann explicit.

The source Simcox cites in relation to Blake is Fuseli, a central figure of Anglo-German life, who described Blake as 'damned good to steal from'.[32] Simcox endorses Fuseli's description and adds Hamann as fitting the same. The fact that she singles out Blake specifically is especially important because the rest of the review shows her awareness of Hamann's wider intellectual circle. She mentions Hamann's influence on key members of Anglo-German circles, including Christoph Martin Wieland, Gotthold Ephraim Lessing, Herder, and Friedrich Heinrich Jacobi. She compares Hamann to 'Carlyle or Richter'.[33] Once more Hamann is seen as an important figure in a wider set of thinkers. Simcox not only shrewdly situates Blake and Hamann in the Anglo-German matrix of the eighteenth century, but also singles them out as particularly noteworthy and connected.

One of the reasons why the comparison fits is that Hamann, similarly to Blake, is singular in his way of connecting philosophical and sensual spheres in new and exciting ways: '[U]nlike most men, he feels in the abstract and thinks in the concrete, and therefore all his thoughts express themselves in images or allegories.'[34] Simcox identifies the overlap of the conceptual and the physical as one of the principles behind Hamann's quality as a thinker and writer. The fact that Simcox herself has little time for the type of images and allegories that he produces—she calls them, mockingly invoking his speech impediment, the results of a 'stammering brain'—shows that she also wanted to canonize Hamann as an eccentric outsider. She viewed him as, ultimately, a strange figure who was too bizarre to be accurate.[35] Nevertheless, in her account it turns out that both Blake's and Hamann's 'images or allegories' are so special and powerful that they are worth stealing from.[36] Not only is Simcox's remarkable essay an archival indication that Hamann was much better known than we have assumed, but also, and more importantly, it continues to instruct us with the assertion Blake and Hamann may share more features than scholars, then or now, credit.[37]

Helene Richter's essay on Blake and Hamann is similarly perceptive to Simcox's, though of much greater intellectual and scholarly scope. It is the most comprehensive comparison of the two figures that has been published to date. In it she stresses that there is between the two an 'inner being-at-one' and an undeniable fellowship

---

[32] Henry's Fuseli's assessment first appears in W. Graham Robertson's introduction to Alexander Gilchrist, *The Life of William Blake*, ed. Robertson (London: John Lane, 1928), pp. v–ix, vii.

[33] Simcox, 'Hamann's Life and Works', p. 463.

[34] Simcox, 'Hamann's Life and Works', p. 466.

[35] Simcox, 'Hamann's Life and Works', p. 463.

[36] Simcox, 'Hamann's Life and Works', p. 466.

[37] In 1875, Simcox mentions Hamann again in another review (of an essay by Charles Joret of Herder, Johann Wolfgang von Goethe, and Jean-Jacques Rousseau). It is a passing reference, but there is evidence that she continued to think about him. See Simcox, 'Herder et la renaissance littéraire en Allemagne au 18me siècle', *Academy* 8, 177 (25 September 1875): 326–8.

that goes beyond sources that would have been common to both, such as the Bible and Lavater.[38] Helene Richter lists a whole number of similarities that span the biographical, temperamental, conceptual, social, philosophical, and spiritual connections between Blake and Hamann:

> Both are towering personalities with the sharpest character, the strangest mixture of incompatible opposites: strong sensualists, of unusual strength in their sexual and affective life as well as visionary spiritualists and transcendentalists; both are dreamy enthusiasts and daredevilish, unrestrained, temperamental men; both are filled with divine fire, carried by the sublime consciousness of a holy mission in the service of divine truth, and, at the same time, full of wondrous quirks and whimsies.... Their nature is characterised by child-like autochthony, their spirit dares to go into the dark abysses of thought. The mystical heightening of feelings in their imaginative intuition starts, for both of them, from a Protestant orthodoxy to which both of them hold on.[39]

In contrast with some of the tone here, Helene Richter's text generally remains fairly historical and more descriptive than philosophical. Ultimately, for her the Blake-Hamann connection is a matter of literary history, and her explanation of why we would see Blake and Hamann as 'standing shoulder to shoulder, warriors for the same ideal' is that they channel a zeitgeist—in the case of Hamann, *Sturm und Drang*, and in the case of Blake, British Romanticism.[40] In her account, both of them turn their initial interest in the Enlightenment (Hamann) or the Revolution (Blake) into a highly critical attitude that will be increasingly turned inwards.

Obviously, the approach in this book is rather different, since I am more interested in disturbing the underlying categories (Enlightenment and Romanticism) and their distinctions (Enlightenment versus Romanticism/Revolution). However, Helene Richter's intervention is still suggestive, not least because she is the only scholar who explores the range of connections between these two thinkers. Even though Helene Richter's essay sometimes portrays Blake and Hamann as more transparent than is warranted, her reading points to important parallels in their biography, modes of expression, and main philosophical-poetical concerns.

What emerges from these nineteenth-century sources is a picture of a reception that is far more rich and complex. We must absorb it if we want to understand the period more fully. Hamann was much better known in Britain than scholarship has

---

[38] '[I]nneren Einsseins' (Helene Richter, 'Blake und Hamann [part 1]', p. 214).

[39] 'Beide sind überragende Persönlichkeiten von schärfster Prägung, eigenartigstes Gemisch unverträglicher Gegensätze: kräftige Sinnenmenschen von ungewöhnlicher Stärke des Trieb- und Affektlebens und visionäre Spiritualisten und Transzendentalisten; beide verträumte Schwärmer und draufgängerische, ungebändigte Temperamentsmenschen; beide des göttlichen Feuers voll, getragen vom erhabenen Bewußtsein einer heiligen Mission im Dienste der göttlichen Wahrheit, und dabei voll wunderlicher Schrullen und Grillen.... Ihr Gemüt steht im Zeichen kindlicher Urwüchsigkeit, ihr Geist wagt sich in dunkle Abgründe des Denkens. Die mystische Gefühlssteigerung der Phantasieanschauung geht in beiden von protestantischer Rechtgläubigkeit aus, an der beide festhalten' (Helene Richter, 'Blake und Hamann [part 1]', p. 214).

[40] 'Schulter an Schulter stehende Kämpfer für dasselbe Ideal' (Helene Richter, 'Blake und Hamann [part 1]', p. 215). For the religious dimension of these questions, see Kees W. Bolle, 'The Romantic Impulse in the History of Religions: An Essay on the Image of Man', *Cultural Dynamics* 2, 4 (December 1989): pp. 400–24.

realized. There was always an interest in connecting Blake with German sources. And there were even efforts to read Blake and Hamann together in a more extensive way. What these comparative efforts have in common, however, is that they think of Blake and Hamann as canonical outsiders. Although they have a comparative interest, and thus countersteer the tendency to lock Blake and Hamann into their national traditions, they nevertheless put their critical focus on their position as typical outsiders.

The serious problem with this form of reception—be it comparative or not—is that it effectively domesticates Blake and Hamann, either in their position within national literary history or in relation to their wider theoretical relevance. In the historical version, Hamann becomes the figure of German counter-Enlightenment, while Blake is the odd one out when it comes to classic accounts of British Romanticism. Blake and Hamann are canonized *as outsiders of the period*—that's their label. Once their work is classified as officially weird, it becomes much easier to discard their ideas as wacky, unusual, and, in the end, a form of thinking that is merely intriguing but needs not be taken seriously. Their exceptional singularity—something that the fans of Blake or Hamann often love to foreground—actually makes it easier to isolate the work and its claims. Ironically, in such a model, their isolation eventually means that it is much more comfortable to think of their ideas as strange experiments rather than to consider them as genuinely powerful attempts at making serious truth claims. If we grow up being told that a particular family member is the crazy-but-harmless uncle, then we are predisposed to understand his statements in this light and, thus, not think of him as a serious member of the conversation. In effect, absorbing Blake or Hamann *as* strange blunts their critical projects.

It is a matter of *not* keeping it in the family: we rarely consider the possibility that our crazy uncle might have friends—or, if we do, then the assumption that they, also, must be crazy (why, otherwise, would they be friends?!) makes us disregard those links. In the very few cases in which both Blake and Hamann are mentioned in the same work of postwar literary criticism—for instance, M. H. Abrams's *Natural Supernaturalism*—no connection has been drawn between them. Abrams cannot have either figure play a major role in his story, and certainly not a combined one, since neither of them will fit the overarching Hegelian narrative about the nature of Romanticism—which is also why Hamann is paired with Wordsworth rather than with Blake. Although initially Abrams presents the German as a Continental intellectual pendant to Wordsworth, in the end 'Hamann's flamboyant irrationalism' is surpassed by 'Wordsworth's quiet testimony'.[41] Once more, Hamann's idiosyncratic Christianity puts him too far apart from the other figures to fit into a teleological narrative of Anglicized Romanticism.

These forms of domestication are deeply limiting habits that we need to challenge. Working across languages and borders allows us not only to unlock them

---

[41] M. H. Abrams, *Natural Supernaturalism: Tradition and Revolution in Romantic Literature* (New York: W. W. Norton, 1973), p. 402. Another account of period transitions (this time of the eighteenth century) that mentions Hamann in passing is that of Elizabeth Harries, *The Unfinished Manner: Essays on the Fragment in the Later Eighteenth Century* (Charlottesville: University of Virginia Press, 1994).

from their national tradition but also, more importantly, to take them seriously as a pair of thinkers within a wider constellation of Anglo-German materials. It means that we get away from treating them either, overly preciously, as the singularly talented genius example of our study or, overly patronizingly, as the singularly odd figures of a period that we can define. As a result, we can read them as thinkers whose ideas stand in productive relation and tension with one another, and whose power works beyond their own work alone. We need to get away from sidelining their radical propositions as national or conceptual oddities. Blake and Hamann are much more than canonical outsiders.

The graphic, shrill, and extreme tone of their writings serves as part of their formal argument against the supposed neutrality of the philosophical essay or a poetic composition. Blake writes prophecies, Hamann 'rhapsod[ies] in kabbalistic prose'.[42] These decisions are made partly in response to what is best called the reign of clarity. Clarity is supposed to be an immediately obvious advantage of any philosophy or poetry. It supposedly reaches for the desired transparency between words and ideas. In contrast, Blake and Hamann insist that in all of these cases transparency is a dangerous illusion, linked directly to the ideology of a systematic distinction between philosophy and poetry. Both of them embrace a form of writing that consciously disturbs these boundaries. True to form, their reaction is neither apologetic nor measured. They both embrace an existential version of Georges L. L. Buffon's maxim that '[l]e style c'est l'homme même'.[43] When Rev Dr Trusler writes to Blake about making his art more accessible, the poet's response is swift and brutal: 'You say that I want somebody to Elucidate my Ideas. But you ought to know that What is Grand is necessarily obscure to Weak men. That which can be made Explicit to the Idiot is not worth my care.'[44] He does not deny that his ideas are difficult to comprehend and that his expression is not accessible. The problem, however, lies with the reader, not with him. Blake neither attempts nor desires to produce forms of writing that are so clear that the ideas will be 'Explicit' even 'to the Idiot'. He simply doesn't care for that form of writing. And, according to him, there are good historical precedents for this attitude: 'The wisest of the Ancients considerd what is not too Explicit as the fittest for Instruction because it rouzes the faculties to act. I name Moses Solomon Esop Homer Plato.'[45] Blake puts himself into an impressive lineage of biblical figures, lawgivers, poets, and philosophers. Note that in his account the foundational figures of poetry and philosophy precisely do *not* write clearly and explicitly. The Ten Commandments are 'necessarily obscure to Weak men'. Blake claims that these forms of discourse, as is his, are 'Grand'. If they are inaccessible, then that comes as little surprise—yet it is not what Blake cares about. Thus, if Trusler finds the writing inaccessible, then that is not a problem. Great writing is, by definition, difficult. And it is part

---

[42] Dickson, p. 82.

[43] Georges L. L. Buffon, *Discours à l'Académie française* (1753), qtd in Anja Weiberg, 'Philosophy and Life', in *In Search of Meaning: Ludwig Wittgenstein on Ethics, Mysticism, and Religion*, ed. Ulrich Arnswald, Europäische Kultur und Ideengeschichte Studien 1 (Karlsruhe, Ger.: Universitätsverlag Karlsruhe, 2009), pp. 67–86, 81.

[44] Blake to Dr Trusler, pp. 702–3, 702.   [45] Blake to Dr Trusler, pp. 702–3, 702.

of a polyglot literary history that keeps being important, and we need to uncover it in its full complexity.

Hamann reacts very similarly to Blake when it comes to the pleas of his contemporary to be more accessible. As Helene Richter points out, 'Hamann professes confidently to his muddled writing style which, just as with Blake, comes into being through wrestling against heavy inner resistances and which, even for similarly matched friends 'not infrequently is real torture' (Jacobi, 16 January 1786). It even prompts Kant to solicit Hamann if he could 'possibly bring forward his views in human language' (7 April 1774).[46] But Hamann refuses to be drawn into this form of argument and responds in the closing sentences of the *Metacritique* with a metaphor that puts the ball firmly in the reader's court: 'I have indicated for the sake of the weak reader: the sacrament of language, the letters of its elements, the spirit of its institution; and I leave it to each to roll the balled fist into a flat hand.'[47] Hamann's image is about the brevity of the text, as Gwen Griffith Dickson and Oswald Bayer point out—the need for the reader to complete it by unrolling his concentrated arguments. This is certainly true, though there is a further dimension to this elliptical form of writing that the image captures well. The reader encounters an aggressive text, a balled fist that will punch her. It is up to her to open it to a hand, to discover what is inside the fist, to discover the inside of the argument.

Both Blake and Hamann react to 'the demand of *reflecting*' about their 'position in the process of production'.[48] Although they produce work in rather different contexts—Blake is a poet and printmaker; Hamann writes theoretical pamphlets—both of them push against the reign of clarity in similarly radical ways. The historically specific dimension of this push is important. The type of clarity that they react against is formulated and perpetuated by a version of the Enlightenment that is attached to a particular form of thought and its relation to language—namely, that obscurity between these two spheres needs to be minimized at all costs. It is a version of the Enlightenment that levels an even more intense criticism against Hamann's and Blake's styles by charging them with wilful obscurantism. G. W. F. Hegel's objection against Hamann ('tiresome riddle') and the verdict of the *Edinburgh Review* against Blake ('able, but, alas! insane') provide good examples of such a misguided critique.[49]

The aim of writing is not, for Blake and Hamann, to present matters in the clearest or most systematic way possible. If we want to explore their full conceptual

---

[46] 'Hamann bekennt sich selbstbewußt zu seiner krausen Schreibart, die—wie bei Blake—oft im Ringen mir schweren inneren Widerständen zustande kommt und selbst den ebenbürtigen Freunden "nicht selten wahre Folter antut" (Jacobi. 16. January 1786), ja Kant zu der Bitte veranlaßt, Hamann möge ihm "womöglich seine Meinung in der Sprache der Menschen vortragen" (7. April 1774)' (Helene Richter, 'Blake und Hamann [part 2]', p. 43).

[47] Dickson, p. 525. 'Habe ich um der schwachen Leser willen, auf das Sacrament der Sprache, den Buchstaben ihrer Elemente, den Geist ihrer Einsetzung gedeutet, und überlasse es einem jeden, die geballte Faust in eine flache Hand zu entfalten' (N, 3:289).

[48] Walter Benjamin, 'The Author as Producer', in *1931–1934*, trans. Rodney Livingstone and others, ed. Michael W. Jennings, Howard Eiland, and Gary Smith, vol. 2, part 2, of *Walter Benjamin: Selected Writings* (Cambridge, MA: Belknap Press of Harvard University Press, 2005), pp. 768–81, 780, and 773.

[49] Anderson, *Hegel on Hamann*, p. 7; Bentley, *Blake Records*, p. 510.

power, then we need to risk going beyond just labelling them canonical outsiders and pretending nothing else has changed. If the relation of thought and language is far less transparent than we thought, then this will affect our reading. Morris Eaves brilliantly puts his finger on it when he states that 'in my experience, Blake's work is a heap of words—and pictures—that starts to become a wall when we readers apply the necessary intellectual pressure to get what we want from it: sense, structure, coherence'.[50] Thus, if we measure writing by its degree of clarity or what goes normally for 'coherence', then we have misunderstood both its character and its power. It is not so much that there is a wilful obscurantism in Blake or Hamann but, rather, that we might want to engage with their idea that the obliqueness of their writing is a more accurate reflection of language and thought than the pretence that there is a clear relation between the two.

To Blake and Hamann it would be a structural mistake to assume that a reader, or even the writer, would ever fully assimilate and understand a text. We are never quite sure whether we comprehend Blake or Hamann, and, almost paradoxically, this insecurity is the result of reading them attentively. The alternative to Hegel's annoyance is to embrace actively this version of a self-reflexive process of reading and its multilayered production of meaning, including epistemology and ethics. As Carol Jacobs observes,

> The ethical act is of commentary, of rhapsody, not only of interpretation but a reading of oneself reading.... Inevitably such an ethics leads to no simple mastery, to no assured sense of one's authority as writer or reader, to no spoils as Hamann puts it, of 'pleasant words, faithfully quoted', as provisions brought from afar. Before such reading looms no messianic horizon of redemption or of decisive judgement.[51]

Reading here becomes an ethical act because it involves the self-reflective 'reading of oneself reading', and both in the moment and over time we cannot ever be assured of our authority on either side of the textual production. Thus, we return to these texts not to decode them or to domesticate them. While we can become more familiar with Blake's prophecies and familiarize ourselves with Hamann's texts, we never get to *know* them. In a Socratic mode, the fruit of growing knowledge is a greater insight into our ignorance. This seemingly obvious approach lies at the heart of the complexity that these writings exhibit. It is not a theoretical insight that we bring to them once we have endorsed the Socratic position. Rather, the texts themselves promote and perform this position as one of their central principles. Their style not only is Socratic in relation to its own insights, but also produces this Socratic attitude in the reader. Remember that both Blake and Hamann style themselves as Socrates: Hamann refers to his Socratic position throughout his work (especially in his *Socratic Memorabilia*), and Blake exclaims 'I was Socrates'.[52]

---

[50] Morris Eaves, 'On Blakes We Want and Blakes We Don't', *Huntington Library Quarterly* 58, 3–4 (1995): 413–39, 416. For one of the most historically and theoretically attuned readings of Blake along similar lines, see Vincent Arthur de Luca, *Words of Eternity: Blake and the Poetics of the Sublime* (Princeton, NJ: Princeton University Press, 1991), esp. ch. 7, 'The Setting of Signs: Language and the Recovery of Origins', pp. 201–24.

[51] Carol Jacobs, *Skirting the Ethical* (Stanford, CA: Stanford University Press, 2008), p. 209.

[52] Crabb Robinson, diary entry, 10 December 1825, qtd in Bentley, *Blake Records*, pp. 419–25, 421.

The reflective reading of these texts, then, poses deep challenges on the level of the sentence but also in a much wider sense of the activity of reading itself. Might we think of the criticism levelled at Blake and Hamann in a more productive way than simply to model it as a misguided understanding about the writing or philosophy? One of the challenges in reading Blake and Hamann beyond their canonical positions at the margins is to sidestep the deadlock of these two models of writing and thinking; it need not all be either clarity or obscurantism. As Michael Ferber puts it in a way that resonates with the title of the introduction to this book: 'Supposing he [Blake] had found readers who had taken the trouble of making sense of him, . . . what would the "trouble" itself have signified? I would argue that the trouble is itself anti-ideological in intent and, at least partly, in effect.'[53] The full potential of Ferber's general suggestion becomes clear when we consider that 'making sense' is tied not only to a specific eighteenth-century context but also to the idea of Blake's and Hamann's contemporary relevance. Blake and Hamann still need readers who at least try to take the trouble.

Exploring these exorbitant areas also means we remind ourselves that in Blake's and Hamann's wider historical and philosophical contexts there were, and are, ideas up for grabs that might seem foreign to us, but with whose force we should really engage. Take, for instance, the discussion surrounding the idea of whether there is intrinsic value to our external world. There had always been, at least since Aristotle, a robust investment in the idea that the natural world carries significance. The thinking about that value or meaning took many different forms, of course, and has its own particular history. At the end of the seventeenth century, however, the view regarding whether nature itself *has* value (rather than *which* value it might have) came under sustained attack by what Akeel Bilgrami, following Blake, has usefully termed 'Newtonianism'.[54] This view does not want to replace the particular *version* of value we might find in nature but, rather, do away with the whole idea of value in nature altogether—and it wants to do this for everyone. This shift, which was so incredibly successful that we often forget it ever took place, may be said to mark the birth of modern science as we know it now. The underlying claim of this account is that there really is no inherent value, no self-generating value, in the natural world around us. Of course, we might project value onto it in all sorts of complex ways, but that is ultimately a matter for psychology, not for philosophy or epistemology. As Bilgrami suggests, in the end it comes down to two diverging metaphysical accounts. The first account presents a 'picture that . . . viewed matter and nature as *brute and inert*', and 'since the material universe was brute', would maintain that 'God was *externally* conceived, giving the universe a push from the *outside* to get it in motion'.[55] It is worth emphasizing that this remains the standard view. After all, most people today, including literary critics and intellectual historians, work with a model of science, and philosophy more broadly, that assumes that

---

[53] Michael Ferber, *The Social Vision of William Blake* (Princeton, NJ: Princeton University Press, 1985), p. 64.

[54] Akeel Bilgrami, *Secularism, Identity, and Enchantment* (Cambridge, MA: Harvard University Press, 2014), p. 187.

[55] Bilgrami, p. 295; italics in original.

matter, when it really comes down to it, is inert (imagining the opposite helps to see the view's pervasiveness: how would one react if a class of students claimed that it was their belief that matter was, in fact, full of life and that this formed the basis of their literary readings or, to pick a different discipline, their engineering designs?). The contrasting view believes that 'matter was *not* brute and inert, but rather was shot through with an *inner* source of dynamism that was itself divine and which was responsible for motion'.[56] In this picture the world is '*suffused with value*'.[57] Blake and Hamann vociferously defend the second version of the world.

It is important to take seriously what that means *philosophically*, not just as a puzzle or a historical insight. What is at stake here for Blake and Hamann—and must be at stake for us too, really—is a whole *world*-view, and, depending on which side one falls, one's world, including one's literary world, can look radically different. Of course, there are several thinkers since before and after the eighteenth century until now that share some of these concerns, and some of them, such as Jacob Boehme, Søren Kierkegaard, Paul Celan, or Martin Heidegger, are even connected historically with Blake or Hamann. More specifically, Charles Taylor in *The Language Animal* has articulated an impressive and exhaustive attempt to construct a specifically Hamannian theory of language today.[58] To follow these philosophical genealogies

---

[56] Ibid.   [57] Bilgrami, p. 297; italics in original.
[58] See Charles Taylor, *The Language Animal: The Full Shape of the Human Linguistic Capacity* (Cambridge, MA: Harvard University Press, 2016). Taylor's tour de force is a systematic and powerful proposition that we should think about language in a way that is akin much more to Hamann, Herder, and Alexander von Humboldt (Taylor calls this 'HHH' view of language) than to Thomas Hobbes, John Locke, or Étienne Bonnot de Condillac (the traditional, 'HLC' view of language) (p. ix). The powerful thing about Taylor's book is that it makes a partisan case for the superiority of a constitutive view, as opposed to a purely functional view of language. In other words, Taylor takes seriously the suggestions he finds in Hamann, Herder, and Humboldt in order to develop a contemporary theory of language that rejects most models that we know. The bite of that theory is that it explains what Taylor calls 'the nature of the human capacity for language' (p. 83). Hamann leads Taylor to concur that there is far more to language than functional exchange of information: 'The information-coding view tends to see language as providing immensely useful *instruments* for defining and communicating knowledge about the world. But language creates a context for human life and action, including speech, which deserves attention in its own right' (p. 90). The crucial insight that Taylor wants to hold on to is that this context is something that is irreducibly connected to our existence; it is not like an instrument that we, as Taylor suggests, pick up or lay down. Like Blake or Hamann, he believes that 'language can only be understood if we understand its constitutive role in human life' (p. 261). Of course, there is a certain circularity to this: '[W]e have to emphasize again that linguistic awareness is not limited to the facet of the semantic dimension, where the designative logic prevails; in other words, to that set of language games where we are concerned with accurate description of independent objects. This is a facet of language that has all too often crowded the stage and monopolized the attention of theorists of language. Language is also used to create, alter, and break connections between people' (p. 261). What Taylor describes here as monopolizing is precisely analogous with the development I term as the narrowing of linguistics in a Newtonian vein. We need to resist this trend if we want to truly understand its philosophical force, though we also need to address the role of history here, conspicuously absent from the heart of Taylor's argument.

The absence of history is, indeed, a little surprising, since, ultimately, Taylor thinks that an attention to Hamann moves us towards 'the important post-Romantic theme of seeking the real language, the living creative one, which reconnects, as against the dead language which simply designates things that everyone can see, and allows us to manipulate them, totally ignoring their sign-character' (p. 344). Given my earlier comments about the misguided investments in historical breaks, I should mention that, for all its power, Taylor's vision here is uncharacteristically historically imprecise. Describing the project as 'post-Romantic' is relatively unhelpful, since it invokes a clear historical break between

or discuss the more contemporary concerns would produce a very different book, so I will steer my focus back to Blake and Hamann, but with the full awareness that these views were and continue to be available, albeit in increasingly rare forms.[59] Part of my task and aim in this book is to argue that we, with Blake and Hamann, can profit from being able and willing to imagine worlds alternative to

Enlightenment, Romanticism, and what comes after that (p. 106). In Taylor's story, Hamann is already a Romantic, not even a precursor anymore. Although this historically shaky judgement does not matter much to Taylor's particular argument, we should still note that it is strange that the author of *The Secular Age* would make it. The fact that Taylor makes an argument about the present, and about *our* contemporary understanding of language, is fundamental. He asks us to think seriously about Ludwig Wittgenstein, Gottlob Frege, Jacques Derrida, and Maurice Merleau-Ponty in relation to their philosophical legacy located in Hamann, suggesting that many of them come out of an orthodox or functionalist tradition. Whatever one's position in these debates, Taylor asks the question of the human as language animal in a way that allows us to combine an interest in historical sources with present-day concerns. As with any project of this magnitude, we can pick holes in it. I prefer to focus on Taylor as an example of what is possible when we take seriously the conceptual propositions of the historical materials. If Bilgrami was my positive example for what can happen when we are open to a different intellectual history, then Taylor is my positive example for what can happen when we are open to a different conceptual armature. This promises to be more productive than, say, Michael Forster's learned, but rather narrow reading of a similar context, which is concerned more with rescuing Herder from a possible Hamannian influence than with engaging with Hamann's work directly. See Michael N. Forster, *After Herder: Philosophy of Language in the German Tradition* (Oxford: Oxford University Press, 2010), pp. 283–319.

   59   Here are some pointers regarding such a genealogy in relation to Hamann that will be useful for readers who want to follow these connections. The genealogy of influence includes thinkers such as Jacob Boehme, Søren Kierkegaard, Walter Benjamin, Martin Heidegger, and Paul Celan. For the latter four, very different writers, Hamann was a pivotal figure in their reading and an important reference point for their thinking and writing. Kierkegaard cites Hamann regularly, including in his opening to *Fear and Trembling* (1843), and adopts his strategy of openly masked authorship as a philosophically significant move. Hamann is the single most relevant figure to Benjamin's thinking on language, especially in his early work: he cites him twice, both times approvingly, in the seminal 'On Language as Such and on the Language of Man' (1916). Heidegger refers to Hamann as one of the 'three Hs' (die drei H) that are the central reference points in Enlightenment language philosophy (the others are Herder and Humboldt). Heidegger's remark is particularly apt, since Hamann wrote a whole treatise on the letter *h*, which I will discuss in Chapter 8. It stands to reason that Heidegger would like to think of himself as *H* number 4. Celan's utterly neglected annotations to Hamann's works (he owned several volumes of Hamann's writings) are extensive and noteworthy. Especially with regard to Heidegger's interest, Celan's continuous study of Hamann is significant. To imagine that *The Meridian* was composed while Celan was reading the *Socratic Memorabilia* opens up this text of contemporary Romanticism completely anew. Celan was also interested in Hamann's intellectual formation in England. Intriguingly, his library also contained books by Blake. The French translations of Blake and Hamann— done, respectively, by Georges Bataille and Pierre Klossowski, the two grand figures of deconstruction— could form another basis for further source study along similar lines.

   A good starting point for the relation between Hamann and Kierkegaard is provided in John R. Betz, 'Hamann before Kierkegaard: A Systematic Theological Oversight', *Pro Ecclesia* 16, 3 (Summer 2007): 299–333. Also see Joachim Ringleben, 'Søren Kierkegaard als Hamann-Leser', in *Die Gegenwärtigkeit Johann Georg Hamanns; Acta des achten Internationalen Hamann-Kolloquiums an der Martin-Luther-Universität Halle-Wittenberg 2002*, ed. Bernhard Gajek (Frankfurt am Main: Peter Lang, 2005), pp. 455–65; and Lydia B. Amir, *Humor and the Good Life in Modern Philosophy: Shaftesbury, Hamann, Kierkegaard* (Albany: State University of New York Press, 2014), pp. 89–100. On Benjamin and Hamann, see the still standard Winfried Menninghaus, *Walter Benjamins Theorie der Sprachmagie* (Frankfurt am Main: Suhrkamp, 1987). In relation to Heidegger and Hamann, see Heidegger, *Vom Wesen der Sprache: Die Metaphysik der Sprache und die Wesung des Wortes zu Herders Abhandlung 'Über den Ursprung der Sprache'*, in *Gesamtausgabe*, 102 vols (Frankfurt am Main: Klostermann, 1975–), vol. 85. For Celan's library, see Celan, *La bibliothèque philosophique: Die Philosophische Bibliothek* (Paris: Rue d'Ulm, 2004), pp. 108–15, and https://www.dla-marbach.de/katalog/bibliothek.

the ones we normally encounter, and that those two figures teach us how to do this in new, original ways. For them, the negative consequences of one's narrowing of the world-view along Newtonian lines are immediately tangible and real. Consider how different we behave towards something we believe has inherent value or something that is inert. Once we believe in the world as brute matter, it is easier to treat it purely in terms of commerce, utility, and monetary worth (and most invocations of value would sound like naive or sentimental projections). These are Blake's satanic mills or the terrible reign of Urizen. The fact that this description immediately connects with the timely topic of ecology illustrates dramatically the contemporary relevance of these views.

Newtonianism deeply shaped the reality of people and continues to do so, especially through institutional forces that perpetuate its assumptions in multiple, subtle forms. Obvious candidates for these ideological mechanisms are language, religion, politics, or science. As we will see, Blake and Hamann sensed acutely that language, in particular, became Newtonianism's philosophical backbone in ways that deeply permeate most of our social and philosophical structures. John Locke's theory of language was, and still is, a central way for adapting Newtonianism.[60] The contrast that Blake and Hamann draw through their disagreements with the Lockean or Newtonian theory, which eventually established itself, allows us to recognize certain historical and theoretical orthodoxies that we have inherited with these forms of thinking and often simply have forgotten about. Newtonianism encompasses the way we organize almost all knowledge and ourselves through philosophy, science, economy, religion, and politics. Most of these highly complex relations have a conceptual and theoretical underbelly that has its own logic: generally speaking, it is a world in which the idea of the sacred seems either constructed, retrograde, or even silly, and in which the idea of linguistic neutrality is celebrated and taken to be the same as—confused with, Blake and Hamann would say—impersonality. Violently opposed to the conceptualization of the world in these functional terms, for Blake and Hamann language becomes *the* primary form of illustrating that and how the world is deeply animated, alive, and supple in ways that lie far beyond any instrumental account. For them, the world is suffused with value because it is suffused with language.[61] If we want to go beyond domesticating Blake and Hamann, then we need to actively engage with what such a philosophical view might mean.

---

[60] Lockean views of language have become incredibly normalized. Most of us share assumptions to a degree that seem to us intuitive way beyond the issue of language: think of the idea, almost a doctrine, of the arbitrariness of the sign, or any number of intellectual schools that proclaim that 'X is structured like language'. The unspoken assumption is that this is a Lockean or Saussurean version of language.

[61] It is, of course, language that fills the world with value, not us via language. It is important to remember this aspect of the argument, since it radically diminishes the role that the individual plays in the construction of what comes to be the world. Thus, the account of nature that includes such a level of activity comes also with the insight that we have to readjust our level of subjectivity and control. Bilgrami hits here on something very interesting in relation to the position of the modern subject, so often the target of a critique of Romanticism as self-absorbed: 'Far from claiming a subject, untethered and unconstrained in its reach and capacities, natural supernaturalism demands merely that the subject's capacities be sensitive to the normative demands that are made on it by the properties of value and meaning in the world, including nature. If anything, it is *constrained* by the world in these ways' (p. 200; italics in original). In this version of events, we end up with a Romanticism, and a version

PROPHETS OF JOY, PROPHETS OF DOOM

Engaging with Blake's and Hamann's work in a less domesticated manner also sheds light on why most of their twentieth-century reception has been shaped by rather teleological and rigid assumptions, especially when it comes to their statements about thought and language. Despite, or maybe because of, their opposition to mainstream thinking, Blake and Hamann have both been viewed as precursors of different strands of twentieth-century thought. This has taken a variety of forms: Blake's practice of combining visual and verbal art has been seen as a prefiguration of multimedia practices in the twentieth century; his treatment and inversion of dualities has led poststructuralist critics to claim him as an early thinker of deconstruction; his attitudes towards the body hold a deep attraction for counterculture throughout the twentieth century; and much recent Blake criticism has been concerned with how far he was a political prophet for or against empire, colonialism, and other forms of political oppression.

In many ways, all of these movements continue the establishment of Blake as a canonical, domesticated outsider. Criticism throughout the centuries has continued a lively debate around the contemporaneity of Blake's thought, much of it revolving around questions of how (im)possible it is to figure out how these theoretical interests relate to the historical context that would have shaped Blake's thinking. How problematic is it to think of Blake, the firm believer in the revelatory quality of the Bible, or the visionary poet, as a deconstructive thinker or a postcolonial poet? Blakean criticism has many varied and sophisticated different answers to these questions that we need not rehearse here. Without wanting to deny the powers of these approaches, this book departs from such scholarship and turns its attention to Blake as a visionary, a philosophical poet whose ideas on language, religion, and sexuality were deeply spiritual and metaphysical. I turn not so much away from politics but, rather, towards an inquiry of what the metaphysically and ontologically unusual dimensions of Blake's work tell us about his philosophical relevance, especially as viewed through a historically comparative lens.

Hamann's limited reception in the English-speaking world has been completely dominated by accounts that conceive of him as a precursor of specific forms of twentieth-century thought. He is generally presented as either a figure of irrationalism whose antipathy against rational discussion is directly connected to twentieth-century totalitarianism or as an author whose writings count as early instances of poststructuralism. Until recently, the most common introduction to Hamann in an Anglophone context was through Isaiah Berlin, whose 1993 essay 'The Magus of the North' subsequently formed part of his popular *Three Critics of Enlightenment* (2000). Berlin characterized Hamann as a deep but anti-rationalist thinker who formulated an attack on the Enlightenment that had profoundly damaging historical

---

of the Enlightenment, too, in which the claims for genius, individual inspiration, and similar ideas, are actually not at all as important as they are generally taken to be. Bilgrami mentions that Wittgenstein would fit into a tradition of Romanticism thus conceived, and there is certainly a sense in which we can see a genealogy of thinkers and poets who are convinced that the subject reacts to a world full of value rather than imposes itself on it. John Keats or Mary Shelley comes to mind, as does W. B. Yeats.

consequences. Berlin's larger conviction was that rational thought and debate were the foundations of any form of liberty and liberalism that would defend itself against political attacks, especially the totalitarianism Berlin had himself escaped. Thus Hamann became the precursor to a form of irrationalism that, eventually, ended up in the forms of Nazism.

In effect, Berlin's objection to Hamann was that he provided the framework for the kind of irrationalism which would result in politically deeply troubling waters. Even though much of this reading is by now debunked, it bears repeating why this is so. Berlin's representation of Hamann is very selective and, as some scholars have pointed out, rather misleading.[62] Although Hamann was deeply critical of the role that the ratio plays in the Enlightenment project, especially in rationalist philosophy, he was certainly not advocating to abandon reasonable discussion and political discourse. It is both historically inaccurate as well as conceptually weak to portray Hamann as a precursor of ideologically dubious politics.

The second form of casting Hamann as a forerunner of twentieth-century thought comes from several poststructuralist thinkers, especially in the areas of literary and religious studies. In contrast to Berlin, these theorists celebrate Hamann as a positive prefigurative author, especially on language and difference. According to this view, his arguments about the inextricability of language and thought not only put him immediately in the orbit of the linguistic turn but also reveal him as expounding an early version of deconstruction, negative theology, or postsecularism.[63] For instance, Jeffrey Mehlman writes approvingly about Richard Rorty as a 'twentieth century transcription of Hamann's message to Kant'.[64] In his discussion Mehlman constructs a genealogy that begins with Hamann and then leads to Benjamin, Richard Rorty, and, ultimately, himself as an advocate for

---

[62] See Günther.

[63] For an Anglophone account of the linguistic turn that mentions Hamann, albeit in passing only, see Michael Losonsky, *Linguistic Turns in Modern Philosophy* (Cambridge: Cambridge University Press, 2006), pp. 104–15. For deconstruction, see Jeffrey Mehlman, 'Literature and Hospitality: Klossowski's Hamann', in 'Des Allemagnes: Aspects of Romanticism in France', special issue, *Studies in Romanticism* 22, 2 (Summer 1983): 329–47; and Garett Green, 'Modern Culture Comes of Age: Hamann versus Kant on the Root Metaphor of Enlightenment', in *What Is Enlightenment? Eighteenth-Century Answers and Twentieth-Century Questions* (Berkeley: University of California Press, 1996), pp. 291–305. For negative theology, see John Milbank, *The Word Made Strange: Theology, Language, Culture* (Malden, MA: Blackwell, 1998). For postsecularism, see Betz, *After Enlightenment.* In plenty of cases Hamann is a precursor for Romanticism, either through Sturm und Drang or as an individual. See Thomas Pfau, who thinks of him as a 'precursor of Novalis's linguistic and poetic theories' (*Romantic Moods: Paranoia, Trauma, and Melancholy, 1790–1840* [Baltimore, MD: Johns Hopkins University Press, 2005], p. 478). Also see Robert C. Holub, 'The Legacy of the Enlightenment: Critique from Hamann and Herder to the Frankfurt School', in *German Literature of the Eighteenth Century: The Enlightenment and Sensibility*, ed. Barbara Becker-Cantarino (Rochester, NY: Camden House, 2005), pp. 285–307; and Paul van Tieghem, *Le Romantisme dans la literature Européenne* (Paris: Albin Michels, 1948), pp. 30–2.

[64] Mehlman, p. 338. Also see Green's claim that Hamann 'adumbrates several themes that have been elaborated by leading theorists of the twentieth century' (p. 291). Of course, this type of suggestion connects up with a more general, common linkage between early Romanticism and critical theory. For such accounts, see Wheeler, *Romanticism, Pragmatism, and Deconstruction*; Andrew Bowie, *From Romanticism to Critical Theory*; and Eckhard Schumacher, *Die Ironie der Unverständlichkeit* (Frankfurt: Suhrkamp, 2000).

deconstruction, closing with the hope that his article will have brought 'the project of the introduction to Hamann to a measure of rhapsodic fulfilment'.[65] In this version of events, Hamann stands at the beginning of a hagiography of deconstruction and rhapsodic writing that ends with Mehlman. Most accounts in literary studies that discuss Hamann more than in passing take a similar view, reading him as an early nominalist proponent of deconstruction.[66] Theologians of Radical Orthodoxy often paint a similar picture when they read his religiously charged work in relation to existentialism or postsecularism. John R. Betz provides one of the most comprehensive introductions to Hamann's thought in his *After Enlightenment: The Post-Secular Vision of J. G. Hamann* (2009). Betz's description of Hamann's metacriticism as a '*merciful* deconstruction' is both suggestive and illustrative but, eventually, reverts to an all-too-familiar structure that positions Hamann as a prophet against Enlightenment in a genealogy that ends with Jacques Derrida.[67]

The main problem with these ahistorical narratives is that, once again, they domesticate thinkers like Blake and Hamann in a way that blunts their critical edge. Even contemporary critics who purportedly support Hamann's or Blake's visions are often not really all that interested in understanding the full implications of their supposed precursors, especially when it comes to theology or metaphysics. This makes them, despite their promising focus on the singular figures of Blake or Hamann, unhelpful guides to these thinkers because, rather than exploring the unusual philosophical ideas of these authors, they only focus on the aspects of their thought that can be absorbed into a twentieth-century intellectual framework. As a result, they often work with conceptions and categories that are reverse-engineered. Take the issue of language, so central to both Hamann and deconstruction: Mehlmann's poststructuralism assumes, as a given, a broadly Saussurean conception of language, ultimately rooted in Locke, which Hamann would identify as a misunderstanding, Blake would think of as sinful, and Benjamin would consider deeply 'bourgeois'.[68] All three strongly believe in the motivated sign, the ontological force of language, or what we might term the 'magic' of words. This is not some childish spleen or a naïveté that they grow out of once they become mature thinkers.[69] It remains an essential touchstone of their work throughout their life, and it is deeply

[65] Mehlman, p. 347.

[66] Another example for this can be found in Job de Meyere, 'The "Enlightened" Derrida: The Formalization of Religion', in *Faith in the Enlightenment? The Critique of the Enlightenment Revisited*, ed. Lieven Boeve, Joeri Schrijvers, Wessel Stoker, and Hendrik M. Vroom (Amsterdam: Rodopi, 2006), pp. 143–56.

[67] Betz, *After Enlightenment*, p. 305. As Kenneth Haynes points out, this aspect of Betz's project seems to rely on 'an old demonology of the Enlightenment' (Haynes, review of *After Enlightenment*, by Betz, *Church History* 78, 4 [December 2009]: 904–6, 906).

[68] Walter Benjamin, 'On Language as Such and on the Language of Man', in *1913–1926*, ed. Marcus Bullock and Michael W. Jennings, vol. 1 of *Walter Benjamin: Selected Writings* (Cambridge, MA: Harvard University Press, 1996), pp. 62–74, 65, and 69.

[69] This is a view that is all too common when it comes to Benjamin (i.e. the idea that the fanciful early theology gets replaced by the mature and serious historical materialism of adulthood). Apart from the fact that it is empirically incorrect (the *Arcades Project* is one of the most theological books of modernity), it is also evidently based on a rather simplified way of conceiving the development of thought.

at odds with the way that most modern people think about language, let alone the world. Thus, a narrative that casts Blake or Hamann as prophetic figures needs to move beyond slotting them into a teleology that creates a lineage which turns out to be far too clean and clear.[70] John Milbank gets to some of this when he returns to the relation between Derrida and Hamann and points out that indeterminacy 'for Hamann is not, as with Derrida, *opposed* to metaphysical presence, rather it is *of the essence* of metaphysical presence'.[71] Rather than reading Derrida as the fulfilment of Hamann's early promise, we should see that there is a historical and conceptual difference between these thinkers that does not align with our normal assumptions about intellectual history. Hamann operates with a historically different model of presence. But that model turns out to be just as radical now as it was then. It is a model of thought and difference that challenges us to reconsider the historical formation of how we align concepts (for instance, indeterminacy versus metaphysical presence) and, in fact, sidesteps through some of the assumptions that are behind these alignments.[72] It is a model that, in its exorbitance, illustrates, and then exceeds, the historical common ground that exists in many forms of philosophy familiar today, some of which are presented as a radical break or critique with the past.

This is just one example of a more general rule that, despite its assurances to the contrary, contemporary theory often relies on a rather conventional version of eighteenth-century thought. In contrast, we must be open to the radical aspects of Blake's and Hamann's work, or at least be open to them. Instead of reverse-engineering our presentism, we need to seriously investigate and not prejudge, for instance, what happens to our criticism if we take seriously the idea that signs are

---

[70] Of course, not all invocations of Hamann are the same. Take, for instance, the comments that Paul de Man, a key figure to argue for the inextricability of thought and language, makes on Hamann. Precisely because he comprehends the historical dimension and theoretical implications of Hamann's thought, de Man resists the temptation to conflate its theoretical ambition with his own poststructuralist project: 'Herder's humanism encounters in Hamann a resistance that reveals the complexity of the intellectual climate in which the debate between symbol and allegory will take place' (*Blindness and Insight: Essays in the Rhetoric of Contemporary Criticism*, 2nd ed. [London: Routledge, 2005], p. 189). De Man understands very well that while Hamann was extremely important for the formation of linguistic thought, including his own, there remain important philosophical differences between them, including the metaphysical convictions that underwrote their different celebrations of allegory. A similar insight is behind Jacques Derrida's, George Bataille's, and Maurice Blanchot's silences on Hamann, all thinkers for whom the irreducibly linguistic quality of thought is central. The simplest explanation would be that they did not know about Hamann's work. However, that seems highly unlikely, since it was none other than Pierre Klossowski—a close friend of Bataille and Blanchot, and a figure Derrida was keenly aware of—who, in 1948, translated into French Hamann's *Biblical Meditations* and Hegel's study of Hamann. It is much more likely these major figures of French poststructuralist thought stayed clear of Hamann as a figure whom, despite superficial similarities, they recognized as an author that could not be absorbed into their projects. It almost seems they shied away from what they perceived to be such a radically different and almost inaccessible way of thinking against established patterns of thought, including their systematic attachment to disruption. Much of this has to do with Hamann's deeply religious thought, connected to his unabashed rejection of systematicity, including its sometimes supposedly subversive character.

[71] Milbank, p. 77.

[72] This point is also at the heart of Katie Terezakis's critique of Milbank's appropriation of Hamann. See Terezakis, 'J. G. Hamann and the Self-Refutation of Radical Orthodoxy', in *The Poverty of Radical Orthodoxy*, ed. Lisa Isherwood and Marko Zlomislic, Postmodern Ethics 3 (Eugene, OR: Pickwick, 2012), pp. 32–57.

not arbitrary, or that the world, indeed, might be '*suffused with value*'. What we need in our studies of Blake and Hamann is to be informed historically and bring this knowledge to bear on the philosophical significance of the material. But we bring it to bear not to primarily historicize their writing in relation to our own assumptions and views, but to allow us to understand better what these authors are trying to say, so that we can figure out whether it is relevant to us. Of course, there is no *one* way of doing this. This book presents a set of case studies that focus on questions that are among the most important philosophical topics for the eighteenth and twenty-first centuries: their accounts of language and instrumental thought, their opposition to institutional religion, and their celebration of the link between language and the human body.

3

Crossing Channels
Fuseli, Hamann, and Lavater

INTRODUCTION

Henry Fuseli, Johann Georg Hamann, and Johann Caspar Lavater are three exceptional critics, writers, and translators who form a special Anglo-German constellation. All three of them are radical in very different, unforeseen, and often-neglected ways. This chapter sets out to describe their disparate exorbitance and to address our neglect of them. Through their translations, political writings, and linguistic theories, they not only give us a good sense of the level of complexity and entanglements of the Anglo-German world in eighteenth-century Britain, but they also provide us with individual examples of the unusual figures that this context produces. Their multiple connections reveal a pattern—a context that keeps producing figures whose thinking on language, epistemology, and ontology is very different from the standard ways in which we account for the period. If we engage with their writings, then we can understand how important it is to challenge our common assumptions about the Enlightenment, Romanticism, and the cultural exchange between them, particularly when we add their individual connections to William Blake into the mix.

A quick snapshot of the different materials that this chapter will connect illustrates the sheer level of interrelatedness and intricacy of transnational culture at the time and how that can make us view things differently. Take the case of Fuseli, one of the most famous British Romantic visual artists. We know him, generally, as the painter of the iconic *The Nightmare* and as a straight-up representative of Gothic Romanticism or British Romantic history painting. Once we dig a little deeper, however, it turns out that he was also a major transmitter between English and German cultures more generally, and with a particularly strong investment in their literary dimension—a multilingual aspect of his work that gets lost in the characterization of him as a painter. He was the first translator who brought Lady Mary Wortley Montagu into German and the first to translate Johann Joachim Winckelmann into English, and he provided the influential translations of Lavater's *Aphorisms*. Fuseli also wrote an anonymous essay on Jean-Jacques Rousseau, published by Joseph Johnson, directly inserting his Anglo-German voice into discussions on British politics.

Back in Germany, Hamann knew of Fuseli through Herder. But even before he was told about the painter, Hamann reviewed both Fuseli's essay and the Montagu translation, even though in the case of the essay Hamann mistakenly thought that piece had been written by Laurence Sterne. Hamann himself was also a major translator, especially of David Hume; he translated the works of Samuel Johnson, George Berkeley, Anthony Ashley-Cooper, Third Earl of Shaftesbury, and many more. Hamann's work as a translator of Hume in particular has far-reaching consequences for the history of ideas since it is was he who translated the part of Hume that woke Immanuel Kant from his dogmatic slumber and indirectly led to the writing of the *Critique of Pure Reason.*

Lavater—the third main character in this chapter—is one of the most connected and widely published figures of the specific Anglo-German context and eighteenth-century European intellectual life more generally. His correspondence with Hamann was long and extensive; Lavater's English translator was his school friend Fuseli, who worked together with Blake on the publication of Lavater's editions published in London by Joseph Johnson. Lavater's neglected religious writings, especially on language, turn out to articulate a theory of linguistic immanence whose relevance to Blake and Hamann is immediate. Yet these connections are little known and their collective implications are almost entirely ignored.

We need to untangle and understand these historical connections, correlations, and crossovers. This includes resisting the simplistic way that these three figures are normally classified, breaking them out of their received reception. Fuseli is much more than a painter; he and Hamann emerge as translators and critics. Lavater turns out to be a theorist of language, not just a physiognomist. The complexity of each of their works is also the key to seeing how, in fact, they are connected. Their often-exorbitant activities make it possible to perceive a set of connections between them that was previously concealed. It also reinforces our sense of the depth and commonality of transnational connections, which were far more typical in the period than we generally realize. While the main line of inquiry of this chapter follows the entanglements of these three figures across languages, genres, and national literatures, all of this source study eventually points towards a larger claim that lies at the heart of this book: that the level of interaction, fluidity, and continuity which the comparative readings unearth across the eighteenth and nineteenth centuries makes it altogether impossible to claim that there was an established Enlightenment culture, against which Romanticism either reacted or can be defined. Returning to the exorbitant excesses of Fuseli, Hamann, or Lavater, and discovering their unknown sides, allows us to explode the difference between these historical and conceptual categories.

HENRY FUSELI: GERMAN TRANSLATOR AND ENGLISH WRITER IN 1760S LONDON

Fuseli is known to most scholars of eighteenth-century literature, art, and culture through his famous *The Nightmare*, one of the most notorious paintings of the age. In the image, one of the most celebrated and ridiculed of the age, the ghoulish nightmare sits above the vulnerable and sexualized female figure who is sleeping, dreaming, and clearly haunted by this malicious presence. In some versions, the viewer finds that his gaze is mirrored in an actual mare, whose wild eyes survey the spectacle from the background. Fuseli, through this painting and many others in a similar vein, has become synonymous with Gothic or 'Dark' Romanticism. His idiosyncratic style is instantly recognizable, be it in his Gothic meditations, his history painting, the illustrations to Shakespeare, or his erotic drawings. His friendships with Reynolds and Blake have always kept him even closer to Romantic visual art. It is also well known that, in 1799, he was chosen as Professor of Painting at the Royal Academy, and four years after that promoted to Keeper, marking for many the canonization of Romantic visual art.

But there is another, equally important side to Fuseli that scholarship has mainly neglected: of Swiss origin, he was a serious writer and the first translator of several texts that were defining for the age. Even before he arrived in London, he had translated Montagu's *Turkish Embassy Letters* from English into German. Once arrived in London he was the first to translate Winckelmann into English, and he convinced Joseph Johnson (with whom he lived) to publish the aesthetician's work. His 1788 translation of Lavater's *Aphorisms*, one of the bestsellers of the age, cements his importance as a translator. Fuseli wrote poetry and prose in German and English; among his works is a highly political pamphlet, *Remarks on the Writings and Conduct of J. J. Rousseau* (1767), which, apart from Rousseau, deals with Hume and William Cowper and also involves Hamann. Few scholars know that, as a translator, Fuseli was a highly significant force in the Anglo-German intellectual context. Once we become aware of it, he begins to emerge as much more than a Gothic painter. He becomes a figure whose early Anglo-German translations and essays disturb the line between Enlightenment and Romanticism.

The relation between English and German materials played a big part in the way Fuseli shaped himself as an idiosyncratic thinker, both in his formative years in Switzerland and in his life in London. He was born in 1741 in Zurich, into an old and established family active in arts and literature.[1] His father promoted the arts across borders by becoming a major patron, correspondent, and publisher of Winckelmann.[2] Later in life, Fuseli would emulate his father by corresponding with the German aesthetician and translating his *Reflections on the Painting and Sculpture of the Greeks* into English. Together with his lifelong friend Lavater,

---

[1] Henry Fuseli's father, Hans Kasper Füssli Sr (1706–82), studied painting in Vienna and was also active as an art historian, whose love for classical art was influential for his children. All of his adult children—two daughters and three sons—were involved in the arts to varying degrees, though Fuseli became the most famous of them by far. This is a rather self-conscious family matter. There is a copper engraving, *Domus Fuesslinorum artis pingendi cultrix*, by Fuseli's elder brother that shows the whole family of artists.

One of Fuseli Sr's major contributions in print is the 1755–57 publication of a multivolume history and dictionary of painters and artists in Switzerland, which was republished after comprehensive revision and extension to five volumes in 1769–79. He also published an aesthetic treatise and other writings for art collectors. For further information, see his entry, 'Füßli, Johann Caspar', in *Allgemeine deutsche Biographie*, 56 vols (Leipzig: Duncker and Humblot, 1878), 8: 258–60.

[2] See Fuseli Sr's *Winckelmann's Briefe an seine Freunde in der Schweiz* (Zurich: Drell, Gessner, Füsslin, 1778).

Fuseli trained as a priest, although he never took orders.[3] Their Anglophile teachers ensured a deep knowledge and interest in British culture and the English language, as well as a keen interest in, and awareness of, dissenting voices.

The most important influence on young Fuseli was Johann Jakob Bodmer, an important figure for intellectual exchanges across eighteenth-century Europe. A philologist, Bodmer taught history in Zurich and was one of the most important champions of John Milton and Edward Young on the Continent. He translated *Paradise Lost* in 1742 and wrote on Young's *Night Thoughts*.[4] Bodmer was at the helm of what would become the new standard of German poetics, heavily influenced by British sources, and Fuseli lastingly adopted these ideas.[5] He was aware of the work of other Anglophiles, such as Hamann, and it is likely that they would have influenced his teaching. Bodmer's pedagogy was part of a transnational way of thinking and education whose quality remained with Fuseli well into his London years. His late (1778–81) painting *The Artist in Conversation with Johann Jakob Bodmer* illustrates this well, functioning as a reminiscence of how the pedagogical relationship between the two transcends time, language, and borders.[6]

The reasons why and how Fuseli eventually ended up in London are the direct result of his first political essay, a public letter entitled *The Unjust Bailiff, or the Complaints of a Patriot*, co-authored with his friends Lavater and Felix Heß. Their attack on a high-ranking public servant led to a major scandal in the wake of which all three authors needed to leave Zurich.[7] Fuseli was never to return permanently, going into German exile first and eventually turning towards London. His teacher Bodmer helped to arrange the logistics, illustrating that these intellectual connections

---

[3] It's worth noting that Fuseli's religious training would likely have exposed him to Moravian thought. See John Knowles, *The Life and Writings of Henry Fuseli*, 3 vols (London: Henry Colburn and Richard Bentley, 1831), 1: 17. Fuseli also comments in his letters, in not too complimentary terms, about contact with the London Moravians (specifically James Hutton, a leading figure of the congregation). See Arnold Federmann, *Johann Heinrich Füssli: Dichter und Maler, 1741–1825*, Monographien zur Schweizer Kunst 1 (Zurich: Orell Füssli, 1927), p. 117.

[4] See C. H. Ibershoff, 'Bodmer and Milton', *Journal of English and Germanic Philology* 17, 4 (October 1918): 589–601; and Ibershoff, 'Bodmer and Young', *Journal of English and Germanic Philology* 24, 2 (April 1925): 211–18. Ibershoff remains one of the few scholars who worked on Johann Jakob Bodmer's Anglo relations. Also see Davis for a discussion of Theodor Haak, the first known translator of *Paradise Lost* into German (p. 76).

[5] Together with his friend Johann Jakob Breitinger, Bodmer publicly opposed Johann Christoph Gottsched, the high priest of German neoclassicism, and argued for a less rule-bound aesthetics, often identified with British authors.

[6] The painting is about a teacher–pupil relationship, between the past and present. Fuseli and Bodmer are seated in front of a bust, which most art historians take to be either Homer (representing the poetic and visionary influence) or Plato (foregrounding the dialogic and pedagogical character of the scene). The statue looms large, outsizing Fuseli and Bodmer, monumentalizing the past and presenting a figure of authority that looks in upon the scene all the way from antiquity. For a scholarly background on the painting, see Marcella Baur-Callwey, *Die Differenzierung des Gemeinsamen: Männliche Doppelporträts in England von Hans Holbein d. J. bis Joshua Reynolds* (Munich: Martin Meidenbauer, 2007), p. 111.

[7] For a more extensive account of the Grebel affair and the subsequent travel, see Federmann, *Johann Heinrich Füssli*; and Marlis Stähli, ' "Wäre es Ihnen gleichgültig ob Füßli in diesem Land oder in England den Plaz fände?" Bodmer und Sulzer als Mentoren des Malers Johann Heinrich Füssli', in *Johann Jakob Bodmer und Johann Jakob Breitinger im Netzwerk der Europäischen Aufklärung*, ed. Anett Lütteken and Barbara Mahlmann-Bauer (Göttingen: Wallstein, 2009), pp. 695–734.

across Europe helped to shape the practical world around them. At the time the scandal broke, Bodmer's fellow academic J. G. Sulzer was visiting Zurich on his way back to Berlin. Upon Bodmer's suggestion, Sulzer agreed to act as a chaperone for Fuseli and took him to Germany via Augsburg and Leipzig. Eventually he would end up in London, but Fuseli first decided to follow Bodmer's example and started to make contacts throughout Europe. He stayed with Johann Joachim Spalding, a theologian of considerable importance, in Barth, Germany, and it was there that Fuseli produced his translation of Montagu's *Turkish Embassy Letters*.[8] It was his first major, direct contribution to the development of Anglo-German discourse and relations that his teachers had encouraged.[9]

In many ways, Fuseli's exile opened up for his tutors the chance to fulfil a fantasy they had long held. As John Knowles points out, '[S]ome of the literati of Germany and Switzerland had it in contemplation to establish a regular channel of literary communication between those countries and England. Fuseli's tutors and friends, Bodmer, Breitinger, and Sulzer, felt a lively interest in this project, and took an active part in carrying the design to execution'.[10] An example of that 'active part' was to send Fuseli to London once he had to leave Zurich. Although exile cannot have been pleasant, Fuseli certainly did not have to be pushed to embrace London as his eventual destination. In 1763 Léonard Usteri wrote to Rousseau about Fuseli as 'un homme de beaucoup de talent, et qui s'est surtout familiarisé avec la littérature anglaise. Il mourait d'envie de voir l'Angleterre'.[11]

In 1763 Fuseli arrived in London with a deep commitment to the literary arts, a few writings under his belt, a broad Anglophile education, and the backing of several of the most important and influential figures in the Anglo-German exchange, who all wanted him to succeed as a transmitter between the two cultures and languages. Upon his arrival, he took on his role of connecting figure with some gusto. His letters of introduction from Switzerland, and an additional one from Sir Andrew Mitchell, the British *chargé d'affaires* in Berlin, helped Fuseli's smooth transfer to England.[12] He immediately 'obtained access to several persons of importance, notably Mr. [Thomas] Coutts, the banker (who remained his steadfast friend and patron throughout), [Andrew] Millar, the bookseller, and [Thomas] Cadell, his successor, and Joseph Johnson, the well-known radical publisher in

---

[8] Spalding himself also was a translator from English to German. See his autobiographical writings in Johann Joachim Spalding, *Kleinere Schriften 2: Briefe an Gleim, Lebensbeschreibung*, ed. Albrecht Beutel and Tobias Jersak, vol. 1, part 2, of *Kritische Ausgabe*, 12 vols (Tübingen: Mohr Siebeck, 2001), pp. 142–53.

[9] Fuseli had tried his hand at transposing *Macbeth*, but that could be classified as a youthful effort. See Knowles, 1: 13.

[10] Knowles, 1: 27. On the role of these three mentors for Fuseli's development in the context of the Enlightenment, see Stähli, 'Wäre es Ihnen gleichgültig'.

[11] Léonard Usteri to Jean-Jacques Rousseau, 8 March 1763, in *Correspondance Générale de J.-J. Rousseau*, ed. Théophile Dufour, 20 vols (Paris: Armand Colin, 1928), 9: 156–8, 157. A silent subtext here is Fuseli's commitment to the literary: he wrote poetry throughout his life, and some of the 'literary' scenes for his paintings are invented by him.

[12] See Davis, pp. 73–4; and Stähli, 'Wäre es Ihnen gleichgültig'. Andrew Mitchell was involved in literary life, such as the Lessing-Gottsched controversy. He knew Gottsched personally but defended Lessing.

St Paul's Churchyard'.[13] Fluent in both languages, he situated himself as an active interlocutor in the Anglo-German context. The link with Joseph Johnson proved to be especially relevant and deep. The two of them at one point lived together, and Johnson published some of Fuseli's English writings. Johnson is best known today for having acted as a facilitator, not only in the radical intellectual and artistic circles that included Joseph Priestley, William Godwin, Mary Wollstonecraft (who fell in love with Fuseli), Lord Byron, and Blake—but also for German publishers in London and visitors such as Georg Christoph Lichtenberg, whose travels to Britain I covered in Chapter 1. Thus, during the years between 1763 and 1770 Fuseli was already part of a radical literary scene, long before he went to and returned from Italy and prior to his friendship with Joshua Reynolds—the two most common turns at which an analysis of Fuseli the painter begins. His early presence in London is a good example of the diversity of the developing Anglo-German relations and the intellectual context that was becoming possible at the time. His activity as a translator and writer, as well as his active involvement in the production of Anglo-German knowledge, helped to directly shape these possibilities.

Before discussing Fuseli's translations in detail, it is worth reminding ourselves that they are part of a larger system of linguistic and cultural exchange that often remains unexamined. Translation, such a central part of the exchange of ideas and the generation of knowledge, in the Anglo-German context as well as beyond it, is hardly ever given its full due in our literary-historical accounts of the period. Our knowledge of it as a central eighteenth-century practice and its role in the creation of new literary forms and intellectual possibilities ought to be much greater than it is. If we do not attend to the breadth of translations between German and English in Britain alone, then we miss out on important information we think we know well. The fact that there were German translations of John Bunyan and William Hogarth published in London, for instance, points towards how the larger structures of how Anglo-German culture in London played an active role in the internationalization of the reading public and the transnational dissemination of literature and aesthetics. Similarly, the Wesley brothers, John and Charles, were two of the most central figures of Anglo-German transmission in Europe, translating Moravian hymns from German, many of which we now consider typically British (I will return to this topic in Chapter 7).

Our desire to pigeonhole people or groups into particular disciplines or cultural contexts is another reason why we often have a blind spot when it comes to translations. Fuseli's work is typical in this regard. Historically, we think of him as a visual artist and thus have not paid enough attention to his written work, let alone his translations. However, these works, and their style, tell us a lot. In presenting Montagu's *Letters* to the German public, Fuseli introduced British Enlightenment discourse on war and exile into the German discussion. By translating Lavater and Winckelmann, Fuseli directly intervened in the British discussions on hermeneutics

---

[13] L. C. [Sanders], 'Fuseli, Henry (Johann Heinrich Füssli) (1741–1825)', in *Dictionary of National Biography*, ed. Leslie Stephen, 63 vols (London: Smith, Elder, 1889), 20: 334–9, 335.

and aesthetics. The translations are historical documents of a larger intellectual Anglo-German culture, and it matters what was translated, by whom, and how. Fuseli, encouraged by Sulzer, tackled Montagu's *Letters* while he was freshly in exile.[14] It set the financial and intellectual framework for this work. The *Letters* had appeared in London a few years before to great success, which must have helped the prospect of sales. Fuseli was by no means unaware of the pecuniary dimension of such exchange, since he writes to Bodmer that 'I have earned 7 Louis with authorial work, because I translated the Montague [*sic*]'.[15] Bodmer gets the hint and actively helps with the dissemination of the translations, writing to acquaintances that 'from the book fair also came the Turkish letters of Montague [*sic*] that Fuseli translated in Pomerenia'.[16] However, the more interesting and significant dimension of Fuseli's choice is that he can relate to it as a text on exile and the reasons around its production. Montagu deals not only with displacement—with both the desire and the necessity to deal with a foreign cultural context—but also with how often such a context is created by negativity, such as war and a misguided sense of reason.[17] Having seen the battlefields of Peterwardein 'being strewed with the skulls and carcasses of unburied men, horses and camels', Montagu reflects not just on the 'injustice of war' but also on how society makes 'murder not only necessary but meritorious'.[18] She ponders our desire to 'pretend' all sorts of 'fine claims…to reason' in the face of slaughter, a topic that Fuseli will take up in his essay on Rousseau when he speaks of the way in which a particular desire to reach '[t]ruth has been—and is—the destroyer of peace'.[19] Fuseli's translation is an early example of his interest in how exile and foreignness are generated and marked—all questions that never left him, just as he never shed his strong German accent.

In May 1764, Hamann wrote a review of the German translation of the *Letters* for the *Königsbergsche Zeitung*. He had read the book 'with pleasure'.[20] He did not know that Fuseli was the translator, but he endorsed the book's style and the linguistic wit on display: 'These letters, in intention of both their content as well as their narrative form, really recommend themselves to the curiosity and attention of all readers of taste'.[21] Montagu's habit of exposing supposedly 'Enlightened' positions as misinformed rhetoric must have been deeply attractive to Hamann and of considerable interest to Fuseli. Both Fuseli's translation and Hamann's review made it

---

[14] On J. G. Sulzer's role in this, see Stähli, "Wäre es Ihnen gleichgültig", p. 722.

[15] 'Ich habe daselbst mit autorarbeit 7 Louis verdienet, weil ich die Montague übersezet habe' (Fuseli to Bodmer, 23 November 1763, qtd in Federmann, p. 110).

[16] 'Von der Messe sind auch die türkischen Briefe der Montague gekommen, die Füssli in Pommern übersetzt hat' (Bodmer to [Heinrich Rudolf] Schinz, 28 November 1763, qtd in Federmann, p. 26).

[17] Also see Humberto Garcia, *Islam and the English Enlightenment, 1670–1840* (Baltimore, MD: John Hopkins University Press, 2011), pp. 60–93.

[18] Lady Mary Wortley Montagu, *The Turkish Embassy Letters*, ed. Teresa Heffernan and Daniel O'Quinn (Toronto: Broadview Press, 2013), p. 95.

[19] Ibid.; and Fuseli, *Remarks on the Writings and Conduct of J. J. Rousseau* (London: printed for T. Cadell, 1767), sig. b1r.

[20] '[M]mit Wohlgefallen' (ZH, 1: 253).

[21] '[D]iese Briefe, sowohl in Absicht des Inhalts als der Erzählungsart, sich wirklich der Neugier und der Aufmerksamkeit aller Leser von Geschmack empfehlen' (N, 4: 297).

clear to German readers that this British text was far more than what Isobel Grundy terms a 'relaxed' 'Enlightenment travel treatise'.[22]

The most obvious example would have been Montagu's famous critique of standard Western representations of the subjugation of Muslim women. As Daniel O'Quinn argues, Montagu 'offers an unusual—for this time period—recognition of Newtonian rationality'.[23] The point here is that such Newtonian rationality was viewed sceptically across Anglo-German borders, especially by figures such as Fuseli and Hamann, and, thus, that a discourse critical of the Enlightenment was a central part of the Anglo-German intellectual context both in London and on the Continent. Fuseli's translation and Hamann's German review of Montagu's letters emerge as concrete examples of a conduit between Britain and Germany that actively engaged in ideas that were deeply critical of the growing Enlightenment climate around them.

Immediately after his arrival in London (1763), Fuseli continued to translate, this time from German to English. He turned his attention to Winckelmann and translated the essay on the torso of the Belvedere and, more importantly, the *Reflections on the Painting and Sculpture of the Greeks*, both of which were published in 1765.[24] Fuseli is thus responsible for introducing Winckelmann into English aesthetics. The book went into a second edition two years later and, as Marcia Allentuck shows, 'had an enormous influence on the growth of British neo-hellenism'.[25] It is fitting, then, that the publication of the *Reflections* in English is part of a whole Anglo-German intellectual exchange on aesthetics, much of which occurs in London.[26] Translations of aesthetic treatises across German and English were not uncommon, as we can see by the publication of Gotthold Ephraim Lessing's *Laocoön* in English (1767) and the 1757 German version of Hogarth's *Analysis of Beauty*, published in London by Linde. These works, including Fuseli's, were reviewed and discussed in the periodicals, directly shaping the discussion on aesthetics. For instance, in 1764 Edmund Burke published a review of another one of Winckelmann's essays, strikingly illustrating that Fuseli's choice of text must have hit a contemporary nerve.[27] As Garold N. Davis suggests, 'Füssli is probably

---

[22] Isobel Grundy, *Lady Mary Wortley Montagu: Comet of the Enlightenment* (Oxford: Oxford University Press, 1999), pp. 199–200.

[23] Montagu, p. 180n1.

[24] There might be another essay, but the attribution is uncertain. As Davis points out, '[T]here were four major translations of Winckelmann's writings known in England; two translated by Füssli, a third very probably translated by Füssli, and a French translation reviewed in London' (p. 74).

[25] Marcia Allentuck, 'Henry Fuseli and J. G. Herder's *Ideen zur Philosophie der Geschichte der Menschheit* in Britain: An Unremarked Connection', *Journal of the History of Ideas* 35, 1 (January–March 1974): 113–20, 114. Allentuck's work obviously suggests further Anglo-German connections. Also see her 'Fuseli and Lavater: Physiognomical Theory and the Enlightenment', in *Studies on Voltaire and the Eighteenth Century* 55 (1967): 89–112.

[26] For a longer and more elaborate discussion of Fuseli as a transmitter of 'pre-Romantic' ideas, see Carol Louise Hall, 'Henry Fuseli and the Aesthetics of William Blake: Fuseli as Transmitter of J. J. Winckelmann, J. J. Rousseau, and J. C. Lavater' (PhD dissertation, University of Maryland, 1979).

[27] The odd thing is that the work Edmund Burke discusses, the *Anmerkungen über die Geschichte der Kunst des Alterthums*, was only published in English in 1801. It is not clear whether Burke had read Johann Joachim Winckelmann in German or whether he had a translator (Fuseli, even?) help him.

more responsible than any other single person for the new wave of Hellenism that became evident in English art and literature in the late eighteenth century'.[28] It becomes increasingly clear that Fuseli's texts were a central piece of intellectual growth and literary exchange that allowed figures such as Blake or Hamann to emerge. It is not surprising that Blake himself had a copy of Winckelmann's *Reflections*, a detail rarely mentioned since it runs counter to the image of Blake as a Romantic. All of these different overlaps and respective influences matter. Fuseli begins to emerge as a crucial, representative figure, and it is worth paying detailed attention to what makes him important: his practice as translator and critic.

Fuseli's choice of Winckelmann's text was significant and complicated, even more so than in the case of the *Letters*. He had a deeply ambivalent relationship to Winckelmann, the ultimate representative of neoclassicism, which reflects his conflicted attitude towards the period as a whole. On the one hand, he had a deep admiration for the German aesthetician whose work his father had already actively supported. Fuseli, quite literally, brought Winckelmann's writings and thinking to London.[29] In this sense, Fuseli's translation was a continuation of his father's work, real or imagined, supporting Winckelmann's cause and the artistic vision that hung by it. On the other hand, Fuseli was also deeply sceptical and often rejected Winckelmann as a derivate thinker.[30] In the introduction to his lectures he remarks that 'Winkelmann was the parasite of the fragments that fell from the conversation or the tablets of Mengs, a deep scholar'.[31] Fuseli demeans Winckelmann as a minor scholar who is dining off the work of giants. This ambivalence, even contradiction, is reflected in Fuseli's translation in a remarkable way, thereby making it a particularly interesting example of the complicated tensions within the Anglo-German context during that period in London. The way Fuseli translates the *Reflections* turns out to be an illustration of the tensions of the period as a whole.

Fuseli's hostility towards Winckelmann is in some ways not surprising, especially if we consider our general image of Fuseli as an arch-Romantic. Winckelmann's treatise is a manifesto for an art that is almost the opposite of a painting such as

On Burke and Winckelmann see Aris Sarafianos, 'Hyperborean Meteorologies of Culture: Art's Progress and Medical Environmentalism in Arbuthnot, Burke, and Barry', in *The Science of Sensibility: Reading Burke's Philosophical Enquiry*, ed. Koen Vermeir and Michael Funk Deckard, International Archives of the History of Ideas 206 (Dordrecht, Neth.: Springer, 2012), pp. 69–91.

[28] Davis, p. 73

[29] One of Fuseli's most prized possessions was a bundle of letters that Winckelmann had written to his father; he even brought these letters with him to London. Fuseli's father had been one of the key supporters of Winckelmann's projects and a major correspondent for many years. For scholars who would like to follow up on the connections of the Fuseli family and Winckelmann, it is interesting to note that Hans Füssli, Henry Fuseli's cousin, was involved in editing and translating into German Daniel Webb's *An Inquiry into the Beauties of Painting* (1760), which became influential for Winckelmann's Hellenism. See Davis, pp. 74–5, on this. For Fuseli Sr's support of Winckelmann, see his work on Rome.

[30] It did not help that by the time Fuseli was finished with his Winckelmann translation, another translation into English had also been published. Fuseli suspected that Winckelmann had known about this rival project without informing him about it, and their relation cooled considerably.

[31] Knowles, p. 2: 13. Rather famous at the time, Anton Raphael Mengs was for many years a close friend of Winckelmann, but the two fell out in 1766, and Fuseli evidently thought he had to take sides.

The Nightmare. In this sense, Fuseli's choice of text is really puzzling. What is going
on here—that a painter, so committed to exploring the depth of the grotesque,
unconscious, and subversive, decides to translate a neoclassical treatise that celebrates 'noble simplicity and sedate grandeur'?[32] Behind this mismatch lies a deep
tension that scholarship has missed because it has not regarded Fuseli in a comparative context.[33] We need to pay attention not just to the fact that Fuseli translated Winckelmann but also to the way he did it. Once we have a detailed look at
his practice, we discover that Fuseli makes his intellectual struggle with the text
part of his translation. In other words, he makes the *Reflections*—nominally the
space of celebrating Anglo-German neoclassicism—the locus for illustrating the
intellectual difficulties and contradictions of eighteenth-century aesthetic theory.
Fuseli, in his practice of translation, performs the tensions and difficulties between
two contrary ways of looking at art.

Winckelmann tried to follow his own mantra of 'noble simplicity' in his prose
and criticism. In his translation, Fuseli often transforms Winckelmann's measured
tone and vocabulary into shrill and extreme statements. What Fuseli does is beyond
what Eudo C. Mason calls 'translation as increase'.[34] Fuseli changes not only the
content but also its performative element when it comes to expressive form. For
instance, Winckelmann writes, 'Da nur...das Viele und Handgreifliche...schlaffe
Sinne und einen stumpfen Verstand beschäftigt'.[35] We might translate this as
'Because only the many and the immediate engage limp senses and a blunted
mind'. Fuseli, instead, writes, '[W]hile the dashing quack tickles only feeble senses
and callous organ'.[36] The most remarkable transition here is from blunted mind
('stumpfen Verstand') to 'callous organ'. In Winckelmann the intellectual power
might be dulled, but it is still visible as a mental faculty: 'Verstand' is 'ratio'. In
Fuseli's translation this power loses its distinctively intellectual character and
becomes a 'callous organ', an ethically objectionable entity. The contrast is between
the real artist and the 'dashing quack' who 'tickles' the 'feeble sense'—that is, an
impostor who is only interested in theatre, in spectacle for the lowest senses.
Changes like these are persistently repeated, especially when it comes to the
descriptions of the artist's mental faculties.[37] It is almost as if Fuseli wanted to
'improve' Winckelmann's prose, to shape his argument for the London context by
making it less measured and less neoclassical in argument and tone.

[32] Johann Joachim Winckelmann, *Reflections on the Painting and Sculpture of the Greeks: With Instructions for the Connoisseur, and an Essay on Grace in Works of Art*, trans. Fuseli, 2nd ed. (London: printed for A. Millar and T. Cadell, 1767), p. 30.
[33] Of course, there are other ways to read this tension: for instance, as the unconscious, suppressed flip-side of Fuseli's *The Nightmare*.
[34] 'Übersetzung als Steigerung', (Eudo C. Mason, 'Heinrich Füßli und Winckelmann', in *Unterscheidung und Bewahrung: Festschrift für Hermann Kunisch zum 60. Geburtstag 27. Oktober 1961*, ed. Klaus Lazarovicz and Wolfgang Kron (Berlin: De Gruyter, 1961), pp. 232–58, 249.
[35] Winckelmann, *Ausgewählte Schriften* (Berlin: Hofenberg, 2014), p. 32.
[36] Winckelmann, *Reflections*, p. 254. We might also note that this passage is one that Fuseli adds under the heading 'Instructions for the Connoisseur', but that Winckelmann's original 'Erinnerung über die Betrachtungen der Werke der Kunst' is separate from the standard *Gedanken*.
[37] In some cases, Fuseli even adds to Winckelmann's text. On Fuseli, classicism, and drama, see Andrei Pop, 'Henry Fuseli: Greek Tragedy and Cultural Pluralism', *Art Bulletin* 44, 1 (March 2012): 78–98.

The easiest conclusion would, of course, be to simply admonish Fuseli for being a lousy or misguided translator and move on. But there is something more interesting going on in this Anglo-German exchange—precisely because Fuseli is by no means naive about the role of the translator as cultural communicator and how his or her procedure has a larger significance. He makes gratuitously misogynistic comments on Friedrich Gottlieb Klopstock's female translators into English, for instance, in which he complains how the female translators are belittling the male genius through their faulty transpositions. This is a good, albeit very unpleasant, example that Fuseli is very aware of the link between the stylistic and the ethical responsibilities of a translator, including his own.

In Fuseli's distorting practice there is a desire to produce an aesthetics of tension and contradiction that will become part of the larger discussions on aesthetics in Britain. The treatise on classicism is shot through with the language of excess and exaggeration that in itself formally breaks with the theory it supposedly advances. His contradictory rendering of Winckelmann's tone is a recreation of his own aesthetic preference as it relates to the principles of classicism and the tension between control and excess that we find throughout his visual art. There is an active, performative element to Fuseli's work here that helps to shape the Anglo-German intellectual context in Britain and beyond. It becomes a context that begins to include polemical and excessive positions, many of which directly interfere in contemporary discussions on aesthetics and politics. Eighteenth-century Anglo-German authors such as Fuseli begin, in other words, to play an active role in contemporary British radical discourses.

The best example of Fuseli's participation in the political dimension of the polyglot Anglo-German context of those years is his essay *Remarks on the Writings and Conduct of J. J. Rousseau* (1767), published by Joseph Johnson.[38] The essay is a shrill, polemic defence of Rousseau and shows Fuseli's direct engagement with the discursive European intellectual and artistic landscape involving Hume, Rousseau, Cowper, and Hamann. The idiosyncratic piece—combining theatrical positioning, close reading, intertextual quotations, and dazzling rhetoric—is a vehemently political essay. Fuseli ventriloquizes Rousseau on 'the despotic system of moralists, built by reason and inhabited by passions—the parental, the domestic, the civil relations of *social* man, with their train of sentiments and refinements'.[39] As the role of reason comes under attack here, so do the normative concepts it can produce. Fuseli produces an extraordinary critique of ideological construction of central philosophical pillars: 'Truth has been—and is—the destroyer of peace—and the parent of revolution'; it is 'owing to the same itch of propagating truth, that America is made a slaughterhouse—and Africa a stable'.[40] Fuseli engages in not a defence of relativism but, rather, a theatrical enactment where such a philosophical

---

[38] As I mentioned before, Fuseli was friends with Joseph Johnson, who was instrumental in publishing Fuseli alongside John Thelwall and Joseph Priestley. Fuseli at one point sent his mentors Johann Jakob Bodmer and Johann Caspar Lavater material by Priestley, so there is a clear sense in which these transmissions had a political dimension.

[39] Fuseli, *Remarks* (1767), p. 22; emphasis in original.

[40] Fuseli, *Remarks* (1767), sig. b1r and b2v.

position might lead us. The role of reason and its political abuse through ideological structures stand at the very centre of Fuseli's concern and his intervention in the political landscape that surrounds him.

The *Remarks* are a deeply complicated and unique text whose forceful rhetoric and political argument put Fuseli at the centre of discussions on abolition during this period. As a result, we need to complement the postcolonial readings of Fuseli's practice as a painter by examining his written work, too, and the way he draws on poetry and literature to make his political points.[41] In the *Remarks*, for instance, he discusses Thomas Southerne's dramatic adaptation of Aphra Behn's *Oroonoko*. Fuseli argues that Southerne's text reverses the powerful abolitionist message of Behn's original work and turns it into an ideologically complicit drama that ends up, against its own will, presenting slavery as an undesirable but ultimately necessary evil. He ventriloquizes an anti-abolitionist, linking him with the playwright:

> Slave-trade is legal, for we must have sugar. To this principle *Southern* [*sic*] sacrificed the laws of nature, conscience, and the truth he had set out with; nay to authorise inhumanity, lodged in the very sufferer's mouth a sentence which, but for its absurdity, must have branded our religion with the abhorrence of reason.[42]

According to Fuseli, Southerne, in the process of adaptation, loses the core principle of the original text, the 'truth he had set out with'. That truth is not only that slavery is undesirable, but also that it is unnatural because the 'laws of nature' show men to be equal. Fuseli argues that Southerne's adaptation veers away from Behn's text and thereby sacrifices its core message.[43] In one crucial change, Southerne's play shows how the slaves turn against each other. According to Fuseli's reading we can detect Southerne's authorial blessing of this perverse position thus 'authoris[ing] inhumanity, lodged in the very sufferer's mouth'. Southerne turns Behn's text on its head. Fuseli's essay is his way of calling out Southerne's and literature's complicit role in perpetuating anti-abolitionist attitudes.

The fact that Fuseli publishes a piece of literary criticism in order to make this point about abolition is important. It tells us that there is an active political awareness in the Anglo-German context at the time and that Fuseli's writing is a loud and unique voice in these discussions. Lastly, there is a formal point to consider.

It is no accident that Fuseli picks the example of literary adaptation to make his ideological point. His analysis of Behn and Southerne is not just about this particular moment of cultural transmission, but also, on a larger scale, about the care we have to take when we engage in translation, adaptation, and adoption. Literature is powerful and effective in cementing ideological positions, and critics need to be

[41] For a postcolonial reading of Fuseli, see Angela Rosenthal, 'Bad Dreams: Race and the *Nightmare* of 1781', in *Representation and Performance in the Eighteenth Century*, ed. Peter Wagner and Frédéric Ogée, Landau Paris Studies on the Eighteenth Century 1 (Trier, Ger.: Wissenschaftlicher Verlag, 2006), pp. 97–126.

[42] Fuseli, *Remarks* (1767), pp. 75–6n; emphasis in original.

[43] On the complicated relation between Fuseli, William Cowper, and Thomas Southerne, see Rosenthal, pp. 118–19. Fuseli's reading of Southerne's play is in many ways much harsher than later postcolonial readings, for instance in Srinivas Aravamudan, *Tropicopolitans: Colonialism and Agency, 1688–1804* (Durham/London: Duke University Press, 1999), pp. 49–59.

attuned to that. As a translator and transmitter, Fuseli points out the ethical responsibilities that authors have when dealing with literary texts. This is particularly important in an age of increased dissemination and communication across languages. Fuseli's political ideas thus link directly back to his activity as a translator between national traditions.[44]

The initial cause for the writing of the *Remarks* was the Hume–Rousseau controversy, a falling-out that was publicized and discussed across all of Europe and that resulted in the eventual end of the friendship between the two thinkers after Hume had brought Rousseau to England. Fuseli's essay was part of the innumerable publications that discussed the affair in a wider, European context. A good example of this wider European dimension is that back in Königsberg, Hamann reviewed Fuseli's *Remarks* soon after their publication.[45] Hamann openly positions the essay in a European literary context, musing that the essay's style 'does not make the conjecture unlikely to recognise as their author the famous Sterne, that spiritual Rabelais of England'.[46] Hamann very consciously situates the *Remarks* (and his own review) in a larger intellectual landscape that is defined by 'biting and accurate'

[44] Intriguingly, Fuseli had met both Aphra Behn and Southerne in person while they were on their way to London, illustrating once more how interwoven intellectual culture was during the period. The fact that Fuseli uses the example of transmission, and its shortcomings, for an ideological and political critique of his own surroundings reflects back not only on the immediate catalyst of the *Remarks* but also on the larger context of the public intellectual sphere that the *Remarks* form a part of and intervene in politically. For a lively and informed account of this debate, see Robert Zaretsky and John T. Scott, *The Philosophers' Quarrel: Rousseau, Hume, and the Limits of Understanding* (New Haven, CT: Yale University Press, 2009).

[45] See Federmann, p. 117. In relation to Hamann's review, see Rudolf Unger's still indispensable *Hamann und die Aufklärung: Studien zur Vorgeschichte des Romantischen*, 2 vols (Jena: Eugen Diederichs, 1911). Unger follows in the steps of earlier reviews when he calls Hamann's review of Fuseli an 'unformed excerpt' (unförmlicher Auszug) yet also describes it as a 'relatively comprehensive analysis' (ziemlich umfänglichen Analyse) of the essay that 'is alleged to have Sterne as its author' (Sterne zum Verfasser haben soll) (1:397). Unger's criticism that Hamann writes something unshapely and 'unformed' puts Hamann and Fuseli in a revealing relation here. Unger's judgement probably stems from the fact that he considers Hamann's review only relevant insofar as it shows Hamann's developing engagement with Rousseau. Hamann is familiar with Rousseau from 'around the middle of the fifties' (etwa gegen die Mitte der fünfziger Jahre) and invokes his name in a 1759 letter to Immanuel Kant (1: 340). In an inverse moment to Fuseli, Hamann's view of Rousseau alters from initial hostility to a more sympathetic treatment. According to Unger, Hamann is highly critical of Rousseau's work, at least until the early 1760s. Hamann senses a secularist or deist undertone in all writings of Rousseau, and thus Unger cites Hamann's remarks against the *Contrat*—namely that it is a work full of 'bitterness against religion' (Bitterkeiten gegen die Religion)—as a representative example (1: 341). For Unger, the review of the *Essay* is a sign that Hamann's position on Rousseau is slightly shifting, since he decides to review, in a fairly positive manner, a piece of writing on Rousseau's work and conduct that is generally favourable. This is noteworthy, especially since one of the main specific contexts of the *Essay* is the quarrel between Rousseau and David Hume, the latter a long-standing idol of Hamann. However, it seems to me that Hamann is here not primarily interested in figuring out his relation to Rousseau (or to Hume, for that matter); rather, his concern is how to play with the different layers of the preface and the review. It interests him to figure out how they raise two concerns that are central to his thinking—namely, style and ethics. The 'unshapely' character of Hamann's review stems more from engaging with the rhapsodic part of the original essay than from his awkward position as a critic. It does also give us a chance to see how Hamann attempts to engage with Fuseli's thought.

[46] '[D]ie Vermuthung nicht unwahrscheinlich macht, den berühmten Sterne, diesen geistlichen Rabelais Englands, für ihren Urheber zu erkennen' (N, 4: 311). Also see Ernst Wirz, the only person other than Mason to have written extensively on the *Remarks* (Wirz, *Die literarische Tätigkeit des*

wit, and in which he himself is a major player.[47] Once more, Hamann's constant interest in English publications led him to read and review Fuseli, again without knowing his identity. The exchange of ideas also crossed the Channel the other way, of course. Bodmer, Fuseli's teacher, was familiar with Hamann, and it seems likely that Fuseli read some Hamann before he went to London.[48] These are European conversations, not national ones. Hume kept tabs on who was saying what in this dispute throughout Europe. He himself read Fuseli's *Remarks* only four days after it was published, commenting sceptically that 'it is said to be the work of Dr. Sterne; but it exceeds even the usual extravagance of that gentleman's productions'.[49] Hume's remark reinforces two things: that Fuseli's writing is stylistically unusual and that, despite these idiosyncrasies, his writings still form part of public discourse. His comment about the 'extravagance' of the *Remarks* is typical for the reception of Fuseli's essay both in England and in Germany. In Britain, one of the reviews in *The Gentleman's Magazine* (1767) terms it a 'rhapsody'.[50] Godwin

Malers Johann Heinrich Fussli (Henry Fuseli): Ein Beitrag zu den Englisch-Schweizerischen Beziehungen und zur Aesthetik des 18. Jahrhunderts (Basel, 1922)).

[47] '[B]eißenden und treffenden Witz' (N, 4: 311).

[48] In a 1762 letter to his friend and colleague Johann Georg Sulzer, Fuseli comments on the heated discussions between Hamann and Christoph Friedrich Nicolai: 'Who has made the *Notes on the Uses of Art Critics*, the *Socratic Memorabilia* and *The Clouds*? He has shattered Nicolai' (Wer hat die 'Anmerkungen zum Gebrauch der Kunstrichter', die 'Sokratischen Denkwürdigkeiten' und 'Die Wolken' gemacht? Er hat den Nicolai zerschmettert) (qtd in Federmann, p. 21). Bodmer also writes to Fuseli in 1763 on the *Aesthetica in Nuce*, misattributing the text to Gellius, though this misunderstanding was later resolved: 'Naumann said that this Gellius wrote the Aesthetica in a Nut' (Naumann...sagte dieser Gellius habe die Ästhetik in der Nuß geschrieben) (qtd in Stähli, ' "Wäre es Ihnen gleichgültig" ', p. 714). There is almost no scholarly work that has examined the links between Fuseli and Hamann. For an exception, see Federmann, pp. 21 and 29.

[49] David Hume, *New Letters of David Hume*, ed. Raymond Klibansky and Ernest C. Mossner (Oxford: Clarendon, 1954), p. 160. Later on that year, Hume mentions that he now knows it was written by Fuseli (see Hume, *The Letters of David Hume*, ed. J. Y. T. Greig, 2 vols [Oxford: Oxford University Press, 1932], 2: 136).
Hume's reference to Laurence Sterne is interesting on several levels. First, it suggests that there is a clear overlap between literary and philosophical culture. Sterne is somebody whom Hume expects to intervene. Second, and somewhat in tension to the first point, the stylistic dimension of writing is very important. Hume believes that Sterne wrote the *Remarks* because the style is so unusual and extravagant. Interestingly, the false link between Sterne and Fuseli is repeated many times in the reception of the *Remarks*. Hamann echoes the view, and John Armstrong's discussion of the *Remarks* in the *Monthly Review* is one of many examples that describe how the author has a manner that is 'somewhat of the SHANDYAN stamp, which is not remarkable for delicacy' (Armstrong, '*Remarks on the Writings and Conduct of J. J. Rousseau*', *Monthly Review* 36 [June 1767]: 459–63, 459). As I say, the misattribution of Fuseli's essay was not uncommon, sometimes maybe even encouraged: in a letter to Bodmer, Fuseli happily mentions that '[h]ere [in London] they [the Remarks] were Sterne's, Smollett's and Armstrong's' (Hier waren sie Sternes, Smolletts und Armstrongs). Fuseli, *Remarks on the Writings and Conduct of J.J. Rousseau/Bemerkungen über J.J. Rousseaus Schriften und Verhalten*, ed. and trans. Eudo Mason (Zurich: Fretz and Wasmuth, 1962), p. 45. Mason does not give a source for this quotation. Fuseli actually had met Sterne, as well as Tobias Smollett. Ironically, on the one hand, according to Knowles, when Fuseli met Sterne he [Fuseli] was 'miserably disappointed, as nothing then seemed to please him [Sterne] but talking obscenely' (Knowles, 1: 373). On the other hand, he formed 'close and lasting friendships with Armstrong the poet, with the liberal booksellers and publishers Millar, Cadell and Joseph Johnson, with the kindly banker Coutts and others' (Eudo Mason, *The Mind of Henry Fuseli: Selections from His Writings with an Introductory Study* [London: Routledge and Kegan Paul, 1951], p. 16).

[50] *The Gentleman's Magazine*, June 1767, p. 318. Overall, the few independent British reviews of Fuseli's essay are pretty damning. While there is a seeming balance of three negative and three positive

writes similarly that it is 'wild, scarcely English, and scarcely common-sense, yet with some striking things interspersed'.[51] Even Mason, the modern editor of the *Remarks*, concludes that 'the decisive thing was that the book is linguistically impossible.... [F]ar too many times he [Fuseli] derails into the involuntarily eccentric, into the pedantic, unclear, incomprehensible, grotesque'.[52] Mason insists on the lack of control that 'derails' the train of argument from its proper path and direction. It becomes a train wreck of an argument, a grotesque accident that is impossible to comprehend because it does not adhere to particular kinds of norms.

Of course, we have heard precisely these kinds of complaints about Blake and Hamann already. In the case of Fuseli, however, his written work did not end up being domesticated into his larger body of work, but was ignored instead. As his Anglo-German translations and strange writings amply demonstrate, he is much more than a British painter. Fuseli's unique voice was part of a lively field of Anglo-German authors, in and outside of London. His works were read in a European context that registered what some Anglo-German writers in eighteenth-century London produced. Some of these writings were canonical; others were much more radical. It would be a mistake to claim that they became central—following the temptation to move Fuseli from the margins to the centre—but that does not mean that they are not important. They had an impact. The *Remarks* in particular show Fuseli as part of the exorbitant constellation that emerges out of the wider Anglo-German context.

'EVEN SPIRITUAL THINGS': HAMANN TRANSLATING HUME

Hamann's links with Britain are ample, varied, and complicated, going much further than the philosophical connections with Blake. He was not only a lifelong Anglophile, but he also had strong personal ties to London. His many important translations of British materials into German—such as Hume, Berkeley, Shaftesbury, or Samuel Johnson—are the most obvious sign of his investment in British culture.

reviews, Mason points out that the latter ones were either written anonymously by Fuseli's friends or, in one instance, by himself (also anonymously). On this, see Mason, *Mind of Henry Fuseli*, pp. 43–8. In addition to the *The Gentleman's Magazine* (June 1767), reviews also appear in the *London Magazine* (June 1767) and the *Political Register and Impartial Review of New Books* (May 1767). The reviewer in the *Political Register*, after reading Fuseli's self-review, returns for a further damning retort. Positive reviews can be found in *Universal Museum* (April 1767), *Monthly Review* (June 1767), and *Critical Review* (May 1767).

[51] Charles Kegan Paul, *William Godwin: His Friends and Contemporaries*, 2 vols (London: King, 1878), 2: 298. As we know, Mary Wollstonecraft, Godwin's wife, had fallen in love with Fuseli in the 1780s. By the time Godwin wrote to Knowles, Wollstonecraft had been dead for a while.

Wollstonecraft was, of course, also a translator from German into English in her own right. In 1790, she translated Christian Gotthilf Salzmann's work as *Elements of Morality for the Use of Children*, which was published by Joseph Johnson. According to Godwin's *Memoirs*, Salzmann in turn translated the *Vindication of the Rights of Woman* into German (1798).

[52] 'Das Entscheidende war, daß das Buch sprachlich unmöglich ist. ... [V]iel zu oft entgleist er ins unwillkürlich Verschrobene, ins Pedantische, Unklare, Unverständliche, Groteske' (Fuseli, *Remarks* (1962), p. 47).

We have already seen that he was on top of the British publishing scene, discussing many of the London publications immediately after their appearance and translating widely. To what degree all of this matters for the wider intellectual context of Anglo-German relations is easily demonstrated: there is much evidence to suggest that Hamann translated the passages of Hume's *Treatise of Human Nature* that awoke Kant from his dogmatic slumber and led him to write the *Critique of Pure Reason*, changing things utterly across Europe and Britain.[53] But his influence is not only a matter of intellectual history; Hamann's translations of British sources also affect literary history, too, since he managed to underwrite these translations with claims about their literary–historical status. As I will show, for instance, Hamann's translations of Hume allow us to reconsider the status of Edward Young. There are, thus, philosophical and poetical dimensions to these translations that are important across the Anglo-German spectrum.

Just as with Fuseli, Hamann's Anglomania has strong biographical roots. It was during his 1757–58 visit to London that he had the most consequential experience of his life, what is commonly referred to as his key experience (*Schlüsselerlebnis*). In the early 1750s, Hamann, already a friend of Kant, his fellow Königsbergian, was an increasingly important presence in the Enlightenment circles that were forming in East Prussia.[54] A prodigy, albeit an ill-disciplined one with a scattered education, it was clear that he was going to be a major intellectual player. All this changed abruptly with his trip to London. Hamann was struggling professionally, and the Riga businessman Christoph Berens—later the joint addressee of Hamann's *Socratic Memorabilia*—offered to send Hamann on a mission to London, most likely to put in order some business affairs on behalf of the Berens company. Hamann accepted and travelled from Riga to Königsberg, Berlin, Lübeck, Hamburg, and

---

[53] Although Kant's remark that Hume awoke him from his dogmatic slumber has become commonplace, it is not widely known (or asked) where Kant actually got his Hume from. This would seem important, especially since Kant did not read English. It turns out that one of the most important early mediations of Hume for Kant came through Hamann. His letters to Kant discuss (and translate) Hume extensively, and Kant repeatedly borrowed Hamann's unpublished translation of Hume. Crucially, Kant asked Hamann for a copy of the *Dialogues* at the precise moment he was finishing the last draft of the *Critique of Pure Reason* and changed several parts of his work after reading them. As late as 1802, Kant suggests that Hamann's translation should be published (see Kant, *Sämtliche Werke*, ed. Karl Rosenkranz and F. W. Schubert, 12 vols [Leipzig, 1838–42], 11: 165). As Günter Gawlick and Lothar Kreimendahl convincingly show, Hamann's translation of the *Treatise of Human Nature* chapter was also crucial in Kant's engagement with Hume, directly influencing the composition of the first *Critique* (see Gawlick and Kreimendahl, *Hume in der deutschen Aufklärung*, pp. 189–98). Consider, then, that it is possible and probable that Hamann (the polyglot Magus of the North) helped Kant (the monolingual chief Enlightener) to wake from his dogmatic slumbers. It is only fitting that this help comes through translation, that it concerns language, the topic of central disagreement between Hamann and Kant. See Gawlick and Kreimendahl, *Hume in der deutschen Aufklärung*, pp. 36 and 183; and Thomas Brose's extensive and thorough treatment of Hume and Hamann (*Johann Georg Hamann und David Hume: Metaphysikkritik und Glaube im Spannungsfeld der Aufklärung* [Frankfurt am Main: Peter Lang, 2006]). Also see Philip Merlan, 'From Hume to Hamann', *The Personalist* 32 (1951): 11–18; and Margarete Pöttinger, 'Hamann's Humeübersetzungen' (University of Vienna, 1939), a doctoral dissertation by one of Joseph Nadler's students in Vienna.

[54] For an initial orientation, see Bernhard Gajek, ed., *Johann Georg Hamann und England: Hamann und die englischsprachige Aufklärung: Acta des Siebten Internationalen Hamann-Kolloquiums zu Marburg/Lahn 1996* (Frankfurt am Main: Peter Lang, 1999); and Gawlick and Kreimendahl, *Hume in der deutschen Aufklärung*.

Amsterdam, finally arriving in London in 1757. Some people have pointed out that Hamann was a curious choice for this task, especially because of his rather unorganized university education. However, he was already a published author on economic theory as well as fluent in English, a combination of skills that must have made him seem a good candidate. Hamann had always been interested in English and in British culture. By the time he travelled to London he had translated some writings by Shaftesbury. Karl Carvacchi makes a convincing case when he suggests in his early biographical account that Hamann had always longed for England, and that his visit to London was the fulfilment of a fantasy: 'Finally he could realise his wish to go to England, the country of his desires; the means for which were, as he says, afforded to him by the most generous funding by the Berens trading firm of Riga'.[55]

Hamann's actual stay in London, however, did not live up to his initial fantasy. His business mission failed, and he was even treated with derision by his counterparts. In *Thoughts about My Vita* (*Gedanken über Meinen Lebenslauf*), Hamann indicates that the Russian business partners he met in London seemed amused by his demands and the way he conveyed them. While there is a certain amount of self-fashioning going on here—Hamann as the odd genius, misunderstood by a simple Russian businessman—the failure of his mission touched him existentially and sent him into a major tailspin. He began to enjoy the darker sides of the British fantasy: London being what it was (and is), his new way of life meant he impoverished himself rapidly. Hamann befriended a wealthy Englishman who became his confidant and donor, sharing his food, lodging, and prostitutes with him: 'I gorged for nothing, I guzzled for nothing, I courted for nothing, I ran around for nothing; gluttony and reflection, reading and knavery, industriousness and wanton idleness, took turns for nothing'.[56] However, this road of excess ultimately led to what Hamann would maintain was his palace of wisdom: a crucial turn to the deep study of language, God, and the Bible.[57] It is not entirely clear what exact experience it was that led Hamann to his turnabout, or even if it was one, singular experience at all. Predictably, speculations invoke a possible sexual dimension, especially since he had discovered that his donor maintained homosexual relationships.[58] While it is unlikely we will ever find out exactly what happened,

[55] 'Endlich konnte er seinen Wunsch nach dem Lande seiner Sehnsucht, nach England zu gehen, ausführen, die Mittel dazu wurden ihm, wie er sagt, mit dem freigebisten Aufbringen von dem Handelshause Berens von Riga aus gewährt' (Karl Carvacchi, *Biographische Erinnerungen*, p. 13).

[56] 'Ich fraß umsonst, ich soff umsonst, ich buhlte umsonst, ich rann umsonst, Völlerey v Nachdenken, Lesen und Büberey, Fleiß und üppiger Müßiggang wurden umsonst abgewechselt' (Hamann, *Londoner Schriften*, p. 339). For an alternative translation, see Betz, *After Enlightenment*, p. 30.

[57] The contemporary reader will be tempted to hear some Heideggerian overtones in this 'turn'. However, I do not want to suggest that Heidegger borrows from Hamann in formulating his departure from *Being and Time*. On translation problems of 'Kehre' in Heidegger, see Frank Schalow, introduction to *Heidegger*, in *Translation, and the Task of Thinking: Essays in Honor of Parvis Emad*, ed. Schalow (New York: Springer, 2011), pp. 11–49, 36–7.

[58] See Hansjorg Salmony, *Johann Georg Hamanns Metakritische Philosophie* (Basel: Evangelischer Verlag Zollikon, 1958); and Wilhelm Koepp, 'Joh. Georg Hamanns Londoner Senel-Affäre Januar 1758', *Zeitschrift für Theologie und Kirche* 57 (1960): 92–108. The suggestions range from prostitution

it is certain that it changed Hamann's life profoundly. He turned from a budding, promising proponent of the Enlightenment to one of its fiercest critics.

One of the most central and innovative aspects of Hamann's thinking, which connects well with Blake's work, is his criticism of the ideological tendency to divide deep spirituality and mundane context. Thinking is never neutral but always happens in a physical context. In reviewing the London episode, many Hamann scholars have focused on his London reading, his inner life, or on the consequences of his stay for the internal structure of his work as a whole. Although these dimensions are important, there is a risk here of relegating his interaction with the concrete, specifically English context in London to a pure, textual sphere and, thereby, create the myth of Hamann as an isolated figure whose dramatic experience happened in a vacuum. Yet Hamann breathed London air during this time of change, he sought out English and German human company, bought goods and Bibles from actual people, and experienced his spiritual turn as a concretely lived experience in a particular daily context. Hamann lived in an area of London that was polyglot, teeming with a European presence which he must have noticed every day. The fact that he sought out the German-speaking Moravian congregation in London during that time gives us a clear sense of how this big shift in his personal conviction was enmeshed in that international context.[59]

Hamann was keenly aware of the intellectual and affective importance of one's immediate, empirical, and sensuous surroundings. After his initial crisis, he needed a place that was more conducive to his spiritual study, and thus he took new quarters. On 8 February 1758, he became a lodger of a certain 'Mr Collins' in 'Marlborough Street'.[60] That means that in 1758 Hamann lived about three

---

to Hamann's own possible bisexuality or his homosexual experiences. Given that Hamann never regarded sexuality as something negative, these readings may be viewed as a little overdetermined.

[59] I discuss Hamann's Moravian connections in detail in Chapter 4.

[60] It is a sign of how difficult it is to get a clear sense of the actual physical context of Hamann's deep change that even Jörg-Ulrich Fechner, whose account of Hamann's London visit is the most important and comprehensive in Hamann scholarship, makes what seems to be a rare mistake when he describes the location of Hamann's new home as 'a small parallel street to Blackfriars' Road, not far from Blackfriars' Bridge on the south bank of the Thames' (eine kleine Parallelstraße zur Blackfriars' Road, nicht weit von der Blackfriars' Bridge auf dem Südufer der Themse) (Fechner, 'Philologische Einfälle und Zweifel zu Hamanns Londoner Aufenthalt: Die "Senel-Affaire" und die "Generalbeichte"', in *Johann Georg Hamann: Acta des Internationalen Hamann-Colloquiums in Lüneburg 1976* [Frankfurt: Klostermann, 1979], pp. 5–11, 13).

As far as I can ascertain, there was no Marlborough Street south of the river until much later in the nineteenth century. The first Thames crossing at Blackfriars was Old London Bridge, not Blackfriars. The houses on this bridge were demolished in 1758, the year Hamann was in London. Old London Bridge remained a thoroughfare until 1831, when a new crossing that had been built alongside it was finished and used exclusively. This new bridge—constructed in 1760, opened to the public in 1769—was first called William Pitt Bridge but became commonly known as Blackfriars. It was in existence until the mid-1800s, after which it was replaced with a new one on the same site, the present Blackfriars Bridge, opened by Queen Victoria in 1869. The standard map and street index for the time, John Rocque's 1746 *A Plan of the Cities of London and Westminster, and Borough of Southwark*, bears this out. Of course, what did exist were Great Marlborough Street, Little Marlborough Street, Marlborough Court, Marlborough House, Marlborough Market, Marlborough Mews, and Marlborough Row.

Unless it was built in the decade following Rocque's map and then destroyed again, it is unlikely that there was a place called Marlborough Street in London in 1758. And while the Electoral Rolls for the area during this period are inconclusive, I think what Hamann is doing is using an imprecise

blocks away from the house in which Blake was born the same year—a suggestive coincidence.[61] It was very much in the geographic orbit of the Anglo-German community, their book shops, congregations and churches, and it was also the neighbourhood in which Catherine Blake weaned her son and no doubt sang the Anglo-German hymns she had learned in the Moravian church at Fetter Lane.

It was also in this concrete, particular context in Moravian London that Hamann turned to Scripture, an act that has an Anglo-German dimension. As Jörg-Ulrich Fechner has pointed out, when Hamann started reading the Bible in London, he most likely used an English King James Version (KJV).[62] That means that the first time Hamann encountered God's word as the most important shaping force in the world it was not in his native tongue. It was through a moment of translation. That would immediately lead him to a comparative reading of the KJV with a *Lutherbibel*, a copy of which he would have obtained via the German booksellers that existed in London. Again, the specificity of these details would have held philosophical significance for Hamann, and we should consider them, too.

For a thinker for whom language turns out to be the most important and powerful form of understanding, knowledge, and ethics, and for whom the word of God is not just a metaphor, it makes a difference in which language he first encounters the story of Babel about the fragmentation of languages or truly understands the sentence: 'In the beginning was the Word, and the Word was with God, and the Word was God'. Reading these passages in English and German, being in London, the multilingual city of Hamann's dreams and nightmares, surrounded by different voices and languages, made this a concrete experience that was not only linguistically complex and spiritually soothing, but also deeply confusing. In this pregnant context, Hamann makes the following note as part of his biblical study: 'The confusion of language is a history, a phaenomeon, a continuing miracle, and a parable, through which God still continues to speak to us'.[63] So, when Hamann

---

abbreviation that is still in use today: he is most likely speaking of Great Marlborough Street or adjacent Little Marlborough Street, both of them in Soho.

Today, there is a Marlborough Street, located in Kensington, south of Hyde Park. Beck, in his notes to *Biblische Betrachtungen*, believes this to be the place Hamann moved to, suggesting that Hamann 'really pilgrimed through the whole city' (Hamann, *Londoner Schriften*, p. 528n7). This seems to me unlikely, since in the 1750s this area of London was hardly developed at all, and from all the maps that are available it looks as though this Marlborough Street was a much later creation.

[61] On the significance of William Blake's residences, see Steven Goldsmith, *Blake's Agitation: Criticism and the Emotions* (Baltimore, MD: Johns Hopkins University Press, 2013), pp. 100–12.

[62] As Fechner points out convincingly, Hamann most likely used an Oxford octavo print from 1755 that remained in his library: 'It was an edition published by T. Baskett, which, according to English tradition, combined the text of the authorized King James Version with the Book of Common Prayer' (Es handelt sich um eine bei T. Baskett erschienene Ausgabe, die nach englischer Tradition den Text der 'Authorized' oder 'King James Version' von 1611 mit dem Abdruck des 'Common Prayer Book' verbindet) (Fechner, p. 4). Also see Sven-Aage Jørgensen, *Querdenker der Aufklärung: Studien zu Johann Georg Hamann* (Göttingen: Wallstein, 2013). For the comparison between English and German Bibles, see Helgo Lindner, 'Hamann als Leser der englischen Bibel: Beobachtungen zu den neuedierten Londoner Schriften', in *Johann Georg Hamann und die englischsprachige Aufklärung*, pp. 17–40.

[63] 'Die Verwirrung der Sprache ist eine Geschichte, ein *Phaenomeon*, ein fortdauerndes Wunder, und ein Gleichnis, wodurch Gott noch immer fortfährt mit uns zu reden' (Hamann, *Londoner Schriften*, p. 282; italics in original).

translates Shaftesbury's philosophy, Samuel Johnson's literary commentary, or James Hervey's theological views, such transmissions between the Anglophone and the German worlds are conscious efforts to contribute to this 'phaenomeon'.[64]

Even more than with Fuseli, the larger historical and conceptual contexts for Hamann's translations are important here. His 1757 visit to London not only resulted in his rejection of a Kantian Enlightenment but also was the beginning of Hamann's activity as a translator in earnest, who rejoiced in the multiplicity of languages and their philosophic-poetical potential. In the midst of London's babble, Hamann became convinced that linguistic variation could be understood as a celebration of the multiple forms of the divine. God speaks to us through all the languages of humankind. We might have inherited a fallen, Babelian language, but there is still grace within each of these languages. Hamann understood his own translation, too, as carrying this deep ambivalence. In a letter to Herder, he speaks about his own plans for biblical translations—begun in London, while reading the KJV and making German notes—as 'faithful and free'.[65] Hamann's formulation combines the traditionally contrary ideas of the translator: it is faithful to the letter but also 'free', attuned to the spirit of what is being said. The phrase makes unmistakably clear that Hamann was trying to separate himself from the 'usual...categorizations of contemporary translation theory', many of which are still in place today.[66]

Hamann wants to escape the traditional and limited dichotomies of translation ('free' versus 'literal') not least because for him translation encompasses everything: 'Speaking is translation from a tongue of angels into a human tongue, that is, thoughts in words—things in names—images in signs'.[67] As we know, for Hamann, language and translation are defined through their poetic and spiritual potential, not their utility. Multilingualism is not just a skill to have for, say, a business trip to London. More importantly, it is theologically relevant since

> the learning of foreign languages should be used as an aid to understand the mother tongue better, to become fruitful in thoughts, to dissect them, to hold their signs against one another, to recognise the difference between them; in short, it should be used to help us understand what looks like merely the work of memorisation, as a preparation and practice of all the strengths of our soul, and higher, more important, more difficult, even spiritual things.[68]

---

[64] For further sources see Andre Rudolph, *Figuren der Ähnlichkeit: Johann Georg Hamanns Analogiedenken im Kontext des 18. Jahrhunderts* (Tübingen: Niemeyer, 2006), especially the section 'Die Londoner Schriften und ihre britischen Quellen' (pp. 103–23). Also see Hans Graubner, ' "Gott selbst sagt: Ich schaffe das Böse": Der Theodizee-Entwurf des jungen Hamann in der Auseinandersetzung mit Hume, Sulzer, Shuckford und Hervey', in *Johann Georg Hamann: Religion und Gesellschaft*, ed. Manfred Beetz and Andre Rudolph (Berlin: De Gruyter, 2012), pp. 255–91.

[65] '[T]reu und frey' (ZH, 3: 76).

[66] '[G]ängigen Kategorisierungen der zeitgenössischen Übersetzungstheorie' (Kai Hendrik Patri, 'Aus einer Menschensprache in eine Menschensprache: Zu Johann Georg Hamanns Hume-Übersetzungen', in Gajek, *Johann Georg Hamann und England*, pp. 319–65, p. 331).

[67] 'Reden ist übersetzen—aus einer Engelssprache in eine Menschensprache, das heist, Gedanken in Worte,—Sachen in Namen,—Bilder in Zeichen' (N, 2: 199).

[68] 'So sollte die Erlernung der fremden Sprachen als ein Hülfsmittel die Muttersprache besser zu verstehen, an Gedanken fruchtbar zu werden, selbige zu zergliedern, die Zeichen derselben gegen

Learning and talking other languages allows communication, critique, and a better understanding of what language can do, including the formation of a space that is predicated on the 'learning of foreign languages'. Multilingualism is dialectical: it helps to think in a new form, but it also defamiliarizes the common, showing it to be conceptually significant. Hamann suggests that defamiliarization helps one to detect empty phrases or linguistic laziness. Accepting the gift of languages by learning their diversity prepares us for 'even spiritual things', a quality of multilingualism that is not motivated by instrumentality. For Hamann, this abstract theological argument was formed in the concrete experience of the polyglot community in eighteenth-century London.

Once this larger context is set, it becomes clear that Hamann translated Hume in order 'to understand' his own 'mother tongue better'. These translations are part of what Günther Gawlick charts in his reception history of Hume in England and what Charles Swain describes as Hamann's deep familiarity with Hume's thought, which 'was lifelong, thorough, and penetrating'.[69] Especially since Hamann insists on the importance of a wider historical context—'Without Berkeley, no Hume', he quips—his extensive translations of Hume gain a special status.[70] There is little debate that Hume's peculiar form of sceptical empiricism is one of the most formative influences for Hamann, especially when it comes to his critical assessment of rationalist and Kantian philosophy. The relation between Hamann and Hume, and the wider networks of which they are a part, is a good example of the profound impact British philosophy made on German intellectual history, bringing the two ever closer together.[71] One of the most powerful aspects of Hume's thinking for Hamann is that it shows the weak basis of what is commonly thought of as the self-evidently rational foundation of our thinking. Hume's scepticism dislodged the primacy of reason, a key moment for a thinker such as Hamann, for whom philosophy's idealization of reason had turned into idolatry. Hume's powerful suggestion that central philosophical assumptions that govern our daily lives are based on what we might call 'natural beliefs' (rather than rationally justifiable assumptions) was an invitation for Hamann to think about the nature of belief itself and its link to reason. Belief takes the place of rationality when rational thought cannot provide its own grounding. This is not just a theoretical argument; it is also at the heart of an experience such as Hamann's in London and his subsequent loss of faith in reason as a guiding principle. In the end, as Frederick C. Beiser puts it, the 'only way to discover the forms of reason, Hamann implies, is through the

---

einander zu halten, den Unterschied derselben zu bemerken, kurz, was ein bloßes Gedächtniswerk zu seyn scheint, eine Vorbereitung und Uebung aller Seelenkräfte und höherer, wichtigerer, schwererer, ja geistlicher Dinge gebraucht werden' (N, 2: 15).

[69] See Gawlick and Kreimendahl, *Hume in der deutschen Aufklärung* 'Hamann and the Philosophy of David Hume', *Journal of the History of Philosophy* 5, 4 (1967): 343–51, 344. It is extraordinary how little of the wide and powerful scholarship on this topic has penetrated literary studies, especially since Hume is often listed as one of the most 'literary' writers of philosophy.

[70] The full context in a letter to Herder (20 April 1782) is as follows: 'This much is certain: that without Berkeley there would have been no Hume, and without the latter, no Kant' (So viel ist gewiß, daß ohne Berkeley kein Hume geworden wäre, wie ohne diesen kein Kant) (ZH, 4: 376).

[71] Here Brose, *Johann Georg Hamann und David Hume*, is a good starting point.

comparative empirical study of natural languages'.[72] The philosophical dimensions of this implication connect directly to Hamann's argument about how multiple languages help us to prepare for the translation of 'spiritual things'. Thus, translation and dissemination are ways not only to understand one's own mother tongue better, but also to understand that thinking in a mother tongue will never be purely guided by rationality.

What Blake saw as a Humean snare of scepticism, Hamann seized as a chance to expand on a notion of thought that he wanted to lead beyond both empiricist philosophy and rationalist Christianity. Hamann's deep antipathy against the latter, which he shared with Blake, led him in 1780 to begin work on a German version of Hume's *Dialogues concerning Natural Religion*.[73] The question of why Hamann would choose this particular text is relevant. On first sight, this seems an extremely odd choice. After all, the *Dialogues* are generally understood to be the final proof that Hume was either agnostic or atheist, at least at the end of his life. Why would Hamann, the devout Christian, have helped to disseminate such literature, especially in times when religious belief was under increasing pressure? The answer lies in Hamann's differentiated view of Christianity and his attachment to the structure of Hume's argument. Hamann, like Blake, would scoff at the idea of proving the existence of God, the type of argument that the *Dialogues* also rebut. But he would not scoff at the idea because God does not exist. Rather, he would ridicule the idea that human rationality could prove His existence; for Hamann that is simply a form of human vanity. The idea of religion as a rational enterprise, which lies behind the type of Deism the *Dialogues* so effectively demolish, is deeply misguided, typical of enlightened times. Just as we are not reasoned into liking a particular form of poetry, we are not reasoned into believing in God. The idea that we could be reasoned into believing in God, or even that God reveals Himself in the rationality of man, is a narcissistic hubris typical of rationalist theology.

For Hamann, the motivation behind the translation of the *Dialogues* is the power of Hume's structural anti-Deist argument, rather than the supposedly unintended consequences of that argument. As he puts it, regarding religion Hume 'falls onto the sword of his own truths', which is not something he will hold against him.[74] We might say that Hamann has a soft spot for Hume's blind spot. In a 1781 letter to Herder, Hamann states that he preferred Hume to Kant because Hume 'at least refined the principle of belief, and took it into his system'.[75] As far as Hamann is concerned, Hume risks more and is more honest, and that is

---

[72] Frederick C. Beiser, *The Fate of Reason: German Philosophy from Kant to Fichte* (Cambridge, MA: Harvard University Press, 1987), p. 43. Alongside Kant and Herder, it is important here to refer to Jacobi, whose role in the discussions about the status of reason, and Hamann's reception within those discussions, are often overlooked. See Beiser, pp. 44–126.

[73] Once more the archival story of Hamann's translation is a little complicated. Because of a rival translation, which was published slightly earlier, Hamann's work never saw the light of day. Yet, despite its ultimate abandonment, his translations still circulated widely in Königsberg and elsewhere. See N, 3: 463–4.

[74] '[S]o fällt Hume in das Schwerdt seiner eigenen Wahrheiten' (ZH, 1: 355).

[75] '[W]eil er wenigstens das Principium des Glaubens veredelt und in sein System aufgenommen' (ZH, 4: 294). Also see Swain, p. 348.

why for Hamann—even though he might disagree with some of Hume's specific conclusions—he has faith in the methods and the man himself. For Hamann, 'Hume is always my man'.[76] The relationship is not, then, as Isaiah Berlin suggests, 'a strange paradox'.[77] Rather, Hamann perceives Hume as an ally with whom he has a connection that goes beyond a constricted understanding of thought. Swain puts it well when he says that Hamann wants a 'confession' from Enlightenment that the status of reason relies, ultimately, on faith rather than on rational argument, even embracing the obvious tensions of such an argument: 'Hamann was aware of the incongruity of using the philosophy of Hume as a basis for Christian apology to the cultured despisers of religion among the enlightened'.[78] The incongruity, however, is in place only for the person who has established a particular model of communication, of believing that language itself can be controlled. For whatever the 'cultured despisers of religion among the enlightened' think, their language often gets the better of them—as in Hume's case—and they end up being of God's party without knowing it. Hamann remarks with some humour that 'I often hear the word of God with more joy in the mouth of a Pharisee, as a witness against his will, than from the mouth of an angel of light'.[79] Hume is the Scottish Pharisee who ends up revealing the power of faith without knowing it.

For Hamann, his foray into English translations within the context of Anglo-German culture is a way 'to become fruitful in thoughts, to dissect them, to hold their signs against one another, to recognise the difference between them'.[80] He pushes these possibilities through not just translation but also reviews and cultural commentary. As a result, he is aware of the tensions within the material he reads (Hume falling onto his sword) and the way such material is perceived by his contemporaries. The *Dialogues* are a good example, since they were considered such a risky proposition, and any translation would spread or maximize that risk. In a 1780 letter to his (and Kant's) publisher, Johann Friedrich Hartknoch, Hamann addresses these concerns head on: 'The dialogue is full of poetic beauties and I do not believe, as does Mr Green, the book to be dangerous, but rather I translate it'.[81] One reason the *Dialogues* are fertile is because they connect poetry and philosophy. For Hamann, poetic beauty is part of the positive power of Hume's philosophical intervention. And it is part of what makes it an important document in the increasingly transnational context of eighteenth-century philosophy. The wider point about Hamann's opposition to contemporary versions of Enlightenment thought is that he proclaims 'poetic beauties' as something to be celebrated. In order to

---

[76] 'Hume ist immer mein Mann' (ZH, 4: 294). 'Mann', of course, also means 'husband'.

[77] Isaiah Berlin, *Against the Current: Essays in the History of Ideas* (Princeton, NJ: Princeton University Press, 2013), p. 228.

[78] Swain, p. 344.

[79] Anderson, *Hegel on Hamann*, pp. 26–7. '[I]ch höre öfters mit mehr Freude das Wort Gottes im Munde eines Pharisäers, als eines Zeugen wieder seinen Willen, als aus dem Munde eines Engels des Lichts' (ZH, 1: 431).

[80] '[A]n Gedanken fruchtbar zu werden, selbige zu zergliedern, die Zeichen derselben gegen einander zu halten, den Unterschied derselben zu bemerken' (N, 2: 15).

[81] 'Der Dialog ist voller poetischen Schönheiten, und ich halte das Buch mir HE. Green, für nicht gar gefährlich, sondern übersetz es vielmehr' (ZH, 4: 205–6).

make such philosophy and its poetic beauties available across languages, Hamann translates the *Dialogues* and makes them part of the Anglo-German exchange of ideas across Europe.

These translations cut across periods, geographies, disciplines, and scholarship to this day. Once more, Hamann's translation of Hume provides a concentrated illustration of this point. In the year 1771, Hamann published in German a little essay entitled *Nachtgedanken eines Zweiflers* (*Night-Thoughts of a Sceptic*). It is a translation of the conclusion to book 1 of Hume's *Treatise*. There is a deeply philosophical and a deeply poetical dimension to this translation. The philosophical element of this passage is that Hume considers that 'since reason is incapable of dispelling these clouds [of scepticism], nature herself suffices to that purpose, and cures me of this philosophical melancholy and delirium'.[82] Hume's argument is that the primacy of reason has been dislodged, that we have been struck at the very heart of our assumptions.[83] And yet he also shows us that 'nature herself' provides the tonic by furnishing us with natural belief in, for example, causation. It is natural belief that makes life—both philosophical life and every other human action—possible. Without it we would indeed suffer a continuous 'delirium'. Hume states in the last chapter of *An Enquiry concerning Human Understanding* that 'it seems evident that men are carried, by a natural instinct or prepossession, to repose faith in their senses'.[84] The connection to Hamann is evident. Hume's philosophy of natural belief resonates with Hamann's conviction that 'belief belongs to the natural conditions of our cognitive powers, to the basic instincts of our souls'.[85] Rather than superior skills in reasoning, it is natural belief—a sign of our limitation—that is a defining quality of humanity, and this will be at the heart of Hamann's exorbitant Enlightenment.[86]

---

[82] David Hume, *A Treatise of Human Nature*, ed. David Fate Norton and Mary J. Norton, Oxford Philosophical Texts (Oxford: Oxford University Press, 2000) p. 175.

[83] Yet we cannot simply abandon the project of critical and sustained enquiry that philosophy represents. Hume's uncharacteristically dramatic tone indicates that this is not just a thought experiment for him. Before we travel on the surface of the 'immense depths' of philosophy we need to 'ponder' the tools that are available to accomplish this trip (Hume, *Treatise*, p. 171). It is a trip that is ambitious, universal, including the whole world, though it thereby also turns close to a circular argument 'compassing the globe' (p. 172). The conceptual position and tools that we have available are at this point neither newly developed nor completely consistent. Yet we have to have the 'temerity' to reuse the 'leaky weather-beaten vessel' of thought, a gendered mode of transport, across the ocean (ibid.). It is relevant that the previous sceptical insights, which have made the vessel 'leaky', are not patched up or painted over: they are part of any future enquiry.
As Hamann suggests elsewhere, this 'leaky…vessel' is not just philosophical method itself but also the form in which we think. Thought and language are 'leaky…vessels' with no guarantee that we will able to carry forward either our journey or carry our records of knowledge. They are faulty, 'weather-beaten', and yet, despite the 'disadvantageous circumstances', philosophy continues to travel on them (ibid.).

[84] David Hume, *An Enquiry concerning Human Understanding*, ed. by Tom L. Beauchamp (Oxford: Oxford University Press, 1999), p. 200.

[85] 'Da der Glaube zu den natürlichen Bedingungen unserer Erkenntniskräfte und zu den Grundtrieben unserer Seele gehört' (N, 3: 190).

[86] A quick comment to avoid a common confusion: this rejection of natural religion for Hamann is not the same as the rejection of the Humean natural belief. The difference is as follows: there are beliefs for which you have no rational grounds—although you often pretend that you do—such as your belief in causality. These are natural beliefs—if you did not have them, then you'd go mad. But the fact that you, and everybody else, has them, does not make them rational. Now, the big question

There is a poetical dimension to this text and its argument, and Hamann makes clear that the essay cuts across philosophy and poetry. '*Night-Thoughts of a Sceptic*' makes us think of both: it invokes Young and scepticism together, drawing attention to the poetic and philosophical qualities of the piece.[87] As we know, Young was one of the most influential and admired poets for figures whom we now consider central to European Enlightenment and Romanticism. For Hamann, what was most fascinating about Young was the depth, the philosophical character, of his poetic vision. By entitling his translation *Night-Thoughts of a Sceptic*, Hamann invites us to think a little harder about the link that he, as a German translator, makes between two English texts (Young and Hume) and disciplines (poetry and philosophy). Hamann presents this passage as Hume's crisis of belief and aligns it with Young's similar crisis described in *Night Thoughts*. In the poem, Young also writes about the painful apprehensions that haunt him and his struggles facing the abyss of doubt. The translation draws a parallel between their moment of crisis and how they resolve it: crucially, it will be belief, not rationality, that will overcome the scepticism.

Having translated both of them, Hamann is able to identify more than a little Young in Hume and vice versa, especially since he is attentive to the 'poetic beauties' in the philosopher's text. Similarly, it is the philosophical power of Young's text that impresses Hamann and ultimately suggests a comparison with Hume. Consider Hamann's letter to Herder in which he states that 'it seemed to me as if all my hypotheses had been a mere afterbirth of his [Young's] night thoughts and all my whimsies had been impregnated by his images'.[88] *Night Thoughts* impregnates Hamann's thinking and his imagery so much that by the time he comes to read and translate Hume, the *Nachtgedanken eines Zweiflers* is born, thus establishing, in a new title, a deep connection between these two British thinkers who are otherwise treated as unrelated.[89]

is whether a belief in God is part of this set of beliefs; and the answer must overwhelmingly be negative. That's fine with Hamann. For him, the rejection of this type of belief does not prevent you from having a belief in God that doesn't pretend to be based on reason. Hamann refers to this later in *Golgotha and Sheblimini!* when it becomes clear that, although the translations of the *Dialogues* will never appear, the intense reading of Hume on belief helped Hamann to tackle Kant's work. (The *Metacritique* was finished shortly after Hamann left the translation.) See Hamann, N 3: 469.

[87] The fact that it relates to Novalis's future *Hymns to the Night* (1800) is even more evocative.

[88] Hamann to Herder, 17 January 1769: '[D]a kame es mir vor, als wenn alle meine Hypothesen eine bloße Nachgeburt seiner Nachtgedanken gewesen...und alle meine Grillen von seinen Bildern impraegnirt worden wären' (ZH, 2: 433). We find plenty more instances in which Hamann uses Young to read across borders—for instance, when he is studying the hymns we will focus on in Chapter 4. As Davis discusses, Hamann writes on 'the hymn, and comparing Johannes Scheffler's "Liebe, die du mich zum Bilde deiner Gottheit hast gemacht" with Edward Young's *Night Thoughts*' (Davis, p. 93).

[89] By connecting Hume with Young, Hamann also opens up a new angle for our understanding of Hume's famously tricky understanding of the relationship between poetry and philosophy. While Hume has been celebrated as one of the most important writers in eighteenth-century letters, his own relation to openly figurative language is rather ambivalent. Although Hume suggests that we give poets a pass precisely because we know that they 'follow implicitly the suggestions of their fancy', he certainly tried to curb the kind of reasoning that runs philosophy and poetry together (*Treatise*, p. 148). He famously states that '[p]oets themselves, tho' liars by profession, always endeavour to give an air of truth to their fictions' (p. 83). The problem is not only that they lie but also that they present this lie as truth. As Paul Hamilton pointedly remarks, 'For Hume, this means that poetry illuminates his philosophy of belief', though not in a way that Hamann would enjoy since it 'leaves poetry either as make-believe or 'a counterfeit belief' (*Coleridge's Poetics* [Stanford, CA: Stanford University Press, 1983], p. 46).

There is no doubt that the intellectual contexts of the Anglo-German arena in Britain were rich, supple, and active. The influence and density of these contexts existed across national boundaries, languages, and histories. We have forgotten much of it, just as we forgot about Anglo-German life in eighteenth-century London. Many times, these connections were mistakes, or they created confusion or simply misattributions. Anonymous publication, in particular, often resulted in an unpredictable dissemination of ideas, much of which is still not known very well. The frequency of these misattributions tells us something about just how complex, rich, and dense Anglo-German intellectual life and exchanges were at the time. It was only possible for these mistakes to occur because there were enough chances for them to happen: remember the common, mistaken belief that Fuseli's essay was written by Sterne. It is thus significant that a similarly telling misattribution accompanies the Hamannian *Night-Thoughts*. The essay was published anonymously in the periodical *Königsbergsche Zeitung*. Eventually, Hamann was identified to be behind the publication, and the essay was included in all standard editions of his works. Remarkably, all editors and scholars assumed that the essay was written by Hamann. It was only in 1967 that Swain showed that *Nachtgedanken* was, in fact, a direct translation from Hume's *Treatise*. Such a misattribution not only tells us something about the affinity of Hamann and Hume, but also provides an example for why we should continue to look for Anglo-German connections— sometimes subterranean, sometimes obvious—in order to get a full sense of the richness of the intellectual context of the period. These connections matter because they remind us that many of the main authors of the period work across languages, disciplines, and borders.

Looking at Hamann's and Fuseli's translations and their practices is not only about getting a sense for them as Anglo-German writers but also about what their activity tells us about their wider conceptual workspace. They reveal to us connections we have not seen before, showing us that we need to rethink our understanding of how connections work during this period. Uncovering this criss-crossing network across periods, genres, and disciplines makes it clear that we cannot ignore the complexity and diffuseness of mutual relevancies and how they recast their intellectual and literary histories. We cannot tell our stories in linear, national, or monolingual fashion anymore.

CASPAR LAVATER: CONNECTING BLAKE AND HAMANN

The Swiss-German figure of Lavater is a reminder of how odd it is that we ever did think of this period as monolingual, especially when we consider his connections to Fuseli, Hamann, and Blake. He was one of the most visible intellectual reference

And yet, as Hamann points out, Hume himself of course uses plenty of 'poetic beauty', which becomes part of his theory of belief, his epistemology. It adds a specific connection to the scholarship that has focused on the literary dimension of Hume's writing, but a connection that is forged via a contemporary German translation. On Hume and language, especially Hume's change of style, see John Bender, *Ends of Enlightenment* (Stanford, CA: Stanford University Press, 2012), pp. 83–91.

points of the age, a nodal point for literature, theology, and philosophy across the German, French, and British spheres and, thus, a particularly good figure to illustrate the multifariousness of the connections that were at work at the time. Lavater maintained public and private friendships—as well as animosities—with most important thinkers of the period.[90] An audience with him was *de rigueur* for anybody who would travel through Switzerland. He was, quite simply, one of the most important presences in eighteenth-century Europe, and he was so in part because the transnational network of connections worked so well. In philosophical terms, Lavater was one of the period's most radical thinkers about hermeneutics and language. His views on the immanence of language, much neglected in scholarship today, connect in direct ways to Blake and Hamann, making him both immediately historically and philosophically relevant.

Lavater was born in 1741, the son of a Zurich doctor. Together with Fuseli he was educated at the Collegium Carolinum, and the two became close friends, which they remained until their death. After co-authoring *The Unjust Bailiff, or the Complaints of a Patriot* in 1762, they both went into German exile.[91] While Fuseli went on to London, Lavater returned to Zurich a few years later, where he established himself as a deacon. Most students of the period will know him as the author of his works on physiognomy, though he was also a poet and composed theological works. As Jean-Jacques Courtine and Claudine Haroche show, the ancient discipline of physiognomy was almost extinct by the mid-eighteenth century.[92] Lavater revived it and gave it fresh and powerful momentum in works such as *On Physiognomy* and *Physiognomical Fragments*. His writings proved immensely popular across Europe and appeared in countless editions as well as in legal and illegal translations, including in German, English (on both sides of the Atlantic), French, Dutch, and Russian.[93] Physiognomy was so popular that we even find

[90] Maria Edgeworth's comment suggests that he had lost none of his quicksilver appeal during his visit to England: 'Lavater is to come home in a coach to-day. My father seems to think much the same of him that you did when you saw him abroad, that to some genius he adds a good deal of the mountebank' (Edgeworth to Mr Ruxton, 29 December 1791, in *The Life and Letters of Maria Edgeworth*, ed. Augustus J. C. Hare, 2 vols [New York: Houghton, Mifflin, 1895], 1: 18–20, 19).
    One of the main controversies involving Lavater was his spat with Moses Mendelssohn, to whom in 1769 he had sent a translation of Charles Bonnet's *Palingénésie philosophique* alongside a public dedication asking him either to refute Bonnet or to convert to Christianity. This aggressive use of a newfound social sphere did not endear him to many, though it did sharpen his public profile considerably. There is a long and bibliographically rich footnote on Lavater's presence in Europe in Graeme Tytler, *Physiognomy in the European Novel: Faces and Fortunes* (Princeton, NJ: Princeton University Press, 1982), p. 161. For a familiar example of how Lavater is picked up in British letters, see Godwin's *Caleb Williams*. The novel is obsessed with physiognomy and the connections to Lavater are rich and varied. In his book-length study, Tytler discusses these aspects in greater detail. For an introductory entry on Lavater in the European context, see Sibylle Erle, 'Face to Face with Johann Caspar Lavater', *Literature Compass* (2005): 131, pp. 1–4

[91] 'Der ungerechte Landvogd oder Klagen eines Patrioten' (Johann Caspar Lavater, *Jugendschriften: Der ungerechte Landvogd Zwey Briefe an Magister Bahrdt Schweizerlieder*, ed. Bettina Volz-Tobler, vol. 1, part 1, of *Ausgewählte Werke in Historisch-Kritische Ausgabe*, ed. Horst Sitta, 10 vols (Zurich: Neue Zürcher Zeitung, 2001–), pp. 77–84.

[92] See Jean-Jacques Courtine and Claudine Haroche, *Histoire du visage: Exprimer et taire ses émotions (XVIe–début XIXe siècle)* (Paris: Rivages, 1988), esp. pp. 118–26.

[93] For a good discussion on the wide distribution of Lavater's writing, see Ellis Shookman, 'Pseudo-Science, Social Fad, Literary Wonder: Johann Caspar Lavater and the Art of Physiognomy', in *The Faces*

physiognomical guides printed as pocketbooks, portable hermeneutic dictionaries to analyse the faces of interlocutors. As Scott Juengel points out, '[I]n addition to the Pocket Lavater and a range of cheap abridgements, there were Juvenile Lavaters and Female Lavaters; as well as anonymous volumes like the *Secret Journal of a Self-Observer*, or *The Confessions of Lavater...* and *Lavater's Looking Glass*'.[94] Lavater's influence was felt throughout Europe; his impact on the London intellectual scene was immediate, especially because of his ties with Fuseli, who acted as Lavater's main translator into English. His selection of Lavater's writings, published as *Aphorisms* by Joseph Johnson, still serves as the standard Anglophone introduction to Lavater.[95]

The *Aphorisms* bring together Lavater, Fuseli, Blake, and Hamann in numerous ways. Fuseli asked Blake to produce an engraving for the frontispiece, thereby actively involving the artist in the presentation of this German material to the English public. Independently, Hamann and Lavater corresponded about many of the passages contained in the *Aphorisms*. Lavater's writings and his translations into English by Fuseli help shape Blake's and Hamann's work to emerge. The *Aphorisms*, one of the most important books of the eighteenth-century intellectual landscape, was an Anglo-German collaborative production (Figure 3.1). Once the book was published, Blake immediately purchased a copy. He was deeply drawn to Lavater's work and had ample opportunity to speak to Fuseli about it, finding out about their wider intellectual background—what J. H. MacPhail calls Blake's 'debt' to Swiss thought.[96]

Blake's annotations to the volume show us that he understood Lavater's book as a hermeneutics and as a study in friendship. Blake's own copy of Lavater's book strikingly illustrates this. The printed text closes with the following aphorism: 'If you mean to know yourself, interline such of these aphorisms as affected you agreeably in reading, and set a mark to such as left a sense of uneasiness with you; and then shew your copy to whom you please'.[97] Blake took Lavater seriously on this. When he purchased a copy of the book, he signed his name into it, claiming it as his own. After he had finished reading and annotating it, he went back to his own signature and drew a heart around it and Lavater's printed name.

Blake's drawing is a vivid, graphic prompt that the ideas of love and friendship were at the centre of his reading, which his annotations bear out: '[T]he name Lavater... is

of Physiognomy: Interdisciplinary Approaches to Johann Caspar Lavater, ed. Shookman (Columbia, SC: Camden House, 1993), pp. 1–24.

94 Scott Juengel, private correspondence to the author (22 October 2015).
95 Johann Caspar Lavater, *Aphorisms on Man: Translated from the Original Manuscript of the Rev. John Caspar Lavater, Citizen of Zuric [sic]* (London: printed for J. Johnson, 1788). The selection is mostly from the two related volumes of *Vermischte unphysiognomische Regeln zur Selbst- und Menschenkenntnis* (1787) and *Vermischte unphysiognomische Regeln zur Menschen- und Selbstkenntnis* (1788).
96 J. H. MacPhail remarks that 'the considerable debt that Blake owed to Switzerland has never been made sufficiently clear' ('Blake and Switzerland', *Modern Language Review* 38, 2 [1943]: 81–7, 81).
97 Lavater, *Aphorisms on Man*, p. 224. See also Blake, 'Annotations', in *The Complete Poetry and Prose of William Blake*, ed. David V. Erdman, rev. ed. (New York: Anchor Books, 1988), 583–601, 583.

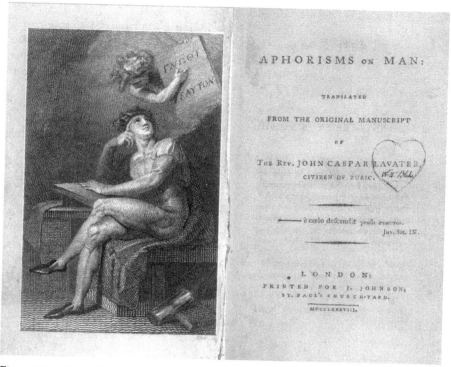

Figure 3.1 Johann Caspar Lavater, *Aphorisms on Man* (London: Johnson, 1788), title page and frontispiece. Huntington Library, San Marino, CA, UDID 223899.

the amulet of those who purify the heart of man'.[98] For Blake, reading and studying Lavater became part of something that is best termed 'critical friendship'.

The Swiss-German demanded an engagement with his text that would produce both agreement and 'uneasiness'. Lavater carefully constructs this engagement. His Socratic suggestion in the last aphorism of the book ('if you mean to know your-self'), in fact, circles back to the title page. On the frontispiece we encounter an image of Lavater (drawn by Fuseli and engraved by Blake) looking up towards an angelic figure holding a tablet onto which are engraved the words 'Know Thyself'. This slogan is a promise about the potential of this book: the *Aphorisms* can lead to a sense of better self-understanding. We do not just read physiognomy; we get to read ourselves through it. Simultaneously, the Socratic imperative 'Know Thyself' reminds us that we need to know ourselves before we can lay claim to any other knowledge. Knowing oneself is also knowing whom one loves—including the 'uneasiness' that might come with it—and being able to share that knowledge. Such knowledge production is a complex process, and to share the results with others is part of Lavater's hermeneutic project that Blake so enthusiastically

---

[98] Blake, 'Annotations', p. 600.

embraces. Drawing the heart is showing who one loves and 'interlin[ing]' the *Aphorisms* accordingly. Blake is aware of the linguistic and cultural backgrounds to which he feels such a close connection. Lavater is not neutral, without country or language: he is Swiss-German, and Blake knows that his translator is a key member of the Anglo-German context in London. Since Blake and Fuseli were friends and worked together on the publication of the *Aphorisms*, these transnational and translinguistic dimensions are something Blake would have known and thought about before drawing that heart.[99]

Hamann and Lavater, too, had a very close relationship. They started their correspondence in 1777 and stayed in contact until Hamann's death ten years later.[100] They were directly influencing each other's work: a letter by Hamann about the nature of Scripture gave Lavater the idea for his massive *Pontius Pilatus*, a hermeneutical *tour de force* and one of the strangest poems of the period. In turn, Lavater was partly responsible for Hamann's composition of *Golgotha and Sheblimini!*, a pendant to the *Metacritique*. Their friendship is reflected directly in Lavater's four-volume German edition of his *Physiognomische Fragmente*, a popular book on physiognomy. The work provides plenty of engravings—some of them by Blake—of portraits and facial features as visual illustrations of what Lavater describes in the text. Lavater takes full advantage of his connections and the growing sense of celebrity, and he features many of the age's most famous figures as examples. In keeping with his international appeal, Lavater describes and interprets the faces of Samuel Johnson, Sterne, and Shakespeare, as well as Fuseli and Hamann himself.[101]

This wider intellectual context is historically and theoretically significant. Lavater's connections with Fuseli, Blake, and Hamann also have philosophical dimensions beyond the obvious topic of physiognomy.[102] Lavater was an important author across many genres that have never been read comparatively. Once we

---

[99] It seems that Blake took Lavater much more seriously than some scholars—for instance, Ann Mellor—suggest. See Ann Mellor, 'Physiognomy, Phrenology, and Blake's Visionary Heads', in *Blake in His Time*, ed. Robert E. Essick and Donald Pearce (Bloomington, IN: Indiana University Press, 1978), pp. 53–74.

[100] The correspondence continued until 1785. After that they stood in contact through their common friend Friedrich Heinrich Jacobi. The tone of their letters is deeply enthusiastic. On Lavater, Hamann, and the idea of a legibility of the body as expression of the immaterial, see Eva Kocziszky, 'Die Schwierigkeit des Nicht-Tuns: Welt und Gesellschaft in Hamanns Kontroverse mit Lavater', in Beetz and Rudolph, *Johann Georg Hamann*, pp. 103–16.

[101] Johann Caspar Lavater, *Physiognomische Fragmente zur Beförderung der Menschenkenntnis und Menschenliebe; Eine Auswahl mit 101 Abbildungen*, 4 vols (Leipzig: Steiner, 1775–8). The entry on Hamann (2: 284–5), presented with an etching and a passage by Herder describing the face, is a striking moment of a historical missed connection. None of the many English editions of the *Essays* or *Fragments* includes the pages on Hamann. It is not entirely clear why the Hamann plate was not included in the English editions. Many of the lesser-known figures (in Britain) were omitted, so most likely it would have been an editor's decision. The Lavater editions and translations vary wildly, and almost none includes as expansive a set as the German original or the French translations.

[102] For a discussion of these connections in direct relation to the *Songs of Innocence and of Experience*, see Sibylle Erle, 'Introducing the Songs with Inspiration: William Blake, Lavater, and the Legacy of Felix Hess', in *(Re-)Writing the Radical: Enlightenment, Revolution, and Cultural Transfer in 1790s Germany, Britain and France*, ed. Maike Oergel (Göttingen, Ger.: De Gruyter, 2012), pp. 251–67.

recover these further dimensions to Lavater's work, we can open a whole new set of theoretical avenues into Blake's text. Particularly, Lavater's religious and spiritual writings, almost completely ignored in Anglophone scholarship, articulate a radical view of hermeneutics and immanent language that is directly relevant to Blake's poetic practice.

Just like Blake, Lavater made a distinction between divine language and human natural language. For him, divine language is 'inexpressively different' from any spoken on earth; it is a language that exists in the 'land of celestial truth', a medium in which '[o]ne can imagine a means of communicating our thoughts, feelings, mental images, etc. that is purely immediate and allows us to dispense with all language we have learned. This immediate language is physiognomic, pantomimic, musical'.[103] What Lavater describes here as 'immediate language' is something akin to Blakean immanence. Since it is immediately and intuitively understood, such language is also simultaneous: it 'must be successive and instantaneous; that is, it must represent with the greatest and unlikely quickness a whole simultaneous accumulation of pictures, thoughts, feelings, like a painting—immediately and at once, and yet nevertheless successively. It must be painting and language at once'.[104] The language that Lavater imagines communicates immediately and on all levels of representation. It resolves the fallenness of our condition by dissolving the boundaries between forms of representation. We see Blake negotiating this idea in all of his illuminated books, exploring the space of the page to present 'painting and language at once'. As Laura Quinney points out, Lavater helps Blake imagine that space or work of immanence, the 'vision of the "Eternal Now", detaching the proper vocation of humanity from linear temporality'.[105] For Blake, the multimedia artist, the understanding of language as a 'simultaneous accumulation of pictures, thoughts, feelings, like a painting' is fundamental for his whole oeuvre.[106] There is a direct and strong relation between Lavater's conception of language and Blake's understanding of the immanence of the word that guides his poetics. Lavater explains that the reason we have to imagine a language of immanence is because our natural languages are limited and fallen: 'Language, language: you can never study it enough! All errors in the world, all originate in the deficiencies of language, all

[103] Johann Caspar Lavater, *Aussichten in die Ewigkeit, 1768–1773/78*, ed. Ursula Caflisch-Schnetzler, vol. 2, part 3, of *Ausgewählte Werke*, pp. 449 and 451–2. As Richard T. Gray rightly comments, these ideas are in concert with many theories of language, including Hamann's and, much later, Walter Benjamin's (see Richard Gray, *About Face: German Physiognomic Thought from Lavater to Auschwitz* [Detroit, MI: Wayne State University Press, 2004], p. 52).
[104] '[M]uß succeßiv und momentan zugleich seyn; das ist, sie muß einen ganzen gleichzeitigen Haufen von Bildern, Gedanken, Empfindungen, wie ein Gemählde zugleich und auf einmal, und dennoch die succeßiven mit der größten und wahrhaftesten Schnelligkeit darstellen. Sie muß Gemälde und Sprache zugleich seyn' (Lavater, *Aussichten in die Ewigkeit*, p. 451).
[105] Laura Quinney, *William Blake on Self and Soul* (Cambridge, MA: Harvard University Press, 2009), p. 22.
[106] Blake is, of course, far less confident about the idea of resolution between different media. See W. J. T. Mitchell, *Blake's Composite Art: A Study of the Illuminated Poetry* (Princeton, NJ: Princeton University Press, 1978; and Saree Makdisi, *Reading William Blake* (Cambridge: Cambridge University Press, 2015).

originate in the want of the peculiar, characteristic signs'.[107] The study of language is a never-ending story. We will always have something to study in language, and that shows us the depth of this medium. Do we err, argue, and make mistakes within it? Of course. Does that mean that language is not revelatory and suggestive of immanence? Absolutely not.

The idea of language as a never-ending story, a celebration of the Babelian condition that leads to translation, connects all the major figures in this chapter. They all work and think across different languages and different conceptions of language, and they all insist on the constant limitations of language, articulated, however, through a multilingual context. The importance of appreciating the width and depth of this polyglot context is a crucial insight of this chapter. The multiple relations between Fuseli, Hamann, Lavater, and Blake make it impossible to think of them as a restricted and unconnected group. Once we learn that their individual authorships are all touched by multilingualism—through writing, translations, reviewing, reading—it becomes clear just how much we can learn when we look at them through such a lens. This is important not just in relation to their works but also in regard to their interconnection and the period as a whole.

---

[107] 'Sprache, Sprache, kannst du nicht genug studieren! Alle Irrthümer in der Welt, alle kommen nur vom Mangel der Sprache, der speciellsten, charakteristischen Zeichen her' (Lavater, *Physiognomische Fragmente*, 4: 156).

4

Blake and Hamann
Poetry as Mother-Tongue and the Fight
against Instrumental Reason

NAMING AS CREATION

For William Blake and Johann Georg Hamann, naming is creation. Blake tells us that God '[t]o man the wond'rous art of writing gave', and Johann Georg Hamann speaks of 'the uterus of language, which is the *deipara* of our reason'.[1] Both agree that '[p]oetry is the mother-tongue of the human race'.[2] The historical context we encounter in these statements reveals a philosophical atmosphere that was much more diverse and radical in its thinking about language than is often assumed.[3] It allows both Blake and Hamann to articulate an exorbitant vision that is not only deeply original but also relevant today.

The first part of this chapter fleshes out these claims by showing how Blake and Hamann argue for language's poetical origin. In the second half, I discuss how their theory of language develops alongside a critique of instrumental reason. This will give us a sense of how Blake and Hamann fit into the wider debates of eighteenth-century language theory, probably *the* most acute and complicated philosophical discussion of the period. They argue not only that language and thought are connected, and that language is poetical, but also that poetry lies at the origin of *all* creative thinking. For both, the Bible turns out to be the most powerful vehicle to illustrate this insight. Most crucially, both Blake and Hamann fiercely resist any account of language or thought as functional or instrumental, an understanding of linguistics and cognition that has become standard and that continues to shape the way we think today. They offer a radical alternative that is out of bounds and yet tells something important about the period.

For Blake, language and poetic vision belong together. The word itself is magical and has ontological power. God created the world through a linguistic act, and we do similar things when we create art or poetry. As part of this vision, Blake holds views on language that are often fundamentally different from our standard ideas about signs. We need to appreciate that difference if we want to read him today.

---

[1] Blake, *Jerusalem*, p. 145; and N, 3: 238.   [2] N, 2: 197.
[3] One of the most powerful accounts of how this complicated intellectual and scholarly field shapes our modern thinking about the humanities and beyond is James Turner, *Philology: The Forgotten Origins of the Modern Humanities* (Princeton, NJ: Princeton University Press, 2014).

In order not to get lost in the infinite complexity of this point, it's important to illustrate some of the stakes by example. One of Blake's most fundamental beliefs is that signs are motivated. We encounter a condensed version of this idea in one of Blake's annotations to Johann Caspar Lavater's *Aphorisms*: '[E]very thing on earth is the word of God'.[4] The word of God encompasses all of what we know— all the objects, words, faces (he is reading Lavater's physiognomy), or poems we write and/or encounter. These issues permeate all of Blake's poetry, from the creation myth in *Jerusalem* down to the deceptively simple *Songs of Innocence and of Experience*. The first stanza of 'Infant Joy' from that collection is a good example:

> I have no name
> I am but two days old.—
> What shall I call thee?
> I happy am
> Joy is my name,—
> Sweet joy befall thee!⁵

'I have no name' is one of the most deeply existential lines in all of Blake. No doubt it is connected to the infant joy of being in a prelingual state (Figure 4.1). The infant has no name yet and then is termed 'joy'. The poem describes this moment of naming that turns into a moment of joy in the face of the fall. In his important reading, David Simpson points out that the child 'does not "speak", but he is "spoken"'.[6] While Simpson undoubtedly gets to the point of the linguistic subject of the poem, he also suggests that Blake's reaction to the linguistic fall is completely negative, that the infant's smile is a 'resignation before an inevitable fate'.[7] Basically, such a reading turns Blake into a linguistic nominalist and somebody who fears the written word. However, there is also something in this Blakean polysyllabic fall that makes existence possible in the first place: 'be-fall'. What is invoked in the poem is akin to a linguistic *felix culpa*. The subject ('I') needs a name in order to be part of the community; this is why it is asked the question 'What shall I call thee?' The answer 'I happy am' suggests that there is a motivated relation between the word and the quality of the existence it describes. The inversion makes this very clear. The fact that it is not 'I am happy' but rather 'I happy am' has nothing to do with the infant still learning the rules of language—quite the opposite, in fact. The infant understands the power of language more than many adults, insisting that the word 'happy' is part of its ontological quality. Thus 'I happy am' and 'Joy is my name' are two sides of the same coin.

Incidentally, the number two is crucial in this poem, in relation both to the dualism of the collection of the *Songs* as a whole and to the illustration of the ambiguous nature of existence itself. Two produces repetition and the Fall; it creates identity and celebrates existence. Remember that on the second day God made the heavens ('Let there be a firmament' [Gen. 1: 6]). The line 'I am but two days old'

---

⁴ Blake, 'Annotations to Lavater's Aphorisms on Man', in *Complete Poetry and Prose*, pp. 583–601, 599.
⁵ Blake, 'Infant Joy', in *Complete Poetry and Prose*, p. 16, lines 1–6.
⁶ David Simpson, *Irony and Authority in Romantic Poetry* (London: Macmillan, 1979), p. 53.
⁷ Ibid.

Figure 4.1 William Blake, 'Infant Joy', *Songs of Innocence and of Experience* (1825). Reproduction by kind permission of the Provost and Scholars of King's College, Cambridge.

is a powerful reminder that existence never occurs *ex nihilo* but is deeply tied to creation, a creation and naming that will have a shape and form but will never be unambiguous. The main direction of the name 'joy' is that—*nomen est omen*—'sweet joy' will befall the infant. It is important to remind ourselves of something almost too obvious here—namely, that Blake chose 'Joy' as part of the title of the poem, the heading for his description of the linguistic process of naming. For all of Blake's awareness of and insistence on the shortcomings of human language, there is also a sense in which this fall gives us the possibility to find 'Sweet joy' and, as the second stanza states, 'sing the while', to produce a lyric that celebrates the linguistic miracle of naming and existence through poetry and song.[8]

A key part of that celebration is the conviction that there is a meaningful relation between the sign and the signified. This view is, of course, deeply alien to many people today. As Robert N. Essick points out, it assumes meaning in the process of naming, while for most there can only be convention:

> The process is circular, and avoids solipsism only for those who have faith in a tran-scendental power, arising from within or descending from above, that makes possible a language without a difference between what it *is* and what it *means*—a language the very existence of which is denied by those who, from Locke to Saussure and Derrida, are equally convinced of the differential nature of all linguistic signs.[9]

Blake believed in that 'transcendental power'—as did many others, such as Hamann—and nevertheless insisted on the affective dimension of language. Peter Otto has observed that

> a Blakean critique of Derrida's description of language and reality (advanced before an appreciation) would begin with the observation that his argument is advanced from the position of the stationary, reasoning self. It is not concerned with what occurs to lan-guage in relationship with others, in embrace, or in movement.... For Blake, emotions and engagements such as these can bring us to the very edge of our linguistic world.[10]

We can quibble about the exact consequences and qualities of his views, and much of Blake scholarship has done so in fascinating ways.[11] But we should not lose sight of the key insight here: Blake's sense of language is profoundly metaphysical and ontological; it puts the meaningful relation between things and words at the very centre of our existence, our creativity, and the world. Even once we historicize this view, it is a conviction that remains at the core of his thinking.

One of the difficulties in reading Blake on language is that these views are everywhere and nowhere. As readers we sense his conviction about the prophetic word and its power throughout his work. At the same time, Blake never sets out to write a theory of language, nor does he directly engage in public exchanges on this topic. The very few propositional statements along these lines give us good reason to assume that he believed that a direct articulation was pointless or even counterproductive: 'the Fault is not in Words, but in Things Lockes Opinions of Words & their Fallaciousness are Artful Opinions & Fallacious also'.[12] Blake

---

[8] Blake, 'Infant Joy', line 11.

[9] Robert N. Essick, *William Blake and the Language of Adam* (Oxford: Clarendon, 1989), pp. 54–5.

[10] Peter Otto, *Constructive Vision and Visionary Deconstruction: Los, Eternity, and the Productions of Time in the Later Poetry of William Blake* (Oxford: Clarendon, 1991), pp. 24–5.

[11] In Essick's view, for instance, Blake does not himself historicize his own belief in a transcendental power sufficiently, a move that is necessary to understand the full impact of Blake's suggestions: 'Blake's confrontations with rationalist grammar and his development of a very different way of thinking about language delineate an historical debate, not a transcendental solution. That debate demonstrates, finally, the historicity of language itself' (Essick, p. 238).

[12] William Blake, 'Annotations to the Works of Sir Joshua Reynolds', in *Complete Poetry and Prose*, pp. 635–70, 659.

attacks John Locke's mistrust of words in at least two ways. First, he claims that what Locke identifies as 'Fallaciousness' is not actually wrong at all. Second, and more importantly, Locke gets 'Fallaciousness' wrong. Locke does exactly what he accuses language of: he produces a 'mist' that is both confusing and misleading.[13] For Blake, the crucial part here is not to find a Lockean solution that outdoes Locke (to 'clarify' Locke, as it were) but, rather, to get away from the ideas Locke has about 'Words' in general, including their historical formation. One of the ways to get away from such a Lockean way of understanding words is precisely to see that there is no 'Fault' in words, that there is no mistake in the construction and existential claim 'I happy am'.

The Blake that comes into view here is committed to the ontological power of the word. For him, words are a central part of a world that is, as Akeel Bilgrami puts it, *'suffused with value'*.[14] Language allows us to see this value because it is at the heart of creation, both human and divine: '[E]very thing on earth is the word of God'. Note that we can emphasize each operative word in that sentence separately, and, for Blake, all of those emphases would be correct: each and *every* thing is the word of God. All *things* are divine; there are no mere objects, in the same way as this *earth* is the place where we encounter revelation. Every thing *is* a word from God, an ontology that reminds us of the Gospel of St John. Lastly, it is the word of *God*, who allows the wonder of creation, not just any old word. Blake's vision not only includes God, but also understands Him to be producing it. For all the unorthodox qualities of this Blakean God, His divine power is a real and constant thing.

For Hamann, language is at the centre of epistemology, ontology, and aesthetics. Recall his totalizing statement that 'without word, no reason—no world'.[15] Given the centrality of language, it matters deeply that '[p]oetry is the mother-tongue of the human race'.[16] Not only is language everywhere, and the key to ourselves and the world, but also this language was poetical in its origin and remains so at its core. The world reveals itself to us through language, and does so in the most powerful way if we understand its poetical character. Thus, language really is *everywhere*, though not quite in the way Jacques Derrida might conceive of it. Since God has given us language as a gift, the deep bond between language and the world around us remains intact, even though we might not always perceive it. Of course, the connection between language and world is often obscure or oblique; we often

---

[13] Words 'interpose themselves so much between our Understandings, and the Truth...that like the *Medium* through which visible Objects pass, their Obscurity and Disorder does not seldom cast a mist before our Eyes, and impose upon our Understanding' (John Locke, *An Essay concerning Human Understanding* [Oxford: Clarendon, 1975], p. 488).

[14] Bilgrami, p. 297. There are different ways of contextualizing Blake's thinking on this matter—in relation to language in particular. For instance, there has been considerable work on the historical influence of Cabbalistic thought for Blake. Sometimes writers even make Blake's poetry and art themselves part of a larger Cabbalistic system. Other research has established the conceptual connection between Blake and ideas that flourished in early German Romanticism, especially in the work of Gotthold Ephraim Lessing and Alexander von Humboldt. Such work sees Blake as a precursor to a particular form of thinking about language that finds its most important theoretical articulation in German Romanticism.

[15] 'Ohne Wort, keine Vernunft—keine Welt' (ZH, 5: 95).

[16] 'Poesie ist die Muttersprache des menschlichen Geschlechts' (N, 2: 197).

misunderstand its relation and even language itself—yet language nevertheless reveals the world to us, even if we may read it in an imperfect way. As Gwen Griffith-Dickson puts it,

> For Hamann...language does not 'screen off' reality; it does not obscure, conceal or distort the rest of reality, but *reveals* it, indeed, is the only organ or mode for its revelation and communication. That there is not access to reality apart from language does not mean that language has managed to insert itself permanently between us and the objects of our knowledge, and is determined forever to make mischief between us. It is because only language can make the world known and understood to a linguistic being. For Hamann, such metaphysical difference as exists between language and the rest of the world is *creative*, and endlessly productive of new layers of meaning.[17]

Hamann attempts in his writings to produce these new layers of meaning, which is why the poetical is not just a theoretical touchstone but also that which is the centre of his style of writing. Philosophy needs to participate in the creation of new layers, just as poetry does, since both of them stand at the beginning of meaning. Blake's poetry is, of course, a prime example of how to put the 'metaphysical difference' at the centre of poetry itself. Whether it be innocence and experience ('the Two Contrary States of the Human Soul') or the visions that involve Urizen or Thel, the gap between language and the world that these poems describe and enact is deeply creative from the very beginning.[18] One of the tasks of our study of language is to figure out how its poetic character has always been part of its development, ever since its poetic inception.

POETRY AS THE MOTHER-TONGUE OF THE HUMAN RACE

Of course, the genealogy of poetry is a well-worn subject in the landscape of the Enlightenment and Romanticism. Broadly speaking, there are two competing models in the period regarding the genealogy, acquisition, and practice of language in its relation to poetry. The first charts a progress from an initially figurative to a

---

[17] Griffith-Dickson, p. 138.
[18] William Blake, subtitle to *Songs of Innocence and of Experience*, in *Complete Poetry and Prose*, p. 7. Just as language is poetical in its origin, revelation is tied to the ability to perceive the poetical dimension of the world. This is not about 'decoding' the world (or a poem) or finding the perfect key to its overall structure. Such endeavours would be hubristic and, quite frankly, pointless. It is much more important to understand that the relation between language and the world is defined through the figural and mediated through the conceptual: 'Imagery comprises the entire treasure of human knowledge and happiness' (Griffith-Dickson, p. 411); 'In Bildern besteht der ganze Schatz menschlicher Erkenntniß' (N, 2: 197). The form of knowledge that comes in images is much more adequate and important than what passes itself off as knowledge without acknowledging its medium. The figural itself is not an abstraction. It is part of language itself, a much better representation of its true nature than the non-figurative. 'Speaking is translation—from a tongue of angels into a human tongue, that is, thoughts in words—things in names—images in signs' (Griffith-Dickson, p. 413). (Reden ist übersetzen—aus einer Engelssprache in eine Menschensprache, das heist, Gedanken in Worte,—Sachen in Namen,—Bilder in Zeichen) (N, 2: 199). In the end, what we do when we speak, think, or represent is be transported by language from one sphere of signification to another. Sometimes the relation between these spheres is not completely clear, but just because we cannot comprehend it doesn't mean that it isn't happening.

more 'neutral' language. It is a view that gains much traction in the philosophical camp of empiricism and eighteenth-century rhetoric. The basic premises are, first, that poetry and epistemology don't mix; second, that philosophy provides a more accurate description of the world; and, third, that while language undoubtedly has poetic elements, we would best get rid of them as much as possible in order to minimize confusion in our philosophical endeavours. If needed, then poetic elements can be employed to produce poems. These poems are, granted, very enjoyable and sometimes even brilliant, yet they do not participate in the same marketplace of ideas as philosophy does. We recognize this argument so quickly today because we are deeply familiar with it in the area of modern scientific discourse. Substitute 'science' for 'philosophy' in the above description and you can easily see the direct relevance to current epistemology. The second model shares the same starting point as the first, yet its following narrative is diametrically opposed. It is basically a story of loss: language has indeed poetic origins, but many of these qualities have been lost over time. The original character of language can only be glimpsed faintly, precisely because the first view has enjoyed such tremendous success and has led to a purging of poetry from our language, thus obscuring its true poetic roots. This narrative of loss is directly adopted across Europe by the Romantics from their eighteenth-century predecessors.[19]

Blake and Hamann both hold an extreme version of the second view. They do not restrict themselves to mourning the loss of poetic language, however. And they also reject what we might call the homeopathic approach to soothe that mourning—that is, the project of continuing to keep poetry alive as a secondary discourse, next to science or functional speech. Instead, both of them go on the offensive, presenting an attempt to recuperate the initial poetical force of language. They want to stop the continuing deterioration of language and thought by reinstating the original power of poetry. As we have seen, this means to recover a sense of the divine and visionary quality of language and to make that part of its history. For Blake and Hamann, human endeavour and history mirror the poetic character of God's initial pronunciation. The history of humankind is the history of how the poetic word changed over time, including our attitudes towards it. In his *Thoughts on My Vita*, Hamann suggests that '[t]he history of art and of human nature in it seems to confirm this even more. Are not the painters the first writing masters and the poets and the speakers the first writers'.[20] Similarly, for Blake in

---

[19] This historical transition is occasionally mapped on to the supposed sharp differences of the Enlightenment and Romanticism that this book is arguing against. Although Essick is surely right when he claims that 'as the natural sign began to disappear from philosophies of language near the beginning of the nineteenth century, it found a new role within theories of poetic diction, finally to reappear in the guise of the romantic symbol' (Essick, p. 87), this account assumes that this transformation was complete. In fact, the natural sign does still linger on in philosophy, albeit in relative obscurity, until today. Nor is the transition from natural sign into romantic symbol all that smooth. Our reading of Blake and Hamann has already shown us that there is good reason to be sceptical about the idea that there should be a Wellek-like absorption of theology into poetry.

[20] 'Die Geschichte der Künste und der menschlichen Natur in derselben scheint dies noch mehr zu bestätigen. Sind nicht die Mahler die ersten Schreibmeister und die Poeten und Redner die ersten Schriftsteller gewesen' (N, 2: 16).

Jerusalem, '[n]ations are Destroy'd, or Flourish, in proportion as Their Poetry Painting and Music, are Destroy'd or Flourish! The Primeval State of Man, was Wisdom, Art, and Science'.[21] In the poem, of course, this is a scene of disaster, and Blake leaves no doubt he thinks he is living through a time of destruction, rather than a time of flourishing.

In these accounts the history of human nature is told through the history of *poetry*. God did not compose a scientific script, nor did he surround us with a philosophical treatise. God wrote a poem, and that poem is the world—including how we represent it back to ourselves through works of the imagination. The most important of those works by far, at least for Blake and Hamann, is the Bible. As Blake puts it, 'Why is the Bible more Entertaining & Instructive than any other book'? The answer is that it is 'addressed to the Imagination which is Spiritual Sensation & but mediately to the Understanding or Reason'.[22] The biblical text reveals more than a scientific examination of the origin of language precisely because it focuses on the poetical revelation.

One of the most intriguing differences between a broadly Lockean outlook and a broadly Hamannian outlook is their radically different approach to what the Bible and reading it could mean, of what was hermeneutically possible under the same description. Biblical study could take such different forms as Isaac Newton's exegesis of Revelation, William Warburton's *Divine Legation of Moses* (1737), or even Alexander Geddes's *Critical Remarks on the Hebrew Scriptures* (1800), three fundamentally different ways of engaging with Scripture. Such heterogeneity makes us reconsider what was possible in Blake's time. The difference between these figures illustrates what Ian Balfour terms an 'extravagance in interpretation that is midrash-like, which means being able to relate anything in the Bible to anything else in the Bible quite apart from the strictures of historical understanding or philology'.[23] In many ways, reading the Bible in these curious ways is nothing else but following its text wherever it takes us. There might not even be another layer between the biblical text and reality that needs to be monitored by human understanding or current epistemology. The big difference from the Lockean tradition is that the latter will 'make sense' of the Bible and domesticate its possible meanings. And this impulse for domestication is directly linked to a particular conception of language that will emphasize clarity over poetry. The point, thus, is not only that the Bible is important, or even that it is a source of poetry for these thinkers, but also that the Bible that they have available is hermeneutically far more experimental and undomesticated than the idea of Scripture we would encounter in a more con-trolled tradition. This Bible is more akin to Sterne's *Tristram Shandy* than to Locke's *An Essay concerning Human Understanding*.

The idea that we are to read the Bible as literature is uncontroversial for Blake and Hamann. The question is only what *type* of literary text we are talking about

---

For the term 'writing master', see Elaine Tennant, *The Habsburg Chancery Language in Perspective* (Berkeley, CA: University of California Press, 1985), pp. 121–24.

[21] Blake, *Jerusalem*, p. 146.   [22] Blake to Dr Trusler, pp. 702–3.
[23] Private correspondence to the author, 25 June 2016.

here, what it means to be literature. The idea that it would be a clear, structured, and coherent work would simply be puzzling, a crass form of desire to project what is whole to us onto the biblical text. Understanding the Bible as literature means, in contrast, to understand that its poetry or literariness because it cannot be tamed is, in effect, its power. If we take 'as literature' to mean a socially sanctioned and regulated lie (the Lockean conception of poetry), then Blake and Hamann would simply point out that Locke works with the wrong definition of literature here, even though it is Locke's that historically has been more successful. Blake puts it well in *Jerusalem*: 'the Daughters of Albion/Names anciently rememberd, but now contemn'd as fictions! / Although in every bosom they controll our Vegetative powers'.[24] The problem is that we have ended up not only with a version of literature that is domesticated but also, by the same token, with a version of it that is 'contemn'd' rather than celebrated as fiction. To counteract this way of reading and condemning is not just a sentimental dream for Blake or Hamann, as their aggressive push in the opposite direction illustrates. For them there is a way of being able to perceive and read the biblical text, or our surroundings, differently, to not confuse a tree for just a green thing and not to mistake a word for a functional sign. They are under no illusion that their form of thinking is not going to be the new standard— poetry will not become the new *doxa*—but this does not mean that they want to give up on the depth of their vision. After all, Blake does 'see Everything' that he 'paint[s] In This World'.[25]

One of the most helpful guides for Blake's and Hamann's respective readings of the Bible was James Hervey. Now almost unknown, he was an important intellectual presence at the time; plenty of figures appearing in this book comment on him, including Henry Fuseli, Mary Wollstonecraft, and Samuel Taylor Coleridge. Blake's mention of Hervey spans from the early *The Island* (1784) to *Jerusalem*. His painting *Epitome of James Hervey's 'Meditations among the Tombs'* (1821) is a large-scale visualization of Hervey's work. Hamann first alludes to Hervey in a letter to Johann Gotthelf Lindner (who also owned some of Hervey's books) in January 1756, when he reports that he has spent some time reading his 'excellent' work.[26] A few months later, he writes to his brother: 'Read Hervey, my dear brother'.[27] The British theologian becomes central for Hamann's readings in his London *Biblical Reflections* and for the composition of his spiritual diary while he undergoes his conversion experience. Hamann directly mentions him,

---

[24] Blake, *Jerusalem*, p. 148, ch. 1, plate 5, lines 37–9.   [25] Blake to Dr Trusler, p. 702.
[26] '[V]ortreflich [*sic*]' (ZH, 1: 134). The discussion on James Hervey, Hamann, and physicotheology is picked up later by various critics, including Sven-Aage Jørgensen, who suggests that Hamann was sceptical about physicotheology (see 'Hamann und Hervey: Zur Bibellektüre während Hamanns Londoner Krise', in *Historische Kritik und biblischer Kanon in der deutschen Aufklärung*, ed. H. Graf Reventlow, Walter Sparn, and John Woodbridge [Wiesbaden: Harrassowitz, 1988], pp. 237–48). Henri Veldhuis holds a contrary view (see 'Hamann's Naturbegriff in seinen Londoner Schriften und Beziehung zur Physikotheologie', in *Historische Kritik und biblischer Kanon*, pp. 99–115. Andre Rudolph suggests that there is a tense hierarchy in Hervey's thinking that develops during his career as a thinker (Rudolph, pp. 108–15).
[27] 'Lies Hervey, mein lieber Bruder' (ZH, 1 :196). He repeats this advice to his brother in August 1758 (see ZH, 1: 243).

especially his view that not only is the world a text but also the Bible is its deepest representation. In a relevant passage Hervey states that 'I admire, I must confess, the very *Language* of the Bible. In this, methinks, I discern a Conformity between the *Book* of *Nature* and the *Book* of *Scripture*'.[28] He insists on an interpretation that understands the power of the biblical text as poetic. He influences Blake in maintaining that if we look for factual coherence, then this is a deeply confused literalism confounding 'the literal' with 'the truth'.[29] For instance, a version of criticism that assumes that the value of the book of Genesis depends on whether or not it provides us with a factually correct account of the 'history of the world' misunderstands not just the power of the text but also the standard by which to measure it. Blake and Hamann both adapt Hervey's view that the Bible is a historical document, but not one whose value lies in its factual accuracy, like a police report. To either criticize or defend the Bible as providing (or failing to provide) such a report is to misunderstand deeply the primary characteristic of the biblical text as a source of poetic insight and truth.

What makes Hervey so interesting here is that he drew particular attention to language as a 'Gift of Speech', a formulation that Blake and Hamann echo repeatedly.[30] The creative God in Hervey is a rhetorical writer, again an image we find in all three of these authors. They come to believe in the Bible as literature precisely because it provides the most powerful way to comprehend the world. The assumption is also that God reveals Himself through nature and in Scripture: 'God reveals Himself—the creator of the world a writer—.'[31] This revelation occurs through the world but also in its biblical representation. We have to develop a hermeneutic apparatus so we can learn how to read them. As Hamann continues in a lightly ironic tone, '[W]hat a fate will His books have to experience, what severe judgements, what sharpminded judges of art will subjugate his books'.[32] He is already foreseeing 'severe judgements' against the quality of creation, a humorous description of the readers that will accuse the Bible of not being quite good enough.

---

[28] James Hervey, *Theron and Aspasio: Or, a Series of Dialogues and Letters, upon the Most Important and Interesting Subjects*, 3 vols (London: printed for John and James Rivington, 1755), p. 19; original emphasis.

[29] Henry St John, first Viscount Bolingbroke, for instance, is a common target for Hervey's and Hamann's criticisms because he deems the Old Testament as ultimately fragmentary, insufficient, and imperfect (see Rudolph, p. 110). Hamann translates Hervey's engagement eleven years after his London visit in *Heinrich St. Johann Vitzgraf Bolingbroke und Jakob Hervey* (1774) (N, 4: 441). Hamann follows Hervey in resisting a new form of literalism: '[H]e turns sharply against the assumption of criticism that one could find a 'history of the world' in the first books of Moses and that they would be worthless if that were not the case' (Außerdem wendet er [Hamann] sich scharf gegen die Annahme der Kritik, man könne in den ersten Büchern Moses eine 'Geschichte der Welt' finden und daß sie wertlos seien, wenn das nicht der Fall wäre) (qtd in Jørgensen, p. 241). As Jørgensen adds, Hamann at the time of *Aesthetica in nuce* circles back to Hervey's critique on Bolingbroke and also explicitly refers to it in the *Socratic Memorabilia* (see Johann Georg Hamann, *Sokratische Denkwürdigkeiten: Aesthetica in nuce*, ed. Sven-Aage Jørgensen [Stuttgart: Reclam, 1998], p. 88).

[30] Hervey, *Theron and Aspasio*, 1: 9. Also see Rudolph, p. 117.

[31] 'Gott offenbart sich—Der Schöpfer der Welt ein Schriftsteller—', Hamann, *Londoner Schriften*, p. 67.

[32] 'Was für ein Schicksal werden seine Bücher erfahren müssen, was für streng[en] Urtheilen, was für scharfsinnig[en] Kunstrichtern werden seine Bücher unterworfen seyn' (Hamann, *Londoner Schriften*, p. 67).

The power of the Bible does not mean, however, that it is straightforward. Scripture is not always positive or immediately revelatory; it is a mysterious, deep text. But rather than criticizing it for that or trying to fix it, Blake and Hamann celebrate that aspect. There is a deference and humility in their attitude that stands in sharp contrast with their normal reaction to the writings of others. In relation to their peers, historical or contemporary, they have a sense of distance, irony, often arrogance, and loud criticism. Think of Blake's annotations, even to books he generally liked, or of Hamann's reviews. There is none of that cocksure contrariness when it comes to the Bible, and the fact that there could not be—it would not make sense— does not come from its coherence but rather its depth and poetical power.

Reading the biblical text is an enormously complex procedure, and we need to think hard about how to enact that hermeneutic practice. For Blake it produces prophetic poetry, and for Hamann it produces a philosophy of poetic language and thought. What these different results have in common is the assumption that God is a writer. In his *On the Interpretation of the Holy Scripture*, Hamann often returns to the idea that God has produced the world as text and simultaneously has written the Bible. Hamann thinks of God as the author of the structures that we can perceive around us. Language will turn out to be the most crucial of those structures. Hence it is important that God is a *writer*—not, say, a scientist or a painter. Hamann invokes the imagery of the world as text in a specific, linguistic way that makes 'language' the most accurate way to speak about structure. Just as for Blake, for Hamann the beginning of the Gospel of St John remains a continual touchstone for an understanding of how meaning is created and should be analysed.

The original insight for both Blake and Hamann is not so much that the world is a text. That much should be clear from the start, and it would seem pointless to deny it. What is more intriguing to them is to figure out how we represent that poetic text back to ourselves. It is not through ratio or analysis alone, but rather through language and creation: 'I will not Reason & Compare: my business is to Create', Blake states.[33] And that creation brings revelation. Thus, revelation is a linguistic act: it speaks to us. Hamann suggests that this has a historical and a philosophical dimension: 'Each Biblical story is a prophecy that is fulfilled through all centuries and in the soul of each human.... [T]he spirit of God reveals itself in His word'.[34] As a result, the Bible becomes not just the most 'Entertaining & Instructive' but also the most generative book, since it encourages us to understand prophecy and poetry together. Balfour rightly insists that there is a 'conviction for the strict identity between poetry and prophecy' in Blake: 'It would...be mistaken to think that where there once was prophecy, there now is poetry, as if the latter had just displaced the former'.[35] One of the distinctive things about Blake's position

---

[33] Blake, *Jerusalem*, p. 153, ch. 1, plate 10, line 21.

[34] 'Jede biblische Geschichte ist eine Weissagung—die durch alle Jahrhunderte—und in jeder Seele des Menschen erfüllt wird...Der Geist Gottes in seinem Wort offenbart sich' (Hamann, *Londoner Schriften*, p. 421).

[35] Ian Balfour, *The Rhetoric of Romantic Prophecy* (Stanford, CA: Stanford University Press, 2002), p. 136.

as a poet of prophecy is that he sees the 'Imagination' as the ultimate addressee of the word. Blake rejects the idea that 'Understanding or Reason' mediates the world and thus imagination becomes the sphere in which revelation occurs and reflects back upon itself. We do well to remember that Blake envisions his own prophetic books to be revelatory also. If *Jerusalem* wants to be 'more Entertaining & Instructive' than most books, then it also will address itself to the 'Imagination which is Spiritual Sensation'. The poem itself is revelatory.

Again, Hervey is helpful here as a mediating figure. Blake made the link between Hervey and Edward Young explicit through the title of his painting, and he put them side-by-side in his poetry. In Hervey and in Young, Blake and Hamann find a confidence in the reflective powers of the night and an implied scepticism regarding the supposedly enlightening powers of an epistemology of the light. In his *Contemplations on the Night* Hervey elaborates on this through a complex analogy that plays on nature and the Enlightenment. Describing a row of hedges that is populated with an abundance of glittering and twinkling glow-worms, he writes, 'Should some weather-beaten Traveller, dropping with Wet, and shivering with Cold, hover round this *Mimicry* of *Fire*; in order to dry his Garments, and warm his benumbed Limbs;... How certainly would... [he] be frustrated of [his] Expectation[]!'[36] The frustration of the traveller is to have fallen for a copy, a mimicry that does not share the desired quality—in this case, heat and warmth. Hervey explains that these are people who are 'deaf to the infallible Decisions of Revelation', and who 'resign themselves over to the erroneous *Conjectures* of *Reason*, in order to find the Way that leadeth unto Life'.[37] To follow the glow-worms for real warmth and heat, and to mistake their copy of light for the real thing, is analogous to confusing the conjectures of human reason with divine revelation. Hervey helps his readers see the wider implications in ways that Blake and Hamann would have heartily approved of:

> To speak more plainly... the Powers of fallen Reason, which *Some* are so apt to idolize; are not only vain, but treacherous. Not only a *painted Flame*, like these sparkling Animals; but much like those unctuous Exhalations, which arise from the marshy Ground, and often dance before the Eyes of the benighted Way-faring man. Kindled into a sort of Fire, they personate a guide, and seem to offer their Service: but, blazing with *delusive Light*, mislead their Follower into hidden Pits, headlong Precipices, and unfathomable Gulfs. Where, far from his beloved Friends, far from Hopes of Succour, the unhappy Wanderer is swallowed up, and lost.[38]

It turns out that the glow-worms are not simply a cause for mild disappointment or frustration but much more dangerous. They almost sound like Blake's little boy who gets 'lost in the lonely fen, / Led by the wand'ring light'.[39] The 'Powers of fallen

---

[36] James Hervey, *Meditations and Contemplations: Containing, Meditations among the Tombs; Reflections on a Flower-Garden; and, a Descant on Creation. Contemplations on the Night. Contemplations on the Starry-Heavens; and, A Winter-Piece*, 21st ed. (London, 1774), pp. 276–7; original emphasis.
[37] Hervey, *Meditations and Contemplations*, p. 277; original emphasis.
[38] Hervey, *Meditations and Contemplations*, pp. 277–8; original emphasis.
[39] Blake, 'The Little Boy Found', in *Complete Poetry and Prose*, p. 11, lines 1–2.

Reason' are so problematic precisely because many contemporaries are apt to idolize them. This idolatry is not merely, as the first analogy suggests, a matter of mimicry: it goes beyond attempting to recreate the fire through a '*painted Flame*' and, instead, becomes an actively misleading will o' the wisp—that is, a '*delusive Light*' leading into a conceptual abyss where we get lost. Many of us deny the reflective possibilities of the night and instead end up blindly following a bunch of glow-worms into the abyss.

We need, then, to look out for the forms of nature or art that address themselves to the 'Imagination'—not to be confused by the glow-worms of artificiality but rather to look for what is immediately around us, even if that does not accord with what we are supposed to be seeing. When Blake says that 'I see Every thing I paint In This World', he is, in effect, presenting a different ontology and epistemology.[40] We can take this to mean that a painting such as *Ghost of a Flea* really does represent a vision of what Blake perceives is ontologically real—just as real, if not more so, than the table in front of him (Figure 4.2).

In a formulation that is important for the second part of this chapter, Blake writes: 'Every body does not see alike.... The tree which moves some to tears of

Figure 4.2 William Blake, *The Ghost of a Flea* (ca. 1819–20). © Tate Britain, London, Image ID: N05889.

---

[40] Blake to Dr Trusler, p. 702.

joy is in the Eyes of others only a Green thing that stands in the way. Some See Nature all Ridicule & Deformity & by these I shall not regulate my proportions, & Some Scarce see Nature at all.' The ability to see is a qualitative difference between humans and it is probably the most important way of discerning between them: 'But to the Eyes of the Man of Imagination Nature is Imagination itself. As a man is So he Sees'.[41] Of course, for Blake, a vision that sees nature through the eyes of the 'Imagination' trumps 'Ridicule & Deformity'. This is a matter of accuracy: '[T]hrough philosophical abstraction the text of nature is more disfigured than through myths and fable creatures', as Helene Richter reminds us about Blake.[42] Certainly, a tree can be 'only a Green thing', reduced to its material objecthood, described sufficiently by its secondary qualities. Yet for Blake, looking at trees in such a way is not just reductive; it is patently wrong: a tree is a vision also of trees past, the tree of knowledge, and the tree full of angels that Blake saw as a child, too. For him the tree is, just like all of God's signs through the biblical text, an expression of the spirit world and its multiple meanings. If we want to record our vision, if we want to account for the world, then the poetic dimension is the most relevant one. The fact that our Lockean account of language has contributed to the loss of our ability to see—that should give us pause. Especially, since all thinkers on language—both Lockean and Hamannian—insist that the link between language and thought is crucial.

BETWEEN LANGUAGE AND THOUGHT: 'LONDON' AND COUNTERFEIT REASON

One account of the difficult connection between language and thought, for Blake and Hamann, lies at the centre of what they perceive to be a version of the Enlightenment that is deeply destructive. The rise and subsequent ossification of a Lockean version of language goes hand in hand with what Blake calls Newtonianism and what we might today term 'instrumental reason'. Instrumental ways of thinking are the most destructive force of their time and need to be resisted. Functionalism or instrumentalism has taken over both empiricism and idealism, theories of language included. It is the kind of thinking that reduces a tree to 'a Green thing that stands in the way'. It is a view that understands thought, just as it does language, as purely functional, assumes it to be disembodied, a neutral tool independent of its medium. It is a version of thought that, ideally, is transparent, unambiguous, and verifiably correct. Since it is instrumental, it is also a version of thought that is primarily directed towards *something*, a goal, an idea, a telos; it is instrumental in getting us somewhere, and, by implication, somewhere better. Although this is somewhat of a caricature, it should nevertheless be clear how variations of such accounts lie at the very heart of our common ideas about the Enlightenment.

---

[41] Ibid.
[42] 'Durch die philosophische Abstraktion ist der Text der Natur mehr verunstaltet also durch Mythen und Fabelwesen' (Helene Richter, 'Blake und Hamann' [part 1] p. 220).

Newtonianism has been our standard for a long time. Even a figure like Emanuel Swedenborg committed the mistake, according to Blake, to 'explain to the *rational* faculty what the reason cannot comprehend[;] he should have left that'.[43]

For Blake and Hamann, instrumental reason leads to the death of poetry. And thus, it also leads to a death of a particular form of thinking that is the obverse of instrumental reason. Again it's important to think beyond a model of dualities (ratio versus irrationalism) here: the obverse of 'instrumental' is not 'obstructionist'. The thought Hamann has in mind is attuned to the forms of physicality and oblique-ness that come via its inextricable connection to the medium of language. It is a form that we encounter in Blake, too. Poems such as 'London' invite us to look into the damaging forms of rationality that disguise themselves as neutral or 'natural'. By reading this suggestion back into some of their other work, I will show how Blake and Hamann provide us with a social and existential critique of thinking. Let's turn to London, whose importance as an international place of thinking becomes increasingly relevant. Blake's most famous engagement with his home encapsulates much of what is in play:

> I wander thro' each charter'd street,
> Near where the charter'd Thames does flow.
> And mark in every face I meet
> Marks of weakness, marks of woe.[44]

Much ink has been spilled on where the 'charter'd street[s]' are that Blake speaks about. Among the many important and productive suggestions stands a reminder that this is both a real and an imagined city. These 'charter'd' streets cross the Babel of the cosmopolitan London that Blake inhabits; they structure Soho, where Hamann has his religious experience, where Blake is born, and which is full of pubs where 'all the languages of Europe talked with the greatest fluency'.[45] One of the many things this stanza is about is how this city and the streets within it are brought under control, how the conceptual and linguistic Babel of London is being tamed. The tension this dynamic produces inhabits the poem from the very beginning: 'I wander thro' each charter'd street', Blake begins both the poem and its musing by *wandering*, an activity we associate more with non-teleological movement. The obvious homo-nym with 'wondering' pushes this activity into the epistemological sphere, but not one in which direct and systematized knowledge is sought. As Saree Makdisi reminds us, the exact way in which Blake walks *through* the streets in this historical context is of some consequence, since it suggests that 'he defies, is not bound by, both the commercial and the spatial chart(er)ing that otherwise seeks to control and define the space-time of the city'.[46] And yet there is also an immediate *volta*: the wondering takes place in 'each charter'd street'. The emphasis here is on

---

[43] Crabb Robinson, diary entry, 10 December 1825, p. 423.

[44] William Blake, 'London', in *Complete Poetry and Prose*, pp. 26–7, 26, lines 1–4.

[45] G. E. Bentley Jr, 'Appendix 2: Blake Residences', in *Blake Records*, pp. 733–56, 743.

[46] Saree Makdisi, *Making England Western: Occidentalism, Race, and Imperial Culture* (Chicago, IL: University of Chicago Press, 2014), p. 66. Makdisi also usefully comments on how mapping a city affects the temporality of that space.

comprehensiveness ('each') and organization ('chart'), both qualities that we do not associate with wandering or with the possibility of materially cutting through. Even the fact that there is a small ambiguity in the emphasis of the phrase 'each charter'd street' cannot hide the systematizing quality of this urban grid. Either we emphasize 'charter'd', which suggests that it is only in chartered (rather than unchartered) streets that Blake is wandering. Alternatively, and more powerfully, we emphasize 'each', stressing the comprehensibility of what Blake is describing, thus realizing that each and every street has been chartered, that London has become a mapped and systematized world. It is a line that powerfully contains many of the tensions of the era: among them, not only the push towards a particular form of order and the rationale behind it, but also a desire to wander and produce a critical account of this push. One certainly has to be careful not to simplify all these different tensions into one struggle between only two forces—the kind of schematic understanding that is responsible for thinking of Romanticism as something that happens *against* the Enlightenment. Blake's memorable phrase encourages us to read these complexities in a wider framework, first and foremost by taking us on a wander through London, the city and the poem.

The streets are being read, and they have to be read through language since every language produces its charts. One version of it, call it instrumental, creates a mapped city in which streets are accounted, organized, and fixed. Another version can create a poem, also a kind of chart to be read, in this case a much more ambiguous structure that suggests a difficult relation between language and thought. The poem reflects this difficulty back to us by its non-representation of language. We are told about the cries of the chimney sweepers and 'the youthful Harlots curse'.[47] Yet the cries and curses are already drowned out; they are neither explicit nor direct. In time, the manacles will organize this language (both the Harlot's and the poet's) and sub-sume it. In the end, what occurs is that the poem's language will not even be con-sidered a part anymore of what a useful chart of London would look like. Few visitors to London choose Blake's poem over a *London A–Z* on their visit. (It should give us pause, I think, that there is such a clear hierarchy of what counts as successful charting in that situation, that the difference in knowledge production between the map and the poem seems so obvious to us.) Blake's poem describes a pivotal moment in a historical process that is an exercise in chartering, in mind-forging, and which will end in the stark division between 'London' and London.

The wider connotations of the 'charting' Blake describes function as a powerful way to evoke what begins to haunt Hamann while he is in London and will con-tinue to trouble him throughout his work. If certain versions of new Enlightenment philosophy and practices invade and map the new cities of modernity, then Hamann immediately understands that this involves a closure of valuable ways of structuring life in this urban space. Through his spiritual 'experience', Hamann had developed a keen sense of the importance of wandering to a place or through a way that was uncharted. Remember that he had arrived in London as a person committed to a certain mapping of thought, the economic sphere of the city. What

---

[47] Blake, 'London', p. 27, line 14.

happened, though, is that the mission failed and in a spiral of depression he lost his way in the streets of London. By his own admission this included a time during which he would have seen some of the 'youthful Harlots' Blake speaks of and wandered around the city in an altogether lost way—a timely reminder that there is a difference between 'wandering' as an economically powerful *flâneur* and 'wandering' as an abject, nearly homeless wanderer.

We remember that it is a spiritual experience that turns Hamann's life around and pushes him towards a different way of experiencing London. There is almost nothing in the poem that suggests a parallel with the religious aspect of Hamann's narrative—even the 'blackning Church' is less about religion than about institutions—but there is something much more important that relates to one of Hamann's central insights which will never leave him after London: how we are restricted and self-restricted by what Blake terms 'mind-forg'd manacles'.[48] Blake's exact formulation and its history stand in helpful and productive relation to Hamann. Two things in particular stand out: first, the manacles are 'mind-forg'd'. This does not mean that they are illusory or exist in the mind. It means that they are created in the mind and then become part of our reality. The 'manacles' already shape the way we are thinking, which turns out to be a double-edged process. The 'forg[ing]' that the mind does is a complicated creation, typical for Blake. His term suggests the ambiguous quality of creation and production. It not only invokes the shaping of the thought, but also suggests the counterfeiting of that thought, a connotation of 'forging' that was already in use in Blake's time, including in his printing trade.

Counterfeiting can create such an imprisoning manacle, partly because we cannot see it, so we do not perceive it as fake anymore. Thought itself begins to pass itself off as neutral but, in fact, it creates an invisible 'manacle'; it chains our way of thinking. In part it is so invisible because it is everywhere:

> In every cry of every Man,
> In every Infants cry of fear,
> In every voice: in every ban[49]

The intense repetition of 'every' is both intensification of and attention to each singular voice. The 'mind-forg'd manacles' are in each utterance and voice. They are not only in every private cry but also in curses, official proclamations or sentences, all connotations contained in the negative word 'ban' that Blake uses. Counterfeit thought creates a set of all-encompassing manacles, and the imagery is by no means arbitrary: '[T]he chains are, the cunning of the weak and tame minds. which have power to resist energy. according to the proverb, the weak in courage is strong in cunning.'[50] The cunning reason is one that counterfeits and actually leaves what would otherwise be an unmediated experience shackled to a system of reason. Instead of a rational liberation, a freeing of humanity from the shackles of superstition, we have quite the opposite: these are the chains of reason that forge things in the mind and begin to charter the world around us. And London had become a capital

---

48 Blake, 'London', p. 27, lines 10 and 8.   49 Blake, 'London', p. 27, lines 5–7.
50 Blake, *The Marriage of Heaven and Hell*, in *Complete Poetry and Prose*, pp. 33–45, 40.

of such systematic and disabling approaches to thought and life. The deeply anti-Newtonian sentiment in 'London' is tied to the city as a specific, contested site of different versions of forging thought and accounting for the world. One of the most important suggestions of Blake's poem, then, is how a certain version of reason and what it does in a historically specific moment to particular ways of thinking and writing will close off avenues—or streets, so to speak, with Blake—of thought. In this sense, the poem encapsulates a chief concern of this book: how 'mind-forg'd manacles' have become the norm.

Several scholars have commented on Blake's decision to use this exact formulation. Jon Mee picks up David V. Erdman's point that in earlier notebook drafts the manacles are 'german forg'd' instead on 'mind-forg'd', 'a phrase more obviously critical of the Hanoverian monarchy'.[51] Most of Mee's (and Erdman's) attention is focused on Blake's political self-censorship here, and there is certainly plenty of evidence to support that reading: anti-royalist sentiment was being brutally quashed, and it thus often was mixed, as I pointed out in Chapter 1, with anti-German sentiment. Here is clearly a German influence or idea that Blake would have wanted to resist, and it makes one suspect that he would have been sceptical of German canonical cultural influence on Britain. Yet while we need to be aware of this change, it is important to remind us that Blake, in fact, made it; and that there are more dimensions to this than only self-censure. The reason why 'mind-forg'd manacles' are so much more powerful than 'german forg'd' ones is that the former can easily include the latter. In the end, Blake is invested in the larger structures of thinking. This is not exactly a generalization in the Blakean sense but rather, it seems to me, a deepening of the description. It is another way to make sense of Steven Goldsmith's recent description of Blake's '*absence* from organized radical activity'.[52] There is something deeply political in asking us to think about reason, including practical reason, differently via our own mind rather than external structures of political repression.

METACRITIQUE: AGAINST PURE LANGUAGE

Blake's sensitivity to the dangers of versions of language and reason that pass themselves off as something they are not, that produce a counterfeit that imprisons, finds productive echoes in Hamann's metacritique, his own powerful diagnosis of 'forg'd' rationality and his philosophical attack on the fetters of reason. Hamann first uses the term 'metacritique' in a letter to Johann Gottfried Herder in 1782: 'Because of Hume & Kant everything in my head turns sour; must live to see the *Prolegomena* of metaphysics, which is still to be written, if it is God's will, before I come out with my *Metacritique*.'[53] Hamann complains that he has to read

---

[51] Sarah Haggarty and Jon Mee, *William Blake: Songs of Innocence and Songs of Experience: a Reader's Guide to Essential Criticism* (Houndmills, Basingstoke: Palgrave, 2013), p. 133.

[52] Steven Goldsmith, *Blake's Agitation*, p. 89.

[53] 'Ueber Hume u Kant versauert alles in meinem Kopf; muß erst die *Prolegomena* der Metaphysik, die noch geschrieben werden soll, erleben, wenn es Gottes Wille ist, ehe ich mit meiner *Metakritik* herauskomme' (ZH, 4: 400).

Immanuel Kant and David Hume, making his metacritical response somewhat of an Anglo-German exercise. As Hamann outlines, he awaits Kant's *Prolegomena*, famously written as a short compendium to the *Critique of Pure Reason*, before he will turn to compose his own direct response, the *Metacritique of the Purism of Reason*. Despite its brevity and the fact that it was unpublished during his lifetime, the *Metacritique* is considered one of Hamann's most important writings. It is a concentrated example of Hamann's thinking, especially when it comes to its self-understanding within the context of the Enlightenment and to reason in relation to language. If we keep this in mind, then we can see how the *Metacritique* resonates meaningfully with the analysis of instrumental reason as a counterfeit of the kind we just encountered in 'London' and also in Locke, who calls figurative language a 'perfect cheat'.

Because Hamann's essay has been the subject of much excellent scholarship, I focus on two issues that are immediately relevant.[54] The first is Hamann's understanding of metacritique in the historical formation of the Enlightenment. The second is the specific role of language within that context. Oswald Bayer has shown that for Hamann the discussion about metacritique is a discussion about different versions or visions of the Enlightenment, especially his specific criticisms of Kant. Hamann believes that Kant begs the question when it comes to reason. The 'chief question', according to Kant, 'is always simply this:—what and how much can the understanding and reason know apart from all experience? not: how is the faculty of thought itself possible?'[55] Hamann, in direct contrast, makes the faculty (das Vermögen) the main question: 'Indeed, . . . a chief question does remain: how is the power to think possible?—The power to think right and left, before and without, with and above experience?'[56] As Bayer points out,

> Hamann answers this main question with reference to *transmission, experience* and *language* which saturates and encompasses them but also is abused for building metaphysical castles in the air. Already this first draft of the metacritique notes that without language rationality is 'impossible'. §9 picks up this thesis—in the metacritically precise version which relates precisely to Kant: 'the whole ability to think rests on language'. The whole text gets its coherence by unfolding and substantiating this thesis metacritically.[57]

[54] A good starting point is provided in Griffith-Dickson, *Hamann's Relational Metacriticism*. By far the most detailed analysis is provided in Oswald Bayer, *Vernunft ist Sprache: Hamanns Metakritik Kants* (Stuttgart: Frommann-Holzboog, 2002).

[55] Immanuel Kant, *Critique of Pure Reason*, trans. Norman Kemp Smith (London: Macmillan, 1963), p. 12: '[W]eil die Hauptfrage immer bleibt, was und wie viel kann Verstand und Vernunft, frei von aller Erfahrung, erkennen und nicht, wie ist das *Vermögen zu denken* selbst möglich?' (Immanuel Kant, *Theoretische Philosophie*, 3 vols [Frankfurt: Suhrkamp, 2004], 1: 16–17).

[56] Griffith-Dickson, p. 522. 'Bleibt es allso ja noch eine Hauptfrage: wie das Vermögen zu denken möglich sey?—Das Vermögen, rechts und links vor und ohne, mit und über die Erfahrung hinaus zu denken?' (N, 3: 286).

[57] 'Diese Hauptfrage beantwortet Hamann mit dem Hinweis auf *Überlieferung, Erfahrung* und, beide durchdringend und umfassend, *Sprache*, die sich selbst noch zum Bau metaphysischer Luftschlösser mißbrauchen läßt. Ohne Sprache, so hält schon der erste Entwurf zur Metakritik fest, ist Vernunft "unmöglich". §9 nimmt diese These auf—in der metakritisch genau auf Kant bezogenen Fassung: "das ganze Vermögen zu denken beruht auf Sprache". Der gesamte Text hat seine Einheit darin, daß er diese These metakritisch entfaltet und begründet' (Bayer, *Vernunft ist Sprache*, p. 201).

Hamann's aim is not to question reason per se (and the philosophical project that hangs by it) but, rather, a version of reason (including a philosophical project that hangs by it), especially when that version passes itself off as the only account of reason that is available.

In the end, the metacritical approach is an intervention against the rise and reign of instrumental reason. Hamann not only believes that Kant gets language and reason terribly wrong; he also understands that Kant's approach is a way of conceiving of not just philosophy but the world.

For Hamann, one of Kant's most severe (and telling) errors is that he does not consider language at all, much less acknowledge the importance of the medium in which he is articulating his theory about the conditions of the possibility of thought. Instead, Kant attempts in the *Critique* to purify thought of its assumptions, to turn it into an invisible, mental operation, independent of the embodied subject. However, much of Kant's work is interested in a critique of pure thought; his project is, for Hamann, a version of how the 'mind-forg'd manacles' are being produced—and, once operational, how they produce themselves. In his analysis, Hamann reads Kant's 'purification' in three stages. First, there is the attempt 'partly misconceived, partly unsuccessful' 'to make reason independent of all custom'.[58] The second step 'is still more transcendental and aims at nothing less than an independence of experience and its everyday induction'.[59] Both of these lead, ultimately, to an apotheosis of reason, an apotheosis that is blind to its original inaccuracies. As Hamann puts it, Kant 'turns God into the ideal without knowing that his pure reason is precisely the same'.[60] Pure reason ends up as the theologically inflected glue that holds the supposedly non-theological critical project together—or, if we want to switch metaphorical registers, it shackles the one to the other.

It is the third purism that is the 'most sublime and as it were empirical': it 'concerns language, the single, first and last *organon* and criterion of reason'.[61] This is the moment when Kant really shows his true colours, since he wants to disassociate experience from the structure that has formed that experience in the first place: language. For Hamann, on the contrary, language is an '*organon*'; that is, it connects the physical and the mental as a 'bodily organ, esp.... an instrument of the soul or the mind'.[62] Kant's first mistake, according to Hamann, is to ignore that language is precisely such an instrument, that it generates thought. As a result, Kant's philosophical account also neglects how the process of that production shapes the outcome in a significant way. Reason and language are not to be separated, since we need them in unison to identify, qualify, and judge their results. Language is not

---

[58] Griffith-Dickson, p. 520: 'dem theils misverstandenen, theils mislungenen Versuch, die Vernunft von aller Ueberlieferung... unabhängig zu machen' (N, 3: 284).

[59] Griffith-Dickson, p. 520: 'ist noch transcendenter und läuft auf nichts weniger als eine Unabhängigkeit von der Erfahrung und ihrer alltäglichen Induction hinaus' (N, 3: 284).

[60] 'Kant macht Gott zum *Ideal* ohne zu wißen, daß seine reine Vernunft eben daßelbe ist' (ZH, 6: 163).

[61] Griffith-Dickson, p. 520 emphasis in original. 'höchste und gleichsam empirische Purismus betrifft also noch die Sprache, das einzige erste und letzte Organon und Kriterion der Vernunft' (N, 3: 284).

[62] *OED*, 2nd ed., s.v. 'organon, *n*.', 1.

only both the productive and the declamatory '*organon*', but also the 'criterion' by which language judges itself and the thoughts it produces with reason.

The difference between empirical experience and conceptual representation cannot be bridged by 'purifying' both of them.[63] To resist the desire for 'purification' is also to resist an accompanying rhetoric that often associates purity with transparency (pure water), concentration (pure gold), or ethics (pure heart). Yet language does not travel in only one sphere since it links the physical and the mental: 'Words... have an aesthetic and logical capacity.'[64] Hamann suggests that this multiplicity and capacity make the aesthetic and the logical part not only of language but also of knowledge and experience. The 'organon' of language makes knowledge production into a process that cannot be 'purified' because it always contains both thought and language, because it is both physical (aesthetic) and mental (logical). Hamann's insistence on the 'aesthetic capacity' points towards his wider criticism of the idealization of reason as a disembodied force. But language and thought cannot be disentangled and isolated in the way that much philosophy seems to suggest.

For Hamann, Kant's neglect of the generative dimension of language is a symptom that is connected to his assumptions of the supposed neutrality of thought. Two of these assumptions stand out: first, that Kant's attempt to 'purify' is particularly resistant to the idea of the physicality of language (Hamann links this to what he sees as an overall resistance to aesthesis in Kant's projected result); second, that Kant's project unwittingly betrays his desire to achieve a clear and coherent outcome at the price of ignoring a piece that is central to its construction but threatens to introduce interference. If language and thought are so intrinsically connected, Hamann insists, then we need to include linguistics in our philosophical field, not simply as an external object of study (such as in Locke) but, rather, as a constitutive part of any method that philosophy develops.[65] This method is, in turn, subject to a form of critique—namely metacritique. Hamann's point is not just simply to ask for more awareness about language in philosophy. For him, as he puts it elliptically, 'Without word, no reason—no world'.[66] Any substantial critique of thought, he intimates, must also include the critique of the form, the medium, in which this thought is generated. Metacritique asks us to think about the forms in which analysing the conditions of the possibility of critique take place. And, while that way

[63] Incidentally, Blake uses a similar idea when he speaks about perception. For him, the organon of seeing is the eye: 'As the Eye is formed such are its Powers' (Blake to Dr Trusler, p. 702). In effect, Blake insists that the eye is the organon of seeing in a way similar to Hamann's suggestion that language is the organon of reason. The point is a metacritical one: neither vision nor thinking is neutral. They shape the way representation is available to us.

[64] Griffith-Dickson, p. 524: 'Wörter haben... ein ästhetisches und logisches Vermögen' (N, 3: 288).

[65] It is important to note that John Locke does not always relegate language this way. In what has become known as *Draft B* of the *Essay*, he does seem to present a variation of his more widely known view on language and its relation to the formation of ideas. This does not affect the overall argument here, but should serve as a reminder that his (and, more widely, eighteenth-century) linguistic theory is more fluid than it is often presented to be. See John Locke, *Drafts for the 'Essay concerning Human Understanding', and Other Philosophical Writings*, ed. by Peter Nidditch and G. A. J. Rodgers, 3 vols (Oxford: Clarendon, 1990), 1: 167–203.

[66] 'Ohne Wort, keine Vernunft—keine Welt' (ZH, 5: 95).

of thinking about metacritique is applicable across a wide spectrum, Hamann posits its linguistic incarnation as the most crucial. Language is privileged because it is the medium through which we construct all reality.

Hamann's thesis of the inextricability of language and thinking puts the analysis of language squarely at the centre of philosophy. It cannot divide intellectual or conceptual inquiry from linguistic form. Philosophy has to account for language not simply as a supposedly controlled object of study. Two years after his letter to Herder in which he first mentions metacritique, Hamann articulates the consequences of this view again when he suspects that 'our philosophy consists more of language than reason'.[67] This is not just a swipe at verbose philosophers, but also an insistence that we had better put language centre stage in our philosophical analysis—but not in a verbose way. To Hamann's mind, his contemporaries show a lack of engagement with the question of how language shapes thinking, and how the structures of language are a meaningful and important aspect of this shaping process. And though Enlightenment philosophy is concerned with language, 'We still lack a *grammar* of reason'.[68] The '*grammar*' is a grammar of reason that takes seriously the inextricability or analogy between language and thinking and understands that the structure—the grammar—of thought reveals its linguistic aspect and meaning.

Hamann's linguistic diagnosis that we lack a '*grammar* of reason' has several consequences. Initially it seems to encourage an account that clarifies and clears up the relation between thought and language. Once we have established that, so the argument would go, we can map language and thought onto one another as clearly as possible, and not risk any interference: the grammar would be clear, unambiguous; the clearer that relation, the better the philosophy—much like later attempts by positivism and certain strands of analytical philosophy. However, this way of approaching the issue runs directly counter to the spirit and meaning of Hamann's remark. It ignores that the relationship of language and thought, for all its importance, is precisely *not* transparent. Philosophy's great error is to maintain that the relation is, or needs to be, clear and unambiguous. This is deeply misguided. To address the lack of our structural understanding of language, our grammar, does not translate into a claim that we can elucidate (or even manipulate) the entirety of that structure. Just because we identify that the structure is important does not mean that we are able clearly to discern how the structure works. Hamann's idea and conception of language is diametrically opposed to Jürgen Habermas's influential idea of an ideal speech situation that comes directly out of Enlightenment philosophy. An ideal speech situation is 'ideal' precisely because it is almost neutral: it produces little interference on which, as a result, political structures can be built. There is a direct line from Kant and Locke to Habermas here, a line that figures such as Hamann and Blake violently cross since they think such a speech situation is not only impossible but also a highly undesirable ideal. For them, in a Habermasian speech situation, we would lose language itself.

[67] '[U]nsere Philosophie mehr aus Sprache als Vernunft besteht' (ZH, 5: 272).
[68] 'Es fehlt uns...noch immer an einer *Grammatik* der Vernunft' (ZH, 5: 272).

For Hamann, then, language is not a neutral medium; it is linked to thinking. That link needs to be part of any philosophy, albeit with an understanding that it will not be elucidated completely. In other words, language is the source of our epistemological, ethical, and aesthetic frameworks. It allows us to articulate our experiences within these frameworks and the thinking that shapes them. However, its link to the faculty of thought is not transparent, and we have to resist attempts, in philosophy and elsewhere, to make it appear as if it were. There is no rational thinking that is neutral or 'outside' of language. The interconnection between language and thought, however, is not open to easy inspection and, certainly, is in need of philosophical scrutiny. In an important sense, philosophy is the continuous investigation of their relation. As Hamann states in August 1784 in a letter to Herder, 'Reason is language, Logos; I gnaw on this marrowbone, and will gnaw myself to death over it'.[69] The remarkable image of the 'marrowbone' turns Hamann into a dog whose repetitious and visceral engagement is, by definition, both profoundly pleasurable as well as ultimately without clear solution. Language and thought provide the backbone of philosophy; they are what lies behind the outer appearance of much thought, but they themselves are irreducible and cannot be further broken down, however much they entice us to try. The engagement with language cannot be teleological or linear; the complexity and resistance of its object of study—the marrowbone—necessitates a return to it over and over again. Hamann positions himself against philosophers who qualify the inescapable obliqueness of that relation as a stultifying frustration. Implicitly, he does not conceive of this oblique relation as something that is necessarily negative. That we gnaw on a bone without having a tangible result does not mean that we should stop gnawing, or that the activity itself is unpleasurable. We gnaw on the bone to sharpen our teeth, but we also find some delight in this repetition. In fact, it makes our mouths water.

CELEBRATING THE OPACITY OF LANGUAGE

It is the simplicity and the control that it promises that help make the Lockean account and linguistic vision so attractive. Locke's view of language and thought explains current shortfalls, while leaving enough room for the linguistic system to take some of the blame. It promises almost a dissolution of the problem once it is brought under control: ideally, we can erase language as a philosophical issue; once we have done so, its relation to poetry will be completely clear. In contrast, Blake and Hamann do not see either language as a 'problem' that needs to be resolved. It is complicated, messy, and difficult—and that's one of the most extraordinary things about it: it allows depth. The primary significance is not that we *need* to be obscure, though Hamann often uses precisely this technique. The more important aspect is, instead, that language's power allows a depth that supposed clarity does not provide. We are reminded of Edmund Burke's pithy expression that a 'clear idea is therefore

---

[69] 'Vernunft ist Sprache Λογoζ; an diesem Markknochen nag' ich und werde mich zu Tod drüber nagen' (ZH, 5: 177).

another name for a little idea'.[70] While the reverse is not true (not all dark ideas are big ideas), what is at stake here is the questioning of the normal paradigms of clarity, evidence, and argument.

Both Blake and Hamann are aware of the seductive power of promised simplicity and control, yet they believe language cannot and, more importantly, should not function in this way. Take the relation between thoughts and words, an example that illustrates well the historical fight that Blake and Hamann are fighting, but also serves as a way to showcase their startling similarities. One central assumption of the Lockean view of words as 'subservient to Instruction and Knowledge' is that words themselves are essentially separate from the thoughts they represent.[71] This is at the heart of any philosophy that will make a distinction between ideas and words, and mostly will fault the latter for the unsuccessful transmission of the former. Plato's cave, Hobbes's marketplace of ideas, or Locke's *tabula rasa* are all metaphors invoked in versions of this approach. One crucial assumption of such a view is that there is, in fact, a knowable relation between those two spheres and that once it is known, it will be clear. It is the promise of simplicity and control. Crucially, this promise works even if, as in Locke's or Hobbes's case, you immediately admit that the relation is not perfect. Yet the promise that it can be, and that this possibility is grounded on a philosophical insight about a structure—the relation between the word and the thought—rather than on faith, is one of the most powerful motors of this philosophy.[72]

Blake and Hamann coincide in identifying the two deepest problems with this view of language: its naïveté and its hubris. The naïveté lies in the assumption that language is powerful because it is, ultimately, something simple. It is a mode of communication that, because of its increasing complexity, has been obscured. The naive assumption is that there is a way to resolve this issue. This second idea not only underestimates the complexity of the task but also mistakes the *nature* of it, committing a category mistake. The relations between words are not compromised purely because of the level of their complexity; it is more a question of the quality of these relations. It is simple to assume that they relate to one another on a level of complexity that accords to our understanding. It's a little bit like assuming they are constructed in the same way that other complicated problems we have come across are constructed—like, say, a giant puzzle. And this is where naivety and hubris make a terrible pair: once we think of the difficulty of language as a puzzle, we think that as humans we can solve the problem. The hubris is equally common to the theorists who maintain that the puzzle is externally thrust upon us (be it nature or God), or the ones that insist that it's produced by ourselves as an

---

[70] Edmund Burke, *A Philosophical Enquiry into the Origin of Our Ideas of the Sublime and the Beautiful*, 5th ed. (London: J. Dodsley, 1767), p. 108.

[71] John Locke, *Essay concerning Human Understanding*, p. 404.

[72] Obviously, this is a simplified, straw-man version of Locke. However, while a technical discussion might reveal a more balanced view, Blake knows and worries that it is this simplified view which is likely to succeed and which needs to be resisted. (Incidentally, the same is true of Hamann's view of Kant.) See Wayne Glausser, *Locke and Blake: A Conversation across the Eighteenth Century* (Gainesville, FL: University Press of Florida, 1998).

anthropocentric puzzle. But language in general, like poetry, is not a puzzle that can, or even must, be solved.

Many critiques of the construction of language and reason take the form of genealogies. We might think of Hamann's writings on the origin of language and reason, or of Blake's many stories about the mythical, linguistic, or spiritual origin (and fall) of man. The precise force of this genealogical method is considered in Chapter 6, in turning to institutional religion, but it also forms an apt conclusion to the current focus on language and thought. Genealogy and narrative become powerful ways to explain the loss Blake and Hamann were feeling regarding our conceptions of language. This dynamic is not just a matter of mournful complaint, but it becomes a critical tool, a philosophical method that points towards how we might reimagine an alternative conception of language. A passage from *Jerusalem* presents one of the most powerful attacks on the 'Reasoning Power' in the age of Enlightenment along these lines:

> And this is the manner of the Sons of Albion in their strength
> They take the Two Contraries which are calld Qualities, with which
> Every Substance is clothed, they name them Good & Evil
> From them they make an Abstract, which is a Negation
> Not only of the Substance from which it is derived
> A murderer of its own Body: but also a murderer
> Of every Divine Member: it is the Reasoning Power
> An Abstract objecting power, that Negatives every thing
> This is the Spectre of Man: the Holy Reasoning Power
> And in its Holiness is closed the Abomination of Desolation.[73]

This radical history of ideas traces how the sons of Albion in their strength 'take the Two Contraries which are calld Qualities, with which / Every Substance is clothed' and name 'them Good & Evil'. Blake's lines are full of philosophical allusions, like Hamann's writings, denouncing Locke. The invocation of 'Qualities, with which Every Substance is clothed' merges the vocabulary of Lockean secondary qualities with the common imagery of the sign as clothing for the thought. Naming those 'Qualities' in a way that sees them only as 'clothed' ideas has disastrous consequences. Blake here presents a negative genealogy, just as he does in the *Marriage of Heaven and Hell*: 'From them they make an Abstract, which is a Negation / Not only of the Substance from which it is derived / A murderer of its own Body: but also a murderer / Of every Divine Member: it is the Reasoning Power.' The contraries become 'an Abstract'—that is, a simplified mode of what actually exists. The sons of Albion (also the driving principles of society) ignore the nuances between certain positions when they put them into abstract principles.[74] Abstraction does not just 'Negat[e]' its original 'Substance'; it is not simply an intellectual mistake. It is a physical act: it turns whoever is abstracting into the 'murderer of its own Body'.

[73] Blake, *Jerusalem*, pp. 152–3, ch. 1, plate 10, lines 7–16.
[74] Hence also the Berkeleyan tone of the passage: remember that George Berkeley, a figure admired by both Blake and Hamann, presents a sharp and powerful denunciation of the Lockean division between primary and secondary qualities.

There is a suicidal threat of thinking in this manner; it is a deadening force we cannot see, an image even more deadly than William Wordsworth's counter-spirit.

The sons of Albion, when they are empowered, contort and distort the qualities of the world around us. They shape the way we view the world, altering our hermeneutic apparatus by interfering with its supposed structure. Once more, this is a question not so much about perception but about the tools of perception and expression, its 'organon' as Hamann calls it. The main distorter is 'Reasoning Power', which creates not only confusion with itself but also much more harm once it is applied in a way that will 'murder[]' through dialectics. Such deadly violence even saturates religion, an area that seemed to maybe offer a route to salvation. Reason distorts spirituality beyond redemption.

5

The Polyglot Moravians in Eighteenth-Century London

THE MORAVIANS, LOCAL AND GLOBAL

The Moravians were one of the most important, yet exorbitant communities in eighteenth-century Britain. They formed a crucial part of the rich Anglo-German network of clergy, authors, language instructors, and tradesmen in pre-1790s London, but they were also defined by being out of the norm, unusual, often excessive, figures who did not want, nor attempt, to become normal or canonical. The Moravians were exorbitant in some of their theology—especially their Christian eroticism—but they also stayed outside the normal tracks of thinking through their polyglot practices. Their nonconformist congregation was among the most active and self-promoting multilingual institutions of the period, exerting a significant influence on literary history—an influence that has been almost forgotten because it sidestepped the mainstream. Although they were always classified as a fringe movement, the Moravians were well known at the time, and their cultural impact was widely discussed across Europe. Most of the eighteenth-century literary or theological figures who have appeared so far in this book mention the Moravians in their writings or letters.[1] Often the remarks about or allusions to the Moravian congregation are fleeting, whether made derisively or in naive admiration. Most of the time, the nonconformists' strong cultural presence was linked to an awareness of their geographic and linguistic roots (John Wesley, for instance, simply called them 'The Germans'). Thus, in the eighteenth century this religious community was identified as a fringe group that, partly due to their multilingual identity, remained hard to pin down. They are a good example of an institution that does not fit into the scheme of Enlightenment and Romanticism, neither in literary historical terms nor in the terms that we normally inherit from intellectual history.

The two main figures of this book have significant links with the Moravian congregation in London. William Blake's mother was an active Moravian, and parts of

---

[1] Emanuel Swedenborg is a good example. He attended the Moravian congregation in London, made friends there, and wanted to join the Brethren, a desire that went unfulfilled. Swedenborg's imagery was steeped not just in Pietism but also in the Moravians' eroticized depictions of the divine, as Lars Bergquist has shown: see *Swedenborg's Secret: The Meaning and Significance of the Word of God, the Life of the Angels, and Service to God; A Biography* (London: Swedenborg Society, 2005), pp. 205–6.

his wider family circle were also members of the congregation. At the time that Blake was growing up, Catherine Blake likely sang Moravian hymns to soothe young William. Chapter 7 (on hymns and Blake's Songs) will discuss this link in detail, but it is worth keeping these connections in mind while developing a sense of the Moravians' general importance at that time in London. Johann Georg Hamann's connections were more direct, since he visited the Moravian Church in London shortly after the key experience that turned him towards biblical study and his unorthodox Christianity. Hamann had read Moravian writings before, and though not a Moravian himself, he certainly felt sympathetic towards them.[2] In London, they were known as a specifically Anglo-German church and also as particularly welcoming to visitors and travellers, so Hamann's turn to them made perfect sense.[3] It means that, when in April 1758 Hamann underwent the most profound intellectual experience of his life, he did so around the same time he saw a pastor in the Savoy Chapel, an important part of the wider context of the Moravian Anglo-German community in London.[4]

This chapter begins with a short historical contextualization of the Moravians' German roots, allowing us to see how deeply the culture they brought to England was embedded in their history and practices. Next, the chapter turns towards primary sources from the Moravian congregation at Fetter Lane in order to illustrate

---

[2] Jörg Ulrich Fechner has shown that Hamann was well acquainted with a range of Moravian publications, including Zinzendorf's *London Prints* (*Londoner Drucke*): he had read these seven years before setting off to Britain (see Fechner, pp. 1–21, 5–6). For a differing view, see Nora Immendörfer, *Johann Georg Hamann und Seine Bücherei* (Königsberg: Ost-Europa, 1938), p. 16. The scholarship of Imendörffer and of Josef Nadler has assembled an extensive record of Hamann's readings (see esp. N, 5). After his return to Germany, Hamann remains interested in Nikolaus Ludwig von Zinzendorf's writing. On this topic, also see Zinzendorf's collection *Der deutsche Sokrates* [*The German Socrates*] (Leipzig: Walther, 1732).

[3] On the Moravians being welcoming, see Colin Podmore, *The Moravian Church in England, 1728–1760* (Oxford: Clarendon, 1998), pp. 120–204.

[4] See Fechner, pp. 16 and 19. Also see N, 2: 46; and Bernhard Gajek, 'Leben und Werk eines Königsberger Philosophen: Zum 200. Todestag des "Magus in Norden"', in *Acta Borussica: Zentralarchiv für altpreußische Volkskunde und Landesforschung* 3 (Munich: Haus der Ost- und Westpreußen in Bayern, 1989): 65–80, 68. Barnett claims that Hamann 'had contact with Moravian Pietism during this period' (*Kierkegaard, Pietism and Holiness* [New York: Routledge, 2016], p. 312); and Gajek states Hamann 'associated with the Moravian Brethren in London' (p. 68). Fechner even claims that Hamann had several 'private contacts' (private Kontakte) with members of the Moravian congregation during his turn to religion (p. 19).

Scholarship on Hamann has spent some time trying to ascertain what precise aspects of Moravian thought or practice would have been critical to him outside of his concrete context; for instance, Fechner suggests that there might be a direct relation between the close biblical criticism that Hamann engaged in and the Moravian daily readings. Most of these connections remain speculative. There is no question that the Moravian community was critical to Hamann's life in 1758, however, though it is less clear that the precise theology of the Moravians captured him for the rest of his life. If there is a direct influence, then it will be found only in relatively circumstantial evidence, since Hamann's theological stance becomes so idiosyncratic and oblique, almost willfully obscuring traces of such influences. See Fechner, p. 11.

Evidently, Hamann outgrows and modulates Moravian influences upon his return from London, but that does not take away the importance that they provide as the concrete context of his experiences within an actively Anglo-German congregation that also included members of William Blake's family. For a discussion of Hamann's funny (ab)uses of Zinzendorf in his writings, see Harald Steffes, 'Hamann und Zinzendorf: Gedanken zu einer sokratischen Verwechslung', in Beetz and Rudolph, *Johann Georg Hamann*, pp. 349–67.

the polyglot world they created and supported, both institutionally and through aesthetic practice. Using previously unpublished material from the London Moravian Archives, including bilingual minutes and books, I show that the multilingual character of the Moravian Church was central to the congregation and its institutional structure all the way down to the daily life of its members. The most important sources here are bilingual official documents and the multilingual books that the Moravian house press produced. None of these practices were naive or unselfconscious. There was a theoretical and conceptual awareness to the polyglot character of the Moravians that was highly suggestive. The multilingual character was a structural dimension of the Anglo-German context and maintained this congregation's importance while also maintaining its non-canonical status. The Moravians' sources show us that we need to pay attention not just to exorbitant individuals but also to the way institutions such as the German churches across England helped in important ways to shape a form of literature and art with which we are not familiar.

The Moravians have had a complex and difficult history, especially because they were so active throughout Europe and beyond. As with other Protestant groups, for them the biblical text stands at the centre of worship and faith. Even more than in other denominations, however, the Moravian Church places deep importance on the personal encounter of believer and God. Often this encounter comes through the figure of Christ and his symbolic presence. Their strong belief in Christ as a real and symbolic carrier reached degrees in the eighteenth century that made many contemporaries uncomfortable, especially since the Moravians developed a highly sexualized and eroticized Christology that made many people nervous at the time and that certainly did reach exorbitant levels. They form one of the most intriguing and fascinating groups of the eighteenth century, and their importance in relation to increasingly globalizing networks, postcolonialism, and the status of women deserves far more attention. So far, the existing research in the area of Moravianism's radical positions on theology, sexuality, and gender rarely considers the multilingual aspect of the congregation as part of their existence. Yet it is important to understand that the Moravians at that time were different from the mainstream, not just in their eschatology but also in the way they concretely articulated their unusual beliefs in a polyglot context in London, outside the normal tracks of thought and language.

In the first half of the eighteenth century, many Moravians showed a highly eroticized articulation of love for the Saviour. The most unconventional and extreme aspect of Moravian Christology was the veneration bordering on an obsession with Christ's blood, his side wound, and how the theological, marital union of Christ and believer translates into a worldly dimension. In an episode that Moravian scholarship now understands as central, there are reports of members of the church literally staging their own entry into an installation, a symbolic representation of Christ's side wound that was revealed during festive celebrations: '[T]he effigy of the Saviour disappeared and in its place appeared a large side hole, serving as an entrance into the brothers' house', as Paul Peucker describes it. 'Through the side hole and inside the house a table was visible on which the body of Christ lay carved (*tranchirt*) and neatly served in pieces.'[5] There are plenty more descriptions of how these excessive forms of devotion mingled with eroticized depictions of the body—the side hole as a vaginal symbol is only the most obvious one—that set the Moravians apart. Among them would have been the 1748 gender-changing ceremony during which, through a performative act, several of the Moravian brothers were declared to be sisters.[6]

This period of extreme symbolism and eroticization coincided with the Moravians' polyglot practices in London. While the congregation in London never reached the extreme eroticism discussed on the Continent—and these practices came under censure on the Continent too—there is a suggestive connection between these aspects, especially since the veneration of Christ in such a manner is deeply bound up with issues of language and poetry. For the Moravians, the celebration of Christ through sung linguistic performance in more than one language is not just a matter of religious practice, but also a topic of theological reflection. A striking example is Donald McCorkle's report how

> in the early history of the Moravian Church in America, the Singstunden [singing hours] were embellished by polyglot singing that is, by the congregation singing the hymn simultaneously in their respective vernacular tongues. The macaronic carol, 'In dulce jubilo', was sung in eleven languages! English, German, Swedish, Bohemian, Dutch, French, Greek, Irish, Latin, Welsh, and Wendish, as well as in two Indian dialects, Mohawk and Mohican.[7]

Importantly, in this macaronic babble, the term for singing hour remains German: *Singstunde*. We find that in London this continued commitment to German combines with an openness to English in order to produce a remarkable Anglo-German hub of productivity that celebrates both multilingualism in education and a polyglot aesthetic.

Evidently, the eighteenth-century Moravians were both inside and outside Protestantism. At no point were they keen to be central players at home, since they were concerned with spreading Christianity abroad. However, they were well known, and most people at the time had heard of them, either for their sexual Christology, their multilingualism, or both. In the mid-eighteenth century, we witness the most powerful and creative period of Moravian writing and a particular physical spirituality of their devotion to Christ's blood and wounds. They imagine the Saviour as a 'bleeding lover' and the applicants to the church imagine that they 'eat and drink…the crucified bleeding Corpse of my Creator and Spouse'. The communion 'was the embrace of the husband, "a conjugal penetration of our bloody husband"'.[8] Much has been written about this aspect of the Moravian imagery, especially its sexual dimensions. It was a crucial reason why the Moravians remained exorbitant, aberrant and exceeded proper bounds and, also, why their polyglot

[5] Paul Peucker, *A Time of Sifting: Mystical Marriage and the Crisis of Moravian Piety in the Eighteenth Century* (University Park: Pennsylvania State University Press, 2015), p. 79.
[6] See Peucker, pp. 1–10.
[7] Donald McCorkle, 'Moravian Music in Salem: A German-American Heritage' (PhD dissertation Indiana University, 1958), p. 60.
[8] Podmore, p. 135.

tradition could never become part of the mainstream. Consider this Easter hymn, for instance, which illustrates how these concerns translate into poetry:

> Our Lamb looks exceedingly sweet
> In his lovely Wounds so bloody,
> Which he wears in Hand and Feet.
> Our Lamb looks exceedingly sweet
> In his whole tormented Body,
> Which we inly kiss and greet. *Fin:*
> His head torn and his Eyes broken,
> His dear Side-Hole, my Lord's Token,
> And the venerable Blood,
> Makes the Tears flow like a Flood.[9]

The physicality and violence, together with sexual overtones, showcase their radical way of understanding the poetry of the biblical text. The idea of Jesus's head 'torn and his Eyes broken' and the focus on the imagery of the side wound and the Saviour's blood go far beyond normal sensibilities and proprieties. Its emphasis on the bodily dimension of Christ, not only in a celebration of his suffering ('lovely Wounds') but also in the singer's attraction and repose in it, is excessive by most standards. As a result of such an unusual articulation of their beliefs, the doctrines and practices of the Moravians became, in their extreme form, repugnant to those who were more conventional in their religious attitudes. Their poetry came to speak with increasing familiarity of Jesus as the Bridegroom of the Soul, which, although no new concept, was offensive to many.[10] These figures could not be absorbed successfully into forms of Anglicanism or even Methodism. The import of German materials was clearly responsible for this, too, as can be understood readily when we consider the translation of a German hymn such as 'Ausgeblutets theil der leichen':

> Wilt thou still pretend to reason?
> Then to praise the Side's Hole learn:
> This be thy most lofty Lesson,
> How wide th' Orifice was torn.
> Blessed spirits! you may covet
> To pry here, and enter down:
> Yet this Cave (you can't disprove it)
> Was for Sinner-Hearts so hewn![11]

---

[9] *A Collection of Hymns with Several Translations from the Hymn Book of the Moravian Brethren*, 3rd ed., 2 vols (London: [James Hutton], 1746), vol. 2, p. 599.

[10] This turn away from the more heterodox readings of the biblical text is something that concerns both Blake and Hamann. Although hard for us to imagine, they were used to an often extravagant and much wilder reading of the text than we are. The move towards a more rational, sensible, and altogether less experimental hermeneutics is part of the larger pattern that they were trying to resist and in which the Moravians, at least until their self-censoring period, played a role.

[11] *A Collection of Hymns* (1746) p. 419: '6. Wollt ihr ja noch resoniren, so gelobts der Pleura an, über nichts zu meditiren, als wie weit sie aufgethan. 7. Reine geister! euch gelüst es in den ritz hinein-zuschaun: aber diese hohl, (ihr wißt es) ist fürs sünder-herz gehaun' ('Anhang und Zugaben zum Herrnhuter Gesangbuch', in Nikolaus Ludwig von Zinzendorf, *Ergänzungsbände zu den Hauptschriften*, ed. Erich Beyreuther and Gerhard Meyer, vol. 2 [Hildesheim, Ger.: Georg Olms, 1964], p. 1788).

Reason, or even our idea of a classic Enlightenment, does not have much of a place in these lines. Such a Christian practice is not sustainable within the British religious landscape at the time. This encouragement that we should stop 'pretend[ing] to reason' outstrips other Protestant forms of reliance on faith as the founding experiences for belief. In translating these hymns, the Moravians also translate the graphic nature of the originals. The English emphasis on the sexually charged 'Orifice' of the side hole that we 'covet' after it opens wide is a direct continuation from the original terms of 'gelüst', 'Pleura', 'ritz', and 'aufgethan'. Consider also that in the hymn book the title to the text is given in the German original and printed in Fraktur. These German hymns and their translation result in the Moravians becoming part of an exorbitant Enlightenment; in other words, they cannot be absorbed with all their strangeness and spiritual excess.

The Moravians are restless not only in their feelings towards God but also in their activities on Earth, including their continuous recording of their practices. They are always travelling, always on the move, yet they also want to keep everybody informed. This restlessness also translates into their linguistic practice, at least in London, as they switch between languages when they keep their records, books, accounts, and even daily practices such as singing and praying. The polyglot character of the Moravian community was, in many ways, not such a surprise since linguistic and geographic displacement—voluntary and not—was one of its defining historical origins. It must have contributed to their comfortableness with existing at or beyond the margins.

As their English name suggests, the first Moravian communities were founded in fifteenth-century central Europe. Moravia and Bohemia were among the earliest centres of Protestant thought, though the Counter-Reformation all but destroyed the movement there. The Moravians might have disintegrated altogether had it not been for Nikolaus Ludwig von Zinzendorf (1700–60), a German Pietist count from Saxony, who gave refuge to a group of Brethren in 1722. Over time Zinzendorf himself became the leading figure of the Moravian Church, its spiritual leader and bishop. Under him, the church flourished and became in effect an early worldwide Protestant church. They were at the very forefront of eighteenth-century globalization, sending missionaries all around the world, including Greenland, the West Indies, Suriname, Australia, and the American colonies. As part of their proselytizing work, they were not afraid to tackle another language or place, situating themselves in the middle of a complicated relation between curiosity, religion, and imperialism. Throughout all their efforts abroad, however, Zinzendorf insisted that they preserve the distinctly German origins of the original Moravian revival. It was a matter of dealing in various languages and cultures at once. As a result, many of the important figures in the church made multilingualism a part of their religious practice by preaching in various languages or working as translators. The London congregation was exemplary in this regard. Thus, it serves as an example of not only how the polyglot Moravians operated in Britain but also to what degree they had a hand in structuring the wider Anglo-German context I describe in Chapter 1.

The first arrival of the Moravians on the British religious scene goes back at least as far as 1728. That year, three brethren came to London, following the request of a small German-Lutheran group at the English Court. They saw a space to build a Moravian congregation and community in Britain, with London an ideal thoroughfare for overseas missionary work. Almost ten years after the first visit, Count Zinzendorf himself came to London and helped to establish a German Society. The Moravian's German heritage was undoubtedly useful in dealing with the Hanoverian Court. Consequently, the Moravians were not classified as Dissenters, and thus it was possible for them to welcome members that belonged to other congregations, opening it up to Anglicans and Dissenters alike.[12] More Brethren arrived in good time, and in 1742 the Fetter Lane Society became the formalized centre of Moravian activity in England. Over time the church steadily grew. Colin Podmore gives us an idea of its considerable size when he states that 'with regular attenders at the preaching and a large number of children, they put the total number of souls in their care in England in 1748 between 5,000 and 6,000'.[13] London was, thus, an important centre of inter-European exchange.

Three distinctive Moravians traits make them a particularly useful source of historical material. First, they suffer from what in Jacques Derrida's wake has been termed 'archive fever'.[14] Loosely put, they actively record and archive the life of their own congregation to an unusual degree. Second, they deeply believe in the significance of the ordinary.[15] The liturgical importance of the everyday means that there was nothing that was not worth sharing and keeping as a record of God's work as part of congregational life. Third, much of their congregational life in London was bilingual, both in its ecclesiastical superstructure and its daily life. We find this polyglot character directly reflected and recorded throughout the London Moravian Archives, currently located in Muswell Hill. The fact the Moravians maintained their own Anglo-German archive from the very beginning, and continue to do so, illustrates better than anything that this is a self-aware, structured, and highly organized part of the supple Anglo-German context in eighteenth-century London.

---

[12] On the topic of the Moravian legal status as non-Dissenters, see Podmore, pp. 205–27.

[13] Podmore, p. 120. Also see Geoffrey Stead and Margaret Stead, *The Exotic Plant: A History of the Moravian Church in Britain, 1742–2000* (Werrington, Cambridgeshire: Epworth Press, 2003), p. 59.

[14] The phrase is often used rather loosely, as I do here. Of course, Jacques Derrida's real interest is how one can suffer from archive fever by being simultaneously committed to archiving everything while at the same time embracing the principle that every archive is highly selective. See Derrida, *Archive Fever: A Freudian Impression* (Chicago, IL: University of Chicago Press, 1998).

[15] The idea of 'the ordinary' is invoked here with a slight nod to Stanley Cavell. However, it is important to note a crucial difference, too. Cavell speaks of the ordinary in relation to philosophy (even though he discusses Samuel Taylor Coleridge and William Wordsworth). For the Moravians, the category is more expansive and slightly less structured than its counterpart in Romanticism. See Cavell, *In Quest of the Ordinary: Lines of Skepticism and Romanticism* (Chicago, IL: University of Chicago Press, 1988).

The ordinary is a massive topic in the study of Moravian thought, especially in relation to Romanticism's celebration of the ordinary, as well as in understanding how practices such as congregation diaries were also forms of surveillance. For further reading, see Keri Davies, 'The Lost Moravian History of William Blake's Family: Snapshots from the Archive', *Literature Compass* 3, 6 (November 2006): 1297–1319. For early women's writings along those lines, see Katherine M. Faull, *Moravian Women's Memoirs: Their Related Lives* (Syracuse, NY: Syracuse University Press, 1997). For a transatlantic perspective, see C. Daniel Crews and Richard W. Starbuck, *Records of the Moravians among the Cherokee*, 3 vols (Tahlequah, OK: Cherokee Heritage Press, 2010).

THE ANGLO-GERMAN CHARACTER
OF MORAVIAN LIFE

It was common practice among the Moravian congregations to keep congregation diaries, which were read out to the local parish along with other documents chronicling the ordinary lives of its members. This practice allowed the community to share their daily activities with others down to the most intimate detail, including personal losses or sexual encounters.[16] For example, in London 'the Congregation Diaries record both the marital problems of Brother and Sister Blake, and their family tragedies, such as the death of their youngest child'.[17] Remarkably, the sharing of such information was not limited to each local congregation. In fact, Moravians sent these reports to other congregations, disseminating them broadly. They were then kept and preserved in important archival centres such as London or, eventually, Herrnhut. Most of the Moravian preachers abroad came from Germany and England, and when their reports made it back to the London congregation we hear about 'General Meeting(s) where Diaries of our German & English Congregations were read'.[18] Since most of the reports from foreign missions and delegations came through London—and copies of many documents were kept there—the holdings in the archive in London brilliantly reflect the international character of the Moravian operation. It also gives us a powerful sense of the specifically Anglo-German character of this London community, not only publicly, but also internally within the congregation itself, which means that, at least in the eighteenth century, this congregation would always have been understood (and understood itself) to be a group that was outside of the orbits even of Dissenter groups.

Here is a report that gives us an impression of the diaries and the practice surrounding them:

> Letters from Bethlehem arrived, dated May 21st, out of which Br. Gambold mentioned at the Lovefeast the Departure of the venerable Father Nitschmann; as also that of our dear Brn. & Sisrs. there are well; tho' the Outrages of the Savages do not yet entirely cease.... In the last meeting Br. Gambold kept a Discourse on the Texts, & concluded with a liturgical & tender Feeling. Afterwards the Labourers read in German the account we had received from Bethlehem with the tenderest Sympathy of Gratitude & Intersession. For the Conclusion was German Singing-Hour.[19]

The letter arrives from Bethlehem, Pennsylvania, the mere name of which reminds all listeners of the global Moravian enterprise. It covers the activities of the congregation, the changes in institutional structure (the departure of Father Nitschmann), and the difficult contact with indigenous people.[20] The entry also describes the

---

[16] See Davies, 'Lost Moravian History', pp. 1302–4.

[17] Davies, 'Lost Moravian History', p. 1304. 'Brother Blake' here most likely refers to William Blake's uncle, also a member of the Moravian Church. 'Sister Blake' would have been his wife.

[18] Moravian Archive, London, C/36/7/10 (29 May 1757).

[19] Moravian Archive, London, C/36/7/10 (3 July 1757 [?]).

[20] Many of the diaries and private documents are much more explicit about this aspect of colonial life, and there is much research to be done in this area.

bilingual practices in London, both reading the incoming reports from the western front in two languages as well as the local 'German Singing-Hour'. After a summary of the recordings from Bethlehem and a subsequent sermon, the 'Labourers' (an institutional position within the church) 'read in German the account we had received from Bethlehem'. It is likely that the German account was, in fact, in the original language and the previous summary given by the brethren was a translation. Either way, the Moravian informational and liturgical structure is resolutely polyglot and specifically Anglo-German. The congregation diaries present one of the most international and impressive archives of colonial activities during the eighteenth century.

Moravians sent people out across the globe to spread the word and, accordingly, heard back from them: 'We had an extraordinary, blessed general meeting with accounts from Wachau, the Caribbee—Islands, Suriname, the Cape, and Letters to & from Cairo.... Br. Gambols spoke briefly on the Texts & the Assembly sung to shine for a Blessing on ourselves & all His People all over the Earth.'[21] The interconnectivity can be concretely felt and seen in London: at a sermon in London in 1757 'Brethren of 9 different Nations were present'.[22] Within that diversity and linguistic multiplicity, German and English are the structuring languages. They remain the two standard languages for preaching, reading, and singing; the bilingual conference books are kept in English and German, and the 1757 congregation even follows a German and an English calendar ('We read with a particular Blessing the Viiith German Week [Wednesday, May the 24th]').[23] The Moravians chose a bilingual system and practice to record the growing complexity around them. Their reaction to increasing levels of interconnectedness was to embrace multilingualism.

Multilingualism is not only a practical cultural fact for the Moravians; it is also a theologically meaningful condition. It is a way to celebrate the glory of God, which adds significance to their insistence on language lessons, bilingual administration, preaching, and singing. Consider the advice that Frankfurt-born Peter Boehler, a bishop of the Moravian Church in England and America, gave in 1743 to his congregation: 'There shd be always somebody among us to learn German. Br Gottshalk will give the Brn every Day an Hour at 7 in ye Morning after ye Bible-Hour', and 'In general an Encouragement was giv'n to ye Brn and Srs to learn German'.[24] The demand for German lessons with the express idea that translation and continuous interpretation should be available represents a significant institutionalization of the Anglo-German character. It ensured the continuity of transmission and translation of ideas from Germany, and it also maintained the ability to welcome, communicate with, and shape German speakers in London who were looking for intellectual and emotional support.[25] It is not the sign of a ghettoized community. But while it confirms our sense of the rich and stable

---

[21] Moravian Archive, London, C/36/7/10, 6 February 1757.
[22] Moravian Archive, London, C/36/7/10, 29 August 1757.
[23] Moravian Archive, London, C/36/7/10, 24 May 1757.
[24] Monday, 4 July 1743, qtd in Davies, 'Lost Moravian History', p. 1315.
[25] See Stead and Stead, pp. 49–77.

Anglo-German culture in eighteenth-century Britain, it also gives us an idea of how the Moravians were in a different orbit than other Dissenter groups, especially ones that were dreaming of becoming mainstream.

Bilingualism was part of daily life at Fetter Lane and combined the practical and the more theoretical aspects of its polyglot character. Around 1757, the congregation diary records switch between German and English for liturgical practices, common readings, and international visits to the church: 'At Fetterlane Br Grumbd preach'd in the morning on "Come unto me, all ye that labour lase? heavy laden, &c.["] Then Br Brodersen in German on Rev. 1. 7. "Behold, He cometh—& every Eye shall see Him, &c.["] He preach'd in English in the afternoon on "We love Him, because He first loved us".'[26] Within one morning, maybe even within one service, the members of the congregation were presented with readings and preaching in both German and English. This is nothing unusual, as the entry from only a week earlier shows: 'Then Br Marshall coming from Lindsey-house, kept the [?] ours Choir-[?]ting, & after it the German Preaching in a very sweet manner on John 20.31. "These are written, that ye might believe that Jesus is the Christ".'[27] The Moravians did more than follow Boehler's advice ('There shd be always somebody among us to learn German'). Sermons, preaching, and singing all took place in English and German. In this context, these hymns were used as tools for memorization more generally, too, so language instruction and knowledge formation were deeply intertwined.[28] The open, public nature of these activities allows us to understand how common it was as part of eighteenth-century London life. When Zinzendorf visited the congregation between 1749 and 1755, '[h]is sermons were immediately translated into English during mass by the London preacher'.[29] The fact that Zinzendorf's sermons are interpreted for the congregation speaks to his popularity and illustrates the ways in which the Moravians embraced multilingualism publicly.

Going through the congregation diary of the 1750s we can see a pattern evolving for certain members of the congregation: English preaching in the morning alternated with sermons or singing in German in the afternoon. The German preaching was always on particular Bible passages detailed in the diaries: 'Br Marshall preached in German on Hebr. i.i.2. "God hath in these last Days spoken to us by his Son".'[30] Both languages are used continuously as part of the life of the congregation. The Moravians became a vocal part of London's theological and spiritual context without denying, hiding, or trying to erase their multilingual character. They structurally connected their polyglot vision to their Anglo-German practice, both at home and abroad. Because this connection continued to hold throughout the eighteenth century, it also remained a structural part of the institutional life of

---

[26] Moravian Archive, London, C/36/7/10, 18 September 1757.

[27] Moravian Archive, London, C/36/7/10, 11 September 1757.

[28] On memorialization, see Jonathan Yonan, 'Evangelicanism and Enlightenment: The Moravian Experience in England, *c.* 1750–1800' (PhD dissertation, University of Oxford, 2006), pp. 153–60.

[29] 'Seine Predigten wurden sofort im Gottesdienst durch den Londoner Prediger ins Englische übersetzt' (Fechner, p. 9).

[30] Moravian Archive, London, C/36/7/10, 13 November 1757.

the church; that is, the Moravians not only were multilingual in their devotional practices and public sermons, but they also brought this polyglot outlook to bear on their self-representation and administration.

In the Moravian Church Archive in London, we find plenty of conference books, elders' minutes, and others, all written in German, German and English, or English, often switching continuously between languages.[31] Good examples of such practices are the elders' conference minutes and the provincial helpers' conference minutes. The elders were in charge of looking after the spiritual aspect of the congregation. They met approximately every two months and recorded, among other things, whether applications to join the congregation had been successful. The provincial helpers were the predecessor of the provincial board, which was eventually responsible for all the Moravian groups in Britain. A good number of the minutes of these bodies are bilingual, presenting a mixture of English and German, not just on the same page but even within one single entry. It is almost as if the line records our Babelian condition within one sentence. I have reproduced and transcribed one of these pages to illustrate the sheer level of multilingualism. The immediate context (the adoption of a congregation member, financial matters) is less important than the formal dimension of the record (Figure 5.1). Transcription:

> Eodem
> Die Aeltesten Conferenz in Fulneck meldet daß
> der Geschw.[ister] Hartley's Sohn 4 Jahr alt............,
> ....wenn er länger bey den Eltern bleibt;
> die Eltern wollen vor des Kind Last Geld zahlen.
> die Oeconomat. Conferenz hat weiter dabey nichts
> zu erinnern.
> Die led.(?) Bro in Fulneck haben Bro, die das Manage-
> Ment der Tuch Fabrique gründlich (???), und
> die Sache daher mit Nutzen fortführen könnten.
> Den gegenwärtigen Defect könnten sie übernehmen (.)
> Leute pflegen sonst considerable Summen for
> Good will zu zahlen um in ein Established Business
> & Custom zu kommen. Man könnte ihnen
> die Zahlung dieses Defects leichter machen und auf
> etliche Jahre hinaus setzen. Capital solten Sie haben
> um die Bill Circulation ein fach zu machen,
> und das Business zu führen. Man könnte vielleicht
> auf dem Provincial Synodo eine Committee von
> 20, 30 Brrn (Brethren?) zusammen nehmen, die gewisse Shares
> zu einem Capital vorschuß übernähmen;.........
> ......würde die bisherige Modification der Manu-
> factur abgeändert und das Business an sich könne
> doch fortgehen.[32]

---

[31] For a conference book entirely composed in German, see Moravian Archive, London, C/26/7/12.

[32] Provincial Helpers conference Minutes (PHC, not catalogued, June 1766). Many thanks to Uwe Steiner and Michael Winkler for their help with this transcription.

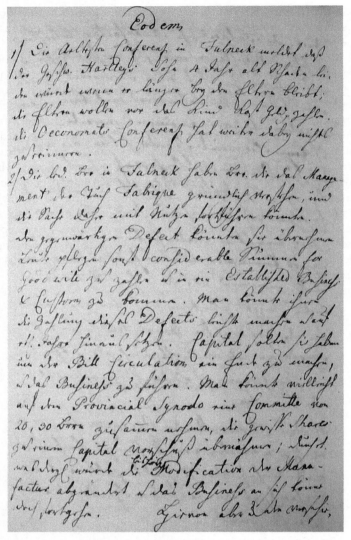

Figure 5.1 *Provincial Helpers Conference Minutes*, volume 1 (not catalogued, June 1766). © Moravian Archives, London.

The bilingual documents draw visual attention to their linguistically mixed quality when, midsentence, the language changes: 'Leute pflegen sonst considerable Summen for Good will zu zahlen um in ein Established Business & Custom zu kommen.' Again, the theological significance of such a practice would not have escaped the senior member of the congregation writing it, despite the pecuniary topic at hand. Such an entry combines the three distinctly Moravian aspects described earlier. It shows us the Moravians' archival impulse itself is multilingual; it reveals the quotidian not only to be meaningful, but also to be polyglot; and, in combination, it suggests that the multilingual condition itself is spiritually meaningful and something to be celebrated, even though it means that one will not fully belong to either language.

The Moravians make multilingualism public beyond their church through their polyglot publications in London. Between 1750 and 1760 two Moravian presses were established in London. First, J. J. Würz founded the Moravian 'house press' (*Hausdruckerey*), sanctioned by Zinzendorf. It was active between 1749 and 1755, printing many of the Moravian theological works that were needed for the Anglo-German community in Britain and that were used by the missionaries who were taking plenty of written materials from London to the Americas, India, and beyond. The Moravian Johann Heinrich Müller opened another press that was active in the years 1758 to 1760 before he moved to Philadelphia (where he was the first to publish the American Declaration of Independence in German, a mere week after it was ratified).[33] While short-lived, it showed the continued, direct impulse of the congregation regarding its Anglo-German project in print. The printing presses show not only that there was a serious commitment—personal, financial, institutional—behind putting the Moravian mission into print but also that there was sufficient volume of demand for these texts printed in German, in English, or bilingually. That is, the Moravian presses were an integral part of the larger set of German booksellers and publishers that I discuss in detail in Chapter 1. They were active and important parts of the establishment of a wider Anglo-German context whose intellectual presence was much more wide-ranging and diverse than people have realized until now, including canonical texts—such as those of Salomon Gessner—as well as material that is far less conventional, such as these hymnals.

It is important to appreciate the wider philosophical meaning of these multilingual practices. These are not primarily practical reactions, though they are that, too. There is something spiritually and theologically significant about multilingualism for the Moravians, a view that they shared with others in the period. What is remarkable is their exact position on this matter, which chimes with unusual figures such as Hamann and Johann Caspar Lavater. In most intellectual contexts, especially eighteenth-century Protestantism, the multiplicity of languages is understood as a reflection of our Babelian condition and therefore an expression of loss or shortcoming. The fact that we need different languages and find it so difficult to communicate across them is a divine punishment, the result of hubris, and a condition to be overcome. Thus, the standard view theorized the multitude of languages as a constant reminder of the fallen condition of Man, the necessity for translation, and its constant shortcomings as the trace of this punishment. The Moravians think of the matter rather differently. They think of their own multilingual practices as a celebration of God's gift to Man, comprehending the variety of languages as a sign of generosity rather than of limitation.

[33] Donald Lineback, 'Johann Heinrich Müller: Printer, Moravian, Revolutionary', *Transactions of the Moravian Historical Society* 23.1 (1977): 61–76. Also see Jefcoate, p. 251.

Historically, the gift of language was a central part of the discussions around linguistic origins, divine and human. The classic question asked by Johann Gottfried Herder, Étienne Bonnot de Condillac, Jean-Jacques Rousseau, and many other thinkers in the period was whether language was given by God or whether it was human in origin, whether it was an external gift so we could understand the world or whether it was a social and worldly construction. This is not the place to rehearse these wide and important debates, yet the phrase at the centre of them—the gift of language—is useful.³⁴ What is often missed in the different readings of the phrase is its insistence on the singularity of both its operative words. There is one gift and one language: one logos. Of course, what is normally meant here is a Language that stands in for all the natural languages, or even systems of signification beyond the obviously linguistic; that is, it really is the gift of Language, not language. This Language, however, in turn contains all the natural languages that we know. And it is here that the figures who are interested in the multiplicity of languages celebrate the gift of languages rather than treat the fragmentation of Language as a curse. Consider the example of the multilingual choir singing in several languages at once mentioned earlier. There is little doubt that, as Peucker suggests, for the Moravians 'multilingualism reflected their eschatological outlook'.³⁵

The Moravians use their Anglo-German context in London to celebrate the existence of languages as a fact of theoretical significance that is reflected in their multilingual schools, the books they publish, and their bilingual hymn-books. The gift of languages allows them to continue to celebrate the word of God in its manifold ways. Thus, the Moravians prepare for a multilingual practice that Hamann terms 'spiritual things' by having both German and English as central parts of liturgical practices, transmissions, and instruction.³⁶ The bilingual operations are not simply a pragmatic reaction to being in a different country, but also they are conceptually motivated operations. Similarly, during his biblical studies in London and a visit to the Moravian church, Hamann makes a note in connection with his works on translation: 'The confusion of language is a history, a phaenomeon, a continuing miracle, and a parable, through which God still continues to speak to us.'³⁷ The crucial aspect of this positive spin on the Babelian condition is the idea that God continues to speak to us through all the languages of the world, and that our multilingual efforts are a pale yet celebratory instance of this condition. The Moravian creation of a multilingual, Anglo-German community in London is an active example of such as positive engagement with the multiplicity of languages.

God's merciful condescension, and especially His gift of language, was a central part of the Moravian doctrine. Zinzendorf locates the spiritual and metaphysical thoroughly in relation to human language. We cannot but understand the world

---

³⁴ I have written about this in my book *Fracture and Fragmentation in British Romanticism* (Cambridge: Cambridge University Press, 2010).

³⁵ Peucker, p. 26.

³⁶ '[G]eistliche [r] Dinge' (N, 2: 15). Also see Chapter 3 on Hamann and translation.

³⁷ 'Die Verwirrung der Sprache ist eine Geschichte, ein Phaenomeon, ein fortdauerndes Wunder, und ein Gleichnis, wodurch Gott noch immer fortfährt mit uns zu reden' (Hamann, *Londoner Schriften*, p. 282).

in human terms, and it is a sign of God's mercy and kindness that He makes Himself known to us in those terms. As Zinzendorf puts it, 'Wir konnten nicht werden GOTT, so ist Er worden wie wir' (Since we could not become GOD, He became as we are).[38] God anthropomorphizes Himself since that is the only register that we understand as humans. This is not just a reference to the figure of Jesus Christ; it also relates to our experience of the world more generally. We can trace a difference between us and Him—and we try and register it in our language, through capitalization, for instance—but we cannot fully articulate that difference other than in 'our' terms. We do not have the transformative power; in fact, we might not even understand sufficiently what the category of transformation or 'becoming' holds. The comparative nature of the analogy is always an insistence on the difference between God and Man. Davis alerts us to a connection between this moment in Zinzendorf and a passage from Blake's 'There Is No Natural Religion' (1788), which articulates a similar thought:

> Therefore
> God becomes as we are,
> that we may be as he
> is.[39]

God transforms Himself into human terms, so that we will understand and perceive Him. I would argue that Blake's thought goes even further than Zinzendorf's. Blake suggests that the condescension includes a potential for us to do the same as God, to become 'divine', not through self-apotheosis but rather through embracing His form of condescension. This is how 'we may be as he / is'. In Blake there is a strong reminder that in the humanization of God we will recognize that we are made in a divine image. This divinity is best emulated not in our desire for becoming the same as God in all His qualities—that would be hubris; rather, it is illustrated by becoming 'as we are' so that 'we may be as he / is': that is, we embrace the state that we are in ourselves—not as something divine itself, but as something that can have a divine quality. Either way, what emerges is that one way in which God becomes as we are is through his gift of language to us. It allows us to articulate the world to ourselves and its divine quality back to God. The dimension of the divine is important here: what we 'become' as humans, or what we 'are' is always linked to the spiritual and holy, which includes Language. While in both Zinzendorf and Blake there is a clear sense that humans are not divine themselves (and that humans might even need divinity to fathom their own connection to the holy), there is an equally clear sense that this is not to be understood as a shortcoming, which would result in negation and self-loathing.

---

[38] Nikolaus Ludwig von Zinzendorf, *Der öffentlichen Gemeinreden im Jahr 1747*, qtd in Craig D. Atwood, *Community of the Cross: Moravian Piety in Colonial Bethlehem* (University Park: Pennsylvania State University Press, 2004), p. 79. Also see Atwood's chapter 'The Moravians and Transatlantic German Pietism', pp. 21–42.

[39] William Blake, 'There Is No Natural Religion [b]', pp. 2–3, 3. Also see Davies, 'Lost Moravian History', pp. 1313–14.

The fact that we have languages, for all their limitations, is a divine gift to be celebrated. It allows us to be different from one another, even outside of the normal orbit of things, and to celebrate the variety of God's ways. The multiplicity of languages, and the differences that come with them, is to be joyfully embraced rather than embarrassingly ignored. Such celebration translates into a practice that supports the instruction of languages, and the translation between them, as an expression of not only a divine gift and condescension but also as an awareness that difference itself is no bad thing. The expression of these relations in different languages was something to aspire to and help to establish the variety of forms of life and thought, including in literature. This is a matter of aesthetics as well as of literary history, as Chapter 6 on the Moravian hymn and Blake will show.

Once we have recovered a sense of the importance of the Moravians, we can see not only how they serve as an excellent example for the institutional stability of Anglo-German context and its theoretically informed practices but also how their religious and archival practices form a direct and influential part of British literary history. Much work remains to be done to recover how their archival activity in Britain and elsewhere showcases important polyglot material that went unexamined in previous accounts of the period. It allows us to reconstruct how this community played a concrete role in shaping the lives of individuals within the Anglo-German context and beyond. What it does most crucially, however, is give us a glimpse of how a group who actively remained very different in London's ecclesiastical setup was able to maintain its difference and celebrate it through multilingualism.

6

A Critique of Habit
Blake and Hamann on Religion, Matrimony, and Pedagogy

SHAPING THOUGHT AND BELIEF

Religion, and its deeply shaping impact on our lives, was central to both William Blake and Johann Georg Hamann: it gave form to their thought and life. In their works, religiosity is serious, and often excessive; it is also metaphysically rather unorthodox and politically unconventional. So, while highly religious and Christian, Blake and Hamann articulate and live an idiosyncratic anti-clericalism that is deeply at odds with both rising secularism and traditional forms of Christianity. They both identify as a major issue of the times that the rise of instrumental reason has produced a version of religion that has destroyed creativity and that has been complicit in the establishment of a set of deeply destructive social constraints. Blake and Hamann produce a genealogy of this process, which this chapter will trace in order to show some of their most acute forms of ideological critique.

To reveal the deterioration of religion and spirituality, both Blake and Hamann latch on to the topics of matrimony and language acquisition. It allows them to go, as they are wont, to the origin of what they perceive as the central problems of human society. The institutionalization of education and religion has turned a process and state that was once revelatory or holy into a banal relation that is actively damaging. This is not simply a theoretical matter for them. They make these insights a guide when they make existential decisions, often sharply deviating from social norms as a result. Their exorbitance stands in sharp contrast to traditionally pious life. Although neither of them belonged to an established congregation, both Blake and Hamann evidently came out of the Protestant tradition, as their focus on the individual experience of God and close textual study of the Bible show. Their idiosyncratic approach to religiosity is marked by the way Blake and Hamann make certain existential decisions. Hamann's 'marriage of conscience' (*GewissensEhe*) or Blake's deep antagonism against the church identify them as trying to carve out a space for maintaining the integrity of their position, a position that cannot be reconciled either with ideas of marginality or as a mode that we can recuperate.[1]

---

[1] ZH, 3: 263.

Blake traces the decline of thought, imagination, and, by extension, ethics, through stories about the Fall of humanity. There are savage critiques of institutional religious structures in *There Is No Natural Religion*, *All Religions are One*, and also *Urizen*, especially through the critique of supposedly 'natural' categories. Three of these intimately related categories are reason, religion, and language. The titles of Blake's first illuminated prints are concentrated examples of this view. *All Religions are One* is a claim about the idea of structural similarities and distinctions between religions (*all* religions are one, they are similar), but it is also on its way to being a question: what are they, all those religions? *There Is No Natural Religion* acts as a counter-part to this thought: it presents a direct statement in what we can imagine to be a straightforwardly theological discussion, standing in an almost humorous relation to the larger argument of the poem. Here is a statement of fact: There is no natural religion. Of course, Blake knows that even the status of 'natural religion' is hotly contested. The thinkers around David Hume and John Locke distinguish between natural religion and natural philosophy, the precursor of what we now think of as science—a topic not too popular with Blake. And there is, of course, the difference between natural religion and revealed religion, a distinction that allows both Blake and Hamann to comment on the problematic status of anything 'natural' in the first place. Consider this passage by Hamann in relation to Blake's: 'What does it mean to speak about the difference between natural and revealed religion? If I understand it correctly, there is, between the two, no more than the difference between the eye of a man who sees a painting without understanding the slightest about painting and drawing, or the history that is being represented, and the eye of a painter; between the natural ear and the musical ear.'[2] There is no natural religion here, since the eye of the man who sees the painting but does not understand in the slightest, understands as little about the world as the person who perceives the tree to be 'only a Green thing'.[3] In these cases, there is no natural religion because it has become normality, a successful counterfeit, successfully passing itself off as neutral.

Contrary to this new normality, neither Blake nor Hamann believe that there is such a thing as natural religion, or natural thought, if that means religion or thought without mediation. We are not paying enough attention, however, to the mediation of thought. As Blake puts it, 'Reason or the ratio of all we have already known. is not the same that it shall be when we know more'.[4] This complex state-ment does two things. First, it encourages us to develop a way of theorizing that is critical of whatever account of thought we have produced. We need to know more about 'Reason or the ratio' and the way it can be misguided, especially when it comes to our spiritual well-being. Second, it invites us to think about what counts

---

[2] 'Was will der Unterschied zwisch[en] natürl. und geoffenbarte Religion sagen? Wenn ich ihn recht verstehe, so ist zwischen beyden nicht mehr als der Unterscheid zwischen dem Auge eines Menschen, der ein Gemälde sieht, ohne d[as] Geringste von der Malerey und Zeichnung oder der Geschichte, die vorgestellt wird, zu verstehen, und dem Auge eines Malers, zwischen dem natürl. Gehör und dem musikalischen Ohr' (Hamann, *Londoner Schriften*, p. 411).
[3] Blake to Dr Trusler, pp. 702–3, 702.
[4] William Blake, 'There Is No Natural Religion [b]', pp. 2–3, 2.

as knowledge and how we attain it, accumulate it. It is, thus, not only *what* we know that changes but also *how* we know that alters, how we construct knowledge. The process of naming is here of particular relevance, as the title of the *First Book of Urizen* already indicates, framing the topic of reason through its history and reminding us that the act of naming, including entitling a poem, holds ontological power. Urizen is probably the most familiar example of how Blake confronts the role of reason. The play on 'your reason' (even 'Ur-reason') immediately marks this figure as a target of Blake's critique, a figure who falls from a positive, fatherly figure to a destructive influence upon the world. After the Fall, the type of reason that Urizen implements is functional and deadly. *Urizen* suggests that the internalization of what becomes 'iron law[]' has disastrous consequences.[5]

Once fallen, reason is used by the 'primeval Priests' to 'assum[e] power'.[6] These prime-evil priests create a whole new set of philosophical assumptions. These include our senses of time and of space, two of the things we feel are most 'natural'. It is Urizen (reason) who '[t]imes on times…divide[s]' and, thus, creates a sense of time that becomes natural, a sense of time that is defined by division and quantitative separation.[7] Spatial quantification also becomes internalized. A web stretches from Urizen's soul, and

> None could break the Web…
> …So twisted the cords, & so knotted
> The meshes: twisted like to the human brain
> …And all calld it, The Net of Religion.[8]

The net, a tool to capture thoughts is a regularized grid, just like the grid that chartered the London streets. It captures the mind and the body. Blake imagines, as in a vision of a pandemic, that this version of thinking ossifies and hardens over time. The people

> Felt their Nerves change into Marrow
> And hardening Bones began
> In swift diseases and torments,
> In throbbings & shootings & grindings
> Thro' all the coasts; till weaken'd
> The Senses inward rush'd shrinking,
> Beneath the dark net of infection.
> …Till the shrunken eyes clouded over
> Discernd not the woven hipocrisy
> But the streaky slime in their heavens
> Brought together by narrowing perceptions
> Appeard transparent air; for their eyes
> Grew small like the eyes of a man

---

[5] William Blake, *The [First] Book of Urizen*, in *Complete Poetry and Prose*, pp. 70–83, 81, ch. 8, plate 23, line 26.

[6] Blake, *Urizen*, p. 70, preludium, plate 2, line 1.

[7] Blake, *Urizen*, p. 70, ch. 1, plate 3, line 8.

[8] Blake, *Urizen*, p. 82, ch. 8, plate 25, lines 19–22.

> And in reptile forms shrinking together
> Of seven feet stature they remaind
> . . . Six days they shrunk up from existence
> And on the seventh day they rested
> And they bless'd the seventh day, in sick hope:
> And forgot their eternal life.[9]

This is one of the bleakest versions of the Fall in the whole of Blake. It is the Fall of imaginative thought itself, the development of rarefied perception into the naturalization of reason. The 'Nerves' harden and the senses weaken and turn inward until they cannot perceive the reality around them. Even the gods cannot discern the 'woven hypocrisy': the net of reason and of religion has become invisible. This deceptive net appears—or, rather, does not appear—as 'transparent air', an analogue to the 'purification of philosophy', the version of reason that Hamann diagnoses as a misguided fantasy.[10] Without noticing it, this version of perception and thinking makes the world poorer and smaller: 'their eyes / Grew small like the eyes of a man'. The paradoxical diminishing growth of the eye is not a sign of increasing focus; rather, it signals the lack of ability to recognize the world in its full richness. The result of this Fall is that creators shrink from existence itself and 'eternal life' is *forgotten*, not forbidden or denied. The fact that it is forgotten—that the new narrowed perceptions '[a]ppeard transparent air'—is important. As a result of the Fall, the world lives '[t]o the jaws of devouring darkness', but this darkness is mistaken as transparent, maybe even illuminating; as a result, the inhabitants of that earth form 'laws of prudence, and call'd them / The eternal laws of God'.[11] The supposedly 'eternal laws' are in fact the result of mistaking darkness for air, of narrowing the senses and thought without realizing it.

Blake suggests that the 'eternal laws of God' are human constructions made under false pretences. Similarly, Hamann insists that the history of religious institutions directly maps onto the powerful and highly destructive ways that reason has been instrumentalized. Blake's poem *The Song of Los* (1795) is a good example of how Blake's and Hamann's thinking productively overlap on this issue. The poem provides a critical genealogy of philosophy and religion. It first turns to 'Abstract Philosophy' and 'abstract Law', which have destroyed thinking through producing the discipline of philosophy.[12] The story of 'Pythagoras Socrates & Plato' is another version of the Fall turning the power of imagination into instrumental reason.[13] The shackles of philosophy result in humanity getting 'chain'd down with the Chain of Jealousy'.[14] And once more, Blake insists that philosophy is a dividing force: 'The human race began to wither, for the healthy built/Secluded places, fearing the joys of Love'.[15] The guilty self-denial is the result of fear borne out of using one's health to seclude

---

[9] Blake, *Urizen*, pp. 82–3, ch. 9, plate 25, lines 24–42.
[10] Griffith-Dickson, p. 520: 'Reinigung der Philosophie', N, 3: 287.
[11] Blake, *Urizen*, p. 83, ch. 9, plate 28, lines 3 and 6–7.
[12] Blake, *The Song of Los*, in *Complete Poetry and Prose*, pp. 67–70, 67, plate 3, lines 11 and 18.
[13] Blake, *Song of Los*, p. 67, plate 3, line 19.   [14] Blake, *Song of Los*, p. 67, plate 3, line 21.
[15] Blake, *Song of Los*, p. 67, plate 3, lines 25–6.

and separate oneself. This is a process that continues until Blake's day. We end up with a version of thought that binds us

> ...more
> And more to Earth: closing and restraining:
> Till a Philosophy of Five Senses was complete
> Urizen wept & gave it into the hands of Newton & Locke.[16]

This narrative gives us the disastrous and avoidable march of humanity towards its current condition. Over time, laws and religions, which both present themselves as founding, tie us to an earth that does not allow the spirit to roam. A simple and eerie subclause, imprisoned between two colons, gives it away: 'closing and restraining'. The mind closes itself, restrains itself, and in doing so will present the limiting result of such restraint as something 'complete'. A philosophy of the five senses parades as something complete, something that would combine our sensuous and intellectual nature. In truth, such a philosophy is restrictive; it has closed our abilities to perceive beyond the five senses. For Blake, the writing is on the wall: in time, we will think of the five senses as rich and complete, whereas actually such a self-image is the result of denial and impoverishment.

The loss of innocence, of imagination, or of thought is not one singular Fall. Blake writes that 'Urizen wept & gave it into the hands of Newton & Locke'. Urizen weeps before handing over this power of thinking to the modern sciences. This melancholy scene reminds us that Blake, in his malleable and changing universe, does not always malign Urizen. It is a scene of a horrible sacrifice, a presentation of reason's ill gift, the gift of a philosophy of the five senses that will bring with it the tyrannies of empiricism and idealism. It is presented as a scene of mourning. Urizen, familiar with his own power, knows that this change will bring not just Newton and Locke but also, as the next line makes clear, 'Rousseau & Voltaire', and with them Enlightenment philosophy in its many different guises.[17]

In Blake's story there seems to be a moment wherein the catastrophe could have been averted. But once Urizen hands philosophy over to Newton and Locke, it is too late. Eventually the techniques of 'closing and restraining' will be so successful that thought or philosophy will be seen as their natural sphere. Philosophy will itself forget this history and origin. Immanuel Kant's disciples will never know of Urizen's existence, let alone that he wept. As Hamann suggested, the self-forgetting of reason's own moment of origin is a crucial moment in its self-account.[18] Once Newton and Locke reign—and Rousseau and Voltaire are not far behind—we enter a situation in which the possibilities of human existence beyond their bounds would seem either spiritual escapism or madness. And so, what happens is a turn to a controlled version of the world, a conventional and structured world that needs explanation. As it happens, the most successful and harmful version of these constructions is institutional religion.

---

[16] Blake, *Song of Los*, p. 68, plate 4, lines 14–17.
[17] Blake, *Song of Los*, p. 68, plate 4, line 18.
[18] This includes the necessity of forgetting the contingency of its origin, along the lines that Friedrich Nietzsche analyses so powerfully in *The Genealogy of Morals* (1887).

The case of religion is analogous to that of philosophy, though here the Fall is even greater, since, in its original form, religion was much closer to the sources of the imagination. Normally, Blake uses the term to describe organized religion, which, to him, is deeply negative. Even more so than for Hamann, Blake identifies this form of religion with the institutionalization of spirituality and, thus, with a process that is deadening and restrictive. In Blake's work the history of institutional religion is the genealogy of these restrictions. Religion comes into existence, paradoxically, precisely because the Gods are 'deceased'.[19] For both Hamann and Blake, imagining the story of the Fall and telling a history of decline is not an exercise in nostalgia, then, but primarily a form of critique. Taking their cue from eighteenth-century conjectural histories, they both produce different accounts that highlight the intersection between historical development and ideological construction when it comes to religion, or at least what has become seen as such.

The Marriage of Heaven and Hell makes very clear that religion, as commonly understood, is an institutionalized set of beliefs that relies on instrumental reason. It is historical and social, and the most powerful way we can see that is by its abuse through clerical structures. We already know that Blake's and Hamann's works, despite (actually, *because* of) their deep spirituality, have a distinct and firmly anti-clerical tone. The pronouncement of a marriage between heaven and hell is an obvious case in point. More than anything, Blake plays with our assumptions and conventional notions: What is it about heaven and hell that makes them unlikely partners? Can I give a historical and critical account of how their tension has come to seem obvious or even natural to me?

There are several obvious reasons why a marriage between heaven and hell seems such an odd, even goofy idea. Heaven and hell are historically constructed opposites; they stand for different spiritual, theological, ethical, and moral spheres. Of course, they also stand for the idea of duality in the first place, the idea that such a dialectical structure of thought is accurate and productive. The third part of the titular trinity is just as difficult. The marriage is a holy, intimate union, a 'blending of two things', a process that in Blake could even describe his artistic practice of blending visual and verbal.[20] In this case, the blending of two irreconcilable opposites is Blake's way of highlighting their constructedness.[21] Marriage, administered by the church, is a perfect illustration of the historical abuse that institutional religion has produced. Crucially, a certain type of reason is the motor behind this abuse. It is the type of reason that seems 'transparent air' but, in fact, shapes the way of thinking so as not to allow us to see a way out of dualities such as heaven and hell, good or evil. Thus, Blake's title challenges us to consider the assumptions that lead to this type of 'purifying' thinking.

It is easy to confuse this approach with the idea that there needs to be a harmony created between heaven and hell, between different forms of thought. Neither Hamann nor Blake subscribe to this tendency towards synthesis. In fact, as I pointed

---

[19] Blake, *Song of Los*, p. 68, plate 4, line 19.   [20] *OED*, 2nd ed., s.v. 'marriage, *n*.', 5a.
[21] On this, see Saree Makdisi, *William Blake and the Impossible History of the 1790s* (Chicago, IL: University of Chicago Press, 2003), pp. 182–8.

out earlier, one of the things that makes them such exciting thinkers is their rejection of the premises of the argument leading to synthesis. As Gwen Griffith-Dickson puts it, 'Either-Or? Neither!'.[22] Their critique of dialectical thinking leaves us with a rejection of a common description for these structures; namely, their differences are subsumed—sublated, in Hegelian terms—in a synthesis. These are exorbitant thinkers for whom things are different: 'Without Contraries is no progression. Attraction and Repulsion, Reason and Energy, Love and Hate, are necessary to Human existence.'[23] This passage is about a dynamic of resistance, making clear that all the members of this dynamic are necessary forces. Both 'Love' and 'Hate' are necessary, yet what is not necessary at all is their simplistic identification in something as banal as religious marriage. The forces Blake speaks about here in an almost allegorical way have little in common with the philosophers' or theologians' accounts of 'Love' or 'Hate'. For Blake, conflict between these forces lies at the very heart not only of human existence but also, therefore, of the poetical.

This conflict is not a dialectic in the received sense, a version which would be resolved as quickly as possible through purely rational means. There is no marriage of this 'Love and Hate'. What Blake describes as a list of contradictions is best conceived of as a process that keeps going from one extreme to the other, oscillating between the two. For Hamann, analogously, language is the 'Alpha and the Omega', and our existence is shaped by what the tension between those contraries produces, but never through a synthesis of the two.[24] They are, to speak astronomically, outside of the track that normally gets subsumed back into the system of philosophy or literary history. Instead of a desire to resolve this tension, there is an investment in the extreme ways through which 'Human existence' is described and describes itself. Concomitantly, 'progression' here does not mean teleology or progress. The way of thinking that always resolves conflict in order to reach a further level of synthesis or growing systematicity is an approach that internalizes and, in effect, erases difference.

Blake and Hamann both describe the *process* of institutionalization as something that is even more insidious and destructive than the resulting structure. In an almost Nietzschean manner, Blake and Hamann both incisively argue that 'institutionalization' means conventionalization and, simultaneously, that assimilation is supposedly intuitive. Their work attempts to disrupt this process. The *Marriage* is not just a critique of the institution of matrimony but rather, comes to be a way of criticizing the catastrophic results of the institutionalization of dialectical thinking, its disastrous effects for the way that we approach the world both hermeneutically and existentially. It is an antidote for what Laura Quinney terms the 'psychic disaster' that follows 'the engorgement of Reason'.[25]

---

[22] Griffith-Dickson, p. 1.   [23] Blake, *Marriage of Heaven and Hell*, pp. 33–45, p. 34, plate 3.
[24] '[L]anguage, the mother of reason and revelation, its A and Ω'. '*Sprache*, die Mutter der Vernunft und Offenbarung, ihr A und Ω' (ZH, 6: 108). Also see ibid., 7: 377.
[25] Laura Quinney, *William Blake on Self and Soul* (Cambridge, MA: Harvard University Press, 2009), p. 51.

The desire to simplify and conventionalize, in effect, banalizes. Blake describes this process in his genealogy of 'Good & Evil', or, rather, 'what the religious', who often believe in a progress 'call Good & Evil':

> From these contraries spring what the religious call Good & Evil. Good is the passive that obeys Reason[.] Evil is the active springing from Energy.
>
> Good is Heaven. Evil is Hell.[26]

The operative word in the first line is 'call'. This is naming, a calling, gone all wrong. '[T]he religious', the institutionalized religion, not the spiritual individual, tells their own history. The contraries give birth *ex nihilo* ('spring') to the categories of good and evil. Concomitantly, these categories are beset by particular values, 'Good' and 'Evil'. This is the way that thinking works once it has, circuitously, identified these values with heaven and hell. If you want to achieve a clear and unambiguous result, then the circle between these two needs to be closed yet invisible. Blake loudly protests: according to him, good and evil turn out to be *mistaken* human constructions, including the function they serve in interpreting the meaning of holy sacraments.

Matrimony is a perfect target for Blake and Hamann, since it so heavily relies on dual structures in creating meaning—the bride and groom or marriage as a symbol of Christ's or Man's union with the church. Hamann, just like Blake, writes directly about marriage in his essay *Sibyll about Marriage*, addressed to a newly wedded friend. He warns this friend that marriage has become both the most basic but also a highly problematic social cornerstone that allows us an insight into larger, underlying societal wrongs. It is 'because marriage is the most delectable ground and cornerstone of all society, [that] the anti-human spirit of our century reveals itself most forcefully in the marriage laws'.[27] Hamann links the laws of marriage to the political structures of the Enlightenment. The insidiousness of supposedly neutral laws is exposed. It is precisely because marriage is so central—the 'cornerstone of all society'—that it has been made ideologically so toxic. This is Hamann's version of heaven and hell. The laws Hamann derides are the clerical laws of institutional religion, which have resulted in a structure that has lost all real spiritual authority. There is certainly here a harking back to early Christianity. As Marilyn Butler puts it, Blake's is 'a remarkable vision of society from the point of view of an isolated artist who cleaves to a deeply unfashionable artisan type of Christianity'.[28] What enforces this sense is that Hamann's spite is aimed at a modern version of marriage that is sanctioned by the institution. For him, this institutionalization of marriage has led to its perversion to something anti-human that he rejects outright.

For Blake and Hamann, things are never either theoretical or practical. The two are always intertwined, whether it is our account of language or of action. This is why

---

[26] Blake, *Marriage of Heaven and Hell*, p. 34, plate 3.

[27] 'Weil der Ehstand der köstlichste Grund und Eckstein der ganzen Gesellschaft ist: so offenbart sich der menschenfeindliche Geist unsers Jahrhunderts am allerstärksten in den Ehgesetzen' (N, 3: 200).

[28] Marilyn Butler, *Mapping Mythologies: Countercurrents in Eighteenth-Century British Poetry and Cultural History* (Cambridge: Cambridge University Press, 2015), pp. 181–2.

their take on institutional practices, such as matrimony or language acquisition, is so revealing. Both of them translate their ideological critique of social and religious institutionalization into their own existential choices. Despite their serious religiosity, or maybe because of it, they led deeply unorthodox, exorbitant lives, and it is only fitting that their respective matrimonies should stand out as particularly illustrative examples. Both marriages were deeply unconventional; Hamann's defied institutionally sanctioned unions even more directly than Blake's.[29] They lived their critique of 'the religious' politically.[30]

Hamann's lifelong partner was Anna Regina Schumacher, the erstwhile nurse of his ailing father. After his father's death, Hamann and Schumacher continued to live together. Although they were open about their cohabitation and had children together, they never actually married. Famously, Hamann spoke of his relationship as a 'marriage of conscience'.[31] At first, it might seem, as John R. Betz notes, that this is one the 'strangest aspect[s] of his life'.[32] On further consideration, however, it fits rather well with Hamann's wider reluctance to perpetuate the ideological structures he found so objectionable. Hamann and Schumacher defied social norms, and they seem to have done it together (rather than one forcing the other), evidently disregarding common assumptions about legal and sexual behaviour openly.

There are plenty of stories that have been used to illustrate the unconventional lifestyle of Blake and his wife Catherine, such as their reading of Milton in the garden together:

> Mr. Butts calling one day found Mr. and Mrs. Blake sitting in this summer-house, freed from 'those troublesome disguises' which have prevailed since the Fall. '*Come in!*' cried Blake; '*it's only Adam and Eve, you know!*' Husband and wife had been reciting passages from *Paradise Lost*, in character, and the garden of Hercules Buildings had to represent the Garden of Eden.[33]

---

[29] Naturally, there are details to each of the cases which make things even more complicated. Earlier in his life, Hamann suffered a setback when his friend Johann Christoph Berens denied him the hand of his sister, a woman whom Hamann believed to be destined to marry him. Berens's refusal was motivated by Hamann's turn away from the Enlightenment project.

It is only fitting that Blake's *Marriage of Heaven and Hell* is also a biographically significant text. It is 'not thirty-three years since' the 'advent' of the 'new heaven' that has supposedly begun (p. 34, plate 3). Blake's age at the time of composition is around thirty-three, and Jesus' death at the same age would have been obviously on his mind when writing it.

[30] This is not a question of competing denominations, or of one Christian community accusing the other of not following the 'real' path of faith. The interesting—and distinctively different—aspect of Blake's and Hamann's cases is that there is not really an alternative programme. There is an alternative—the celebration of poetry, of the imagination, of the human body—but at no point does this turn into an argument about a system. This attitude leaves them open for other objections, which we will cover in due course, but it is important to keep it in mind while discussing their push to dismantle ideological assumptions.

[31] 'GewissensEhe' (ZH, 3: 263).   [32] Betz, *After Enlightenment*, p. 105.

[33] Alexander Gilchrist, *Life of William Blake, 'Pictor Ignotus'* (London: Macmillan, 1863), p. 115, qtd in Bentley, *Blake Records*, pp. xxvi–xxvii. The hasty addition, *de rigueur* in current scholarship, that the story is probably apocryphal has the whiff of Anglican embarrassment about it. Surely, it intimates, Blake could not have been *that* unconventional, *that* odd?! This attitude may tell us more about accepted reading practices among scholars today. Why do we assume that it is *that* odd to read Milton naked, then or now? Is it? Maybe we should try.

Although William and Catherine were married, it certainly was not a conventional partnership. She seems to have been one of the very few people who could cope with Blake's notoriously difficult personality, but not through docility—rather by being an active part of his creative life. There is little doubt in his poetry and life that Blake embraced an anti-traditional concept of marital union.

There is no question that, even in unconventional relationships, the historical reality of gender inequality would have played out in these partnerships, too. It is important to remember that such decisions have real, tangible, consequences for the people involved. The 'marriage of conscience' was socially isolating for Hamann, Schumacher, and their children.[34] But part of the mutual attraction might well have been that the other was willing to engage in a union that defied social expectation or conventionality. If we look at the biographical material, then in neither case do we get the sense that there was shame or regret regarding these decisions, at least not for the men. We have to be careful, of course, not to be naive and forget that the negative consequences of such unusual lifestyles were far greater for Schumacher and Catherine Blake than for their husbands. Marsha Keith Schuchard's work in particular has helped to illuminate how Blake's wife might have been under enormous social and private pressures.[35] Even if we do not accept all of Schuchard's findings, it is certain all was not well in the Blakean garden of Eden. Hamann discusses with Johann Gottfried Herder his reluctance to marry, and it shines through that if Hamann had wanted to, Schumacher would probably have agreed to nuptials.

And yet it is vital that here unconventionality is not simply a cover for another version of ideological repression. Take, for instance, the fact that both Schumacher and Catherine Blake were illiterate—Schumacher remained so, and William taught Catherine to read and write. Famously, Catherine signs her wedding papers with an *X*, a nicely proleptic sign of their chiastic union. Their illiteracy is more than a noteworthy coincidence given their husbands' deep and intense dedication to the written word. It suggests a gender-marked asymmetry of power: the men can write; the women cannot. Yet it also suggests Blake's and Hamann's willingness to go against the norms for one particular person, irrespective of his or her education: in their circles, it cannot have been all that fashionable to have an illiterate wife, and it would certainly have been perfectly possible to maintain more

---

[34] Hamann never pretends otherwise, though in 1784 Hamann writes to Franz Kaspar Buchholtz, a potential benefactor, about his relationship with Schumacher to disabuse him of any illusions before money passes hands (ZH, 5: 207–8). Also see Hamann's explanation of his conviction that '[m]y work in love may be blasphemed as much as people want; God will recognize it and will bless me for it' (Meine Arbeit in der Liebe mag gelästert werden wie sie will; Gott wird sie erkennen und mich dafür seegnen) (ZH, 2: 193).

[35] See Marsha Keith Schuchard, *Why Mrs Blake Cried: William Blake and the Sexual Basis of Spiritual Vision* (London: Century, 2006). In its explicit subject matter but often associative style, the book caused a certain amount of controversy that is best summarized by G. E. Bentley: 'All serious readers of Blake will wish to read *Why Mrs Blake Cried*. If they pay close attention to the evidence, they will come away enlightened, puzzled, and frustrated' (G. E. Bentley, review of Marsha Keith Schuchard, *Why Mrs Blake Cried: William Blake and the Sexual Basis of Spiritual Vision*, *Blake/An Illustrated Quarterly* 40.4 [2007]: 150–1).

heavily patriarchal relationships with wives who were literate and socially more acceptable. There is no doubt that questions of gender and silencing trouble these relationships, but they do emerge in a context immensely more unconventional and exorbitant than the standard Romantic-era matrimony. Consider the comparatively conventional relations of Mary Hutchinson or Fanny Brawne with her husband or betrotheds; Thomas De Quincey's Ann might come close, but then we never get the chance to find out since they never reconnect. There is a real sense in which the four figures of Hamann and Schumacher, as well as Catherine and William Blake lived lives that were actively resisting the ideological pitfalls of the institutionalization of affect.

There is little doubt that Hamann and Blake loved their life partners. Hamann's letters mention Schumacher with regularity and indicate respect and deep affection. As for William Blake's views of his marriage, we have plenty of evidence that he valued his wife, including his verdict on his deathbed that 'you have ever been an angel to me', both of them knowing that Blake would not define an angel as domestic help.[36] We know that Catherine Blake was of great importance to her husband's work, being actively involved in the production of some of his illuminated books, including the *Songs of Innocence and of Experience*. This volume, of course, includes 'The Garden of Love', another indictment of religious institutionalization. In this poem, '[a] Chapel was built' in the midst of an Edenic scene (the titular 'Garden of Love'), replacing playfulness with a solid structure on whose closed entrance we encounter the declaration 'Thou shalt not writ' above the door. Catherine and William Blake surely tried to escape the 'Priests in black gowns' described in the poem, who are 'binding with briars, my joys & desires'.[37]

Neither Blake nor Hamann have a marriage *comme il faut*. The reason for that lies less in their privilege or flexibility to do otherwise than in the translation of what they were thinking, writing, and doing. The different ways that Blake and Hamann uncover the ideological trappings of religious institutions in *The Marriage of Heaven and Hell* or *Sibyll about Marriage* translate into their existential decisions. In some aspects, it is a direct extension of their exorbitant thought that is deeply spiritual, even Christian, and yet sidesteps the normal ways in which we think about these categories. As a result, Blake, Hamann, and their respective partners emerge as leading more unconventional and unorthodox lives than some of the more secular and supposedly socially progressive figures of the period. They leave the specified track of institutional religion and thought, both intellectually and existentially.

The institutionalization of religion is partly too toxic because it spreads everywhere through education. As Hamann writes, religious educational structures produce many of the 'cornerstone[s] of . . . society', not just in ethical education (teaching, supposedly, 'Good' and 'Evil'), but also in actually teaching language,

---

[36] Allan Cunningham, 'William Blake', in *The Lives of the Most Eminent British Painters, Sculptors, and Architects*, 6 vols, 2nd ed. (London: John Murray, 1830), 2: 143–88, 180.

[37] Blake, 'The Garden of Love', in *Complete Poetry and Prose*, p. 26, lines 3 and 11–12.

the tool to articulate any pedagogy or programme. For figures such as Blake and Hamann, the practical and theoretical significance of language acquisition is enormous, and it is important that they try to actively interfere with its link to institutionalization and habit. For them, it fits into a wider pattern of the continuing loss of language's spiritual and visionary qualities. Going back to Blake's bleak vision of the Fall in *Urizen*, we realize that one of the consequences of forgetting 'eternal life' is that a new life needs to be learned. After this Fall, novel structures are acquired, many of them further accelerating and intensifying the process of oblivion. New ways of learning create new habits and standards, helping to ossify those structures until they seem natural and intuitive.

This abstract issue of the linguistic Fall connects directly with the concrete topic of how we actually learn to read and write and, thus, is intimately bound up with the structures in which this instruction takes place, such as schools or pedagogical institutions. Blake's and Hamann's interests in children were always linked to learning and writing. Blake was childless, yet deeply fascinated with children, as the *Songs* amply show. Similarly, Hamann saw them as living instantiations of a spiritual principle, and by all accounts he was a tolerant father who did not mind the constant interruptions at home, which many blame for his never having had the peace to write a longer treatise. Both actively participated in the wider discussions about children's education—Blake through his *Songs*, and Hamann in exchanges on William Warburton and education—and how it repeats and institutionalizes the linguistic Fall. They both knew about the often constricting power of educational models. To Blake and Hamann, how we first discover, learn, and implement the mysteries of language was deeply important. Schools are a practical illustration of the structures that ignore those mysteries and have replaced the forgotten sense of an eternal life with something functional and crude.

The title page of the *Songs of Innocence* depicts a female figure with (her?) two children, showing them a book (like the *Songs*) in the middle of a reading lesson (Figure 6.1).

The image reminds us that we are ourselves children (of God) and that learning how to read is a hermeneutically formative moment that goes far beyond the ability to manipulate words on a page. As Hamann writes, 'Once children are instructed one should choose patterns through which light in understanding and virtue in the heart can be received; not the first book that comes to hand, and just for reading's sake, but the reading itself, if it is the main aim, must be seen as ancillary'.[38] The skill of reading is only marginally reflected in one's ability to read and write natural verbal language. 'Reading itself' goes a long way beyond a deciphering of letters; it will also allow us to discern the power of figurative language. Of course, this attitude also underlies part of the form of Blake's *Songs*: they ask us to read images and music as integral parts of the poems, pushing us to consider what it means to 'read' a piece of art or a constellation in the stars. Blake and Hamann think that to learn

---

[38] 'So bald Kinder lesen gelehrt werd[en], sollte man Muster wählen, wodurch sie Licht in Verstand v Tugend im Herzen empfieng[en], nicht d[as] erste d[as] beste Buch, und bloß des Lesens willen, sondern d[as] Lesen selbst, wenn es die Hauptabsicht ist, muß als eine Nebenabsicht angeseh[en] werd[en]' (Hamann, *Londoner Schriften*, p. 317).

Figure 6.1 William Blake, 'Title Page, *Songs of Innocence*', *Songs of Innocence and of Experience* (1825). Reproduction by kind permission of the Provost and Scholars of King's College, Cambridge.

best such reading, one should be in direct contact with the natural world as an unmediated space. Take the beginning of 'The School Boy':

> I love to rise in a summer morn,
> When the birds sing on every tree;
> The distant huntsman winds his horn,
> And the sky-lark sings with me.[39]

[39] Blake, 'The School Boy', in *Complete Poetry and Prose*, p. 31, lines 1–4.

The speaker is attentive to the language and song of the birds 'on every tree', and he learns to read his surroundings both human ('The distant huntsman winds his horn') and non-human ('the sky-lark sings with me'). He learns how to distinguish and differentiate between these different languages. The horn of the huntsman, for instance, is related to the boy by being human—all these sounds provide 'sweet company'—yet qualitatively different from the boy's and the sky-lark's joint singing.[40] The promise of this education is cut short:

> But to go to school in a summer morn,
> O! it drives all joy away;
> Under a cruel eye outworn,
> The little ones spend the day,
> In sighing and dismay.[41]

The boy's learning process is interrupted, as the title has already threatened: he is dragged into the institutionalized context of learning and, as a result, has to 'go to school in a summer morn'. This school is the waste of time, the 'trouble' and 'tedium' that Hamann writes about—or, as Blake puts it, 'O! it drives all joy away'.[42]

The poem not only describes a lack of entertainment or superficial enjoyment but also addresses the structural consequences that occur as a result of how the institutions begin to regulate time, reading, and thinking. Blake tells Henry Crabb Robinson that '[t]here is no use in education[.] I hold it wrong—It is the great Sin'.[43] In such education the children 'spend the day, / In sighing and dismay' rather than breathing freely and singing melodiously. In the poem, the dis-may is almost enough to suggest that the season of summer itself is over. The sound of the 'distant huntsmen' is replaced by an unsympathetic sight of control and supervision: the children find themselves 'Under a cruel eye outworn'. The cruelty of this sight is twofold: it wears itself out as well as outwearing the children it observes. As Hamann notes, this form of education shapes the very form of thought itself, particularly the way they think about language:

> I think that the use of writing costs children much time, much trouble, and tedium; even that the very use is, for certain ones, the more disadvantageous the earlier they are led to learn it. The disadvantage to health, because this work requires constant sitting, affords an opportunity to do nothing, or at least be lost in thought, while at the same time the hand is employed with displeasure. What child has a desire to be able to make an 'a' or a 'b'. Could one not let children start with painting and drawing, with the hieroglyphic art of writing. This would be easier, because we are all born to imitate, especially imitate nature; the sense of the eye, its judgement, the sense and the taste of the relation of visible beauty, the comparison of the similarities and dissimilarities, in which consists such a great advantage of the power of thought.[44]

---

[40] Blake, 'School Boy', p. 31, line 5.   [41] Blake, 'School Boy', p. 31, lines 6–10.

[42] 'Mühe und Ueberdruß' (Hamann, *Londoner Schriften*, p. 318).

[43] Crabb Robinson, diary entry of 10 December 1825, pp. 419–25, 422.

[44] 'Ich glaube daß der Gebrauch des Schreibens viele Zeit, viel Mühe und Ueberdruß Kindern kostet, ja daß derselbe bey einig[en] desto nachtheiliger ist, je früher sie dazu angeführt werden. Der Nachtheil der Gesundheit, weil diese Arbeit ein anhaltendes Sitzen erfordert, eine Gelegenheit nichts zu thun oder wenigstens müßig in Gedank[en] zu seyn, unterdessen die Hand mit Verdruß beschäftig[en] muß. Was hat ein Kind vor Lust ein a oder b mach[en] zu können. Könnte man Kinder nicht lieber

Hamann proposes a radical education that emphasizes the poetic power of language. He focuses on the link between writing and thinking, between linguistic and cognitive habits, when he expresses that children are right not to want to repeat signs over and over again, an exercise that leads to the disconnect between the body (the 'employ[ed]' hand) and the mind ('lost in thought'). This is precisely the type of language learning that 'drives all joy away'. It also drives all the knowledge away since it teaches a distorted version of natural language and thus also distorts the understanding of language itself. The larger context of Hamann's remarks is a discussion with Warburton, who maintained that language needs to be rescued from its initial, hieroglyphic status. Hamann, by contrast, aggressively insists that we should continue to emphasize 'painting and drawing, with the hieroglyphic art of writing'. If this art is quashed by institutional confinement, then children—such as Blake's 'school boy'—are not free to paint or draw; as a result, as Hamann suggests, too, their 'hand is employed with displeasure'.[45] The way they learn what language is and how to read it is limited and limiting. It's what Blake invokes with the 'summer mo(u)rn' in 'The School Boy': the mourning of this loss begins with 'learning'.

It would be tempting to absorb this model into a wider account of Romantic or even modern liberal education, thus recuperating Blake and Hamann as central thinkers of such schools. However, while we recognize seemingly similar thinking later on in modern discussions about pedagogy, we should not forget that Blake and Hamann most of the time cannot be domesticated in this way. Just as they are not founders of intellectual schools, they would never have become headmasters. Their criticism is not really a proposition to build a different school. And just as in so many other areas, their exorbitant positions mean that their criticism bites but that their positive programme is not really articulated in relation to a reality that we would recognize as standard. For them, any institutionalization of learning that promotes a model of language as primarily communication will end up in a version of the pain that the 'School Boy' experiences.

Hence Blake and Hamann's critique is not only about mediating a better pedagogy. An example is instructive: at one point, Kant approached Hamann to coauthor a book on physics for children. Hamann declined, suspecting that his friend and fellow thinker wanted to lure him into writing a book that would solidify looking at the world—physics—through the lens of natural philosophy. Blake and Hamann refuse any form of institutional learning, in the same way that they themselves are known for their own scattered educations when it came to books. In this case, the limits and frustrations of the two exorbitants come starkly into view. There is no positive programme, at least not one that would be 'realistic'.

---

mit mahlen und Zeichnen, mit der hieroglyphisch[en] Schreibekunst den Anfang mach[en] lassen. Dies würde leichter seyn, weil wir alle zum nachahm[en] gebor[en] sind, besonders die Natur nachzuahmen; der Sinn des Auges, das Urtheil desselben, der Sinn v der Geschmack der Verhältnis v sichtbarer Schönheit, die Vergleichung der Ähnlichkeiten und Unähnlichkeiten, worinn ein so großer Vortheil der Denkungskräfte besteht' (Hamann, *Londoner Schriften*, p. 318).

The similarities and links to Walter Benjamin's theory of mimesis mentioned in the introduction are astonishing.

[45] '[D]ie Hand mit Verdruß beschäftig[en] muß' (Hamann, *Londoner Schriften*, p. 318).

We might think it hopelessly naive to let our children follow their hieroglyphic tendencies. But, of course, it is only naive if you believe that *eventually* they will need to communicate functionally. It is a good example of just how out of orbit Blake and Hamann are and remain: they reject even a homeopathic approach to education that would ameliorate it or introduce a slightly more sensitive approach. This still will be too institutional; it might even introduce a more deadening way of thinking since it is more insidious—recall that Hamann prefers atheism to deism. In effect, they embrace learning but reject education as we know it, just in the same way (and for similar reasons) that they embrace religiosity but reject religion as we know it.

To their contemporaries—as well as to many today—their approaches, arguments, and readings were often deeply baffling and alien. They cleaved to an unfashionable type of early Christianity and a version of impossible education. That does not mean, of course, they were not Christian. They claimed the affiliation. In fact, much of the critical fire in their bellies stemmed from their idiosyncratic Christianity, including their critique of ideology and institutional religion. To put it simply, if under 'religion' we understand the institutionalized version of Christianity, then neither Blake nor Hamann would have subscribed to it. For them, Christianity was deeply individual, tied to language and poetry, and it could not be expressed in a modern, institutional form. In this sense, they defended a radical Christianity similar to the version Søren Kierkegaard would outline in his later work: an impossible, individual relation between God and the singular being. The problem is, of course, that such a version of religious relation sounds very much like a private language, something that is impossible.

7

Hybrid Hymns
Anglo-German Voices in Blake's *Songs*

THE MORAVIAN POLYGLOT HYMN
IN BRITISH LITERARY HISTORY

Moravian hymns are among the most powerful yet least recognized Anglo-German forms of literature and culture across the eighteenth century. Hymns that many consider typically British are, in fact, the products of translation and assimilation from a German, often exorbitant, context. As I show in this chapter, the Wesley brothers play an important role here, especially as translators, offering a new and relatively unknown side of these central figures of eighteenth-century cultural life. Uncovering the multilingual origin of the Moravian hymn allows us to trace echoes of these polyglot dimensions in William Blake's *Songs of Innocence and of Experience*. Blake's recently uncovered biographical connections to the Moravian congregation via his mother, a member of the church, further substantiate this link. The Moravians were difficult figures in the eighteenth century and remain outside the common tracks of our cultural histories. Despite their exorbitance and their small size, their impact in Britain was remarkable. Methodist hymnal tradition is partly a monolingual domestication of the Moravians' polyglot, excessive practice. The Moravian Church's loss of influence over the course of the nineteenth century eventually resulted in an obfuscation of the multilingual history of the hymn. Once we develop a renewed sensibility for this multilingual history, we can not only rehear hymns but also sense a new radicalism in lyrics we thought we already knew, including Blake's *Songs*.

The Moravians were instrumental in developing the hymn—helping to create the conditions for its impact on British literary history—although their radical style was to be sidelined. Of course, the genre of the hymn existed in Britain before the nineteenth century, and its main influences and development between different figures (Isaac Watts and the Wesleys) and among denominations (Moravians, Methodists, Calvinists, and Lutherans) represent several complex relations and networks. The development of what Benjamin Kolodziej terms '18th-century English congregational song' is a highly revealing topic, since it focuses on the translation of theoretical or spiritual belief into the daily practices of worship and aesthetics.[1] What I want to concentrate on here is not only how the Moravian role in this story

---

[1] Benjamin Kolodziej, 'Isaac Watts, the Wesleys and the Evolution of the 18th-Century English Congregational Song', *Methodist History* 42, 4 (July 2004): 236–48.

has been underestimated but also, crucially, how this underestimation comes at the price of being unable to hear the multilingual dimensions of the history of the genre.[2]

Basically, we have ended up with a distorted, monolingual literary history that is deaf to the complexity of these contexts and that we need to rectify. Concretely, we need to develop an ear for the multilingual echoes across the eighteenth century. In Blake's case, that means to listen for foreign voices where we might not expect them, both historically and formally. I show how the unexpected Anglo-German origin of the Moravian hymns allows us to discover a new Blake steeped in multilingualism. Once more, it would be tempting to argue for putting the Moravian hymn at the centre of eighteenth-century hymnody. However, as the main methodological point of this book reminds us, the purpose of uncovering the genre is to see how it remains on the outside, yet makes an impact. What we can see, however, is how the domestication of this form through literary history has blunted its once powerfully radical potential.

The hymn celebrates Christian beliefs in a quotidian manner and setting, making its music and poetry part of daily liturgical life. By the eighteenth century the genre included, as J. R. Watson puts it, 'the expression of all the varieties of human religious experience, the dark places of the soul, the exaltation, the sense of penitence, and the sense of joy'.[3] The Moravians are a particularly interesting case in point, since they link that variety of human religious experience to the *aesthetic* and the *musical* dimensions of the genre. Their theoretical investment in the sensual dimension of music puts them on a very different track from many other Pietist or Dissenting movements at the time. For the Moravians, music, singing, and poetry became ways to celebrate the world's complexity, individually or collectively. As Robert Rix notices, Nikolaus Ludwig von Zinzendorf, the most influential bishop of the Moravian Church,

> had brought the appreciation of the arts...to bear on the Moravian congregations. Moravian worship differed from the usual Pietist rejection of aesthetic pleasures.... Song especially became an important dimension of Moravian devotion, as Zinzendorf insisted that the truths of the Christian religion are best communicated in poetry and song, rather than systematic theology or scholastic polemics.[4]

We find a good illustration for this attitude in the beginning to the Moravian 1789 *Collection of Hymns*:

> It is our ardent wish and fervent prayer unto the Lord, that he may render this publication a means to enliven that part of our worship which consists in *singing*, and that we

[2] This includes other multilingual connections such as Isaac Watts's own connections to Germany and the fact that his own work was being translated before 1740.

[3] J. R. Watson, *The English Hymn: A Critical and Historical Study* (Oxford: Oxford University Press, 1999), p. 5.

[4] Robert Rix, *William Blake and the Cultures of Radical Christianity* (Burlington, VT: Ashgate, 2007), p. 10. While the focus here is on William Blake, it is worthwhile to mention that this musical element would have been crucial for Johann Georg Hamann, too. The emphasis on aesthetics, and music in particular, would have been deeply relevant in his biblical study within the context of Moravianism and his continuing appreciation of Nikolaus Ludwig von Zinzendorf. Throughout his career Hamann repeats how musical poetry—song—stands at the centre of the world.

may sing unto him with humble hearts and cheerful voices, both when assembled before him, and in our private devotion.[5]

The importance of the acoustic experience of song was paramount for the Moravians since they embraced the aesthetic as a crucial part of our concretely lived experience. The choirs, male and female, were a central part of the congregation. As a result, the Moravians developed a reputation for their hymns and their singing. John Wesley, whose conviction that hymnal singing was a sign of faith had resulted from his having witnessed Moravian voices, put it thus: 'If you want to hear fine psalmody...go to Fulneck and hear the Moravians sing'.[6] The theoretical significance of this devotional practice lies in the Moravian insistence that the ordinary, daily aspect of human experience—including singing and listening to music—is a living proof for the existence of God. Spirituality is neither a theoretical matter nor limited to particular spheres of our existence. As Rix points out, 'The Deity is never abstract, but...the full manifestation of divinity was revealed in Christ', who walked and lived on Earth.[7] It is also revealed in the concrete form of the hymn and its text. Poetry and song, rather than philosophy, stand at the centre of revelation.

The multilingual German Moravians brought their Germans hymns with them and continued to sing them in London, teaching them and translating them as well. In Chapter 5, I mention the diaries that describe the habits of Moravian congregation members at Fetter Lane. In one of them we read, 'For the Conclusion was German Singing-Hour'.[8] The day ends with a German singing hour—what is still known as the *Singstunde* in Anglophone congregations—for both the native speakers and the British members of the congregation. This was a conscious effort since, as Geoffrey Stead and Margaret Stead point out, 'German and English leaders cooperated over the production of suitable material for congregational use'.[9] Correspondingly, many of the printed materials and hymnals that were published by and for the Moravians during the eighteenth century in London were bilingual, either in part or throughout. We find hymnals that have prefaces in both German and English, or in both of them together. Several of them have the languages printed on opposite sides of the pages of the book. This cooperation involved not just the Moravians in the immediate congregation but also a set of figures who were responsible for the production and dissemination of those forms. One of these was James Hutton, a German bookseller in London, whose 'production of the early hymnals...and the German style of creating material for immediate use was an important part of the developing pattern of worship in the English society', as Stead and Stead show.[10] Since Moravian hymnody becomes crucial to British

---

[5] Preface to *A Collection of Hymns, for the Use of the Protestant Church of the United Brethren* (London, 1789), pp. iii–vi, vi; ECCO ESTC T124259.
[6] John Wesley, qtd in Louis Elson, ed., *University Musical Encyclopedia* 10 vols (New York: The University Society, 1910), vol. 5, p. 52.
[7] Rix, p. 11.   [8] Moravian Archive, London, C/36/7/10 (3 July 1757 [?])
[9] Stead and Stead, p. 59.
[10] Stead and Stead, pp. 59–60. The complexity of this Anglo-German link, intertwining cultural and economic production, brought with it a certain potential for conflict. This was highlighted during the expansion of the Moravians across Britain under what Stead and Stead claim was a rather

literary life and religious-aesthetic expression within it, these multilingual texts and practices demand our attention.

The act of singing was, as it is now, one of the most effective and powerful ways to learn another language. The Moravians understood this well and combined linguistic, spiritual, and literary education in their children's choir. In 1756, the Moravian press produced a small (3.7 × 2.4 in; 9.5 × 6 cm) pocketbook titled *A Hymn-Book for the Children Belonging to the Brethren's Congregations: Taken Chiefly out of the GERMAN Little Book*. It presents the children with both the German and the English versions since the editors have decided '[*i*]*t may not be improper to subjoin here a few* German Verses, *such as are most in Use among us*'.[11] Here are two arresting examples of such verses:

> WENN ich mich will erquicken,
> Und schöne Blümlein pflücken,
> Geh' ich zum rosen-rothen
> Herz Gärtlein meines Todten.
> When Garlands I'm for twisting, or Nosegays fresh, I hasten To th' Roses in
>   th' Heart's Garden of my so faithful Dead-one.

> WAS wein'st du warum giert die Kehl?
> Ich jamm're vor Gebrech und Fehl;
> Ich giere nach der Seiten-hohl [*sic*];
> Ich weine, ach! nach seiner Seel.
> Why weep'st thou? wherefore all these Plaints? I mourn because of Faults and
>   wants; Into the Side's warm Nest I'd creep; After His Soul I wish & weep.[12]

The hymns suggest that at this point there was no hesitation in embracing the rhetoric of the side-hole or the idea of joining a dead Christ. Moravian children were clearly expected to adopt these ideas as part of learning the language.

Starting with its title, the hymn book highlights its place within the larger linguistic context. The way that the 1754 hymnal is structured acknowledges this openly: the table of contents lists dedicated sections of '*German* Hymns in the xvi[th] Century... *German* Hymns in the xvii[th] Century... Hymns, *German* and *English*, about the End of the xvii[th], or in the xviii[th] Century'.[13] Many hymn books provide bilingual versions of the songs, or at least retain the German titles. The 1756 *Hymn-Book* for children expands the bilingual practice with a section that

---

authoritarian German style of governance (see p. 59). While this story falls a little too neatly into national stereotypes and is rather contrary to the account we have of the Moravians as a generally inclusive and open congregation, the fact remains that by the late eighteenth century the Brethren were large and complex enough to have to accommodate internal differences whose character reached across languages and national cultures: 'tensions and changes which arose from the interaction between a growing desire to conform to British denominationalism and the appeal of the Moravians' Anglo-German tradition' (Stead and Stead, p. 225). Importantly, this difficult multinationalism is bound up with the production of a particular form of artistic and poetic practice.

   [11] *A Hymn-Book for the Children Belonging to the Brethren's Congregations: Taken Chiefly out of the* GERMAN *Little Book* ([London], 1756), pp. i–xxx, vii; ECCO ESTC T189669.
   [12] Hymns 5 and 14, in *Hymn-Book for the Children*, pp. ix and xiv.
   [13] Table of contents to *A Collection of Hymns of the Children of God in All Ages* (London, 1754), p. [1]; ECCO ESTC T053156.

produces 'Luther's *Paraphrase of the Creed and Ten Commandments, (by which a Child may accustom himself a little to read the Language)*', together with an alphabet in German print.[14] Clearly, this is not just about teaching a language or a set of musical compositions; it is also about teaching a certain aesthetic and spirituality that is connected to the exchange between different tongues, another sign for the power of a polyglot literary history. The passage also suggests that these hymns might open up an alternative way of thinking that we have lost.

Many of these hymns are odd, radical, strange, and unusual. They celebrate Christianity in ways we are not used to and provide an example of how the Moravians were members of the exorbitant Enlightenment. Since their 'spirituality was Christocentric, focusing on Christ's blood and wounds, particularly the side-wound...Moravians aimed at becoming ever more childlike and simple, playing games and developing a secret language laced with diminutive terms of endearment. All this found its most controversial expression in the Moravian hymns of these years'.[15] Many German original hymns, such as the two just cited here, play an important part in this eroticized celebration. It is no surprise that many moderate Moravians as well as an increasing number of Anglicans wanted to ignore or suppress these forms of exorbitant hymnal celebrations—and, together with it, the rich heritage of German material that continued to affect the genre in Britain.

Crudely speaking, what we can chart is the transformation of polyglot, exorbitant Moravian hymns to monolingual, canonical Methodist practice, as I suggest in Chapter 5. This general narrative allows us to see how the radical, nonconformist ideas of the Moravians were tempered and regulated and made less troubling, including their unusual ideas about hymnody and language. The story of the relationship of the Wesley brothers with Moravianism is a good illustration of this main point since they transform their initial interest in Moravianism to a more acceptable centre—rather than staying outside of the orbit with the Moravians—by way of the hymn. This is not to doubt the Wesleys' importance as central figures of British hymnody of the period, of course. Rather, it is to recover some of the complicated, multilingual qualities of the Moravian hymn that continue to be evocative, and turn out to be especially suggestive in connection with poetry that is similarly strange, such as Blake's.

John and Charles Wesley were key members of the Moravian congregation until 1740. Their productive, yet difficult, relation to the Moravians began in 1735 with great enthusiasm. It was followed by a very active period in the organization but eventually by a split from the congregation. From the very beginning, different languages and devotional song played an important role in John Wesley's relation to the Moravians. His first encounter with Moravians, possibly one of the most profound experiences of his life, is a good example. It occurred during his 1735 voyage to the New World, in the midst of a storm on the Atlantic. He recorded in his diary that the passengers and crew of his boat, the *Simmonds*, were in a panic and had lost all hope. However, he also details how there was a small group of religious Moravian missionaries whose behaviour was significantly different. They

---

[14] *Hymn-Book for the Children*, p. xxvi.   [15] Podmore, p. 132.

were calm and collected, and their behaviour ended up being a major turning point in Wesley's life:

> At Seven I went to the *Germans*. I had long before observed, The great Seriousness of their Behaviour.... There was now an Opportunity of trying, Whether they were deliver'd from the Spirit of Fear, as well as from that of Pride, Anger and Revenge. In the Midst of the Psalm wherewith their Service began, the Sea broke over, split the Main Sail in Pieces, cover'd the Ship, and poured in between the Decks, as if the great Deep had already swallow'd us up. A terrible Screaming began among the *English*. The *Germans* calmly sung on. I asked one of them afterwards, 'Was you not afraid?' He answer'd, 'I thank GOD, No.' I asked, 'But were not your Women and Children afraid?' He replied, mildly, 'No; our Women and Children are not afraid to die.'
>
> From them I went to their crying, trembling Neighbours, and pointed out to them the Difference in the Hour of Trial, between him that feareth GOD, and him that feareth him not. At Twelve the Wind fell. This was the most glorious Day which I have hitherto seen.[16]

This experience led Wesley to eventually join the Moravian Church.[17] He had already learned German to communicate with them and to translate their hymns. His exposure to both the multiplicity of languages and the importance of song matters because it draws our attention to the characteristic combination of the multilingual and the importance of sung poetry that I have identified as typically Moravian. The 'Germans' don't miss a beat, not even at the disruptive climax of this story, the moment when the elements toy with the ship, almost swallowing it. Their 'Psalm' continues, and their eloquent song contrasts sharply with the 'terrible Screaming' of the English. Because they have learned to sing in this way, Wesley suggests, even the women and children act more steadfastly than the grown English men.

Back in London, Wesley joined the Moravians and became central in shaping this multilingual congregation. After learning German he translated at least thirty-three Moravian hymns into English, a collection that formed the beginning of his interest in the genre. (Also, consider that his brother would go on to become the most important composer of hymns in the English language.)[18] Wesley, the founder of English Methodism, at this point

> talked and sang in German; read German books; wrote in German; mastered and reviewed a German grammar and a German dictionary, then transcribed them to fix their contents in his memory; and, finally, he wrote a German grammar and compiled a German dictionary of his own.
>
> From this time until 1740... he was almost continuously in contact and communication with German-speaking people.[19]

[16] John Wesley, *An Extract of the Rev. Mr. John Wesley's Journal, from His Embarking for Georgia to His Return to London* (Bristol: S. and F. Farley, [1740]), pp. 7–8; ECCO ESTC T017121.

[17] It foreshadows the so-called Aldersgate experience: during a Moravian service in Aldersgate Street, Wesley had a profound religious experience that led him to develop the idea of salvation by grace alone, a cornerstone of Methodism.

[18] See John L. Nuelsen, *John Wesley and the German Hymn: A Detailed Study of John Wesley's Translations of Thirty-Three German Hymns*, trans. Theo Parry, Sydney H. Moore, and Arthur Holbrook (Calverley, Yorkshire: A. S. Holbrook, 1972).

[19] Thomas Herbert, *John Wesley as Editor and Author* (Princeton, NJ: Princeton University Press, 1940), p. 49, qtd in Davis, p. 26.

A good example of the impact of his translation work is the 1737 *A Collection of Psalms and Hymns*. This book became a standard English hymn book in the United States and thus helped to regulate and establish the Moravian congregation in London and abroad. It marks, as Garold N. Davis points out,

> the beginning of one of the most important cultural and literary links between England and Germany in the eighteenth century. The union of the Wesleys with the German Moravians was not only important for the transmission of further German poetry into England, but was in large measure responsible for the entire evangelical revival of the eighteenth century and the consequent influence of this revival on English culture and literature.[20]

Wesley's role as a transmitter of Anglo-German culture, albeit a tempered version of Moravian ideas and songs, has yet to be explored fully. His work directly contributes to a development of English literary history that is much more grounded in comparative, transnational practices than we often are wont to admit. When Donald M. McCorkle suggests that it is 'well known' that 'Wesley was rather heavily indebted to the Moravians for some of his early hymnody', he is being a little optimistic, certainly when it comes to knowledge of the German dimension of this relation.[21]

One of the few exceptions to this trend, Martha Winburn England and John Sparrow's *Hymns Unbidden*, does take up Wesley's Anglo-German connection, but it ends up trying to protest too much:

> Germanic studies in England were non-existent in 1737 when John Wesley introduced into English the first influence of German hymnody. His German hymns were soon in use in all congregations that allowed the use of hymns, were adopted as hymnody was adopted, and remain in wide popular use and high critical esteem.[22]

If all the other scholarship ignores Wesley, then this tries to move the needle too far in the other direction. It shifts Wesley (not the Moravians, note) from the margin to the centre. Such overcompensation means that England and Sparrow's account makes Wesley the Ur-moment of Anglo-German relations, a suspicious move for an exorbitant Enlightenment. In any case, at least there is a commitment on England and Sparrow's part to speak of Wesley's explicitly 'German hymns' and show their wide cultural impact. Importantly, the story that *Hymns Unbidden* tells post-Wesley emphasizes continuity in this influence: 'When Coleridge and Carlyle (himself a bringer-in of Lutheran hymnody) focused attention on Germanic studies, the reputation of Wesley's translations reached new heights'.[23] There is a direct Anglo-German line from Wesley to Samuel Taylor Coleridge and Thomas

---

[20] Davis, pp. 23–4.

[21] McCorkle, *Moravian Music in Salem*, p. 64. See, for instance, the relative absence of the Moravian hymns in Isabel Rivers, *Reason, Grace, and Sentiment: A Study of Religion and Ethics in England, 1660–1780*, 2 vols (Cambridge: Cambridge University Press, 1991–2000); David L. Wykes, *Dissenting Praise: Religious Dissent and the Hymn in England and Wales* (Oxford: Oxford University Press, 2011).

[22] Martha Winburn England and John Sparrow, *Hymns Unbidden: Donne, Herbert, Blake, Emily Dickinson, and the Hymnographers* (New York: New York Public Library, 1966), p. 38.

[23] England and Sparrow, pp. 38–9.

Carlyle, making these three British authors a part of a much larger context that also included Fuseli, Hamann, Blake, and many others, and which is a central part of our account of eighteenth-century Britain and its relation to Germany.

All of these relations present another set of examples of how comparative work can elucidate a forgotten or neglected aspect of authors or historical contexts we think we understand well.[24] As Keri Davies points out, 'The historian R. T. Jenkins, in writing of the Moravians in the eighteenth century, stressed the key role they played in the establishment of the tradition of English (and Welsh) hymnody'.[25] The problem is that many of us have lost a sense of the difficult and troubled beginning of that process. For instance, we mainly think of Wesley today as the father of Methodism and of Methodism as the group that most influentially adopts and develops the very English genre of the hymn.[26] In fact, Methodism and the hymn are the result of a multilingual, Anglo-German context that insisted on the importance of translation and transmission, both theologically and practically. And this development lessens the radical aspects of hymns from Moravian exorbitance to Methodism's canonization.

The development was both internal and external. The internal development had begun before 1750, during a time when the Moravian Church was trying to curb what many perceived to be its excessive character. There was an important shift within Moravian thinking and vision in the eighteenth century. This shift tempered the radical, eroticized Christianity and led to a more mainstream understanding of doctrine. This 'Sifting Time' resulted in a self-censorship that was immediately reflected in the hymns.[27] Moravian hymnody, as Jonathan Yonan shows, had to increasingly 'bow…to the pressure to readjust itself according to respectable Protestant standards'.[28] The most visible and audible sign of this change was the switch from the hymnbooks in the 1740s and even the 1750s to the one published in 1789, which reflected a big change from experimental and liminal voices as central to Moravian practice to a much more conventional formulation of Christianity in these hymns.

The move away from radical, even exorbitant Moravian hymns to more tempered Methodist material coincided with the increasingly monolingual understanding of the hymnal form. Although it would be too crude to argue for a simple, direct causal connection, the parallel is suggestive. Many of the more adventurous ideas we encounter in Moravian texts were directly identified *as* German by critics, internal and external. In 1788 one of the committee members, charged with deciding what would be included in the new hymnal, complains that his only ally on the committee 'could not affect anything against the Adorers of Germanisms, no not even against

[24] Davis invokes a possible genealogy here that leads straight into Romanticism: 'Consequently, this phase of the development of the mind of John Wesley under the influence of the German Moravians is important for a complete understanding of the development of the English Romantic movement. Unfortunately it has been a neglected chapter in the long history of this movement' (p. 25).
[25] Davies, 'Lost Moravian History', p. 1298.
[26] On the relation between Methodism and Moravians, see Podmore, pp. 72–96.
[27] Yonan, p. vi. See also ch. 4 of Yonan, 'Remaking Moravian Hymnody: Remaking the Moravian Church', pp. 149–220.
[28] Yonan, p. 150.

the mystical and fanatical Publications w[hi]ch have brought infamy upon us'.[29] The Germanism is clearly identified with the earlier, radical period. Such changes are part of a complex and long process, and Yonan makes a convincing case that Moravian self-censoring was part of a multidimensional process.[30] One of the crucial aspects of this development is not just that there was an internal drive within the Moravian Church to ease some of the more idiosyncratic imagery of their hymns, but also that there were external pressures that began to sideline Moravian hymnody on a much broader scale.

Methodism, and John Wesley in particular, played a crucial role in the historical decline of the radical Moravian hymn and, by extension, the awareness of its multilingual origin. Wesley actively contributed to a shift in perception of the Moravians from pious outsiders to religious fanatics and sacrilegious sinners, even after their own period of self-censuring. He condemns some of the typical Moravian hymns as extravagant, and after his withdrawal from the Moravian congregation he published a satirical version of the Moravian hymn book. Although this was an odd and ineffectual approach—by that time he was known to have contributed to the distribution of the hymns to begin with—it does suggest a continuous engagement with the form and an understanding of how relevant it was for religious practice. In a way, Wesley's publication was as much a reaction to his changed views on Moravianism as it was a proof of his success as their former agent in the Anglo-German network. The rejoinder that the Moravians published in reaction to Wesley's attack makes this clear, since it contained a considerable number of Wesley's own translations.

Wesley is a powerful example of how certain parts of the originally radical Anglo-German context became domesticated, absorbed, and canonized into a monolingual literary and cultural history. Stead and Stead conclude that the 1754 Moravian hymnal, 'drawing on German and other Central European sources to an extent unique in contemporary British hymnody, was the foundation on which all subsequent provincial hymnals were built. It remains a very important publication for the understanding of eighteenth-century Unity spirituality as presented to English-speaking members'.[31] And yet there is little awareness that the hymnal contained some of the most radical poetic imagery or that this was done in an openly multilingual way. These hymnals were the basis for years of congregational service, thus deeply seeping into the musical, poetical, and linguistic habits of the congregation. Alongside the Bible or the *Book of Common Prayer*, these lines would have been better known than any other texts, would have shaped the songs of day-to-day life. It would be part of a daily practice—but then its multiple origins are quite quickly forgotten.

[29] C. I. Latrobe, letter of 9 October 1792, in *Letters to My Children*, ed. J. A. LaTrobe (London: Seeleys, 1851), qtd in Yonan, p. 209.
[30] See Yonan, p. 190.
[31] Stead and Stead, p. 278. They continue: 'Changes were slow and irresolute, because the mid-eighteenth-century atonement style of the original Unity in its German homeland exercised a strong and persistent appeal, in spite of a desire in the British Province for modernization in line with contemporary taste, and a willingness to bring in new hymns' (ibid.).

To see how the pressures of absorption and canonization work, it is worth reminding ourselves of the pervasiveness and sheer quantity of hymns that were written, translated, and available at the time. According to John Julian, 'The number of German hymns cannot fall short of one hundred thousand', and we know that Zinzendorf alone composed over two thousand hymns, many of which were translated into English.[32] The German hymns sometimes became the standard against which English hymns were working—or, at least, they were highly influential in determining how English hymnody adopted its materials and combined them with more traditional elements from John Donne, Richard Crashaw, George Herbert, or Abraham Cowley.[33] The distribution of the type of hymn books I have just discussed was relatively fast and easy, since there were plenty of printers and booksellers already familiar with the Anglo-German or Moravian context. The Moravian hymn production was steady and continuous, both through in-house printing and other London publishers.

All these examples point towards a larger insight: the historical origin of the British hymn reveals it to be a hybrid genre. It is also, in its Moravian incarnation, a genre that can be excessive and experimental. This push towards the exorbitant and the hymn's polyglot origin, however, are not aspects that survive in literary history. The Moravian congregation is one of the best places to illustrate this claim. It turns out that the English and Welsh hymns that have been part of everyday life in Britain since the eighteenth century have a deeply transnational origin. Our reading of a great number of eighteenth- and nineteenth-century poems and poets should reflect this, including their radical predecessors. If England is correct in claiming that '[w]hen the development of hymn meters is seen in historical sequence, it is apparent that Blake is closer to Wesley than to any other poet', then this becomes a claim not only about prosodic form but also about how this literary relation is predicated on translation, on a German body of writing (often Moravian), and on an Anglo-German reception in London that produced and translated these hymns to begin with.[34] It certainly adds to our reading of Blake's *Songs of Innocence and of Experience* in ways I explore next.

BLAKE AND HIS MORAVIAN 'CITY, GRACE'

That the genre of the hymn is important for our reading of Blake is surely uncontroversial, and, as Andrew Lincoln puts it, the '*Songs* attest to his interest in the English hymn, and in children's literature'.[35] The fact that the polyglot Moravians are part of this tradition, however, brings something new to this relation, especially since recent scholarship has uncovered a direct link between Blake and the Moravians.

---

[32] John Julian, *Dictionary of Hymnology* (London, 1892), p. 412, qtd in Davis, p. 12. On Zinzendorf's extensive number of compositions, see Davis, p. 61.
[33] See England and Sparrow.
[34] England and Sparrow, p. 48.
[35] Andrew Lincoln, 'Alluring the Heart to Virtue: Blake's *Europe*', *Studies in Romanticism* 38, 4 (Winter 1999): 621–39, 630. Lincoln provides a subtle reading of the feminine connotations that the genre of the hymn carried.

In fact, the two most important women in Blake's life—his mother and his wife—both had connections to the Moravian Church. As Davies has conclusively shown, Blake's mother was an active member of the congregation in London. In her book on Blake's wife, Marsha Keith Schuchard brings to our attention the unusual and often very transgressive sexual doctrines and practices of the Moravians—both documented and imagined—some of which Blake supposedly followed to his wife's dismay (hence Schuchard's title: *Why Mrs Blake Cried*). In relation to the topic of eroticized Christianity, we can add as an influence here the figure of Emanuel Swedenborg, whom Blake was reading early on in his career and who was himself substantially influenced by this aspect of Moravian thought.[36] We will come back to the issues of eroticism and Christology, especially in relation to Blake, in Chapter 8 of this book, but for the moment I would like to focus primarily on the connection between Blake's mother and the congregation, since it is closer to the focus on Blake's own relation to Moravian hymns and poetry.[37]

The discovery of Blake's mother's membership is another example of the richness of the Moravian Archives. Davies and Schuchard follow the trail of casual remarks about Blake's connections to the Moravians by Thomas Muir, Thomas Wright, and Margaret Ruth Lowery. According to Muir, 'Blake's parents "attended the Moravian Chapel in Fetter Lane"—and such a chapel did exist, having been established around 1738'.[38] The Moravian Archive reveals a direct trace of Blake's mother, including her letters of application to the congregation. It turns out that Catherine (then Armitage, later Blake) and her first husband were not just occasional visitors of the main Moravian congregation but were deeply and actively involved in the group.[39] They even worked on becoming members of the so-called Congregation

---

[36] The link to Emanuel Swedenborg might be more than a coincidence, especially when it comes to the link between the erotic and Christianity. We can easily see how Swedenborg would have been attractive to Blake, consciously or not, precisely because there was already a Moravian influence at work here. On that account, Blake became interested in both Swedenborg and the reclamation of the erotic for Christian thought precisely because he was already predisposed to the Moravians' aspects of such ideas or their tone.

Reclaiming the erotic as part of Christianity is, of course, also central to Hamann. This is the body of the celebration of divine grace, rather than the abject body. Sex is an expression not primarily of one's limitation, since the senses are not negative, but rather offers a deep affirmation of life. It is understood that sex is limited, but one doesn't have to mourn that limitation: sex is an expression of a divine gift. The senses are not signs of depravity but rather of the amazing complexity of the divine gifts to and of the world.

[37] Davies's and Marsha Keith Schuchard's works are a corrective to one of the main arguments of E. P. Thompson's influential study *Witness against the Beast* (1993). Thompson proposes that Blake's mother was a Muggletonian and that he was heavily influenced by this connection. While there is no doubt about the general importance of nonconformist circles on Blake's thinking, it is clear by now that Thompson was mistaken about the exact denomination. See Davies and Schuchard, 'Recovering the Lost Moravian History of William Blake's Family', *Blake: An Illustrated Quarterly* 38, 1 (Summer 2004): 36–43, 38.

[38] Here Davies and Schuchard cite Thomas Muir, as quoted in Margaret Ruth Lowery, *Windows of the Morning: A Critical Study of William Blake's 'Poetical Sketches', 1783*, Yale Studies in English 93 (New Haven, CT: Yale University Press, 1940), pp. 14–15. See also Keri Davies, 'William Blake's Mother: A New Identification', *Blake: An Illustrated Quarterly* 33, 2 (Fall 1999): 36–50; and Schuchard, *Why Mrs Blake Cried*.

[39] Catherine was called Catherine Armitage at the time, since this was during her first marriage. The time between her attendance at the Moravian congregation with her first husband, his death, and

of the Lamb, an elite group within the church. As Davies explains, 'Catherine and her husband urgently wanted to join this inner circle, where they could participate more intensely in the mystical marriage and salvific blood'.[40] To become a member, both Catherine and her husband had to write letters of application that described why they were worthy of membership and that detailed their own experiential relation to Christ in Moravian terms. Here is Catherine's letter, dating from around November 1750:

> I have very littell to say of my self for I am a pore crature and full of wants but my Dear Saviour will satisfy them all I should be glad if I could allways lay at the Cross full as I do know thanks be to him last friday at the love feast Our Savour was pleased to make me Suck his wounds and hug the Cross more then Ever and I trust will more and more till my fraile nature can hould no more at your request I have rit but I am not worthy of the blessing it is desird for I do not Love our Dear Savour halfe enough but if it is will to bring me among his hapy flock in closer conection I shall be very thankful I would tell you more of my self but itt is nothing thats good so now I will rite of my Savour that is all Love.[41]

Catherine's statement shows a deep familiarity with and investment in Moravian iconography and imagery.[42] The focus on Christ's wound invoked so starkly by Catherine was a favourite Moravian topic, one often associated with a sexual dimension. The mixture of spirituality and sensuality—the sucking of the wound, the hugging of the cross—is particularly powerful and suggestive. This was not the first time Catherine had engaged with these ideas: she writes the letter and feels she is ready to be accepted into the Congregation of the Lamb, because 'last friday' she felt the power of 'Our Savour… more then Ever'. Before she reaches a state of impossible intensity ('till my fraile nature can hould no more') she applies to be a lamb in the 'flock in closer conection'—that is, the congregation. The woman who would later become Blake's mother was clearly deeply engaged and marked through her involvement with this church. Even though after her husband's death she left the inner circle of the Congregation of the Lamb, she showed a level of existential involvement that is relevant. Her views also suggest a certain openness to spirituality that reflected itself in her relation to her son. Remember that William Blake told Alexander Gilchrist that it was his mother who saved him from a thrashing when he had claimed to have seen a tree full of angels. What is certain is that the religious and institutional circumstances of such formative experiences for Catherine would not have simply disappeared. Similarly, it would not have escaped

---

the marriage to her second husband—Blake's father—is not long enough to really make a massive difference to the argument here, so I have tried to avoid confusion by naming her Catherine Blake throughout.

[40] Davies, 'Lost Moravian History', p. 1316.

[41] Qtd in Davies, 'Lost Moravian History', pp. 1308–9.

[42] Laura Quinney suggests that the Moravians are a 'less radical' sect, though Schuchard's research reveals them to be a congregation whose rituals and teachings, especially about sexuality, remain among the most unusual. For Quinney this less radical bent does not mean, however, that Blake's ties to Gnosticism (one of her main objects of interest) are any less substantial. See Quinney, *William Blake on Self and Soul*, p. 55. Regarding the sexual mysticism and practices, see Schuchard, *Why Mrs Blake Cried.*

her notice that there was an Anglo-German dimension to this context. While I have no evidence that she actively participated in German lessons or the like, it remains a fact that the Anglo-German character of that congregation would have been visible and audible.

Once Catherine's first husband dies, her ties to the Moravian congregation are less clear, but it would seem strange for her to change from total commitment to active disengagement, especially since the Moravians would have welcomed Catherine's new husband, and we have no evidence that he objected to her Moravian ties. Davies believes that both of them continued to take an active part, suggesting that '[g]iven the demands of their business and growing family, it may just have been that James and Catherine Blake henceforth kept up attendance only at the public services on the weekend'.[43] Davies goes so far as to suggest that at the time of the Gordon Riots, William Blake was actively looking after some members of the congregation in response to his mother's request.[44] Whether or not these specific claims are true, it is certainly the case that Blake grew up with a parent who was deeply influenced by the Moravian teachings and practices, and who took these teachings and practices into the poet's life. These include the Anglo-German hymnal tradition that was being developed and practised as a central part of the Moravian congregation. Blake's connection to the Moravians is also a connection to their hybrid, Anglo-German hymnals. My work here adds to the research of scholars such as Muir, Wright, and Lowery—who all suggest a direct link between Moravian hymnody and Blake's *Songs*—by bringing to the table an awareness of the importance of the multilingual origin and contexts of the Moravian songs at work in a complex world of different and competing versions of poetry and religion in the eighteenth century.[45] We should, then, listen for some of the multilingual echoes that we know their songs and hymns were producing throughout London, both when Blake's mother was part of the congregation and many years after. There is a direct conversation between the Moravian hymns—the pieces that Catherine Blake sang and heard—and Blake's later compositions.

One of these hymns might very well have been the German hymn 'O stilles Gottes Lamm' and its translation:

> MEEK patient Lamb of God! to thee
> I run, thy Meekness give thou me;
>
> ....
>
> Thou seest my heart, thou know'st my love.
> From Thee I never will remove;
>
> ....
>
> Make clean as wool my filthy Heart,
> Wash white as Snow my ev'ry Part,

[43] Davies, 'Lost Moravian History', pp. 1312–13.

[44] See Davies, 'The View from Fetter Lane: Moravian Eye-Witnesses of the Gordon Riots', paper presented at 'The Gordon Riots and British Culture Conference', Roehampton University, July 2008, p. 9; accessed on *Academia.edu*, http://www.academia.edu/1691609/The_view_from_Fetter_Lane_Moravian_eye-witnesses_of_the_Riots.

[45] See Lowery, p. 15.

> Give me in stillness to sustain
> Whate'er thy Wisdom shall ordain.[46]

The hymn repeats the focus on the lamb and the Christ-centric forms of worship that are typical for the Moravians. The idea that the focus on the lamb is very physical, that the washing away of sins includes 'ev'ry Part' is paired with the idea that the heart will be made as clean as the white wool that comes to represent the soft, comforting presence of Jesus. Compare the sentiment, form, and the vocabulary of this Moravian, Anglo-German hymn with that of Blake's 'Spring':

> Little Lamb
> Here I am,
> Come and lick
> My white neck.
> Let me pull
> Your soft Wool.
> Let me kiss
> Your soft face.
> Merrily Merrily we welcome in the Year.[47]

That there are significant echoes and connections between these texts is evident. The licking, pulling, and kissing in Blake's poem suggest a level of erotic physicality that appears newly relevant in the context of the Moravian literature. The figuration of the traditionally Christian figure as playful and soft and fully embracing its physicality is something that we can clearly hear louder in the Moravian antecedent than in many of the more domesticated hymns that are contemporary with Blake.

This does not mean, of course, that Blake was a Moravian. When it comes to literary-historical claims, this book is interested in very different, much more general senses of influence, confluence, and simultaneity. Scholarship needs to appreciate the difficult and important relations between Blake and these polyglot hymns whose music and often exorbitant words were beginning to fade at the very time he was writing what many considered to be equally strange texts. This means we should also consider aspects of Blake's writing that are not obvious points of connection, whether that be through symbolism (the lamb) or through topicality (religious physicality). There are other, even less obvious connections, such as Blake's own physical location in London, which of course he shared with the Anglo-German congregation his mother attended. Both the Moravians and Blake, as we know, had a keen sense of how our immediate physical and personal environment and location have deeply spiritual significances. Once we consider such a common concern, this Moravian hymn can appear in a new light:

> Morning Star I follow thee,
> Lead me here or lead me there:
> Thou my Staff in trav'ling be,
> I'll no other weapon bear;

---

[46] 'O stilles Gottes Lamm', in *Collection of Hymns of the Children of God*, hymn 545, pp. 311–12.
[47] William Blake, 'Spring', in *Complete Poetry and Prose*, pp. 14–15, 15, lines 19–27.

> Me may Angels guard from ill,
> When I am to do thy Will:
> So shall I with steady pace,
> Reach the dearest City, Grace.[48]

The seeming simplicity of form and diction is remarkably close to Blake's shorter lyrics.[49] The strange mixture of the abstract and the concrete in both the imagery and the ideas that this poem expresses echoes similar moves in 'The Fly' or 'Infant Joy'. Ontology is located in the other ('thee/ ... / ... be'), and there is something prophetic yet searching about this poem. The singer follows the star, whose direction almost seems random, or at least not clear to the speaker. He apostrophizes, 'Lead me here or lead me there', thereby disclosing that he is not even interested in the accumulation of experiences (that would be 'here' *and* 'there'), but gives himself in total faith ('here or ... there': it doesn't matter). The shepherd here does not need to use his 'Staff' as a weapon, since the presence of 'Angels' will guard him from ill. I cannot but think that these angels meaningfully relate to the angels Blake sees in his childhood visions or 'The Angel' in the *Songs* ('Guarded by an Angel mild / Witless woe, was ne'er beguil'd!').[50] The 'dearest City' is clearly an invocation both of Jerusalem (hence 'Grace') and Augustine's textual and utopian City of God. In our context, though, the 'dearest City' is also cosmopolitan London, home to the Moravians at Fetter Lane.[51] And the 'dearest City' is also the place where angels 'guard from ill' a Blake who was wandering and writing its chartered streets well into Romanticism.

The attention to the power of song is the most obvious place to start for a reading of Blake's poetry along the lines suggested by Moravian hymnal practice. After all, we interpret the *Songs of Innocence and of Experience* not just as text but also as music. In the 'Introduction' a child encourages the poet to 'Pipe a song about a Lamb', and the poems that follow are all 'happy songs / Every child may joy to hear'.[52] The musical form of these songs 'about a Lamb', the most important Moravian symbol, is a crucial devotional quality. These *Songs* are not just lullabies but also religiously inflected songs, akin to hymns and psalms, as we can see in their great popularity as bases for liturgical music well into the twenty-first century— John Tavener's powerful 1982 version of 'The Lamb' comes to mind. One of the reasons why these songs are so powerful is that they establish a very tight and coherent pattern, even a rhetoric. Most of the pastoral care, so important to Moravians, was rooted in linguistic practices—prayer, song, and conversation—that show a continuity in their use of figurative language. The most prominent example of this regularity—and one that is also at the centre of Blake's and Hamann's writing—is the image of the lamb. The Moravians adopt the common Christian symbol and

---

[48] Qtd in Stead and Stead, p. 277.

[49] On the few scholars who discuss Moravian hymnody and Blake's early poetry, see Davies, 'Lost Moravian History', p. 1298.

[50] William Blake, 'The Angel', in *Complete Poetry and Prose*, p. 24, lines 3–4.

[51] London, of course, is also the city in which Hamann found God (his own Augustinian moment), an event that shaped the intellectual history of the Enlightenment and Anglo-German relations within it.

[52] William Blake, 'Introduction', in *Songs of Innocence and of Experience*, p. 7, lines 5 and 19–20.

make it into one of the most important elements of their aesthetic and symbolic rhetoric and imagery; the Moravian motto still remains *Vicit agnus noster, eum sequamur* (Our Lamb has conquered; let us follow Him), and we remember that Catherine Blake's application to the Congregation of the Lamb ended with a musical hymn. It is, then, noteworthy that the lamb is one of Blake's central images, too, much more important than others that he adopts from classical Christian iconography—such as, say, the cross. For him, just as for the Moravians, the lamb is a structuring image that concentrates the celebration of the mysterious nature of creation. One recurring example from Blake that readers will easily recall includes the wondering question about the mystery of creation and its seeming contradictions. In 'The Lamb' he asks directly, 'Little Lamb who made thee', and in the nearby 'Tyger' he famously wonders, 'Did he who made the Lamb make thee?'[53] We can add to these familiar examples another invocation of the lamb as a powerful symbolic presence in *Jerusalem* that contains intriguing echoes of Catherine Blake's application letter mentioned before: 'O that the Lamb / Of God would look upon me and pity me in my fury.'[54] The way that the speaker here wishes the Lamb of God to give mercy recalls Catherine's wish to 'bring me among his hapy flock in closer conection'. The animal here becomes the conduit through which God can look upon his flock, and through which we can feel his presence. These examples of meaningful relations among the distinct treatments of the central figure of the lamb point towards a set of more specific and tighter connections between Moravian and Blakean aesthetics.

Once we pay attention to the Moravians' and Blake's fascination with innocent childhood, pastoral care, and the Christian imagery of the lamb, poems that we know very well, such as 'The Lamb', 'The Shepherd', or 'A Little Boy Lost', appear in a new light. The pastoral care that somebody (we? the readers?) seeks and receives lies at the heart of all these poems. They cover the concerns of what Blake in 'The Shepherd' calls 'the Shepherds sweet lot', whose 'tongue shall be filled with praise': the shepherd 'hears the lambs innocent call', and one of the reasons why the Christian lamb (and the 'ewes tender reply') can rest in peace is that 'they know when their Shepherd is nigh'.[55] Of course, the lambs over which the shepherd is looking are multiple in their meaning, since they stand for themselves as well as for Christ, Himself, in turn, the ultimate shepherd. Remember that Blake makes explicit in 'The Lamb' that 'He is called by thy name, / For he calls himself a Lamb'.[56] Among the multiple elisions in these last lines lies one that blurs two versions of the not exactly human: Christ and the animal. Blake plays on God's power of naming: just as Adam names the animals, Christ calls himself a Lamb

---

[53] William Blake, 'The Lamb', in *Complete Poetry and Prose*, pp. 8–9, 8, lines 1 and 9; and Blake, 'The Tyger', in *Complete Poetry and Prose*, pp. 24–5, 25, line 20. The lamb is, of course, also a symbol that is deeply tied to national identity and is used by a particular, predominantly Christian representation of England. The current use of the lines 'And was the holy Lamb of God, / On Englands pleasant pastures seen!' as a de facto English national anthem at sporting events is an example of such a use (and abuse) (Blake, *Milton a Poem*, pp. 95–144, 95, lines 3–4).

[54] Blake, *Jerusalem*, pp. 144–259, 150, lines 59–60.

[55] William Blake, 'The Shepherd', in *Complete Poetry and Prose*, pp. 7–8, 7, lines 1, 4, 5–6, and 8.

[56] Blake, 'The Lamb', p. 9, lines 13–4.

and, thereby, is called (by us) by the name of the lamb ('by thy name').[57] '[C]alled by thy name' also means, however, that we can resurrect Christ through the name; we can call upon him to appear as our shepherd and saviour. In the end, 'He became a little child', completing the circle and allowing the reader to turn back to the animal to exclaim, 'I a child & thou a lamb'.[58] Compare Blake's lines, then, with a letter by the Moravian John Cennick, who writes to Hutton in June 1745, 'When that dear Lamb please, I know he will bring me and give me into my Mothers Lap and say to her, take care of him. I feel I want to be nursed, I want to be in a little Child's place, & be carried any where, where my Father and my Mother please'.[59] The lamb, just as in Blake, also becomes a shepherd and delivers us as innocent children. To be united with Christ, Cennick wants to be 'in a little Child's place'. *The Songs of Innocence and of Experience* are Blake's poetic descriptions of the different versions of this 'place', both biographical and geographical. His poems are about the possibility of finding this place and losing it, of inhabiting this place and mourning it.

The Moravian hymns are at work in this complex world of different and competing versions of the Enlightenment. They are the songs that the future Catherine Blake would have sung and heard. William Blake would certainly have been familiar with them, and their imagery and forms provide a powerful part of the tapestry on which he himself composes. Thus, when Davies states that 'how Blake will have responded to his mother's spiritual yearnings will be a matter of future debate', part of that debate should be its multilingual dimensions.[60] What we can add to the astute readings of influences that scholarship has already produced is an insistence on the deeply Anglo-German character of the Moravian sources. So far, Blake scholarship does not really discuss the multilingual background of these intertextual histories. The work that does follow the Anglo-German traces in Moravian hymnody hardly ever mentions Blake. A similar gap exists in the formal study of these poems. The hymn is, of course, central to British eighteenth-century and Romantic poetry as a whole. Yet the case of Blake invites us to see it in a wider European context. What the Moravian connection opens up is a Blake who grows up, and continues to live, in a London that is full of non-British influences and figures. This includes the Dissenter circles, which are not just a local phenomenon but rather an international affair. Contextualizing Blake like this might allow us to revise accounts of Blake that present him as a lone voice, completely at odds with his age, or as part of an utterly local or parochial environment. The type of worship, practice, and religious input that Blake's mother experienced, and no doubt passed on to her son, was a way of thinking that was part of a much wider, even international project. Even though it was by no means mainstream, Moravianism was not a religion for the lone Dissenter committed to a clearly defined alternative spiritual system. It made much of the idea of community and the ordinary, both of which were crucial to Blake. There are many more surreptitious influences, religious or not, that help to shape the literature of the period. We stand to gain much from understanding

---

[57] See Essick, *William Blake.*   [58] Blake, 'The Lamb', p. 9, lines 16–7.
[59] Moravian Archives, AB97.A3.5.1.   [60] Davies, 'Lost Moravian History', p. 1312.

that the spiritual, poetic, ethical, and ontological beliefs that we recognize as 'Blakean' have their origin in a complicated net that goes beyond national and linguistic boundaries. Once we perceive and work out these dimensions, an even richer and more complex Blake emerges.

The *Songs of Innocence and of Experience* suggest that our innocence is either marred by experience or it is retained, however illusorily or temporarily, by our own internal force.[61] The most obvious example in this context is probably 'The Little Boy Lost' and its counterpart 'The Little Boy Found'. The poems invoke pastoral care, the desire to self-infantilize, and the longing to be found and led, all of which may be read in tandem with Cennick's fantasy to be welcomed into the fold of the Moravian congregation. They share an ideal of pastoral care that we find across the Moravians, together with the imagery of the child and its rescue through a divine figure. The image in 'The Little Boy Found' makes this link even more explicit:

> The little boy lost in the lonely fen,
> Led by the wand'ring light,
> Began to cry, but God ever nigh,
> Appear'd like his father in white.[62]

The omnipresence of the divine down to the most concrete form is one of the baselines for the little boy's experience and Blake's poem. God is spatially and temporally 'ever nigh'—an echo of the German *immerda*, which contains the connotations of 'perpetually' and also 'unchangingly'. That He is always near is rooted in the experience of feeling God's proximity in situations of crisis. Upon the child's 'cry', God becomes close—spatially and emotionally—and visible for the boy and opens him to salvation and redemption. The boy's perception opens God up for the reader as well, as a guiding light not only in this particular instance of the individual child but also for a larger context: surely the 'wand'ring light' through which the boy got lost is analogous to the versions of supposedly enlightening attitudes 'leading' the way around Blake. The poem offers the chance to think about a potential corrective to this situation, one based in concrete experience and available to the boy through God's apparition.

It is crucial that the vision of this corrective is delivered by telling us about the apparition of the child. The child is open for such salvation because his innocent cry has the ability to conjure up the presence of God. Naturally, the boy here is himself a cypher for any erring human, traditionally likened to a child in nature— consider that the 1754 hymn book of the Moravians is entitled *A Collection of Hymns of the Children of God in All Ages*. It is crucial that Blake uses the specific image of the child and insists on the importance of who is reading here. Just as the development of the lamb as a symbol has a long history, the child is also

---

[61] The qualification about the illusory nature of innocence is important: Blake presents innocence as something that is neither naive nor sentimental in the Schillerian sense; for him it is a category that denies that there can, in fact, be such a clear division.

[62] Blake, 'Little Boy Found', p. 11, lines 1–4.

traditionally presented as the intuitive and, thus, superior reader. It is as suggestive as it is likely that Blake would have heard Moravian hymns sung as a child and felt their influence.[63] The Moravian Church actively participated in this aesthetic construction: 'Zinzendorf stressed that the unlearned, or even small children, can gain from singing these hymns, despite their apparent obscurities.'[64] Like a new language to be learned, children adopt and mould the poetical forms in front of them—only to be, in turn, moulded by them. One learns without any prior knowledge or practice. This is what we call linguistic memory, which is akin to the muscle memory of a child that learns a sport: with repetition, thinking retreats and the movement is not performed consciously anymore. Yet the child is still learning, though it does not really 'know' what it is doing. The boy who can perceive an alternative to the 'wand'ring light' in his most direct experience links this ability to envision to this way of knowing.

THE DECLINE OF THE MORAVIANS AND THE OBFUSCATION OF MULTILINGUALISM

How, then, is it that we have lost much of this history, especially when it comes to something like the genre of the hymn, a poetic form—rather than an author— whose link to the Anglo-German Moravians seems so clear to see? The answer to this question lies in the decline of the Moravians as a cultural force and the resulting nineteenth-century obfuscation of their multilingual influence and presence in eighteenth-century Britain.

The Moravians and Blake inhabited a moment and sphere that were partly defined by polyglot and complex poetic exchanges, in regard to both form and history. It is clear that by developing a sense for the multilingual transmission of specific genres, such as hymns, we can develop a richer and poetically more nuanced account of national literatures than if we consider them in monolingual splendid isolation.

There was a directly parallel development in literary history. The Moravian hymn began to be seen as lugubrious and was increasingly sidelined. Hymns with unorthodox and openly sexual connotations were characterized as typically Moravian, whereas other, more orthodox hymns, which often came from the same place, were considered the new standard, easy to absorb into a more canonical, conventionally Protestant literary tradition. Davies picks up on this when he chastises England, Sparrow, and E. P. Thompson for dismissing Moravian and early Methodist hymnody: the characterizations of such forms as either 'vulgar' or as 'perverted eroticism'

---

[63] Once again, see England and Sparrow on this, although they do not consider the Moravian dimension.

[64] Davies, 'Lost Moravian History', p. 1312.

show us that the idea of sexual deviance continued to haunt the reception.[65] We can hear a similar tone in Stead and Stead's historical description:

> By the early nineteenth century, the eighteenth-century association of hymn-singing with dissent, nonconformity and evangelicalism was weakening. The emotive hymns of that earlier period were now generally regarded as rude and homely; something more refined was looked for, and this change in taste was evolving with exceptional vigour among Anglicans, who had hitherto been singers of metric psalms and only marginally of hymns. At the beginning of the Victorian period, therefore, the writing of new 'Romantic' hymns became important in all the British Protestant Churches, changing the style of an evangelical and dissenting minority into an art form which had something in common with the more universal hopes and aspirations of the Romantic poets.[66]

What Stead and Stead are describing is, in effect, a continuous and continuing push towards the conventional.[67] Even though many would take exception to the characterization of the 'universal hopes and aspirations', such a narrative was certainly powerful and dominant. What this story illustrates is how quickly and successfully the hymn—or its perception—was tamed from a multilingual, potentially radical form into a modest, conventional, and peculiarly English genre. Once that is in place, possible links of such qualities to figures such as Blake also go unexamined.

For my reading of a more linguistically comparative British literary history, the most important aspect of the decline of the Moravians is that the polyglot character of hymnody was also obscured. This coincided with a rise in accepting Methodism as a mainstream denomination that became increasingly identified as the cultural carrier of a—this time monolingual—hymnal tradition. The fact that Methodism tried to separate itself almost completely from its early Moravian influence, to the degree of obscuring and denying that impact altogether, makes it all the more ironic that it should have claimed the hymn as one of its most powerful expressions. Once more, the role of the Wesleys is crucial here since they are the most direct and influential figures in the relation between Moravianism and Methodism and are particularly involved in the translation and dissemination of hymns in both contexts. The fact that they are directly aware of the German origins of much of the material plays a special role here.

The Wesleys' conventionalization of the hymns via Methodism went hand in hand with burying these texts' Anglo-German heritage. I am not suggesting that they saw the polyglot origin itself as unorthodox, but embracing their Babelian condition certainly did not help the Moravians' cause. And while John Wesley might not have actively denied the German heritage, it was not in the interest of the

---

[65] England and Sparrow, p. 91; and Thompson, p. 407—all qtd in Davies, 'Lost Moravian History', p. 1312.

[66] Stead and Stead, p. 281. Also see Kirstie Blair, ed. *John Keble in Context* (London: Anthem, 2004), p. 164.

[67] This history foreshadows a set of difficulties that continue to haunt the reception of Blake and Hamann; the earliest attempts to turn them into more palatable and conventional versions of themselves happen precisely in the period of supposed revolution and radicalism—the early nineteenth century.

developing Methodist establishment to highlight this foreign influence. Thus, this development and its subsequent canonization certainly seem to have contributed to the fact that the Anglo-German character of hymnody is so little known today.

By the early nineteenth century, Robert Southey had fully adopted the conventional stance laid out by Wesley and 'passed judgement on the hymnody of the Moravians: "Even in the humours and the extravagances of the Spanish religious poets", he wrote, "there is nothing which approaches to the monstrous perversion of religious feeling in these astonishing productions".'[68] Some time after Southey wrote this passage, the Moravians were broadly discredited as a highly esoteric, strange religious group with questionable practices from which Methodism had successfully protected itself. In fact, in due course the original connection was forgotten, and with it an awareness that the Moravians themselves—as well as some of the Methodists' culture—had bridged at least two different national poetic traditions. As a result, scholarship missed much of the polyglot dimensions of religious life, and its literary forms, during that time. Correspondingly, British literary history lost a sense of how this would be relevant to a study of figures such as Blake, Wesley, or William Cowper. Thus, we have to build on the scholarship that uncovers the subtleties of Blake's religious thought and thinking, with a sense that these spiritual qualities were often mediated in multilingual ways. The works of Isabel Rivers, E. P. Thompson, Jon Mee, and, more recently, Michael Farrell present a set of powerful examples that explain how the general worlds of religious dissent, Pietism, enthusiasm, and antinomianism formed an important intellectual background to Blake's poetry.[69] We have seen that we need to develop a stronger sense for how these intellectual currents and conflicts are inflected by a history that is also linguistically different from the mainstream culture, or at least what we now imagine it to have been. The Moravians show us that a poet like Blake grew in an environment that was much more international and linguistically complicated than we often want to admit, and that these complications found their ways into his poetry. In other words, the Moravian—and therefore the Anglo-German—influence upon Blake allows us to read him in a new light. We understand the whole genre of the hymn better once we detect its hybrid history and this, in turn, invites us to extend our comparative angle to exorbitant authors we might not have considered in this light.

---

[68] England and Sparrow, p. 11.

[69] See Rivers, *Reason, Grace, and Sentiment*; Thompson, *Witness against the Beast*; Jon Mee, *Dangerous Enthusiasm*; and Michael Farrell, *Blake and the Methodists* (Houndmills, Basingstoke: Palgrave, 2014).

8

Every Letter Has a Body
Blake and Hamann on the Sexuality of Language

LANGUAGE AND THE PHYSICAL: AN INTRODUCTION

This last chapter focuses on the physical and sexual dimensions of language in William Blake and Johann Georg Hamann. The inextricability of language and the physical body is an important topic in their works, and they take radical, exorbitant positions in the wide and heterodox field of the materiality and physicality of language. Once more, the Anglo-German context provides sources to enrich that discussion, particularly through the strange and radical figure of Johann Caspar Lavater, whose relation to Blake and Hamann is surprisingly deep and direct. Hamann articulates his views on the physicality of language across his *oeuvre*, but we will mostly focus on his essay *New Apology of the Letter* h and its subsection 'New Apology of the Letter *h* by Itself', a funny, direct, and powerful intervention on this topic. The essay directly relates to Blake's views on language and writing, especially his claim in *Jerusalem* that 'Every word and every letter is studied and put into its fit place'.[1] The 'fit place' that Blake speaks about is very much a physical one, on the page as well as in the body. Both Blake and Hamann provide powerful arguments to preserve a sense of the physical aspect of the letter. They reply to the Enlightenment's increasing rationalization and standardization of language, which includes its physical aspect, with an excessive and loud celebration of the link between the human body and the letter. Blake and Hamann turn out to be among the most radical thinkers in the long and complicated history of the relation between language and the body, a history that encompasses philosophy, theology, literature, science, and the arts. In the context of the eighteenth century, their anti-instrumentalism represents an extremely untimely position, a form of thinking about language and the body that was becoming increasingly unusual—and that remains so to this day.

The body becomes the instrument through which we can understand ourselves as made in the divine image; it is of a piece with the understanding of language as a divine gift that allows revelation. Yet Blake's and Hamann's arguments exceed that position when they go a crucial step further and argue that language is not only physical but also irreducibly sexual. As Helene Richter states, 'Blake as well as Hamann,

---

[1] Blake, *Jerusalem*, p. 146.

characters of strong sensuality, are open to erotic mysticism'.[2] Their insistence on the link between language and sexuality turns into a brilliant form of critique, since both Blake and Hamann recognize that a supposedly neutral or nonphysical rationalization emerges from a historical rejection of the physical. In contrast, they argue that we should rejoice in the sexual aspect of human and language.

For Blake, each letter is meaningful, not just as an abstract sign but also as a material presence. Recall Blake's specification that 'Every word and every letter is studied and put into its fit place'.[3] Hamann expresses a similar sentiment about the irreducibly material aspect of language in a more philosophical vocabulary. In the context of his critique of the purification of reason he reminds us that 'words... have an aesthetic and logical capacity'; they are physical and conceptual.[4] To some degree, Blake and Hamann are part of the eighteenth- and early nineteenth-century discussions on the physical properties of language—discussions that were far more frequent and creative than we might imagine today. Especially since semiotic discourse and religious discourse were not as divided as they are now, the conceptual spectrum and overlaps between thinkers from the theological, philosophical, and linguistic spheres allowed for very different thinking on this matter.[5]

Many thinkers at the time attempt to describe exactly how words are (or are not) caught up in a complicated relation between the material and the immaterial, the corporeal and the ideal. Blake and Hamann take matters further than normal, since they insist on the sexual dimension of this physicality as something that is not an incidental consequence of corporality but an essential aspect of the word. Once more, they are exorbitant, and they leave the track of normal thinking. Blake and Hamann look at language from an extreme vantage point; they insist that words, even letters, not only are not arbitrary but also have an actively sexual role to play in the production of self-generated meaning.

One figure whose own exorbitance on this topic is a good way into Blake's and Hamann's work is Lavater, whose writings were held in great esteem by both of them. (I discuss these links extensively in Chapter 3.) Lavater is an important author, well beyond his more widely known work on physiognomy, especially on hermeneutics, semiotics, and the idea of natural language:

> Just as Christ is the most graphic, most vivid, most perfect image of invisible God, an image where everything is expression, everything has unfathomable and infinite meaning,

---

[2] 'Sowohl Blake als auch Hamann, Naturen von kräftiger Sinnlichkeit, sind erotischer Mystik zugänglich' (Helene Richter, 'Blake und Hamann', [part 2] 37–45, 40).

[3] Of course, the materiality of language is bound up with the production of his illuminated books also.

[4] Griffith-Dickson, pp. 517–25, 524. 'Wörter haben...ein ästhetisches und logisches Vermögen' (N, 3: 288).

[5] In my own work, I have spent some time discussing William Wordsworth's claims of words as 'the incarnation of thought' or his insistence that words are '*things*, active and efficient', which show that these concerns were active well into the nineteenth century. See Alexander Regier, 'Words Worth Repeating: Language and Repetition in Wordsworth's Poetic Theory', in *Wordsworth's Poetic Theory: Knowledge, Language, Experience*, ed. Regier and Stefan H. Uhlig (Houndmills, Basingstoke: Palgrave Macmillan, 2010), pp. 61–80. There are plenty of other examples from the period and beyond, from Alexander Pope and Samuel Taylor Coleridge to Giorgio Agamben and Jacques Ranciere. See William Keach, *Arbitrary Power: Romanticism, Language, Politics* (Princeton, NJ: Princeton University Press, 2004).

such a truthful, unfathomable expression that the supreme archangel's successive description in words, lasting through all eternity, could not achieve the wealth and sublimity of this expression—could not, that is, cause the impression that the original makes, in only a few moments, on whoever is capable of understanding it—so, too, is every human being (an image of God and Christ) thus entirely expression—expression that is instantaneous, truthful, comprehensive, unfathomable, impossible to attain in words, and inimitable. Such a human being is entirely natural language.[6]

Let's start with the implicit juxtaposition of the divine language (expressions that are 'truthful, unfathomable... [and] infinite') with its earthly instantiation, which is 'impossible to attain in words'. Lavater performs the complications of a fallen language here, the barrage of subclauses showing us the impossibility of expressing real simultaneity. Strikingly, Lavater conceives of the human body itself as the most likely site for our understanding of divine expression. What is clear is that, since we are fallen creatures, the language of pure immanence—or even the slightly lesser one of the supreme archangels—is not ours, and we need to resort to a different, much more confused version of expression: our human natural language. Yet that language still has the trace of immanence through its creativity. The human body presents us with an expression that we interpret. It's not just that we have a body; it is also that, as Eva Kocziszky puts it, 'the person is a body'.[7] This is why Lavater speaks of geniuses as a 'substantives in the grammar of humanity', making the physical human body a linguistic expression of the world's text.[8]

In the light of Lavater's statement, consider Blake's description in 'A Vision of the Last Judgment', itself a scene of resurrection where the lines between corporeality and immateriality are powerfully blurred:

> If the Spectator could Enter into these Images in his Imagination approaching them on the Fiery Chariot of his Contemplative Thought if he could Enter into Noahs Rainbow or into his bosom or could make a Friend & Companion of one of these Images of wonder which always intreats him to leave mortal things as he must know

---

[6] 'Wie Christus das redendste, lebendigste, vollkommenste Ebenbild des unsichtbaren Gottes ist, ein Ebenbild, wo alles Ausdruck, alles von unerschöpflicher und unendlicher Bedeutung ist, ein so wahrhafter, unerschöpflicher Ausdruck, daß eine successive, durch alle Ewigkeiten fortgehende Wortbeschreibung des höchsten Erzengels den Reichthum und die Erhabenheit dieses Ausdruckes nicht erreichen, das ist: die Eindrücke nicht verursachen könnte, die das Urbild auf den, der dazu organisirt ist, es zu verstehen, in wenigen Augenblicken, machen muss, so ist jeder Mensch (ein Ebenbild Gottes und Christi) so ganz Ausdruck, gleichzeitiger, wahrhafter, vielfassender, unerschöpflicher, mit keinen Worten erreichbarer, unnachahmbarer Ausdruck; er ist ganz Natursprache' (Johann Caspar Lavater, *Ausgewählte Werke*, 1: 183), qtd in Ellis Shookman, ed., *The Faces of Physiognomy: Interdisciplinary Approaches to Johann Caspar Lavater*, Studies in German Literature, Linguistics, and Culture (Columbia, SC: Camden House, 1993), p. 27. Carsten Zelle discusses a similar passage, which is helpful in directing our attention to the language theory as a set of assumptions that stands behind the intricacies of physiognomy as a science: 'The motive for Lavater's physiognomic reflections must be sought in both this physico-theological sphere and in pietism (as well as the heretic tradition). He actually derived the principles of physiognomy from reflections on "heavenly language"—i.e. on a utopian ability to communicate' ('Soul Semiology: On Lavater's Physiognomic Principles', in *The Faces of Physiognomy*, ed. Shookman, pp. 40–63).

[7] '[D]ie Person ein Leib ist' (Eva Kocziszky, 'Ein Leib-Sein: Lavaters Dialog mit Hamann', *Seminar: A Journal of Germanic Studies* 38, 1 [February 2002]; 1–18, 10).

[8] 'Substantive in der Grammatik der Menschheit!' (Lavater, *Physiognomische Fragmente*, p. 83).

then would he arise from his Grave then would he meet the Lord in the Air & then he would be happy.[9]

Blake's fantasy extends from the image itself to the mind of the possible viewer. He turns our 'Imagination' into a biblical vehicle. In a helpful analysis of this passage, Robert N. Essick connects it to the wider ambition and context of Blake's art:

> By giving up independent 'Self-hood' and entering into incarnational signs, man can become a companion to their immanent meanings, arise like [Jacob] Boehme's Christ from '*the Death* of the Letters' to return them to their original significance as covenants with God's Word, and overcome the multiple dualities dominating the fallen vision of language—signifier and signified, *langue* and *parole*, spirit and matter, artist and audience, man and his signs.[10]

Any further erosion of signs that allow us to see or imagine the 'Fiery Chariot of... Contemplative Thought' will take us further away from understanding the complexity and richness of the word. We need to become a 'Friend & Companion' to the image rather than an analytical or detached bystander. What Essick terms 'entering into incarnational signs' is analogous to Lavater's idea of the physical form as 'natural language'. These wider ideas and their variations are clearly alive in the Anglo-German intellectual constellation that this book describes. In Blake and Hamann they experience an extreme condensation, through which the incarnational sign will become linked inextricably to the human organs of reproduction.

In his articulation of the physical and sexual nature of the letter, it is almost as if Hamann combined Lavater's idea of the physical body as sign and Blake's later linguistic vision of the Resurrection. He adopts the idea that the human body becomes, simultaneously, the site of linguistic expression and of imaginative interpretation. Rather than only reacting to outer stimuli we express our imaginative power through our body and language: 'Our imagination operates upon our physiognomy.'[11] We translate our imagination and affect into our bodies and those of our fellow men, which in turn we read. Following Lavater, Hamann pays particular attention to the face, but he adds a twist by turning this attention onto himself. In his *London Writings*, Hamann jots down an observation he makes in looking at the men and women he encounters in the city: 'As the image of my face re-appears in water, so my I is thrown back in each fellow human.'[12] Our fellow human creatures reflect back to us what we really are, though there remains the danger of a narcissistic contemplation—it is no accident Hamann chooses water as his image. These reflections and contemplations occur through the physical body, not just theoretically; Hamann turns the Enlightenment encouragement to 'know thyself' into a statement that applies to both body and mind.

---

[9] Blake, '[A Vision of the Last Judgment]', in *Complete Poetry and Prose*, pp. 554–66, 560.

[10] Essick, pp. 52–3.

[11] 'Die Einbildungskraft wirkt auf unsre eigne Physiognomie' (Lavater, *Physiognomische Fragmente*, p. 64).

[12] 'Wie das Bild meines Gesichts im Wasser wiederscheint; so ist mein Ich in jedem Nebenmenschen zurückgeworfen' (Hamann, *Londoner Schriften*, p. 10). Also see Kociszky, p. 4.

But Hamann goes further than turning a *locus classicus*—reading a face—onto himself. He moves to the body as a whole and insists that our whole body enters into a relation with language in a world that is an organism, physical and spiritual, and in whose context we ourselves are analogous to symbols and signs:

> The hieroglyphic Adam is the history of the entire race in a symbolic wheel:—the character of Eve, the original of beautiful nature and systematic economy, that is not written with methodical piety on the page of the forehead; but rather is formed below in the earth and lies concealed in the entrails,—in the kidneys of the matter itself.[13]

We are characters; we always have been. As such, we need to read each other to understand ourselves and the world. This goes beyond language in its narrow sense. As Walter Benjamin writes in 'On the Mimetic Faculty', ' "To read what was never written." Such reading is the most ancient: reading before all languages, from the entrails, the stars, or dances'.[14] The mysteries of these characters, the same that Blake attempts to penetrate, not only are on our faces but also lie under the surface, in the entrails of the earth itself. We find an echo of these formulations in Blake's own interest in the organs and inner workings of the world.[15] The original beauty and power of nature, even its own order (the 'systematic economy'), are both inside nature and out. This creation involves a visceral dimension that crosses the material and the immaterial, the inside of the world and its bodies (the entrails) and its outside (the surfaces and faces). Decisively for Blake and Hamann, the attention to the physical aspect of the human is only a necessary but never a sufficient condition to understand the fundamental structures of language. Two more aspects are also required: first, this physicality always also means sexuality. Second, this sexuality is to be celebrated, not shunned.[16]

In order to give a sophisticated account of language, we need to understand that the sexual quality of language is not an afterthought or an embarrassment but, rather, an essential, positive feature. This view actively turns from sanitizing and purifying language to highlighting its physical and sexual dimensions. Blake and Hamann both find highly original ways to develop this thought throughout their work, in ways that puts them at odds, both consciously and unconsciously, with most Enlightenment philosophical and proprietary discussions on language.

---

[13] 'Der hieroglyphische Adam ist die Historie des ganzen Geschlechts im symbolischen Rade:—der Charakter der Eva, das Original zur schönen Natur und systematischen Ökonomie, die nicht nach methodischer Heiligkeit auf dem Stirnblatt geschrieben steht; sondern unten in der Erde gebildet wird, und in den Eingeweiden,—in den Nieren der Sachen selbst—verborgen liegt' (Hamann, *Aesthetica in Nuce*, qtd in Griffith-Dickson, pp. 409–31, 414).

[14] Walter Benjamin, 'On the Mimetic Faculty', in *1931–1934*, pp. 720–22, 722.

[15] On Blake, organs, and the idea of organization, see Tilottama Rajan, 'Blake's Body without Organs: The Autogenesis of the System in the Lambeth Books', *European Romantic Review* 26, 3 (May 2015): pp. 357–66.

[16] J. H. Macphail goes so far as to suggest it is through Lavater that 'we find the first traces of his [Blake's] cult of sexual enjoyment as an earthly exemplar of the Infinite Joy which is Eternity' ('Blake and Switzerland', p. 86).

HAMANN SAVES A LETTER: NEW APOLOGY
OF THE LETTER *H*

One of the funniest and most powerful examples for the argument about the importance of each letter is Hamann's *New Apology of the Letter* h (and its subsection 'New Apology of the Letter *h* by Itself') a sharp attack against the Enlightenment programme of the rationalization of language. The title itself already suggests the playful character of these essays, and the two texts encapsulate well Hamann's oddities as a writer. As in all of his other works, he writes them in the guise of a fictional character and indicates a wrong place of publication—in this case, Pisa instead of Frankfurt. The first part of the *Apology* is written under the pseudonym of the schoolmaster Heinrich Schröder, an actual historical figure whose name Hamann adopts for this purpose. The narrator-figure of the second is the letter *h* itself. Again in keeping with the most of Hamann's *oeuvre*, both sections are written in response to another text, providing a historically specific context for Hamann's motives.[17]

In 1773 the theologian C. J. Damm published *Betrachtungen über Religion* (*Reflections on Religion*), in which he advances the thesis that the silent *h* in German was not only superfluous but ought to be abolished. According to Damm, it had been unthinkingly and incorrectly introduced and, therefore, should be excluded through orthographic reform, purging the language of such an embarrassingly irrational constituent. It would, argues Damm, be unreasonable to keep such a potentially confusing and outdated part of the language. We know that questions about spelling and its harmonization had been discussed in Europe since the seventeenth century, but it was the eighteenth and the nineteenth centuries when many languages—including German—were standardized in the way that we now consider conventional. So, orthography was something of a hot topic in eighteenth-century Germany, and Damm's project certainly not far-fetched. We find, for instance, similar projects in the works of Johann Christoph Adelung, Friedrich Gottlieb Klopstock, and others. It was only in the 2000s that German orthography had its latest wave of such rationalization: *Rechtsschreibreform*—literally, 'correct-write-reform'. In the 1770s, several figures picked up the discussion under the banner of the Enlightenment, including Damm, who advocates his programme in the name of reason and rationality.[18] Hamann, of course, mocks the alleged combination of linguistic rationalization and reason's emancipation, calling the reform a sign indeed 'befitting to the taste of his [Damm's] enlightened century'.[19] For him, this is a century, an Enlightenment, which has neglected to think hard enough about reason. Damm, for Hamann, is a perfect straw man since he exemplifies an attitude

---

[17] A further dimension of Hamann's title is the etymological link that the term 'apology' (*apo*, 'away'; *logos*, 'speech', 'reason') affords; he alludes to the legal connotation and uses it humourously in relation to his own writings (away from the *logos*, 'reason'). See N, 3: 89–108.

[18] For an overview of the discussions on orthographic reform during that period, see Max Hermann Jellinek, *Geschichte der Neuhochdeutschen Grammatik von den Anfängen bis auf Adelung*, 2 vols (Heidelberg: Winter, 1913–14), 2: 49–73.

[19] 'Geschmack seines erleuchteten Jahrhunderts angemessen zu seyn' (N, 3: 93).

that *unthinkingly* adopts several assumptions without critically examining them; Damm ignores his self-incurred immaturity.

The first part of the *Apology* is structured like a typical eighteenth-century review. Hamann outlines Damm's proposals and replies to each of them in turn. The first reason that somebody might want to do away with the letter *h*, Hamann ventriloquizes, might be because it is not pronounced. Polemically, he states that he does not even want to attribute this view to Damm—although it is, in fact, outlined in Damm's essay. According to Hamann, nobody in his or her right mind would adopt such an argument, since it would show complete lack of critical judgement. The confusion here, Hamann points out, lies in equating the absence of pronunciation with the absence of meaning. In fact, silent letters both determine the pronunciation of the letters around them *and* generate a semantics that is audible not through the letters but through their contextual use. Hamann's example, apart from the *h*, is double consonants: you cannot pronounce *mm*. Why else, asks Hamann, would Damm have written his own treatise disregarding the suggestions he advances in it? Why else would he use *h* and *mm*—the latter in Damm's own name— throughout? In the end, Damm's treatise '[d]oes not even touch with one finger, all of the weight of his method in the issue at hand about the letter h'.[20] The biblical allusion is to God's finger, with which He writes down the Ten Commandments for Moses on the stone tablets. Invoking such divine Scripture and writing methods puts Hamann cheekily but firmly on the side of the divine word. If even God uses His finger, then it seems ludicrous to engage in an account that separates us from this physicality. Surely we would not want either to deny Him that physicality or, subsequently, to attempt to correct the text.

What is at stake is whether a letter can be the sign of a divine trace and, if so, what conception of language lies behind such an idea. The fact that this is about the letter *h* adds to this significance since, as Daniel Heller-Roazen reminds us, this 'breathy letter posed delicate problems from the beginning'.[21] It was always in danger of extinction or elision, and many figures—grammarians, such as Quintilian and Aulus Gellius, as well writers like Heinrich Heine—discuss it at length. But, as Jonathan Sheehan shows, Hamann, unlike the grammarians,

> cherished a language that did not exist for the clear expression of thoughts, and a writing exceeding its function as a mirror of speech. Rather, writing was to preserve the speech of God or, even more precisely, the breath of God: keeping *h* on the page, this served as a constant reminder of this Godly creation and invigoration of man and his language.[22]

Every letter—especially the ones that mark the complex relation between different forms, embodiments, of language—is a divine trace.

In the second essay, Hamann turns to Damm's subsequent argument with a similar mixture of bemusement and derision. According to Damm, the silent *h* is

---

[20] '[D]ie ganze Last seiner Methode in der obwaltenden Sache des Buchstabens h nicht mit einem Finger berührt' (N, 3: 91).

[21] Daniel Heller-Roazen, *Echolalias* (New York: Zone Books, 2005), p. 35.

[22] Jonathan Sheehan, 'Enlightenment Details: Theology, Natural History, and the Letter *h*', in 'Practices of Enlightenment', special issue, *Representations* 61 (Winter 1998): 29–56, 38.

a historically determined accident, inserted by scribes and hack writers throughout history. It is an addition rather than part of the original. This is a perfect opening for Hamann, of course: how, he asks, could the hack writers have overcome reason, social custom, and institutional habit with such power?—especially since Damm just told us how unreasonable it is to retain such letters (so imagine adding them!).

Hamann's mock-objection is a historical argument, although his real target is Damm's consistent desire to rationalize language. In some ways, Hamann's appeal to history seems a little odd, since the elongated *h* was, indeed, introduced into German around the sixteenth century, and it is not as if Hamann was unaware that natural languages evolve, that they add and shed. As Sheehan puts it, '[H]e could hardly have thought of it (the letter *h* as lengthening sign) present since Creation. It is his understanding of it as a historical object that makes him aware of its contingent presence, despite its hearkening to God, and its possible absence'.[23] History, language, and revelation are deeply connected for Hamann. The fact that something is contingent does not mean it is not revelatory. In fact, it can be that something is revelatory *by* being contingent, exemplifying that God is everywhere. Hamann enjoys the tension between history and revelation as something that is ultimately another sign of the impossibility of clear and unambiguous relations in the world. Of course, the development of letters is contingent to some degree. But they can be, simultaneously, signs and traces of divine spirit. The difficulty of rationalizing two poles into one dimension is the misguided aim and undertaking of the type of Enlightenment that Hamann rejects. His version maintains that such a rationalization is impossible, and he mocks any attempt to bring it about. Such attempts at linguistic 'clarification' through rationalization are analogous to the attempts to 'clarify' the distinction between the material and immaterial of language, or, even, to parse out physicality and sexuality.

Any form of linguistic rationalization misapprehends the deep-seated link between the complexities of language, reason, and revelation. The misunderstanding of reformers such as Damm is twofold: first, they mistakenly assume a transparency between reason and language; second, they assume such transparency to be desirable. Such views are an inadequate and unreflective response to the relation of language *and* reason. Hamann illustrates this by invoking a passage from Proverbs (30: 12) that, for him, describes directly the projects of linguistic rationalization and the age of Enlightenment: '*There is* a generation, *that are* pure in their own eyes, and *yet* is not washed from their filthiness.' For Hamann, the self-delusion of being pure in the eyes of one's own contemporaries is precisely the impulse to simplify and avoid linguistic excess as a 'kind of ignorance'.[24] This kind of ignorance puffs itself up and speaks with swelling cheeks: 'that is wretched, and miserable, and poor, and blind, and naked'. This last reference, also invoked by Hamann, is to Revelation

---

[23] Sheehan, p. 45. Sheehan's subtle reading is a good example of a non-presentist approach to Hamann that wants to avoid 'simplistic analogy in favor of a logic of strategic invention' (p. 48). In the larger picture, Sheehan understands that 'there is a recuperative element in the scholarly return to religion that, I believe, hinges on our own concern about the incongruity of the domains of reason and faith in their late-twentieth-century manifestations' (p. 50).

[24] Hamann, *Writings on Philosophy and Language*, trans. Kenneth Haynes (Cambridge: Cambridge University Press, 2007), p. 156.

(3: 17), upping the ante considerably, since it is not just about self-incurred ignorance but also about being 'miserable, and poor': to misconstrue language can be harmful and impoverishing, making us poorer thinkers and diminishing our imagination. This version of language and reason turns out to be ignorance or even, as Hamann later terms it in *Golgotha and Sheblimini!*, 'superstition'.[25] The *h* has Damm in its unhappy spell without him knowing anything about it.

For Hamann, it is a philology of the physical that saves us from such superstition. It combines textual analysis, historical argument, and philosophical reflection with a sense for the material quality of language. The meanings of signs 'manifest themselves in the physical acts of articulation—the position of the tongue and the movement of the breath', as Essick points out.[26] Blake and Hamann not only believe in motivated signs but also maintain that the actual corporeal movement when we pronounce a letter is part of this discussion. The position of the tongue when we pronounce a word has a meaningful link to creation at large, including Creation. We are reminded of the Moravians, their erotic Christology, their openness to sensuality, and their insistence on the importance of our ordinary physical experience—all aspects which I discuss earlier in this book. But Hamann's suggestion in the *Apology* goes further. It includes every breath that we take, meaningfully connecting even this non-verbal activity to the world's language. Hamann uses the silent letter—the seemingly weakest case—to intervene in wider Enlightenment discussions of theology and history, as Sheehan points out: 'While the letter h may be a historical convention, its power to mark out God in the written text simultaneously affirms the necessity of historical conventions and erodes contemporary hopes for a completely rationalized culture.'[27] Only if we can see the deeper physical and spiritual connection between letter and the world can we understand—or, to use Blake's word, 'see'—creation.

The physical-philological impulse that Hamann invokes originates in and gravitates towards Scriptural criticism, and thus he returns to the biblical connotations of the letter *h*. Hamann suggests that the breath of creation can be heard with every silent *h*, symbolizing the link between creation and language, ontology, and a single letter:

> Because letters are signs not only of articulated sounds, but often also of syllables and sometimes of words, and indeed can even represent the name of an extraordinary religious teacher of our time, it is therefore easy to believe that his philosophical concept of a letter will be sufficiently general to suit also a mere breath or *spiritus*.[28]

[25] Hamann, *Writings on Philosophy and Language*, p. 183. 'Aberglaube[s]' (N, 3: 305).

[26] Essick, p. 49.

[27] Sheehan, p. 46. Also see Hedwig Röben, 'J. G. Hamann und die Reformversuche in der deutschen Orthographie' (PhD dissertation, University of Vienna, 1942).

[28] Hamann, *Writings on Philosophy and Language*, pp. 149–50. 'Weil Buchstaben nicht nur Zeichen articulirter Töne sind, sondern auch oft Sylben und bisweilen Wörter, ja so gar den Namen eines ausserordentlichen Religionslehrers vorstellen können: so ist leicht zu erachten, daß sein philosophischer Begriff von einem Buchstaben allgemein gnug seyn wird, auch auf einen blossen hauch oder *Spiritum* zu passen' (N, 3: 93).

Damm, as we know, commits precisely the mistake of thinking that a 'philosophical concept of a letter' can contain and grasp the creative breath.[29] Hamann's joke about how a syllable itself can represent the name of a religious teacher is the lead here. In the first and most important instance, it is about the letter *h* itself, which is, of course, the supposed author of the second part of the *Apology*. As an immediate exemplification of Hamann's point, this little essay provides a loud warning about what might be lost if we do not attend to the 'mere breath or *spiritus*'. The silent letter *h* (pronounced 'ha' in German) points out rather loudly in its essay, 'Your life is that which I am—a breath'.[30] The reader, just like the letters she is reading, is nothing but a small, silent letter in the much bigger book of creation. This is the deep relation between a seemingly innocuous detail such as spelling and foundational ontological questions.

To some degree Hamann is simply complaining that Damm has not done his historical homework. He should know that the *h* is a reference to the power of the creative breath represented in the biblical image of God, who 'formed man *of* the dust of the ground, and breathed into his nostrils the breath of life'.[31] The reference is not only biblical but also connected to previous thinkers on the topic, such as Jacob Boehme, who 'in reference to written Hebrew...claims that the loss of "the *five* Vowels in the Alphabet" indicates the loss of "the great holy Name of JEOVA or JESUS (*viz*. The living Word)" from our language'; the reason why the *h* is important is because 'the return of "the Spirit of the five Vowels, *viz*. the Name JEHOVAH (which with the *H* has breathed the JESUS thereinto)" will destroy the beast and return language to its true form'.[32] Hamann's essay is not so much an 'onslaught against phonocentrism' but rather an exposition that takes seriously the divine breath of the letter as an idea that comes from Scripture itself.[33] The *Apology* wants to follow the divine breath in its human incarnation. It is simply not good enough, Hamann suggests, to dismiss the biblical material as superstitious or irrelevant because it does not fit the historical paradigm, which is what Damm does in his project of rationalization.

For all its humour, it is clear that Hamann makes a serious point against a functionalist understanding of language and in favour of the physicality of the letter. The specific historical moment of this argument is important. The increasingly powerful functionalist account, and the rationalization and standardization of language, are all associated with the Enlightenment. This is true not just for Hamann but also for others during the period. That is why Hamann's critique is legible as a critique of certain forms of the Enlightenment to contemporaries such as Moses Mendelssohn. In his 1775 review of the *Apology*, Mendelssohn

---

[29] Haynes's translation is sensitive to the wider dimension here. He uses the verb 'suit', thereby echoing the conversation about words being the clothes of ideas.
[30] Hamann, *Writings on Philosophy and Language*, p. 160. 'Euer Leben ist das, was ich bin—ein Hauch' (N, 3: 105).
[31] Genesis 2:7.   [32] Essick, p. 50.   [33] See Mehlman, pp. 329–47, 339.

picks up the wider existential dimension of Hamann's ventriloquism and adds a historical context:

> He [Hamann] even believes to have discovered that there is a more intimate connection between orthography and orthodoxy than many people might imagine; and that not only is orthodoxy very necessary in orthography, but also that if one acts all too hastily in orthography, innovations in orthodoxy must be the inevitable consequences thereof.[34]

Mendelssohn neatly diagnoses how Hamann's philology advances a wider claim about language: its connection to thought and ontology, and its historical theorization. As Mendelssohn stresses, for Hamann this link cannot possibly be exaggerated because the spheres of thinking and language are coextensive. After all, Language is Logos. Mendelssohn sharply picks up on Hamann's reasons for his resistance against reducing language to functionality. The link between orthodoxy and orthography is not simply one of historical tradition but, rather, one of the continuation of the metaphysical dimension of the letter. Orthodoxy and orthography are linked much deeper 'than many people might imagine', and changes in one of these areas have consequences in the other.

Every single letter is a meaningful sign in the much wider picture and history of the world's text, and human language reflects this wider structure back to us. There is, for Hamann, little sense in saying that this is 'only' about a disembodied letter. The main point of his essay and argument is that there is nothing like 'just' a letter, as there is analogously no such thing as 'just' a metaphor. The physical dimension of the biblical description is powerfully reflected in our own seemingly simple activity of breathing an unheard letter, the rhythmical reminder of our corporeal existence. Breathing, of course, is also at the centre of language and poetry. It is a physical activity that is connected to the letter, and, in return, concentrating on that letter reminds us how language is corporeal. There is a body that breathes, but the breath, the letter, cannot be grasped physically. It is produced by a body, keeping it alive—and yet is not fully material.

The body becomes an instrument, an organon, through which we can understand ourselves as made in the divine image. To complain about its shortcomings is to miss the point entirely since, for all its faults, it is the organon that allows that understanding in the first place. The argument is almost parallel to Hamann's earlier view of language as something, despite all its internal faults, to be celebrated as a divine gift that allows revelation. He illustrates these views in the *Apology* via an elaborate joke on himself and his own name.

Hamann's name falls into two syllables: Ha-mann. The first spells out the German pronunciation of the letter *h* ('ha'); *mann* translates as 'man'. Thus 'Hamann' is *Ha-mann*, *h* man, the man of the letter. The definition of Hamann himself as a subject with a name depends on the letter. The joke ('ha, ha') is significant insofar

---

[34] 'Er [Hamann] glaubt überhaupt entdeckt zu haben, daß zwischen der Orthographie und der Orthodoxie, eine innigere Verbindung sey, als sich viele Leute vorstellen mögen, und daß nicht allein die Orthodoxie in der Orthographie sehr nöthig sey, sondern auch, daß wenn man in der Orthographie allzuvorschnell verfährt, die Neuerungen in der Orthodoxie unausbleibliche Folgen davon seyn müssen' (Moses Mendelssohn, 'Sammelrezension zu Hamann', *Allgemeine Deutsche Bibliothek* 24 [1775]: 287–96, 289).

as the apology for the letter also becomes an apology for the style of arguing for its continued existence. Once we do away with *h*, we do away with the man that goes with it. And as much as Hamann uses pseudonyms, he does ultimately put his name to these essays. His interest becomes, in the most immediate and curious way, existential.[35] Playfully, Hamann defends a version of language that he sees as deeply bound up with his own existence. That the occasion obliquely brings his own name into play concentrates the rhetorical force of his approach. For all its apparent flippancy, the joke relies on an assumption about the nature of language that is fundamental and deadly serious for Hamann. The qualities of the letter and of the breath that carries it, as well as the relation it discovers between materiality and immateriality—the revelatory potential—make it a shorthand for a much wider concern. The letter comes to stand for language itself, for the way we understand ourselves in the world. As Johannes von Lüpke points out, 'The rescue of the letter is simultaneously the rescue of the divine spirit, which binds itself to the sphere of sensuality'.[36] The letter is the microcosmic instance that mirrors the linguistic nature of the entire world.

The intricate joke has one final layer, and again it is on Hamann himself. The uncontrollable laughter ('ha ha ha') is also an allusion to the fact that Hamann suffered from a stutter, a linguistic 'handicap' he had all his life. The stutter undoubtedly made him deeply aware of the physical nature and often painful limitation of language.[37] To again invoke Essick's formulation, 'the position of the tongue and the movement of the breath' really do make a difference to the understanding of the world. It is a reminder that the relation between idea and word is by no means transparent; the physical, halting repetition of one particular syllable or letter reinforces the awareness that speaking is a bodily and quite often exhausting activity. A stutter can be experienced as something rather violent, both mentally and physically. It is often also a revealing part of our lack of patience—we want clarity—as if the stutter is a reminder of how difficult thinking and language can be, a reminder that is highly marked through the body.

Of course, Hamann's stutter also had social consequences: in many ways, Hamann looked destined to become an academic, but his speech impediment made it impossible. He was considered unable to hold a position at the university in Königsberg because he would have been unable to lecture effectively—or 'fluently', as people might have said. Thus, the linguistic impediment is revealing in many ways, not just as a private symbol for the complications of language itself,

---

[35] The joke, of course, refers back to the passage cited earlier about how a syllable itself can represent the name of a religious teacher, thereby tying Hamann and Damm together since both have a letter to spare under Damm's vision.

[36] 'Die Rettung des Buchstabens ist zugleich Rettung des göttlichen Geistes, der sich an die Sphäre der Sinnlichkeit bindet' (Johannes von Lüpke, 'Die Wahrheit in einem Hauch oder von der Eitelkeit der Vernunft "Neue Apologie des Buchstaben h von ihm selbst"', in *Hamann: Insel Almanach auf das Jahr 1988*, ed. Oswald Bayer, Bernhard Gajek, and Josef Simon [Frankfurt am Main: Insel, 1987], pp. 172–84, 183). The same sentence occurs in a piece by Yoshikatsu Kawanago, but the quotation does not seem attributed ('Sprache und Leib bei Georg Hamann', *Interdisciplinary Cultural Studies* 4 [1999]: 111–31, http://www004.upp.so-net.ne.jp/kawanago/LEIB-H01.HTM).

[37] For a discussion of the philosophical implications of stuttering that mentions Hamann in passing, see Marc Shell, *Stutter* (Cambridge, MA: Harvard University Press, 2005); and Steven Connor, *Beyond Words: Sobs, Hums, Stutters, and other Vocalizations* (London: Reaktion, 2014), pp. 39–47.

but also as a marker of the degree to which functionality, 'smooth' communication, and a preference to make the medium of communication disappear had already taken root in public life. It is a multiple reminder of the lack of control that we have, both publicly and privately, over the medium that we often pretend to manipulate with such ease. Hamann's reaction to his stutter is not to ignore it as a defect but, rather, to explore it as a means of revelation. That is, the stutter helps him to become the exorbitant figure who will step outside the discourse which governs normal speech.

UTERI AND PUDENDA: GRAPHIC SEXUALITY AND LANGUAGE AS CRITIQUE

What does it mean to believe that language is not only physical but also sexual? Blake and Hamann give a characteristically exorbitant answer. Hamann writes that '[a] world without God is a human without head—without heart, without entrails, without pudenda'.[38] For him, as well as for Blake, sexuality is an absolutely central way to comprehend the relation between the world, language, and the body. Understanding this relationship opens up a form of critique, since there is a push for sexuality as the first and most fundamental form of the physical. Blake and Hamann use the link between language and sexuality to reject the idea of the human body, including its sexuality, as a secondary shell of our existence, a worldly obstacle that needs to be overcome or purified. Just like creation itself, the body is something to be celebrated either in language or through the imagination. In contrast, sexuality is a way to celebrate the physicality of human existence, not just in language but also beyond.

Sexuality is part of the radically holistic vision of Blake's and Hamann's ways of thinking, their deliberate moves to accentuate the most graphic parts of the human body. Their celebration of the body is not restricted to the parts of the human frame that are traditionally associated with showing its status as the head of creation—say, the hands or the head of the human frame. This is not just the body of the knowing eye, proudly surveying its position in creation; it is also the breathing body that produces our voice and song. Even more unusually for the sensibilities of the time, it is also the body of genitalia and organs of sexual reproduction. These are neither the abject parts of a vision that celebrates the mind, nor a rejection of the bodily as interfering with establishing knowledge. Sexuality as part of the human body is to be celebrated. In fact, its mysterious nature—perhaps even its poetics—puts it at the centre of the interest of both Blake and Hamann.

The graphic articulation of the topic of sexuality and language is part of the conceptual argument. As we know, Blake's and Hamann's discourses are not of soft allusions, but of explicitness and excess: words are spoken of in terms of uteri, sexual organs, pudenda, and so forth. There are several reasons for these transgressions of

---

[38] 'Eine Welt ohne Gott ist ein Mensch ohne Kopf—ohne Herz, ohne Eingeweide—ohne pudenda' (ZH, 5: 326).

conventional discourse. Much of it is connected to the historical rejection of eighteenth- and early nineteenth-century intellectual culture in a way that this book describes as 'exorbitant'. In relation to sexuality, for instance, Blake's and Hamann's way of thinking and writing are completely unlike the two most important attitudes on this topic at the time. First, it does not square with a version of the Enlightenment that wants to neutralize, to secularize, both language and sexuality. Second, it does not fit into the standard Christian attitude of the rejection of the body. Blake and Hamann are outside of both of these orbits of thinking.

To understand their opposition to the Enlightenment attempt to neutralize sexuality, it is useful to turn to William Godwin as a representative figure of such views, especially concerning procreation. Here is Godwin on sexuality: 'Reasonable men will then propagate their species, not because a certain sensible pleasure is annexed to this action, but because it is right the species should be propagated; and the manner in which they exercise this function will be regulated by the dictates of reason and duty.'[39] It is a startling statement, a sign of the times for Blake and Hamann of what counts as 'reasonable'. In Godwin's formulation it is reason rather than pleasure or revelation that will lead to sex. And, in an odd echo of certain strands of Christianity, the only reason to have sex is to procreate. We have sex because it is a rational, heteronormative, and clear and functional way to behave. Enlightenment sex turns out to be the opposite of a headfuck.

Blake and Hamann would find Godwin's account almost ludicrously reductive if it were not so dangerous. It is almost as if Godwin imagines that, once fully enlightened, our sexual habits would be completely regulated. For Blake, such an idea is an ultimate nightmare. In a fine and subtle reading of *Los*, Karen Swann reminds us that 'the "natural" body in Blake is always a cruelly fashioned body, "organized" to serve the interests of interconnected social, economic, and political regimes'.[40] That 'natural' body is Godwin's body, the body that leads to disciplined sexuality. It is the body that will stay functional, out of trouble, and within pre-scribed tracks—and the body that is detached from language and its poetry. The cruel irony lies in the supposed liberation that such neutralizing produces. In con-trast, Blake and Hamann insist on the celebration of human physicality and on the impossibility of making the sexual body 'natural' in a way that Swann suggests.

The second major paradigm that Blake and Hamann oppose is Christianity's traditional opposition to the sensual. For them, in contrast, the flesh is a matter of deep spiritual importance. They identify that the denial of the body is another instance of how institutional religion has produced a warped sense of the human self. In the *Apology* and elsewhere, Hamann implies that he wants his writing to be a 'vigorous critique of the hypocritical piety—in fact, blasphemy, according to Hamann's theology—of prudishness and sexual shame', as Gwen Griffith-Dickson puts it.[41] In Blake, we encounter a similar attitude when it comes to sexual shame

---

[39] William Godwin, qtd in Don Locke, *A Fantasy of Reason: The Life and Thought of William Godwin* (London: Routledge and Kegan Paul, 1980), p. 109.

[40] Karen Swann, 'Blake's Jerusalem: Friendship with Albion', in *A Companion to Romantic Poetry* (Oxford: Blackwell, 2010), pp. 538–53, 548.

[41] Griffith-Dickson, p. x.

in relation to nakedness. Recall William Blake and Catherine Blake sitting naked in their garden: '*[I]t's only Adam and Eve, you know!*'[42]

For both Blake and Hamann, sexual shame in particular is part of how we begin to close ourselves off from the world, impoverishing it, and thereby lose a sense of the physicality of language. It is an experience of the world and ourselves that is limited to 'the five senses', as Blake says.[43] Instead, we should understand that our sexual body is a reminder of the reproductive nature of language and therefore to be celebrated. The sexual body is part of creation and, as such, serves as an adequate illustration of how both the material and the immaterial qualities of language are, quite literally, embodied in our form. Blake and Hamann directly oppose the standard Christian characterization of the body as a sinful and abject site. Instead, they celebrate it as revealing human glory.

The theoretical dimension to these arguments is that the insistence on the sexual character of language becomes a form of critique. It uncovers that a supposedly neutral rationalization of language is a direct result of a historical rejection of the physical—in particular, the sexual aspect of human existence. In contrast, Blake and Hamann argue that we should rejoice in the physical aspect of man and language, even though they will inevitably illustrate the limited nature of human existence. And, crucially, 'flesh' means genitalia, penises, vulvas, and pudenda.[44]

Their graphic and excessive style is an important historical marker for Blake and Hamann, especially in the light of contemporary scholarship on eighteenth-century attitudes towards sexuality. What look like open attitudes towards sexuality were far more common than we might think. In the case of Blake, for instance, Susan Matthew has shown that he was influenced by 'a specific pro-sex discourse within the bourgeois world with which he had most contact.'[45] However, we should not confuse this openness with Blake's and Hamann's exorbitance. In much of their writing Blake and Hamann go much further than a general discursive endorsement of sexuality. In fact, they are not interested in normalizing sexuality in a way that would make it more acceptable by lessening it in importance. The sexuality that they embrace is not so much a domesticated, bourgeois version but, rather, a spiritual one that is embarrassed about neither its nakedness nor its sacred status. The graphic nature of their prose is not about normalizing sexuality in the discursive field with a view of taking away its special status (secularizing it, as it were). Their explicit vocabulary insists, instead, that the power of sexuality, and its link to language, lies in the magical connections between the two.

---

[42] Alexander Gilchrist, *The Life of William Blake, 'Pictor Ignotus'* (London: Macmillan, 1863), p. 115, qtd in Bentley, *Blake Records*, p. xxvii.

[43] The phrase appears in *The Marriage of Heaven and Hell*, *Visions of the Daughters of Albion*, *Europe a Prophecy*, *The Song of Los*, and *The Four Zoas*.

[44] Another exorbitant figure in this connection is Rowland Jones, part of the Celticists, a group of eighteenth-century linguistic thinkers. Jones believes that the shapes of letters themselves are linked to their hieroglyphic nature, down to sexuality: 'Many of Jones's roots and hieroglyphic letter forms refer to water or parts of the body, including "the sea and river, the vulva and penis, and the mouth and the tongue"' (Essick, p. 80).

[45] Susan Matthews, *Blake, Sexuality, and Bourgeois Politeness* (Cambridge: Cambridge University Press, 2011), p. 6. Notably, this context includes key members of the Anglo-German community in London, such as Henry Fuseli, the Moravians, and Emanuel Swedenborg.

In a 1780 pamphlet entitled *Two Mites* (*Zwey Scherflein*), Hamann describes thinking as located in the 'uterus of language, which is the DEIPARA of our reason'.[46] The origin of language is sacred, holy, and unmistakably bodily. The German word for 'uterus' is 'Gebärmutter', which translates literally as 'birthmother', making the link to 'DEIPARA' even more clearly gendered. 'DEIPARA' is not only a name for the Virgin Mary—mother, bearer of God (*deus-parere*)—but also the undeniably physical reminder that this God was made flesh, just like His word. This physicality was real, and thus the sexual dimension of linguistics is the most apt way to describe language's reproductive power in general. When Hamann speaks of language as an '*organon*', this is part of a rhetoric of reproduction that can be found throughout his work.[47] Hartmut Böhme pinpoints how 'Hamann rehabilitates the passionate body as a pre-rational origin of (poetic) language: there is a striking accumulation of sexual and affective metaphors'.[48] This accumulation becomes part of the argument; for instance, the admission that his 'coarse imagination is never able to imagine a creative spirit without genitalia' suggests that the sexual body is a defining trait of our humanity.[49] Hamann's exact formulation is important here since he speaks about 'Geschlecht' (genitalia). In German, *Geschlecht* is a term for 'genitalia', but it also denotes 'gender', 'dynasty', 'generation', 'species', or 'race'. Hamann's reference to 'genitalia' is not to denounce a crude anthropomorphism but, rather, to remind us that if we want to talk about humans, then we need to talk about our bodies in their whole complexity, including our genitals. The Moravians picked up on a similar point where Nikolaus Ludwig von Zinzendorf argues that a person 'must accept that the manliness of Jesus was so natural, complete, and simple as his own which he carries on himself'.[50] In 1784 Hamann wrote that 'the *pudenda* of our nature hang together so precisely with the chambers of our heart and of our brain that too strict an *abstraction* of such a natural bond is impossible'.[51] In this radical holism, natural bonds cannot be abstracted and separated. To abstract is to dissect into a facile way of thinking about thought (brain), heart (affect), and sex (pudenda). In fact, the sexual organ itself, just like the word it produces, is the site where all of these areas meet, which is indeed a troubling yet powerful idea. It is a radical and complete insistence that our bodies are—especially in their sexuality—an integral part of the way we produce knowledge linguistically.

[46] 'Gebärmutter der Sprache, welche die DEIPARA unserer *Vernunft* ist' (N, 3: 239).

[47] Griffith-Dickson, p. 520; emphasis in original. 'Organon der Vernunft' (N, 3: 284).

[48] 'Gegen den Asketismus der Aufklärung rehabilitiert Hamann den leidenschaftlichen Leib als vorrationalen Ursprung der (poetischen) Sprache: auffällig häufen sich sexuelle und affektive Metaphern' (Hartmut Böhme, *Natur und Subjekt* [Frankfurt: Suhrkamp, 1996], p. 196).

[49] Griffith-Dickson, p. 209. '[M]eine grobe Einbildungskraft ist niemals im Stande gewesen, sich einen schöpferischen Geist ohne genitalia vorzustellen' (ZH, 2: 415).

[50] Nikolaus Ludwig von Zinzendorf, qtd in Craig D. Atwood, 'Sleeping in the Arms of Christ: Sanctifying Sexuality in the Eighteenth-Century Moravian Church', *Journal of the History of Sexuality* 8, 1 (July 1997): 25–51, 29. Also see Nikolaus Ludwig von Zinzendorf, 'Einundzwanzig Diskurse über die Augspurgische Konfession', reproduced in *Hauptschriften in sechs Bänden*, ed. Erich Beyreuther and Gerhard Meyer, 6 vols (Hildesheim, 1962); sermon 7, p. 147

[51] '[D]ie *Pudenda* unserer Natur hängen mit den Cammern des Herzens und des Gehirns so genau zusammen, daß eine zu strenge *Abstraction* eines so natürlichen Bandes unmöglich ist' (ZH, 5: 167).

The female body, in particular, is the focus of Hamann's attention and his way of linking sexuality and language through images of female reproductive organs and poetic creation. In a 1786 letter to Johann Gottfried Herder he varies the formulation that he used in the *Two Mites* ('uterus of language') and writes, 'Nothing that comes out of the womb and the uterus of our brain may make claim to pure perfection'.[52] Language is always lacking, but nevertheless reproductive. Language is reproductive precisely because it is linked to the human body, which here is female. The fact that this body cannot make a claim to 'pure perfection' is not a reason to reject it—quite the contrary. And yet the focus on female sexuality is relevant. For Blake, '[t]he nakedness of woman is the work of God' and it is her nakedness that gets his imagination going.[53] Blake's relationship to gender is, of course, famously problematic. Anne Mellor objects that in the end Blake condones 'the continuation of female slavery under a benevolent master', and while it is problematic to claim that Blake has such set principles, what is certainly true is that not all that looks like 'free love' is indeed liberated.[54] His poetry both consciously and unconsciously records these sexual politics, and the same is true for Hamann. The fact that Blake and Hamann show little historical or conceptual interest in the assumptions underlying the erotic tradition that links the female body and language indicates that they are uncharacteristically uncritical of their own thinking and expressions here. Blake's and Hamann's rhetoric in this instance falls into the trap of functionalizing the female body. The explicit focus on the uterus in an almost clinical way—there is no mention of pleasure at all—turns the female body into a birth machine. The primary role of the uterus of thought seems suddenly to be functional productivity, not creative poetry. This suspicion is confirmed when we realize that, while the organ of reproduction is female, the creator of that fruit is imagined as male. Here is Hamann on the production of writing: 'Not even a mother can rejoice as much about her first sight of her child than the writer who sees his work printed'.[55] The tension in the structure of denial of this sentence is revealing. When the mother sees the creation that is literally the 'fruit of the body' (*Leibesfrucht*) with her eyes, she is joyful.[56] However, Hamann immediately constructs an analogy with a male figure: the writer or author who also feels happiness and relief in seeing his creation being reproduced for the first time, mechanically printed upon paper. If we look closely, then we realize that Hamann constructs the analogy not quite symmetrically: the mother cannot feel as much joy as the male author. In comparison, the mother is deficient; or a human baby turns out to be less capable of producing joy than a book. Here the male clearly produces the longer-lasting creation, which is, significantly, the form of

---

[52] 'Nichts was aus Mutterleibe und aus der Gebährmutter unsers Gehirn kommt, darf auf reine Vollkommenheit Anspruch machen' (ZH, 6: 340).

[53] Blake, *Marriage of Heaven and Hell*, pp. 33–45, 36, plate 8, line 25.

[54] Anne K. Mellor, 'Sex, Violence, and Slavery: Blake and Wollstonecraft', in 'William Blake: Images and Texts', special issue, *Huntington Library Quarterly* 58, 3/4 (1995): 345–70, 369–70.

[55] 'Nicht eine Mutter kann sich über den ersten Anblick ihrer Leibesfrucht so freuen, wie ein Schriftsteller seine Arbeit gedruckt zu sehen' (ZH, 5: 169–70).

[56] ZH, 5: 169–70.

reproduction that leads to joy and pleasure: the writer who rejoices. Thus, Blake and Hamann do not consider sufficiently that not only the act of creation but also the form and dissemination of such creation is a matter of the differences between sexual bodies.

It is important to insist on the limitations of Blake's and Hamann's thinking because they themselves have pointed out that the sexual bodies in their work are not just theoretical figures. Their criticism, including its shortcomings, both encompasses the position of the reader—male or female—and informs our translation of these insights into our reading experience. As Blake and Hamann would be the first to admit, our reading body is a sexual body, and recognizing, even celebrating, its physicality is a central part of our linguistic reading experience. Hence, we should consider the sensual qualities of the text or image in front of us as a central part of the aesthetic dimension of our hermeneutic understanding.

When we read we perform a translation from 'a tongue of angels into a human tongue, that is, thoughts in words—things in names—images in signs'.[57] This process is never neutral or transparent. Understood in Blake's and Hamann's terms, reading here focuses on, and points beyond, approaches in phenomenology that speak to the physicality of our interaction with texts. They inquire after the sexual dimension of that affective relation.[58] Put more directly: what about our own pudenda here? And what about the endemic reluctance to own up to what our own genitalia might do to us as thinkers? This is a point that goes beyond the analysis of the gendering or sexualizing power of rhetoric—for example, the familiar point that the sublime is always marked as male, whereas the beautiful is described in female terms. It does not deny the power of such an analysis, of course. But there is a claim here that goes fundamentally further than speaking about discourse or the larger semantics of meanings. It is an exorbitant claim, a claim that concerns the sexual dimension of each letter that others might compose but that we read, breathe, speak, and write. The sexuality of the *h* or each letter in *Jerusalem* is something that not only stops with Hamann or Blake, but also inhabits our own reading and writing. It can propel us out of the orbit of reading normally, including history and culture. As such, the call to think about the physicality and sexuality of each letter—from the authors we study all the way to ourselves—puts these ideas in a context of a resistance to the Enlightenment that is still relevant today. It is part of a larger set of claims about the rejection of dualism or the purification of language that make us think differently about our intellectual heritage, including our own enlightened bodies. It is, in other words, an encouragement to continue to chart an exorbitant Enlightenment.

The different case studies and forms of historical, philosophical, and philological readings that these eight chapters have followed have presented ways of charting specific Anglo-German constellations in such an exorbitant Enlightenment. It has

[57] Griffith-Dickson, p. 413. '[A]us einer Engelssprache in eine Menschensprache, das heist, Gedanken in Worte,—Sachen in Namen,—Bilder in Zeichen' (N, 2:199).
[58] Another approach might be through an increased attention to the physical reaction of the reader's body, like work in neuroscience and literature. For obvious reasons, the materialist premises of such an approach would contradict Hamann's approach to science exhibited here.

become clear that this involves a way of understanding literary, historical, and conceptual influence that goes beyond more standard, causal claims and, instead, emphasizes a larger context that involves people who are on the outside, describing them *from* the outside. The resulting formations and relations include descriptions of the material realities discussed in Chapter 1, the intellectual connections revealed in Chapters 2 to 4, the institutional formations analysed in Chapter 5, the reformulation of literary history explored in Chapters 6 and 7, and the conceptual dimensions regarding the body in this final chapter. All of these case studies encourage us to read the whole period differently, to disrupt traditional ways of looking at the change from Enlightenment to Romanticism, revising our literary and conceptual histories. This does not just increase the level of confusion; it also clarifies several things, especially when we employ a comparative outlook. Over the course of this book, a set of exorbitant figures emerges from an Anglo-German context. They have never been compared before because they were thought to be from different national traditions, periods, or intellectual genealogies. However, they turn out to speak to one another in remarkable ways once we appreciate them on their excessive terms. The constellations they create across languages, disciplines, and historiographies allow us to understand this period, and ourselves, in new ways that do not follow an already specified track but imagine them, and us, in new, exorbitant ways.

Bibliography

A Collection of Hymns, for the Use of the Protestant Church of the United Brethren (London, 1789).

A Collection of Hymns of the Children of God in All Ages (London, 1754).

A Collection of Hymns with Several Translations from the Hymn Book of the Moravian Brethren. 3rd ed. (London: [James Hutton], 1746).

A Hymn-Book for the Children Belonging to the Brethren's Congregations: Taken Chiefly out of the GERMAN Little Book ([London], 1756).

Abrams, M. H. *Natural Supernaturalism: Tradition and Revolution in Romantic Literature* (New York: W. W. Norton, 1973).

Allentuck, Marcia. 'Fuseli and Lavater: Physiognomical Theory and the Enlightenment'. *Studies on Voltaire and the Eighteenth Century* 55 (1967): 89–112.

Allentuck, Marcia. 'Henry Fuseli and J. G. Herder's *Ideen zur Philosophie der Geschichte der Menschheit* in Britain: An Unremarked Connection'. *Journal of the History of Ideas* 35, no. 1 (January–March 1974): 113–20.

Amir, Lydia B. *Humor and the Good Life in Modern Philosophy: Shaftesbury, Hamann, Kierkegaard* (Albany: State University of New York Press, 2014).

An English and Danish Dictionary: Containing the Genuine Words of Both Languages with Their Proper and Figurative Meanings. Edited by Andreas Berthelson (London: printed by John Haberkorn and A. Linde, 1754).

Anderson, Lisa Marie. *Hegel on Hamann.* Translated by Lisa Marie Anderson (Evanston, IL: Northwestern University Press, 2008).

Aravamudan, Srinivas. *Enlightenment Orientalism: Resisting the Rise of the Novel* (Chicago, IL: University of Chicago Press, 2011).

Aravamudan, Srinivas. *Tropicopolitans: Colonialism and Agency, 1688–1804* (Durham, NC/ London: Duke University Press, 1999).

Archenholtz, Johann Wilhelm von. *England und Italien.* 2 vols (C. G. Schmieder, 1787).

Archenholtz, Johann Wilhelm von. *England: From the 1787 Expanded Edition of 'England und Italien'.* Edited and translated by Lois E. Bueler (Lanham, MD: University Press of America, 2014).

Armstrong, John. Review of 'Remarks on the Writings and Conduct of J. J. Rousseau'. *Monthly Review* 36 (June 1767): 459–63.

Atwood, Craig D. *Community of the Cross: Moravian Piety in Colonial Bethlehem* (State College: Pennsylvania State University Press, 2004).

Atwood, Craig D. 'Sleeping in the Arms of Christ: Sanctifying Sexuality in the Eighteenth-Century Moravian Church'. *Journal of the History of Sexuality* 8, no. 1 (July 1997): 25–51.

Austen-Leigh, J. E. *A Memoir of Jane Austen and Other Family Recollections.* Edited by Kathryn Sutherland (Oxford: Oxford University Press, 2002).

Ayres, Brenda. 'Edith Simcox's Diptych: Sexuality and Textuality'. In *Women in Journalism at the Fin de Siècle: 'Making a Name for Herself'*, edited by F. Elizabeth Gray, pp. 53–70. Palgrave Studies in Nineteenth-Century Writing and Culture (New York: Palgrave Macmillan, 2012).

Bairnes, Trial of Charles, 26 February 1783. In *Proceedings of the Old Bailey*, pp. 292–6. Rept in *The Old Bailey Proceedings* (Harvester Microform, 1983), pp. 64–8. *Old Bailey Proceedings Online*, t17830226-38.

Balfour, Ian. *The Rhetoric of Romantic Prophecy* (Stanford, CA: Stanford University Press, 2002).

Barnett, Christopher B. *Kierkegaard, Pietism and Holiness* (New York: Routledge, 2016).

Barnett, Christopher B. 'Socrates the Pietist? Tracing the Socratic in Zinzendorf, Hamann, and Kierkegaard'. In *Kierkegaard's Late Writings*, edited by Niels Jørgen Cappelørn, Hermann Deuser, and K. Brian Söderquist, special issue, *Kierkegaard Studies Yearbook* 15, pp. 307–23 (Berlin: Walter de Gruyter, 2010).

Baur-Callwey, Marcella. *Die Differenzierung des Gemeinsamen: Männliche Doppelporträts in England von Hans Holbein d. J. bis Joshua Reynolds* (Munich: Martin Meidenbauer, 2007).

Bayer, Oswald. *A Contemporary in Dissent: Johann Georg Hamann as a Radical Enlightener* (Grand Rapids, MI: Eerdmans, 2012).

Bayer, Oswald. *Vernunft ist Sprache: Hamanns Metakritik Kants* (Stuttgart: Frommann-Holzboog, 2002).

Beetz, Manfred, and Andre Rudolph. *Johann Georg Hamann: Religion und Gesellschaft* (Berlin: De Gruyter, 2012).

Beiser, Frederick C. *The Fate of Reason: German Philosophy from Kant to Fichte* (Cambridge, MA: Harvard University Press, 1987).

Bender, John. *Ends of Enlightenment* (Stanford, CA: Stanford University Press, 2012).

Benjamin, Walter. 'Doctrine of the Similar (1933)'. In Walter Benjamin special issue of *New German Critique* 17 (Spring 1979): 65–9.

Benjamin, Walter. *Gesammelte Schriften*. Edited by Rolf Tiedemann and Hermann Schweppenhäuser. 7 vols (Frankfurt: Suhrkamp, 1991).

Benjamin, Walter. *Walter Benjamin: Selected Writings*. Translated by Edmund Jephcott and others. 4 vols (Cambridge, MA: Belknap Press of Harvard University Press, 1996–2003).

Bentley, G. E., Jr. *Blake Records: Documents (1714–1841) concerning the Life of William Blake (1757–1827) and His Family, Incorporating Blake Records (1969), Blake Records Supplement (1988), and Extensive Discoveries since 1988*. 2nd ed. (New Haven, CT: published for the Paul Mellon Centre for Studies in British Art by Yale University Press, 2004).

Bentley, G. E., Jr. Review of Marsha Keith Schuchard, *Why Mrs Blake Cried: William Blake and the Sexual Basis of Spiritual Vision*. *Blake/An Illustrated Quarterly* 40, 4 (2007): 150–1.

Berlin, Isaiah. *Against the Current: Essays in the History of Ideas* (Princeton, NJ: Princeton University Press, 2013).

Berlin, Isaiah. *Three Critics of Enlightenment: Vico, Hamann, Herder* (New York: Random House, 2000).

Bersier, Gabrielle. 'Arcadia Revitalized: The International Appeal of Gessner's Idylls in the 18th Century'. In *From the Greeks to the Greens: Images of Simple Life*, edited by Reinhold Grimm and Jost Hermand, pp. 34–47 (Madison: University of Wisconsin Press, 1989).

Bett, Henry. *Hymns of Methodism in Their Literary Relations* (London: Charles H. Kelly, 1913).

Bett, Henry. *The Hymns of Methodism*. 3rd rev. ed. (London: Epworth, 1945).

Betz, John R. *After Enlightenment: The Post-Secular Vision of J. G. Hamann* (Malden, MA: Wiley-Blackwell, 2012).

Betz, John R. 'Hamann before Kierkegaard: A Systematic Theological Oversight'. *Pro Ecclesia* 16, 3 (Summer 2007): 299–333.

Bilgrami, Akeel. *Secularism, Identity, and Enchantment* (Cambridge, MA: Harvard University Press, 2014).

Blackall, Eric A. *The Emergence of German as a Literary Language 1700–1775*. 2nd ed. (Ithaca, NY: Cornell University Press, 1978).

Blackie, J. S. 'Jung Stilling: Religious Literature of Germany'. *Foreign Quarterly Review* 21, 42 (July 1838): 247–83.

Blair, Kirstie, ed. *John Keble in Context* (London: Anthem, 2004).

Blake, William. *The Complete Poetry and Prose of William Blake*, rev. ed. Edited by David V. Erdman (New York: Anchor Books, 1988).

Bodenheimer, Rosemarie. *The Real Life of Mary Ann Evans: George Eliot, Her Letters, and Fiction* (Ithaca, NY: Cornell University Press, 1994).

Boening, John. 'Pioneers and Precedents: The "Importation of German" and the Emergence of Periodical Criticism in England'. *Internationales Archiv fur Sozialgeschichte der deutschen Literatur* 7 (1982): 65–87.

Böhme, Hartmut. *Natur und Subjekt* (Frankfurt: Suhrkamp, 1996).

Bolle, Kees W. 'The Romantic Impulse in the History of Religions: An Essay on the Image of Man'. *Cultural Dynamics* 2, 4 (December 1989): 400–24.

Bowie, Andrew. *From Romanticism to Critical Theory: The Philosophy of German Literary Theory* (London: Routledge, 2012).

Bridgewater, Patrick. *De Quincey's Gothic Masquerade* (Amsterdam: Rodopi, 2002).

Brose, Thomas. *Johann Georg Hamann und David Hume: Metaphysikkritik und Glaube im Spannungsfeld der Aufklärung* (Frankfurt am Main: Peter Lang, 2006).

Buffon, Georges L. L. *Discours à l'Académie française* (1753).

Burckhardt, Johann Gottlieb. *Kirchengeschichte der deutschen Gemeinden in London nebst historischer Beylagen und Predigten* (Tübingen: Fues, 1798).

Burke, Edmund. *A Philosophical Enquiry into the Origin of Our Ideas of the Sublime and the Beautiful*, 5th ed. (London: J. Dodsley, 1767).

Burwick, Frederick. 'Blake's Laocoön and Job: Or, on the Boundaries of Painting and Poetry'. In *The Romantic Imagination: Literature and Art in England and Germany*, edited by Burwick and Jürgen Klein, pp. 125–55 (Amsterdam: Rodopi, 1996).

Butler, Marilyn. *Mapping Mythologies: Countercurrents in Eighteenth-Century British Poetry and Cultural History* (Cambridge: Cambridge University Press, 2015).

Butler, Marilyn. *Romantics, Rebels, and Reactionaries: English Literature and Its Background, 1760–1830* (Oxford: Oxford University Press, 1981).

Carlyle, Thomas. 'State of German Literature'. *Edinburgh Review* 46, 92 (October 1827): 304–51.

Carvacchi, Karl C. *Biographische Erinnerungen an Johann Georg Hamann, den Magus in Norden* (Münster: Friedrich Regensberg, 1855).

Casanova, Pascale. *The World Republic of Letters* (Cambridge, MA: Harvard University Press, 2004).

Cavell, Stanley. *In Quest of the Ordinary: Lines of Skepticism and Romanticism* (Chicago, IL: University of Chicago Press, 1988).

Celan, Paul. *La bibliothèque philosophique: Die Philosophische Bibliothek* (Paris: Rue d'Ulm, 2004). https://www.dla-marbach.de/katalog/bibliothek.

Chandler, James. *England in 1819: The Politics of Literary Culture and the Case of Romantic Historicism* (Chicago, IL: University of Chicago Press, 1999).

Class, Monika. *Coleridge and Kantian Ideas in England, 1769–1817* (New York: Bloomsbury, 2012).

Coleridge, Samuel Taylor. *Letters of Samuel Taylor Coleridge*. 2 vols (London: William Heinemann, 1895).

Coleridge, Samuel Taylor. Marginalia 2. Edited by George Whalley. In *The Collected Works of Samuel Taylor Coleridge*. 23 vols (Princeton, NJ: Princeton University Press, 1969).

Coleridge, Samuel Taylor. *The Wanderings of Cain* [reading text]. Edited by Nikki Santilli (Baltimore: University of Maryland, Romantic Circles, 2003). Available at: https://www.rc.umd.edu/editions/cain/readingtext.html.

Connor, Steven. *Beyond Words: Sobs, Hums, Stutters, and Other Vocalizations* (London: Reaktion, 2014).

Courtine, Jean Jacques, and Claudine Haroche. *Histoire du visage: Exprimer et taire ses émotions (XVIe-début XIXe siècle)* (Paris: Rivages, 1988).

Crews, C. Daniel, and Richard W. Starbuck. *Records of the Moravians among the Cherokee* (Tahlequah, OK: Cherokee Heritage Press, 2010).

Cunningham, Allan. *The Life of Sir David Wilkie; with His Journals, Tours, and Critical Remarks on Works of Art; and a Selection from His Correspondence*. 3 vols (London: John Murray, 1843).

Cunningham, Allan. 'William Blake'. In *The Lives of the Most Eminent British Painters, Sculptors, and Architects*, 2nd ed. 6 vols (London: John Murray, 1830), 2, pp. 143–88.

Davies, Keri. 'The Lost Moravian History of William Blake's Family: Snapshots from the Archive'. *Literature Compass* 3, 6 (November 2006): 1297–319.

Davies, Keri. 'The View from Fetter Lane: Moravian Eye-Witnesses of the Gordon Riots'. Paper presented at 'The Gordon Riots and British Culture Conference', Roehampton University, July 2008. Available at *Academia.edu*, www.academia.edu/1691609/The_view_from_Fetter_Lane_Moravian_eye-witnesses_of_the_Riots.

Davies, Keri. 'William Blake's Mother: A New Identification'. *Blake: An Illustrated Quarterly* 33, 2 (Fall 1999): 36–50.

Davies, Keri, and Margaret Keith Schuchard. 'Recovering the Lost Moravian History of William Blake's Family'. *Blake: An Illustrated Quarterly* 38, 1 (Summer 2004): 36–43.

Davis, Garold N. *German Thought and Culture in England 1700–1770: A Preliminary Survey*. Studies in Comparative Literature 47 (Chapel Hill: University of North Carolina Press, 1969).

Defoe, Daniel. *A Brief History of the Poor Palatine Refugees, Lately Arriv'd in England* (London: J. Baker, 1709).

Defoe, Daniel. 'Explanatory Preface' to 'The True Born Englishman'. In *The Works of Daniel Defoe, Carefully Selected from the Most Authentic Sources, with Chalmer's Life of the Author, Annotated*, edited by John S. Keltie (Edinburgh: Nimmo, 1870).

Defoe, Daniel, *Robinson Crusoe*. Edited by Thomas Keymer (Oxford: Oxford University Press, 2007).

Defoe, Daniel. *The True-Born Englishman: A Satire* (Leeds: Alice Mann, 1836).

Deneke, Otto. *Lichtenbergs Leben* (Munich: Ernst Heimeran, 1944).

De Luca, Vincent Arthur. *Words of Eternity: Blake and the Poetics of the Sublime* (Princeton, NJ: Princeton University Press, 1991).

De Man, Paul. *Blindness and Insight: Essays in the Rhetoric of Contemporary Criticism*, 2nd ed. (London: Routledge, 2005).

De Meyere, Job. 'The "Enlightened" Derrida: The Formalization of Religion'. In *Faith in the Enlightenment? The Critique of the Enlightenment Revisited*, edited by Lieven Boeve, Joeri Schrijvers, Wessel Stoker, and Hendrik M. Vroom, pp. 143–56 (Amsterdam: Rodopi, 2006).

De Quincey, Thomas. *The Works of Thomas De Quincey*. 21 vols. Edited by Grevel Lindop (London: Pickering and Chatto, 2000–2003).

Der kirchen-Catechismus: Welchem einige der auserlesensten Sprüche der Heiligen Schrifft hinzugesetzet worden [multiple contributors] (London: Downing, 1709).

Derrida, Jacques. *Archive Fever: A Freudian Impression* (Chicago, IL: University of Chicago Press, 1998).

Derrida, Jacques. *The Beast and the Sovereign*, 2 vols, trans Geoffrey Bennington (Chicago, IL/London: University of Chicago Press, 2009–11).

Dickson, Gwen Griffith. *Johann Georg Hamann's Relational Metacriticism* (Berlin: De Gruyter, 1995).

Eaves, Morris. 'On Blakes We Want and Blakes We Don't'. *Huntington Library Quarterly* 58, 3–4 (1995): 413–39.

Edgeworth, Maria. *The Life and Letters of Maria Edgeworth*. Edited by Augustus J. C. Hare. 2 vols (New York: Houghton, Mifflin, 1895).

Elson, Louis. ed., *University Musical Encyclopedia* 10 vols (New York: The University Society, 1910).

Erle, Sibylle. 'Face to Face with Johann Caspar Lavater'. *Literature Compass* (2005): 131, pp. 1–4.

Erle, Sibylle. 'Introducing the *Songs* with Inspiration: William Blake, Lavater, and the Legacy of Felix Hess'. In *(Re-)Writing the Radical: Enlightenment, Revolution, and Cultural Transfer in 1790s Germany, Britain and France*, edited by Maike Orgel, pp. 251–67 (Göttingen: De Gruyter, 2012).

Essick, Robert N. *William Blake and the Language of Adam* (Oxford: Clarendon, 1989).

Farrell, Michael. *Blake and the Methodists* (Houndmills, Basingstoke: Palgrave, 2014).

Faull, Katherine M. *Moravian Women's Memoirs: Their Related Lives* (Syracuse, NY: Syracuse University Press, 1997).

Fechner, Jörg-Ulrich. 'Philologische Einfälle und Zweifel zu Hamanns Londoner Aufenthalt: Die "Senel-Affaire" und die "Generalbeichte"'. In *Johann Georg Hamann: Acta des Internationalen Hamann-Colloquiums in Lüneburg 1976*, pp. 5–11 (Frankfurt: Klostermann, 1979).

Federmann, Arnold. *Johann Heinrich Füssli: Dichter und Maler, 1741–1825*. Monographien zur Schweizer Kunst 1 (Zurich: Orell Füssli, 1927).

Ferber, Michael. *The Social Vision of William Blake* (Princeton, NJ: Princeton University Press, 1985).

Forster, Michael N. *After Herder: Philosophy of Language in the German Tradition* (Oxford: Oxford University Press, 2010).

Fuseli, Henry. *Remarks on the Writings and Conduct of J. J. Rousseau* (London: printed for T. Cadell, 1767).

Fuseli, Henry. *Remarks on the Writings and Conduct of J. J. Rousseau/Bemerkungen über J.J. Rousseaus Schriften und Verhalten*, edited and translated by Eudo Mason (Zurich: Fretz and Wasmuth, 1962).

Gajek, Bernhard. 'Leben und Werk eines Königsberger Philosophen: Zum 200. Todestag des "Magus in Norden"'. In *Acta Borussica: Zentralarchiv für altpreußische Volkskunde und Landesforschung 3*, pp. 65–80 (Munich: Haus der Ost- und Westpreußen in Bayern, 1989).

Gajek, Bernhard, ed. *Johann Georg Hamann und England: Hamann und die englischsprachige Aufklärung: Acta des Siebten Internationalen Hamann-Kolloquiums zu Marburg/Lahn 1996* (Frankfurt am Main: Peter Lang, 1999).

Garcia, Humberto. *Islam and the English Enlightenment, 1670–1840* (Baltimore, MD: Johns Hopkins University Press, 2011).

Gawlick, Günther, and Lothar Kreimendahl. 'Hamann and the Philosophy of David Hume'. *Journal of the History of Philosophy* 5, 4 (1967): 343–51.

Gawlick, Günther, and Lothar Kreimendahl. *Hume in der deutschen Aufklärung*: Umrisse einer Rezeptionsgeschichte (Stuttgart: Fromann-Holzboog, 1987).

'German Pantheism and Its Influence on Criticism'. *Christian Remembrancer* 15, no. 60 (April 1848): 353–95.

Gessner, Salomon. *Salomon Geßners Schriften* 3 vols (Zurich: Orell, Geßner, Füeßlin, 1774).

Gessner, Salomon. *The Death of Abel: In Five Books; Translated from the German of Mr. Gessner* Translated by Mary Collyer (London: printed for C. Cooke [1796]).

Gibbons, B. J. *Gender in Mystical and Occult Thought: Behmenism and Its Development in England* (Cambridge: Cambridge University Press, 1996).

Gilchrist, Alexander. *Life of William Blake, 'Pictor Ignotus'* (London: Macmillan, 1863).

Gilchrist, Alexander. *The Life of William Blake*. Edited by W. Graham Robertson (London: John Lane, 1928).

Gilchrist, Alexander. *The Life of William Blake* (Mineola, NY: Dover, 1998).

Glausser, Wayne. *Locke and Blake: A Conversation across the Eighteenth Century* (Gainesville: University Press of Florida, 1998).

Goethe, Johann Wolfgang von. *Goethes Werke*. 6 vols (Frankfurt am Main: Insel, 1965).

Goethe, Johann Wolfgang von. *Goethe's Collected Works*, ed. Victor Lange; Eric Blackall; Cyrus Hamlin, 12 vols (Princeton, NJ: Princeton University Press, 1994–5).

Goldsmith, Steven. *Blake's Agitation: Criticism and the Emotions* (Baltimore MD: Johns Hopkins University Press, 2013).

Graubner, Hans. '"Gott selbst sagt: Ich schaffe das Böse": Der Theodizee-Entwurf des jungen Hamann in der Auseinandersetzung mit Hume, Sulzer, Shuckford und Hervey'. In *Johann Georg Hamann: Religion und Gesellschaft*, edited by Manfred Beetz, and Andre Rudolph, pp. 255–91 (Berlin: De Gruyter, 2012).

Gray, Richard. *About Face: German Physiognomic Thought from Lavater to Auschwitz* (Detroit, MI: Wayne State University Press, 2004).

Green, Garett. 'Modern Culture Comes of Age: Hamann versus Kant on the Root Metaphor of Enlightenment'. In *What Is Enlightenment? Eighteenth-Century Answers and Twentieth-Century Questions*, edited by James Schmidt, pp. 291–305 (Berkeley: University of California Press, 1996).

Grundy, Isobel. *Lady Mary Wortley Montagu: Comet of the Enlightenment* (Oxford: Oxford University Press, 1999).

Günther, Timo. 'Mythos und Irrationalismus: Isaiah Berlins Blick auf Hamann'. In *In the Embrace of the Swan: Anglo-German Mythologies in Literature, the Visual Arts and Cultural Theory*, edited by Rüdiger Görner and Angus James Nicholls, pp. 353–68 (Berlin: De Gruyter, 2010).

Haggarty, Sarah, and Jon Mee. *William Blake: Songs of Innocence and Songs of Experience: a Reader's Guide to Essential Criticism* (Houndmills, Basingstoke: Palgrave, 2013).

Hall, Carol Louise. 'Henry Fuseli and the Aesthetics of William Blake: Fuseli as Transmitter of J. J. Winckelmann, J. J. Rousseau, and J. C. Lavater'. PhD dissertation, University of Maryland, 1979.

Halmi, Nicholas. *The Genealogy of the Romantic Symbol* (Oxford: Oxford University Press, 2008).

Hamann, Johann Georg. *Londoner Schriften*. Edited by Oswald Bayer and Bernd Weissenborn (Munich: Beck, 1993).

Hamann, Johann Georg Hamann. *Briefwechsel*. Edited by Walther Ziesemer and Arthur Henkel, 7 vols (Wiesbaden: Insel, 1955).

Hamann, Johann Georg. *Sämtliche Werke.* Edited by Josef Nadler. 6 vols (Vienna: Herder, 1949–57).

Hamann, Johann Georg. *Sokratische Denkwürdigkeiten: Aesthetica in nuce.* Edited by Sven-Aage Jørgensen (Stuttgart: Reclam, 1998).

Hamann, Johann Georg. *Writings on Philosophy and Language.* Translated by Kenneth Haynes (Cambridge: Cambridge University Press, 2007).

Hamilton, Paul. *Coleridge and German Philosophy: The Poet in the Land of Logic* (London: Bloomsbury, 2007).

Hamilton, Paul. *Coleridge's Poetics* (Stanford, CA: Stanford University Press, 1983).

Hamilton, Paul. *Metaromanticism: Aesthetics, Literature, Theory* (Chicago, IL: University of Chicago Press, 2003).

Hamilton, Sir William. *Discussions on Philosophy and Literature, Education, and University Reform* (London: Longman, 1853).

Harries, Elizabeth. *The Unfinished Manner: Essays on the Fragment in the Later Eighteenth Century* (Charlottesville: University of Virginia Press, 1994).

Haynes, Kenneth. Review of *After Enlightenment*, by John Betz. *Church History* 78, 4 (December 2009): 904–6.

Heidegger, Martin. *Vom Wesen der Sprache: Die Metaphysik der Sprache und die Wesung des Wortes zu Herders Abhandlung 'Über den Ursprung der Sprache'*, vol. 85 of *Gesamtausgabe*. 102 vols (Frankfurt am Main: Klostermann, 1975).

Heidenreich, Bernd. *Sophie von La Roche: Eine Werkbiographie* (Frankfurt am Main: Peter Lang, 1986).

Heller-Roazen, Daniel. *Echolalias* (New York: Zone Books, 2005).

Henkel, Arthur. 'Goethe und Hamann. Ergänzende Bemerkungen zu einem Geistergespräch'. *Euphorion* 77 (1983): 453–69.

Henrich, Dieter. *Konstellationen: Probleme und Debatten am Ursprung der idealistischen Philosophie (1789–1795)* (Stuttgart: Klett-Cotta, 1991).

Herbert, Thomas. *John Wesley as Editor and Author* (Princeton, NJ: Princeton University Press, 1940).

Hervey, James. *Meditations and Contemplations: Containing, Meditations among the Tombs; Reflections on a Flower-Garden; and, a Descant on Creation. Contemplations on the Night. Contemplations on the Starry-Heavens; and, A Winter-Piece*, 21st ed. (London, [1774]).

Hervey, James. *Theron and Aspasio: Or, a Series of Dialogues and Letters, upon the Most Important and Interesting Subjects.* 3 vols (London: printed for John and James Rivington, 1755).

Holub, Robert C. 'The Legacy of the Enlightenment: Critique from Hamann and Herder to the Frankfurt School'. In *German Literature of the Eighteenth Century: The Enlightenment and Sensibility*, edited by Barbara Becker-Cantarino, pp. 285–307 (Rochester, NY: Camden House, 2005).

Hume, David. *A Treatise of Human Nature*, edited by David Fate Norton and Mary J. Norton. Oxford Philosophical Texts (Oxford: Oxford University Press, 2000).

Hume, David. *An Enquiry concerning Human Understanding*, edited by Tom L. Beauchamp (Oxford: Oxford University Press, 1999).

Hume, David. *New Letters of David Hume*, edited by Raymond Klibansky and Ernest C. Mossner (Oxford: Clarendon, 1954).

Hume, David. *The Letters of David Hume*, edited by J. Y. T. Greig. 2 vols (Oxford: Oxford University Press, 1932).

Hunter, Ian. *Rival Enlightenments: Civil and Metaphysical Philosophy in Early Modern Germany* (Cambridge: Cambridge University Press, 2001).

Ibershoff, C. H. 'Bodmer and Milton'. *Journal of English and Germanic Philology* 17, 4 (October 1918): 589–601.

Ibershoff, C. H. 'Bodmer and Young'. *Journal of English and Germanic Philology* 24, 2 (April 1925): 211–18.

Immendörfer, Nora. *Johann Georg Hamann und seine Bücherei* (Königsberg: Ost-Europa, 1938).

Irvine, George. 'Recollections of the Life of Johann Gottfried von Herder'. *Dublin Review* 14, 28 (May 1843): 505–34.

Israel, Jonathan I. *Radical Enlightenment: Philosophy and the Making of Modernity 1650–1750* (Oxford: Oxford University Press, 2001).

Jacobs, Carol. *Skirting the Ethical* (Stanford, CA: Stanford University Press, 2009).

Jacobus Mary. *Tradition and Experiment in Wordsworth's 'Lyrical Ballads' (1798)* (Oxford: Clarendon, 1976).

Jager, Colin. *The Book of God: Secularization and Design in the Romantic Era* (Philadelphia: University of Pennsylvania Press, 2007).

Jarvis, Simon. 'Introduction: Poetic Thinking'. In *Wordsworth's Philosophic Song*, pp. 1–32 (Cambridge: Cambridge University Press, 2007).

'Jean Paul Richter'. *British Quarterly Review* 12 (November 1847): 375–407.

Jefcoate, Graham. *Deutsche Drucker und Buchhändler in London 1680–1811: Strukturen und Bedeutung des deutschen Anteils am englischen Buchhandel* (Berlin: De Gruyter, 2015).

Jellinek, Max Hermann. *Geschichte der Neuhochdeutschen Grammatik von den Anfängen bis auf Adelung.* 2 vols (Heidelberg: Winter, 1913–14).

Johns, Alessa. *Bluestocking Feminism and British-German Cultural Transfer, 1750–1837* (Ann Arbor: University of Michigan Press, 2014).

Jørgensen, Sven-Aage. 'Hamann und Hervey: Zur Bibellektüre während Hamanns Londoner Krise'. In Reventlow, Sparn, and Woodbridge, eds. *Historische Kritik und biblischer Kanon in der deutschen Aufklärung* (Wiesbaden: Harrassowitz, 1988), pp. 237–48.

Jørgensen, Sven-Aage. *Querdenker der Aufklärung: Studien zu Johann Georg Hamann* (Göttingen: Wallstein, 2013).

Julian, John. *Dictionary of Hymnology* (London, 1892).

Junod, Karen. 'Crabb Robinson, Blake, and Perthes's *Vaterländisches Museum* (1810–1811)'. *European Romantic Review* 23, 4 (August 2012): 435–51.

Kant, Immanuel. *Critique of Pure Reason.* Translated by Norman Kemp Smith (London: Macmillan, 1963).

Kant, Immanuel. *Sämtliche Werke.* Edited by Karl Rosenkranz and F. W. Schubert. 12 vols (Leipzig, 1838–42).

Kant, Immanuel. *Theoretische Philosophie.* 3 vols (Frankfurt: Suhrkamp, 2004).

Kawanago, Yoshikatsu. 'Sprache und Leib bei Georg Hamann'. *Interdisciplinary Cultural Studies* 4 (1999): 111–31. Available at: http://www004.upp.so-net.ne.jp/kawanago/LEIB-H01.HTM.

Keach, William. *Arbitrary Power: Romanticism, Language, Politics* (Princeton, NJ: Princeton University Press, 2004).

Khalip, Jacques, and Forest Pyle, eds. *Constellations of a Contemporary Romanticism* (Oxford: Oxford University Press, 2016).

King, John [Johann Konig]. *A Compleat English Guide for High-Germans/Ein vollkommener englischer Wegweiser fur Hoch-Teutsche* (London: printed for W. Freeman [Wilhelm Frieman] and B. Barker, 1706).

Knowles, John. *The Life and Writings of Henry Fuseli.* 3 vols (London: Henry Colburn and Richard Bentley, 1831).

Kocziszky, Eva. 'Die Schwierigkeit des Nicht-Tuns: Welt und Gesellschaft in Hamanns Kontroverse mit Lavater'. In *Johann Georg Hamann: Religion und Gesellschaft*, edited by Manfred Beetz and Andre Rudolph, pp. 103–16 (Berlin: De Gruyter, 2012).

Kocziszky, Eva. 'Ein Leib-Sein: Lavaters Dialog mit Hamann'. *Seminar: A Journal of Germanic Studies* 38, 1 (February 2002): 1–18.

Koepp, Wilhelm. 'Joh. Georg Hamanns Londoner Senel-Affäre Januar 1758'. *Zeitschrift für Theologie und Kirche* 57 (1960): 92–108.

Kolodziej, Benjamin. 'Isaac Watts, the Wesleys and the Evolution of the 18th-Century English Congregational Song'. *Methodist History* 42, 4 (July 2004): 236–48.

Lacoue-Labarthe, Philippe, and Jean-Luc Nancy. *The Literary Absolute: The Theory of Literature in German Romanticism* (Albany: State University of New York Press, 1978).

La Roche, Sophie von. *Begegnungen mit Zürich im Ausgehenden 18. Jahrhundert* (Zurich: Berichthaus, 1962).

La Roche, Sophie von. *Sophie in London, 1786: Being the Diary of Sophie v. la Roche*. Translated by Clare Williams (London: Jonathan Cape, 1933).

La Roche, Sophie von. *Tagebuch einer Reise durch Holland und England* (Offenbach: Brede, 1788)

LaTrobe, C. I. *Letters to My Children*. Edited by J. A. LaTrobe (London: Seeleys, 1851).

Lavater, Johann Caspar. *Aphorisms on Man: Translated from the Original Manuscript of the Rev. John Caspar Lavater, Citizen of Zuric* [*sic*] (London: printed for J. Johnson, 1788).

Lavater, Johann Caspar. *Historisch-Kritische Ausgabe*. Edited by Horst Sitta. 10 vols (Zurich: Neue Zürcher Zeitung, 2001).

Lavater, Johann Caspar. *Physiognomische Fragmente zur Beförderung der Menschenkenntnis und Menschenliebe; Eine Auswahl mit 101 Abbildungen*. 4 vols (Leipzig: Steiner, 1775–8).

Lavater, Johann Caspar. *Vermischte unphysiognomische Regeln zur Selbst- und Menschenkenntnis* (Stuttgart: Reclam, 1787).

Lavater, Johann Caspar. *Vermischte unphysiognomische Regeln zur Menschen- und Selbstkenntnis* (Stuttgart: Reclam, 1788).

Lehr, Andreas. 'Kleine Formen. Adornos Kombinationen: Konstellation/Konfiguration, Montage, und Essay'. PhD dissertation, University of Freiburg, 2000.

Lethen, Helmut, Annegret Pelz, and Michael Rohrwasser, eds. *Konstellationen: Versuchsanordnungen eines Schreibens* (Vienna: Vienna University Press, 2013).

Levine, Caroline. *Forms: Whole, Rhythm, Hierarchy, Network* (Princeton, NJ: Princeton University Press, 2015).

Lichtenberg, Georg Christoph. *Schriften und Briefe*. 5 vols (Munich: Hanser, 1967–74).

Lincoln, Andrew. 'Alluring the Heart to Virtue: Blake's *Europe*'. *Studies in Romanticism* 38, 4 (Winter 1999): 621–39.

Lindner, Helgo. 'Hamann als Leser der englischen Bibel: Beobachtungen zu den neuedierten Londoner Schriften'. In *Johann Georg Hamann und die englischsprachige Aufklärung*, edited by Bernhard Gajek, pp. 17–40 (Berlin: Peter Lang, 1999).

Lineback, Donald 'Johann Heinrich Muller: Printer, Moravian, Revolutionary'. *Transactions of the Moravian Historical Society* 23.1 (1977): 61–76.

Locke, Don. *A Fantasy of Reason: The Life and Thought of William Godwin* (London: Routledge & Kegan Paul, 1980).

Locke, John. *An Essay concerning Human Understanding* (Oxford: Clarendon, 1975).

Locke, John. *Drafts for the 'Essay concerning Human Understanding', and Other Philosophical Writings*. Edited by Peter Nidditch and G. A. J. Rodgers. 3 vols (Oxford: Clarendon, 1990).

Losonsky, Michael. *Linguistic Turns in Modern Philosophy* (Cambridge: Cambridge University Press, 2006).

Lowery, Margaret Ruth. *Windows of the Morning: A Critical Study of William Blake's 'Poetical Sketches', 1783*. Yale Studies in English 93 (New Haven, CT: Yale University Press, 1940).

Lowry, Helen. '"Reisen, sollte ich reisen! England sehen!" A Study in Eighteenth-Century Travel Accounts: Sophie von La Roche, Johanna Schopenhauer and Others'. PhD dissertation, Queen's University, Ontario, 1998.

Lüpke, Johannes von. 'Die Wahrheit in einem Hauch oder von der Eitelkeit der Vernunft "Neue Apologie des Buchstaben h von ihm selbst"'. In *Hamann: Insel Almanach auf das Jahr 1988*, edited by Oswald Bayer, Bernhard Gajek, and Josef Simon, pp. 172–84 (Frankfurt am Main: Insel, 1987).

Luther, Martin. *The Shorter Catechism of Martin Luther, translated from the Latin into English by a Clergyman of the Church of England; and now published together with the German, for the use of the school belonging to St. George's Lutheran Chapel, in Little Ayliffe-Street, Goodman's Fields, London. By Gustavus Anthony Wachsel, D. D. Pastor of the said Church* (London, 1770).

Mackintosh, James. 'De l'Allemagne'. *Edinburgh Review* 22, 43 (October 1813): 198–238.

Macphail, J. H. 'Blake and Switzerland'. *Modern Language Review* 38, 2 [April 1943]: 81–7).

Maertz, Gregory. *Literature and the Cult of Personality: Essays on Goethe and His Influence* (Stuttgart: Ibidem, 2017).

Makdisi, Saree. *Making England Western: Occidentalism, Race, and Imperial Culture* (Chicago, IL: University of Chicago Press, 2014).

Makdisi, Saree. *Reading William Blake* (Cambridge: Cambridge University Press, 2015).

Makdisi, Saree. *William Blake and the Impossible History of the 1790s* (Chicago, IL: University of Chicago Press, 2003).

Mander, John. *Our German Cousins: Anglo-German Relations in the 19th and 20th Centuries* (London: John Murray, 1974).

Manz, Stefan, Margrit Schulte Beerbühl, and John R. Davis, eds. *Migration and Transfer from Germany to Britain 1660–1914* (Munich: K. G. Saur, 2007).

Martin, Alison. *Moving Scenes: The Aesthetics of German Travel Writing on England 1783–1830* (London: MHRA, 2008).

Mason, Eudo C. 'Heinrich Füßli und Winckelmann'. In *Unterscheidung und Bewahrung: Festschrift fur Hermann Kunisch zum 60. Geburtstag 27. Oktober 1961*, edited by Klaus Lazarovicz and Wolfgang Kron, pp. 232–58 (Berlin: De Gruyter, 1961).

Mason, Eudo C. *The Mind of Henry Fuseli: Selections from His Writings with an Introductory Study* (London: Routledge & Kegan Paul, 1951).

Matheson, Percy Ewing. *German Visitors to England 1770–1795 and Their Impressions* (Oxford: Clarendon, 1930).

Matthews, Susan. *Blake, Sexuality, and Bourgeois Politeness* (Cambridge: Cambridge University Press, 2011).

McCorkle, Donald. 'Moravian Music in Salem: A German-American Heritage'. PhD dissertation, Indiana University, 1958.

Mee, Jon. *Dangerous Enthusiasm: William Blake and the Culture of Radicalism in the 1790s* (Oxford: Clarendon, 1992).

Mehlman, Jeffrey. 'Literature and Hospitality: Klossowski's Hamann'. In 'Des Allemagnes: Aspects of Romanticism in France', special issue, *Studies in Romanticism* 22, 2 (Summer 1983): 329–47.

Mellor, Anne K. 'Physiognomy, Phrenology, and Blake's Visionary Heads'. In *Blake in His Time*, edited by Robert E. Essick and Donald Pearce, pp. 53–74 (Bloomington: Indiana University Press, 1978).

Mellor, Anne K. 'Sex, Violence, and Slavery: Blake and Wollstonecraft'. In 'William Blake: Images and Texts', special issue, *Huntington Library Quarterly* 58, 3/4 (1995): 345–70.

Mendelssohn, Moses. 'Sammelrezension zu Hamann'. *Allgemeine Deutsche Bibliothek* 24 (1775): 287–96.

Mendicino, Kristina. *Prophecies of Language: The Confusion of Tongues in German Romanticism* (New York: Fordham University Press, 2017).

Menke, Bettine. 'Magie des Lesens'. In *Namen, Texte, Stimmen: Walter Benjamins Sprachphilosophie*, edited by Thomas Regehly and Iris Gniosdorsch, pp. 109–37 (Stuttgart: Akademie der Diözese Rotenberg, 1993).

Menninghaus, Winfried. *Walter Benjamins Theorie der Sprachmagie* (Frankfurt am Main: Suhrkamp, 1987).

Merlan, Philip. 'From Hume to Hamann'. *Personalist* 32 (1951): 11–18.

Milbank, John. *The Word Made Strange: Theology, Language, Culture* (Malden, MA: Blackwell, 1998).

Milbank, John, Catherine Pickstock, and Graham Ward, eds. Introduction to *Radical Orthodoxy: A New Theology* (New York: Routledge, 2002), pp. 1–20.

Mitchell, W. J. T. *Blake's Composite Art: A Study of the Illuminated Poetry* (Princeton, NJ: Princeton University Press, 1978).

Montagu, Lady Mary Wortley. *The Turkish Embassy Letters*, edited by Teresa Heffernan and Daniel O'Quinn (Toronto, ON: Broadview Press, 2013).

Montgomery, James. '*The World before the Flood, a Poem, in Ten Cantos; with Other Occasional Pieces*, by James Montgomery'. *Quarterly Review* 11, 21 (April 1814): 78–87.

Moretti, Franco. *Graphs, Maps, Trees: Abstract Models for Literary History* (New York: Verso, 2005).

Morgan, Bayard Quincy, A. R. Hohlfeld, and Walter E. Roloff. *German Literature in British Magazines, 1750–1860* (Madison: University of Wisconsin Press, 1959).

Mortensen, Peter. *British Romanticism and Continental Influences: Writing in an Age of Europhobia* (Houndmills, Basingstoke: Palgrave, 2007).

Mulsow, Martin, and Marcelo Stamm, eds. *Konstellationsforschung* (Frankfurt: Suhrkamp, 2005).

Nuelsen, John L. *John Wesley and the German Hymn: A Detailed Study of John Wesley's Translations of Thirty-Three German Hymns*. Translated by Theo Parry, Sydney H. Moore, and Arthur Holbrook (Calverley, Yorkshire: A. S. Holbrook, 1972).

Otto, Peter. *Constructive Vision and Visionary Deconstruction: Los, Eternity, and the Productions of Time in the Later Poetry of William Blake* (Oxford: Clarendon, 1991).

Patri, Kai Hendrik. 'Aus einer Menschensprache in eine Menschensprache: Zu Johann Georg Hamanns Hume-Übersetzungen'. In Gajek, *Johann Georg Hamann und England*, pp. 319–65 (Berlin: Peter Lang, 1999).

Paul, Charles Kegan. *William Godwin: His Friends and Contemporaries*. 2 vols (London: King, 1878).

Péter, Ágnes. 'A Second Essay in Romantic Typology: Lord Byron in the Wilderness'. *Neohelicon* 26, 1 (January 1999): 39–54.

Peucker, Paul. *A Time of Sifting: Mystical Marriage and the Crisis of Moravian Piety in the Eighteenth Century* (University Park: Pennsylvania State University Press, 2015).

Pfau, Thomas. *Minding the Modern: Human Agency, Intellectual Traditions, and Responsible Knowledge* (Notre Dame, IN: University of Notre Dame Press, 2015).

Pfau, Thomas. *Romantic Moods: Paranoia, Trauma, and Melancholy, 1790–1840* (Baltimore, MD: Johns Hopkins University Press, 2005).

Pipkin, James. *English and German Romanticism: Cross-Currents and Controversies* (Heidelberg: Carl Winter, 1985).

Pocock, J. G. A. *Barbarism and Religion*. 6 vols (Cambridge: Cambridge University Press, 2000–15).

Pocock, J. G. A. 'Enlightenment and Counter-Enlightenment, Revolution and Counter-Revolution; A Eurosceptical Enquiry'. *History of Political Thought* 20, 1 (January 1999): 125–39.

Podmore, Colin. *The Moravian Church in England, 1728–1760* (Oxford: Clarendon, 1998).

Pop, Andrei. 'Henry Fuseli: Greek Tragedy and Cultural Pluralism'. *Art Bulletin* 44, 1 (March 2012): 78–98.

Pöttinger, Margarete. 'Hamann's Humeübersetzungen' (1939). PhD dissertation (University of Vienna).

Proceedings of the Committee Appointed for Relieving the Poor Germans, Who Were Brought to London and There Left Destitute in the Month of August 1764 [Multiple contributors] (London: J. Haberkorn, 1765).

'Prussian Schools'. *British Critic, and Quarterly Theological Review* 25, no. 49 (January 1839): 76–95.

Quinney, Laura. *William Blake on Self and Soul* (Cambridge, MA: Harvard University Press, 2009).

Rajan, Tilottama. 'Blake's Body without Organs: The Autogenesis of the System in the Lambeth Books'. *European Romantic Review* 26, 3 (May 2015): 357–66.

Raven, James. *The Business of Books: Booksellers and the English Book Trade 1450–1850* (New Haven, CT: Yale University Press, 2007).

Reaney, Percy, ed. *A Dictionary of English Surnames*, 3rd. ed. (Oxford: Oxford University Press, 2005).

Reed, Bertha. *The Influence of Solomon* [*sic*] *Gessner upon English Literature*. Americana Germanica, 4 (Philadelphia, PA: Americana Germanica, 1905).

Reed, Susan. 'The Poor Palatines: An 18th-Century Refugee Crisis' (London: British Library, 4 September 2015). Available at: http://blogs.bl.uk/european/2015/09/the-poor-palatines.html#

Reed, T. J. *Light in Germany: Scenes from an Unknown Enlightenment* (Chicago, IL: University of Chicago Press, 2015).

Regier, Alexander. 'Words Worth Repeating: Language and Repetition in Wordsworth's Poetic Theory'. In *Wordsworth's Poetic Theory: Knowledge, Language, Experience*, edited by Regier and Stefan H. Uhlig, pp. 61–80 (Houndmills, Basingstoke: Palgrave Macmillan, 2010).

Regier, Alexander. *Fracture and Fragmentation in British Romanticism* (Cambridge: Cambridge University Press, 2010).

'Reminiscences of the Latter Days of Kant'. *Athenæum* 129 (17 April 1830): 232–3.

Reventlow, H. Graf, Walter Sparn, and John Woodbridge, eds. *Historische Kritik und biblischer Kanon in der deutschen Aufklärung* (Wiesbaden: Harrassowitz, 1988).

'Review of '*The Death of Abel*, by Solomon [*sic*] Gessner'. *Eclectic Review* 6, no. 2 (October 1810): 946–7.

Richter, Helene. 'Blake und Hamann: Zu Hamanns 200. Geburtstag', 3 parts: *Archiv für das Studium der Neueren Sprachen und Literaturen*, vol. 158 (1930), [part 1] 213–21; vol. 159 (1931) [part 2] 36–45 and 195–210 [part 3].

Richter, Jean Paul Friedrich. 'Jean Paul Friedrich Richter's Review of Madame de Stael's "Allemagne"'. *Fraser's Magazine for Town and Country* 1, 4 (May 1830): 407–13.

Richter, Jean Paul Friedrich. *Vorschule der Aesthetik*. 3 vols (Stuttgart: Cotta, 1813).

Ringleben, Joachim. 'Søren Kierkegaard als Hamann-Leser'. In *Die Gegenwärtigkeit Johann Georg Hamanns; Acta des achten Internationalen Hamann-Kolloquiums an der Martin-Luther-Universität Halle-Wittenberg 2002*, edited by Bernhard Gajek, pp. 455–65 (Frankfurt am Main: Peter Lang, 2005).

Ripley, Wayne C. 'William Blake and the Hunt Circle'. *Studies in Romanticism* 50, 1 (Spring 2011): 173–93.

Rivers, Isabel. *Reason, Grace, and Sentiment: A Study of Religion and Ethics in England, 1660–1780*. 2 vols (Cambridge: Cambridge University Press, 1991–2000).

Rix, Robert. *William Blake and the Cultures of Radical Christianity* (Burlington, VT: Ashgate, 2007).

Röben, Hedwig. 'J. G. Hamann und die Reformversuche in der deutschen Orthographie'. PhD dissertation, University of Vienna, 1942.

Robertson, W. Graham. Introduction to *The Life of William Blake*, by Alexander Gilchrist, pp. v–ix. Edited by Robertson (London: John Lane, 1928).

Robinson, Henry Crabb. *Essays on Kant, Schelling, and German Aesthetics*. Edited by James Vigus (London: MHRA, 2010).

Robinson, Henry Crabb. 'Reminiscences' (1852). Appendix 1, part F, of Bentley, *Blake Records*, pp. 692–706 (New Haven, CT: published for the Paul Mellon Centre for Studies in British Art by Yale University Press).

Robinson, Henry Crabb. 'The Inventions of William Blake, Painter and Poet'. *London University Magazine* 2 (March 1830): 318–23.

Robinson, Henry Crabb. 'William Blake, Künstler, Dichter, und religiöser Schwärmer'. *Vaterländisches Museum*, vol. 1 (January 1811). Appendix 1B to Bentley, *Blake Records*, pp. 594–603 (New Haven, CT: published for the Paul Mellon Centre for Studies in British Art by Yale University Press).

Robson-Scott, W. D. *German Travellers in England 1400–1800* (Oxford: Basil Blackwell, 1953).

Röhrs, G. J. H. *Predigt bei der Beerdigung des am 9ten May 1790. Ganz unerwartet verstorbenen Herrn Dr. C. G. Woide* (London: Young, 1790).

Rosenthal, Angela,. 'Bad Dreams: Race and the Nightmare of 1781'. In *Representation and Performance in the Eighteenth Century*, edited by Peter Wagner and Frédéric Ogée, pp. 97–126. Landau Paris Studies on the Eighteenth Century 1 (Trier: Wissenschaftlicher Verlag Trier, 2006).

Rudolph, Andre. *Figuren der Ähnlichkeit: Figuren der Ähnlichkeit: Johann Georg Hamanns Analogiedenken im Kontext des 18. Jahrhunderts* (Tübingen: Niemeyer, 2006).

Ruskin, John. 'Expenditure'. In *The Works of John Ruskin: Time and Tide, by Weare and Tyne. Twenty-Five Letters to a Working Man of Sunderland on the Laws of Work*, Letter IV, pp. 18–20 (New York: John Wiley and Sons, 1889).

Salmony, Hansjörg. *Johann Georg Hamanns Metakritische Philosophie* (Basel: Evangelischer Verlag Zollikon, 1958).

Sarafianos, Aris. 'Hyperborean Meteorologies of Culture: Art's Progress and Medical Environmentalism in Arbuthnot, Burke, and Barry'. In *The Science of Sensibility: Reading Burke's Philosophical Enquiry*, edited by Koen Vermeir and Michael Funk Deckard, pp. 69–91. International Archives of the History of Ideas 206 (Dordrecht: Springer, 2012).

Schalow, Frank. Introduction to *Heidegger*. In *Translation, and the Task of Thinking: Essays in Honor of Parvis Emad*, edited by Schalow, pp. 11–49 (New York: Springer, 2011).

'Schlegel's *Lectures on Ancient and Modern Literature*'. *Monthly Review, or, Literary Journal* 81 (December 1816): 506–16.

Schmidgen, Wolfram. Exquisite Mixture: The Virtues of Impurity in Early Modern England. *Eighteenth-Century Studies* 48, 2 (Winter 2015): 239–45.

Schuchard, Marsha Keith. *Why Mrs Blake Cried: William Blake and the Sexual Basis of Spiritual Vision* (London: Century, 2006).

Schumacher, Eckhard. *Die Ironie der Unverständlichkeit* (Frankfurt: Suhrkamp, 2000).

Sheehan, Jonathan. 'Enlightenment Details: Theology, Natural History, and the Letter *h*'. In *'Practices of Enlightenment'*, special issue, *Representations* 61 (Winter 1998): 29–56.

Shell, Marc. *Stutter* (Cambridge, MA: Harvard University Press, 2005).

Shookman, Ellis, ed. *The Faces of Physiognomy: Interdisciplinary Approaches to Johann Caspar Lavater*. Studies in German Literature, Linguistics, and Culture (Columbia, SC: Camden House, 1993).

Shookman, Ellis. 'Pseudo-Science, Social Fad, Literary Wonder: Johann Caspar Lavater and the Art of Physiognomy'. In *The Faces of Physiognomy: Interdisciplinary Approaches to Johann Caspar Lavater*, edited by Shookman, pp. 1–24 (Columbia, SC: Camden House, 1993).

Simcox, Edith [H. Lawrenny, pseud.]. 'Hamann's Life and Works'. *Academy* 3, 62 (15 December 1872): 463–6.

Simcox, Edith. 'Herder et la renaissance littéraire en Allemagne au 18me siècle'. *Academy* 8, 177 (25 September 1875): 326–8.

Simpson, David. *Irony and Authority in Romantic Poetry* (London: Macmillan, 1979).

Sinnett, Jane. 'Johann Gottlieb v. Herder'. *Foreign Quarterly Review* 37, 74 (July 1846): 281–304.

Sonenscher, Michael. *Before the Deluge: Public Debt, Inequality, and the Intellectual Origins of the French Revolution* (Princeton, NJ: Princeton University Press, 2007).

Soni, Vivasvan. 'A New Passion for Enlightenment'. Review of John Bender, *Ends of Enlightenment*; Hina Nazar, *Enlightened Sentiments: Judgment and Autonomy in the Age of Sensibility*; John C. O'Neal, *The Progressive Poetics of Confusion in the French Enlightenment*; and Wolfram Schmidgen, *Exquisite Mixture: The Virtues of Impurity in Early Modern England, Eighteenth-Century Studies* 48, 2 (Winter 2015): 239–45.

Spalding, Johann Joachim. *Kleinere Schriften 2: Briefe an Gleim, Lebensbeschreibung*; vol. 1, part 2, of *Kritische Ausgabe*. Edited by Albrecht Beutel and Tobias Jersak. 12 vols (Tübingen: Mohr Siebeck, 2001).

Sparling, Robert Alan. *Johann Hamann and the Enlightenment Project* (Toronto, ON: University of Toronto Press, 2011).

Stähli, Marlis. '"Wäre es Ihnen gleichgültig ob Füßli in diesem Land oder in England den Plaz fände?" Bodmer und Sulzer als Mentoren des Malers Johann Heinrich Füssli'. In *Johann Jakob Bodmer und Johann Jakob Breitinger im Netzwerk der Europäischen Aufklärung*, edited by Anett Lütteken and Barbara Mahlmann-Bauer, pp. 695–734 (Göttingen: Wallstein, 2009).

St Clair, William. *The Reading Nation in the Romantic Period* (Cambridge: Cambridge University Press, 2004).

Stead, Geoffrey, and Margaret Stead. *The Exotic Plant: A History of the Moravian Church in Britain, 1742–2000* (Werrington, Cambridgeshire: Epworth Press, 2003).

Stelzig, Eugene. *Henry Crabb Robinson in Germany: A Study in Nineteenth-Century Life Writing* (Lewisburg, PA: Bucknell University Press, 2010).

Stephen, Leslie. 'The Importation of German'. In *Studies of a Biographer*, 4 vols, pp. 38–75 (London: Duckworth, 1898).

Stockley, V. *German Literature as Known in England 1750–1830* (London: G. Routledge and Sons, 1929).

Stokoe, F. W. *German Influence in the English Romantic Period 1788–1818, with Special Reference to Scott, Coleridge, Shelley, and Byron* (1929; Cambridge: Cambridge University Press, 2013).

Swann, Karen. 'Blake's Jerusalem: Friendship with Albion'. In *A Companion to Romantic Poetry*, edited by Charles Mahoney, pp. 538–53 (Oxford: Blackwell, 2010).

Swedenborg, Emanuel. *Swedenborg's Secret: The Meaning and Significance of the Word of God, the Life of the Angels, and Service to God; A Biography* (London: Swedenborg Society, 2005).

Tayler, Rev. John James. 'Some Account of the Life and Writings of Herder'. *Monthly Repository and Review*, n.s., 4, 47 (November 1830): 729–38.

Taylor, Charles. *A Secular Age* (Cambridge, MA: Harvard University Press, 2007).

Taylor, Charles. *The Language Animal: The Full Shape of the Human Linguistic Capacity* (Cambridge, MA: Harvard University Press, 2016).

Tennant, Elaine. *The Habsburg Chancery Language in Perspective* (Berkeley: University of California Press, 1985).

Terezakis, Katie. 'J. G. Hamann and the Self-Refutation of Radical Orthodoxy'. In *The Poverty of Radical Orthodoxy*, edited by Lisa Isherwood and Marko Zlomislic, pp. 32–57. Postmodern Ethics 3 (Eugene, OR: Pickwick, 2012).

The Palatines' Catechism, or, a True Description of Their Camps at Black-Heath and Camberwell: In a Pleasant Dialogue between an English Tradesman and a High-Dutchman (London: printed for T. Hare, 1709).

Thompson, E. P. *Witness against the Beast: William Blake and the Moral Law* (New York: New Press, 1993).

Thorne, Christian. *Dialectic of Counter-Enlightenment* (Cambridge, MA: Harvard University Press, 2009).

Trawick, Leonard. 'William Blake's German Connection'. *Colby Library Quarterly* 13 (1979): 229–45.

Turner, James. *Philology: The Forgotten Origins of the Modern Humanities* (Princeton, NJ: Princeton University Press, 2014).

Tytler, Graeme. *Physiognomy in the European Novel: Faces and Fortunes* (Princeton, NJ: Princeton University Press, 1982).

Unger, Rudolf. *Hamann und die Aufklärung: Studien zur Vorgeschichte des Romantischen*. 2 vols (Jena: Eugen Diederichs, 1911).

Van Tieghem, Paul. *Le Romantisme dans la literature Européenne* (Paris: Albin Michels, 1948).

Veldhuis, Henri. 'Hamanns Naturbegriff in seinen Londoner Schriften und Beziehung zur Physikotheologie'. In Reventlow, Sparn, and Woodbridge, *Historische Kritik und biblischer Kanon in der deutschen Aufklärung*, pp. 99–115 (Wiesbaden: Harrassowitz, 1988).

Watson, J. R. *The English Hymn: A Critical and Historical Study* (Oxford: Oxford University Press, 1999).

Watts, Francis. 'Life and Writings of John Albert Bengel'. *Eclectic Review* 3 (January 1838): 21–37.

Weiberg, Anja. 'Philosophy and Life'. In *In Search of Meaning: Ludwig Wittgenstein on Ethics, Mysticism, and Religion*, edited by Ulrich Arnswald. Europäische Kultur und Ideengeschichte Studien 1, pp. 67–86 (Karlsruhe: Universitätsverlag Karlsruhe, 2009).

Wellek, René. *Immanuel Kant in England 1793–1838* (Princeton, NJ: Princeton University Press, 1931).

Wendeborn,Gebhard Friedrich. *Beyträge zur Kentniss Grosbritanniens vom Jahr 1779. Aus der Handschrift eines Ungenannten* (Lemgo: Meyer, 1780).

Wesley, John. *An Extract of the Rev. Mr. John Wesley's Journal, from* His Embarking for Georgia to His Return to London (Bristol: S. and F. Farley, [1740]).

Wheeler, Kathleen M. *Romanticism, Pragmatism, and Deconstruction* (Oxford: Blackwell, 1993).

Will, Peter, trans. 'Horrid Mysteries: A Story from the German of the Marquis of Grose (1797)'. In *Gothic Readings: The First Wave 1764–1840*, edited by Rictor Norton, pp. 122–8 (London: Leicester University Press, 2000).

Williams, Edmund S. 'German Literature'. *Foreign Quarterly Review* 20, 39 (October 1837): 121–36.

Williams, John. *Wordsworth Translated: A Case Study in the Reception of British Romantic Poetry in Germany, 1804–1914* (London: Continuum, 2009).

Winckelmann, Johann Joachim. *Ausgewählte Schriften* (Berlin: Hofenberg, 2014).

Winckelmann, Johann Joachim. *Reflections on the Painting and Sculpture of the Greeks: With Instructions for the Connoisseur, and an Essay on Grace in Works of Art*, 2nd ed. Translated by Henry Fuseli (London: printed for A. Millar and T. Cadell, 1767).

Winckelmann, Johann Joachim. *Winckelmann's Briefe an seine Freunde in der Schweiz* (Zurich: Drell, Gessner, Füsslin, 1778).

Wirz, Ernst. *Die literarische Tatigkeit des Malers Johann Heinrich Fussli (Henry Fuseli): Ein Beitrag zu den Englisch-Schweizerischen Beziehungen und zur Aesthetik des 18. Jahrhunderts* (Basel, 1922).

Wordsworth, William. *Poems, in Two Volumes* (London: printed for Longman, Hurst, Rees, and Orms, 1807).

Wordsworth, William. *Lyrical Ballads, with Other Poems*, 2nd ed. 2 vols (London: printed for T. N. Longman and O. Rees by Biggs, 1800).

Wordsworth, William. *The Thirteen-Book Prelude*, edited by Mark L. Reed. 2 vols (Ithaca, NY: Cornell University Press, 1991), pp. 95–324.

'Works Recently Published on the Continent'. *Foreign and Colonial Quarterly Review* 1, no. 2 (April 1843): 660–7.

Wykes, David L. *Dissenting Praise: Religious Dissent and the Hymn in England and Wales* (Oxford: Oxford University Press, 2011).

Yonan, Jonathan. 'Evangelicanism and Enlightenment: The Moravian Experience in England, c. 1750–1800'. PhD dissertation, University of Oxford, 2006.

Zaretsky, Robert, and John T. Scott. *The Philosophers' Quarrel: Rousseau, Hume, and the Limits of Understanding* (New Haven, CT: Yale University Press, 2009).

Zelle, Carsten. 'Soul Semiology: On Lavater's Physiognomic Principles'. In Shookman,*Faces of Physiognomy*, pp. 40–63 (Columbia, CO: Camden House, 1993).

Zinzendorf, Nikolaus Ludwig von. *Der deutsche Sokrates* (Leipzig: Walther, 1732).

Zinzendorf, Nikolaus Ludwig von. *Ergänzungsbände zu den Hauptschriften*; vol. 2, edited by Erich Beyreuther and Gerhard Meyer (Hildesheim: Georg Olms, 1964).

Index

Wollstonecraft, Mary
  and Fuseli 97–8, 107n.51
  and Hervey 133–4
  as translator 107n.51
Wolff, Christian 35–6
Wordsworth, William 16–17, 19, 31–2, 65,
    149–50
  and Bürger 31–2
  and Gessner 38–40
  preface to *Lyrical Ballads* 31–2
  and pre-Schillerian German literature 32–3
  vs. Hamann 80
Wright, Thomas 193–5

Yonan, Jonathan 160n.28, 190–1
Young, Edward 34, 107–8, 117
  Blake and 75, 136
  Blake's engravings for *Night Thoughts* 75

Bodmer and 96
Hamann and 117
Young, J. 51

Ziegenhagen, Friedrich Michael 50–1
Zinzendorf, Nikolaus Ludwig, von 156,
    160, 163
  and Blake 164–5
  composes hymns 161
  and Hamann 152n.2, 184, 215–16
  on language 164–5
  London Prints (*Londoner Drucke*) 152n.2
  on the manliness of Jesus 219
  and poetry and song 154–5, 184
Zurich:
  Collegium Carolinum 119–20
  intelligentsia 37, 37n.19, 96–7, 108–9
  see also Fuseli Lavater